THE FUTURE OF NORTHERN IRELAND

edited by

JOHN McGARRY
AND
BRENDAN O'LEARY

with a Foreword by

AREND LIJPHART

CLARENDON PRESS · OXFORD
1990

Oxford University Press, Walton Street, Oxford OX2 6DP

Oxford New York Toronto
Delhi Bombay Calcutta Madras Karachi
Petaling Jaya Singapore Hong Kong Tokyo
Nairobi Dar es Salaam Cape Town
Melbourne Auckland

and associated companies in
Berlin Ibadan

Oxford is a trade mark of Oxford University Press

Published in the United States
by Oxford University Press, New York

British Library Cataloguing in Publication Data
The Future of Northern Ireland.
1. Northern Ireland. Politics
I. McGarry, John   II. O'Leary, Brendan
320.9416
ISBN 0–19–827329–0

Library of Congress Cataloging in Publication Data
The Future of Northern Ireland/edited by John McGarry and Brendan
O'Leary; with a foreword by Arend Lijphart.
Includes bibliographical references and index.
1. Northern Ireland—Politics and government—1969–   I. McGarry,
John.   II. O'Leary, Brendan.
DA990.U46F87 1990   941.50824–dc20   90-36853
ISBN 0–19–827329–0

Typeset by Cotswold Typesetting Ltd, Cheltenham
Printed in Great Britain by Biddles Ltd,
Guildford & King's Lynn

To Liam Agnew,
who taught both of us the importance
of ancient history

Foreword

One Basic Problem, Many Theoretical Options—And a Practical Solution?

by Arend Lijphart

RICHARD ROSE'S frequently quoted statement concerning Northern Ireland that 'the problem is that there is no solution' (Rose 1976b: 139) is as provocative as it is wrong. The main problem—as all of the authors of the present volume appear to agree in spite of the many differences of interpretation and of policy preferences among them—is that Northern Ireland is a segmented (or plural or deeply divided) society. That is the basic problem that any proposed solution has to deal with. And, contrary to Rose's assertion that no such solution exists, there are a whole series of possible solutions. This is particularly true for Northern Ireland—more so than for most other segmented societies—because the internal problem of segmentation has complex external and international dimensions. As a result, there are even more solutions, at least in theory, than the principal options presented so ably and penetratingly in the different chapters of this book. An additional great merit of the book is that it allows the divergent viewpoints to be argued by the advocates of these views themselves and that they do so with great force and persuasiveness.

While it is important to acknowledge the multitude of available options, I believe that it is equally important to recognize that these are interrelated in two ways. First, just about all of them entail some form of consociation or power-sharing. Northern Ireland will remain an area in which two separate and antagonistic segments live in close proximity regardless of its status as part of the United Kingdom or part of the Irish Republic or as an independent state, and regardless of whether it belongs to the United Kingdom or Eire as a more or less separate entity or as a more closely integrated part of either country. And it is difficult to see any solution other than power-sharing to this basic problem of segmentation. Partition appears to be an alternative—and hence unrelated—to power-sharing, but this is the case only if partition can completely separate the segments from each other. In most segmented societies, including Northern Ireland, this is impossible without large-scale population transfers. When partition is incomplete, the need for power-sharing remains; to argue otherwise would be to say that minorities lose their rights or can be ignored when they are reduced in size. I would even argue that power-sharing is also a vital part of any solution that is based on a policy of assimilation: the best hope for assimilation is to start with power-sharing as a first step.

The second close link between the principal options concerns the special relationship between power-sharing and partition. I agree with the editors' argument that partition—repartition in the case of Northern Ireland—is the least undesirable default option when power-sharing cannot be made to work in a plural society. In addition, I believe that the formulation of an explicit and detailed scheme for partition can be an important inducement to make power-sharing work after all. I have presented the same argument with regard to South Africa, where I believe that radical partition is not an attractive proposition either. Nevertheless, if I may take the liberty of quoting myself,

radical partition may serve one useful purpose, and it should therefore not be rejected completely. If negotiations were begun for a consociational democracy, it would be a good idea to formulate not only a consociational constitution, but also a radical partition scheme as a fallback solution. If, contrary to all good intentions and reasonable expectations, a consociation were to fail, the availability of an agreed upon fallback plan for partition may help to avoid or minimize violence. It should therefore decrease the nego-tiators' reluctance to attempt a consociational solution. More important, such a fallback plan would increase the likelihood that a consociational democracy could be negotiated and that it would work well because the participants in the negotiations and in the actual operation of consociational government would have the sobering knowledge of exactly what the partitionist alternative would entail. (Lijphart 1985: p. 46)

In my opinion, a repartition plan for Northern Ireland could serve the same purpose.

It is no great surprise to me that power-sharing emerges as the main option from this volume. It is a solution that has been repeatedly reinvented and rediscovered by politicians and political scientists. At approximately the same time that I began to think and write about consociationalism, Gerhard Lehmbruch (1967) and Jürg Steiner (1971) started working along the same lines. Sir Arthur Lewis's (1965) study of plural societies in West Africa and their need for power-sharing was the first consociational statement by a modern social scientist. And, at least initially, we formulated our ideas completely independently of each other. What is even more striking is that the politicians had been way ahead of us. The necessity of power-sharing was recognized and consociational rules and institutions were invented by Dutch politicians in 1917, by Lebanese politicians in 1943, by Austrian politicians in 1945, by Malaysian politicians in 1955, by Colombian politicians in 1958, and, of course, by British politicians for the Northern Ireland problem in 1972. The pattern is one of reinvention instead of learning from prior foreign examples. The logic of power-sharing is so compelling that it is readily recognized even when established political traditions, such as the strong British majority-rule tradition, militate against it.

A factor that complicates the adoption of power-sharing in practice to some extent is that power-sharing can come in very many forms. I have already stated earlier that it can be seen as a core component of several options. Moreover, as I argued several years ago in a multi-authored book entitled *Political Co-operation in Divided Societies: A Series of Papers Relevant to the Conflict in Northern Ireland*—to which the present volume is a most worthy successor—consociation itself can be implemented in a large variety of forms: formal versus informal, territorial versus non-territorial, and so on (Lijphart 1982). Instead of there being no solution for Northern Ireland, the greater problem may well be that there are too many options and that political support is too widely scattered among these. But this constitutes a challenge to the political decision-makers instead of an insoluble problem. There are plenty of possible and reasonable solutions; what is needed in addition is the political will and creative statesmanship to use the available options constructively.

Preface

John McGarry and Brendan O'Leary

THIS book was conceived with three fundamental objectives. First, we aimed to provide an opportunity for authoritative academic and political figures to present their considered arguments for the most feasible and reasonable proposals for political progress in Northern Ireland in the 1990s. Not everybody approached accepted this opportunity, and academics were naturally more forthcoming than political figures. We must also report the sad fact that one of our political contributors, John McMichael, who had agreed to provide a chapter on co-determination, was assassinated by the Provisional IRA. However, despite some of the difficulties we encountered, we believe we have assembled an up-to-date, diverse, and well argued set of statements on how to achieve political progress in Northern Ireland.

The second major objective of the book is to counter one facile, thought-stopping, and pessimist article of faith which has come to dominate academic, administrative, and intelligent journalistic commentary on Northern Ireland. This 'idea' is the notion that there is *no* solution to the conflict in Northern Ireland. In fact, as the chapters in this book amply demonstrate, there are *many* solutions to the Northern Ireland conflict. Indeed we have not been able to present them all—partly of course because not all the proposed solutions are worthy of sustained examination and because some of them have no academic or political exponents. However, this book should make clear that it is the multiplicity of solutions on offer—and the multiplicity of problems to which the solutions are the alleged answer— which makes discussion of progress in Northern Ireland so diffuse and inchoate, that is if rational discussion takes place at all. We have some faith that the rationalism of our authors' contributions may improve the quality if not the quantity of dialogue within and outside Northern Ireland.

Our third ambition was to organize a coherent collection which we would edit in an interventionist way. We aimed to provide background knowledge where necessary, to comment with Editors' notes on our contributors' arguments, and to drive the collection towards an analytical framework and conclusion which might help the general reader, students, and policymakers to make sense of the possible futures for Northern Ireland. This intention explains the historical introduction, the structure of our conclusion, our four appendices and our repeated commentary on or—cross-referencing of—authors' contributions. It is for readers to judge whether our aims have been satisfactorily accomplished.

A book is always a collective endeavour, especially an edited collection. We would like to thank our contributors first and foremost. Henry Hardy's faith in the project was very important in sustaining our commitment. Oxford University Press's referee was also of considerable assistance. We are entirely indebted to the Fax machine, which enabled the editors to communicate rapidly across the Atlantic—and thereby avoid the heartstopping activities of the Canadian and British Post Offices. John McGarry is grateful to the Social Sciences and Humanities Research Council of Canada for financial support, and Brendan O'Leary is grateful for London School of Economics and Political Science Staff Research grants between 1988 and 1989, and to the Nuffield Foundation for a travel grant which facilitated several trips to Ireland in 1989. We must also express our gratitude to our colleagues, friends, and interviewees who contributed in various ways to improving the arguments developed here—especially Jack Allen, Jim Allister, Brian Barry, Peter Barry, Alan Beattie, Ken Carty, James Crimmins, Jeffrey Donaldson, Alan Dukes, Pat Dunleavy, Desmond Fennell, Garret FitzGerald, Tom Garvin, Steven Greer, George Jones, Desmond King, Marian Larragy, Brian Lenihan, Conor Lenihan, Ian Lustick, Tom Lyne, Chris McCrudden, Chris McGimpsey, Kevin McNamara, Stephen Milne, Margaret Moore, Sid Noel, Brendan O'Duffy, Cornelius O'Leary, Séan O'Leary, John Peterson, Clive Symmons, Jennifer Todd, Lorelei Watson, John Whyte, and Claire Wilkinson.

November 1989

J.McG.
B.O'L.

Contents

Contents

Appendices

List of Abbreviations

AIA	Anglo-Irish Agreement (see Appendix 1)
APNI	Alliance Party of Northern Ireland
BIIC	British–Irish Intergovernmental Council
BIA	British Irish Association
BLP	British Labour Party
CEC	Campaign for Equal Citizenship for Northern Ireland
CLP	Constituency Labour Party
CLR	Campaign for Labour Representation for Northern Ireland
CRG	Campaign for Responsible Government
DUP	Democratic Unionist Party
EOC	Equal Opportunities Commission
EPA	Emergency Provisions Act
FCS	Federation of Conservative Students
FEA	Fair Employment Agency
FEC	Fair Employment Commission
IIP	Irish Information Partnership
IIP	Irish Independence Party
ILP	Independent Labour Party
INLA	Irish National Liberation Army
IPLO	Irish People's Liberation Organization
IRA	Irish Republican Army
MRBI	Market Research Bureau of Ireland
NICRA	Northern Ireland Civil Rights Association
NILP	Northern Ireland Labour Party
NIO	Northern Ireland Office
NUPRG	New Ulster Political Research Group (also known as the UPRG)
OUP	Official Unionist Party (also known as the Ulster Unionist Party)
PR	Proportional Representation
PTA	Prevention of Terrorism Act
RUC	Royal Ulster Constabulary
SACHR	Standing Advisory Commission on Human Rights
SDLP	Social Democratic and Labour Party
STV	Single Transferable Vote
UDA	Ulster Defence Association
UDR	Ulster Defence Regiment
UFF	Ulster Freedom Fighters
UULCC	United Ulster Loyalist Central Co-ordinating Committee
UPRG	Ulster Political Research Group (also known as the NUPRG)

UUUC   United Ulster Unionist Council
UUP   Ulster Unionist Party (also known as the Official Unionist Party)
UVF   Ulster Volunteer Force
UWC   Ulster Workers' Council
VUP   Vanguard Unionist Party
WP   Workers' Party

Glossary of Key Concepts

Simplified definitions of the key concepts used throughout this book are given below. The glossary also indicates some of the complementary relationships between these concepts.

Co-determination

A political system in which major political parties share executive power on a constitutionally entrenched proportional basis. A synonym for power-sharing (*q.v.*) or consociation (*q.v.*). An antonym of majority-rule (*q.v.*).

Confederal state

A set of states unified by treaty for certain specifically demarcated purposes, but the constituent states retain their individual sovereignty and international identity. It differs from a federal state (*q.v.*) in the latter respects.

Consociation

A political system used in divided societies to share and divide governmental power and authority. Political power is shared by the rival subcultures on a proportional basis—in the executive, the legislature, and public employment. Each subculture or segment enjoys rights of veto and autonomy in the organization of its culture. Public expenditure may also be allocated on a proportional basis. Consociation is the antonym of majority rule (*q.v.*), and unlike integration does not endeavour (immediately) to assimilate subcultures.

Devolution

The formation of a sub-central government, with executive and legislative powers within a unitary state. Devolved governments can be formed on either a majority rule (*q.v.*) or a consociational (*q.v.*) basis.

Equal citizenship

A slogan with distinct meanings in Northern Ireland. It was first used by the civil rights movement in the 1960s to demand legal, political, and civic equality for Catholics as British citizens in Northern Ireland. The term has now been appropriated by various organizations who seek to ensure that the citizens of Northern Ireland have the right to vote for the political parties most likely to form the government of the United Kingdom.

Federal State

A composite state in which executive and legislative powers are shared and divided between central and sub-central governments, and intergovernmental relations are necessarily constitutionally regulated. The antonym of a unitary state (*q.v.*).

Independent state

A sovereign state, which can be organized in multiple ways: as a unitary or federal state, and with either consociational or majority-rule decision-making.

Integration

A synonym for assimilation. The organization of a territory or culture under one unified set of norms. In Northern Ireland two main types of integration are advocated: into Britain and into Ireland. There are various ways in which the territory might be fully integrated into Britain. *Administrative integration* would ensure that Northern Ireland was administered like the rest of the UK (or like England, or like Scotland, or like Wales). *Electoral integration* would ensure that British political parties would compete for support in Northern Ireland. *Educational integration* would assimilate Protestants and Catholics under the same schooling institutions. British integrationists are generally hostile to devolution, consociationalism, and federalism. Irish integrationists suggest, by contrast, that

Northern Ireland should be administratively and electorally integrated into the Irish Republic, in a new unitary state. They are also generally hostile to consociational or federal ideas.

Joint authority

The sharing of ultimate governmental authority over a territory by two or more states. In principle within the designated territory a devolved government can be created, on either a majority-rule or power-sharing basis.

Majority rule

A synonym for simple majority rule, a decision-making norm which in some democracies is used in every sphere of political activity—especially in the electoral, constitutional, government-formation, and policy-making systems. The universalization of the merits of this norm is criticized by consociationalists and federalists. Majority rule sounds less pleasant when it is described as the 'minimum winning coalition' norm, or the 'tyranny of the majority'.

Partition

The division of the territory of a divided society with a view to creating ethnically or culturally homogeneous states.

Power-sharing

Expression used in Britain, Ireland, and Northern Ireland to refer to consociational (*q.v.*) or co-determination (*q.v.*) systems.

Unitary state

A state in which sub-central governments enjoy no autonomous sovereign power.

Notes on Contributors

Paul Arthur is Senior Lecturer in Politics at the University of Ulster, the author of *The People's Democracy* (1974), *The Government and Politics of Northern Ireland* (1985), the co-author of *Northern Ireland since 1968* (1988), and a regular political columnist for the *Irish Times*.

Paul Bew is Reader in Political Science at the Queen's University, Belfast, the author of *Land and the National Question* (1978), *Parnell* (1980), *Conflict and Conciliation in Irish Nationalism* (1987), and the co-author of *The State in Northern Ireland, 1921–72* (1979), *Sean Lemass and the Making of Modern Ireland* (1982), *The British State and the Ulster Crisis* (1985) and *The Dynamics of Irish Politics* (1989).

Kevin Boyle is Professor of Law at the University of Essex, and co-author of *Law and State: The Case of Northern Ireland* (1975), *Ten Years on in Northern Ireland* (1980), *Ireland: A Positive Proposal* (1985), and *The Anglo-Irish Agreement* (1989). He is also the editor of *Irish Law Texts*, an international authority on the law of human rights, and was a legal consultant to the New Ireland Forum.

Anthony Coughlan is Senior Lecturer in Social Studies at Trinity College, Dublin, and the author of *Fooled Again? The Anglo-Irish Agreement and After* (1986) as well as numerous other publications in Irish politics and social policy.

James Crimmins is Lecturer in Politics at Huron College, University of Western Ontario, and is editing Bentham's *Church of Englandism* for *The Collected Works of Jeremy Bentham*. His publications include the edited anthology *Religion, Secularization and Political Thought* (1989), and the essay *Secular Utilitarianism* (1990) a study of Bentham's writings on religion.

Charles Graham is a member of the New Ulster Political Research Group. He is the co-author of *Common Sense* (1987).

Tom Hadden is Professor of Law at the Queen's University, Belfast, and co-author of *Law and State: The Case of Northern Ireland* (1975),

Ten Years on in Northern Ireland (1980), *Ireland: a Positive Proposal* (1985), and *The Anglo-Irish Agreement* (1989). He is also the author of *Company Law and Capitalism*, and was the founding editor of *Fortnight: An Independent Review for Northern Ireland.*

Liam Kennedy is Lecturer in Economic and Social History at the Queen's University, Belfast, and amongst his publications are *Two Ulsters: A Case for Repartition* (1986) and *The Modern Industrialisation of Ireland* (1989).

Anthony Kenny is Warden of Rhodes House, Oxford, and the author of many books, including *Descartes* (1968), *Wittgenstein* (1973), *Aquinas* (1980), *More* (1983), and more recently *The Road to Hillsborough: The Shaping of the Anglo-Irish Agreement* (1986). He was vice-chairman of the Kilbrandon Committee, an unofficial all-party British body set up in 1984 to respond to the New Ireland Forum Report.

Arend Lijphart is Professor of Political Science at the University of California, San Diego. He is the pioneer of the theory of consociationalism. *The Politics of Accommodation* (1968), *Democracy in Plural Societies* (1977), *Democracies* (1984), and *Power-Sharing in South Africa* (1985) are amongst his best-known publications.

John McGarry is Lecturer in Politics at King's College, University of Western Ontario, the author of numerous academic publications in the comparative politics of divided societies, and the co-author of *The Politics of Antagonism: Explaining Northern Ireland* (forthcoming).

Margaret Moore was a Canadian Council Post-Doctoral Fellow. Her doctorate at the London School of Economics & Political Science was on 'The Foundations of Liberalism'. She is a Lecturer in Political Science at York University, Toronto.

Brendan O'Duffy is researching a Ph.D. on 'Political Violence in Northern Ireland' at the London School of Economics & Political Science.

Brendan O'Leary is Senior Lecturer in Political Science & Public Administration, London School of Economics & Political Science, the author of *The Asiatic Mode of Production* (1989), and the co-author of *Theories of the State: The Politics of Liberal Democracy* (1987) and *The Politics of Antagonism: Explaining Northern Ireland* (forthcoming).

Claire Palley is Principal of St Anne's College, Oxford, and, while Professor of Public Law at the Queen's University, Belfast, published 'The Evolution, Disintegration and Possible Reconstruction of the Northern Ireland Constitution', *Anglo-American Law Review* (1972).

Henry Patterson is Senior Lecturer in Politics at the University of Ulster, the author of *Class Conflict and Sectarianism* (1980) and *The Politics of Illusion* (1990), and co-author of *The State in Northern Ireland, 1921–72* (1979), *Sean Lemass and the Making of Modern Ireland* (1982), *The British State and the Ulster Crisis* (1985) and *The Dynamics of Irish Politics* (1989).

Hugh Roberts is Senior Lecturer in Politics at the University of East Anglia, and the author of *Northern Ireland and the Algerian Analogy: A Suitable Case for Gaullism* (1986). He is the founder of the Campaign for Democratic Rights in Northern Ireland.

1

Introduction

Northern Ireland as the Site of State- and Nation-Building Failures

Brendan O'Leary and Paul Arthur

THE future of Northern Ireland cannot be understood without reference to its past. The keys to its past lie in three periods of British and Irish state- and nation-building failure. The first period, from 1801 to 1922, ended with the failure of British state-builders to forge a pan-British national identity throughout the British Isles and the failure of Irish nationalists to build a pan-Irish national identity in the island of Ireland. The second period, from 1920 until 1972, ended with the abolition of the Stormont Parliament, a system created and maintained by British and Irish state- and nation-building failures. The third period has lasted since 1972, although some believe that the Anglo-Irish Agreement, signed in November 1985, has marked a new departure in creative statecraft.

State-building and nation-building are distinct processes. State-building is the creation and maintenance of public institutions subordinated to a centralized and sovereign decision-making authority which enjoys an effective monopoly of coercion within a given territory, the capacity to extract stable revenues from subjects, and the ability to enforce laws. In Europe modern state-building began through the consolidation and acquisition of territory by royal and aristocratic élites. These states originated in conquest or military domination, the survivors emerging from the Darwinian environment of the 'states-system'. State-builders were facilitated by but did not require mass legitimacy, although they increasingly came to seek it. They simply required compliance (Finer 1975*b*; Hintze 1975; Mann 1986; Oppenheimer 1975; Rokkan 1975; Tilly 1975*a,b*).

Nation-building by contrast necessarily required legitimization. The manufacture of a national identity amongst heterogeneous people could not succeed unless the imaginary national community was extensively internalized by the target population. Whatever the historical dynamics of the formation of the nations, they had two simple consequences. Nation-builders came to argue that they required a state to protect or to express the nation. State-builders, conversely, usually came to believe that nation-building was indispensable to the maintenance and expansion of the power of their regimes.

The combination of state-building and nation-building gave rise to dissonance as well as harmony. The bloody history of twentieth-century Europe is visible testament to the social contradictions and catastrophes which state-building and nation-building can engender. Many nations failed to become states, and many states failed to become nations. Northern Ireland is the paradigm case of state- and nation-building failure in Western Europe. Neither a nation nor a full state, its creation, development, and disintegration, as we shall see, were the by-products of intended and unintended British and Irish state- and nation-building failures.

1. THE FIRST FAILURES, 1801–1922

The United Kingdom of Great Britain and Ireland, established in the Act of Union of 1801, created a multi-ethnic core to the British Empire, 'integrating' three kingdoms (England, Scotland, and Ireland)[1] under one Crown and Parliament. The break-up of this political formula after World War I was by no means teleologically inscribed in the 'laws of history', contrary to the subsequent rationalizations of Irish nationalists. British state-building failure in Ireland owed most to the nineteenth-century failure to create stable foundations for a durable sense of common citizenship throughout the United Kingdom, especially within the island of Ireland. The impact of the triangular relationship between Protestant settlers, Catholic natives and the metropolitan core, a colonial legacy which produced an imbalanced Union, and the failure to tie Catholic emancipation and equality to the creation of that Union are widely acknowledged to be central constituents in any explanation of British state-building and nation-building failure in Ireland (Lustick 1985).

The failure of the British state to assimilate Irish Catholics as 'west Britons' provided the milieu in which Irish 'native' leaders sought equality and subsequently protection for the Irish national identity through the establishment of a separate parliament under the British Crown. This idea was central to O'Connell's 'Repeal of the Union' and Parnell's 'Home Rule' movements of the nineteenth century. However, the blockage of these projects by the Protestant settler population, fearful of being dominated in any arrangements which made Ireland autonomous from the rest of Britain, fertilized a more militant Irish nationalism which sought an independent and republican Irish nation-state. The British rulers of Ireland were simultaneously torn between the twin imperatives of placating the loyal settler population and satisfying the demands for reform and equality made by Irish Catholics. In consequence the British were unable to assure either party of their sincerity. This vicious triangle of British rulers, Irish natives, and Protestant settlers lay behind the partition of Ireland.

There were six deep-rooted objective historical and cultural constraints working against the successful integration of Ireland into the British state and nation. First, Ireland was a conquered territory which had been colonized but not assimilated by successive waves of Norman, English, and British rulers. Its native élites were not co-opted but displaced. Second, the Protestant reformation, successful in the main island of the British Isles, was dramatically unsuccessful in Ireland in the sixteenth century. Consequently religion and ethnic identity were henceforth to be fused on the island: to be Catholic was to be a native, to be Protestant was to be a settler. Third, the Anglo-Irish ascendancy (the Protestant landlord class of English stock created by the confiscatory Cromwellian and Williamite settlements of the seventeenth century), who dominated Ireland until the end of the nineteenth century, were radically differentiated from the Catholic and originally Gaelic-speaking peasantry by deep caste-like divisions. These divisions had their roots in imperial conquest and the system of religious apartheid of the eighteenth century, the Penal Laws, which left a lasting legacy of bitterness and encouraged a peasant culture which legitimized agrarian violence. Fourth, in Ulster, the only successful site of extensive colonial plantation in Ireland, profound sectarian conflict between Catholic and Protestant peasants existed long before industrialization, entrenching a mentality of siege amongst Protestants and of dispossession amongst Catholics. Fifth, when industrialization materialized in Ireland in the nineteenth century it was concentrated in the environs of Belfast and the Lagan Valley, differentiating the economic interests of north-eastern Ireland from the rest of the island. Therefore, it was not surprising that in the late nineteenth century, following the advent of universal suffrage, native, Catholic, agrarian, and originally Gaelic-speaking Ireland was mobilized behind Irish nationalism whereas planter, Protestant, industrial, and originally Scots and English Ireland was mobilized against it in defence of the Union. Finally, British political development, for a variety of reasons, produced no powerful federalist or consociational political ideologies which might have bridged the major ethnic and religious divisions within and between the two largest islands in the British archipelago.

Northern Ireland was therefore the by-product of British state- and nation-building failure in Ireland for two interrelated reasons. First, the British state failed to maintain its control over the whole of Ireland through the Act of Union, and eventually, after the Easter Rising of 1916 and the war of independence launched by Irish nationalists, tried to retreat to the political formula of two home-rule governments for Northern Ireland and Southern Ireland. As Southern Ireland was stillborn, unacceptable to Irish nationalists, Northern Ireland came to mark the territorial line of retreat of the British state in Ireland. Second, British state-building failure in Ireland was caused by the failure to build a British national identity in Ireland, one which would have enabled the descendants of Catholic natives and Protestant settlers to transcend their differences as equal citizens, either under a home-rule parliament under the Crown, or under the jurisdiction of the Westminster Parliament.

On the other hand Northern Ireland was also the by-product of Irish state- and nation-building failure. First, and most obviously, Irish nationalists lacked the coercive and ideological resources to achieve a popularly supported nationalist revolution throughout the whole island of Ireland between 1916 and 1925. The north-eastern counties of Ireland, heartlands of the Protestant settler population, were obdurately hostile to Irish nationalism and willing to resist it militarily. The inability of nationalists to coerce Protestant Ulster owed something to the military weakness of guerrillas, and the power of the British Empire, but had perhaps its most profound roots in the ideological development of Irish nationalism. The commonsensical definitions of the Irish nation elaborated by poets, intellectuals, and politicians stressed a synthesis of three elements: the Gaelic language, the Catholic religion, and a territorial Irish state defined by its autonomy from Britain. Such 'common sense' spelled blunt messages to the Protestant population of Ireland. The English language, the Protestant religions, and the British state were the implicit antonyms of Irish nationalism. Protestants consequently understood themselves to be regarded at best as non-nationals ripe for reculturation, and at worst as anti-nationals, with no place in the Irish nation. Most of them accordingly resisted incorporation within the Irish nation, and sought to maintain the Union with the British state to protect their community.

Thus Northern Ireland, the political entity created in 1920, was nobody's first preference: the British government saw it as a necessary staging-post to Irish unity, albeit within the British Empire; Irish nationalists saw it as a temporary and unworkable denial of the Irish people's right to self-determination; and Ulster unionists saw it as a sacrifice of Unionists elsewhere in Ireland, and, by virtue of its constitutional singularity, an unwelcome differentiation of the province from the rest of Britain. The creation of Northern Ireland and the Irish Free State was the product of failed British and Irish state- and nation-building. This précis contains no surprises. However, what is less well understood is that the subsequent development of Northern Ireland, and the roots of today's seemingly insoluble conflicts, owe a great deal to further British and Irish state- and nation-building failures.

2. INTERPRETATIONS OF THE NORTHERN IRELAND CONFLICT

There are many competing definitions and analyses of the Northern Ireland problem which have been lucidly summarized elsewhere (Whyte 1978, 1988, 1990), but explanations of the dynamics of the conflict can be distinguished by their stress upon exogenous or endogenous causes (O'Leary 1985). Exogenous explanations seek to locate the causes of the conflict outside Northern Ireland, in Anglo-Irish relations, British imperialism, or Irish irredentism. Endogenous explanations by contrast seek to locate the causes of the conflict inside Northern Ireland, in atavistic historical, cultural, religious, and segmental antagonisms.

The bulk of this chapter examines the important exogenous and endogenous causes which shaped the genesis and development of Northern Ireland between 1920 and 1972. The major argument is that the current conflict does not simply, or even primarily, stem from causes endogenous to Northern Ireland, important though these are. Although internal-conflict or endogenous theories are now the prevailing academic orthodoxy (Whyte 1978, 1988, and 1990), they are at most one half of the story. The argument which follows is emphatically not a restatement of either traditional Irish nationalist or Ulster unionist accounts of the exogenous sources of the conflict. British imperialism and Irish irredentism, over-emphasized by nationalists and unionists respectively, are no longer the key exogenous causes of the conflict. The consequences of the patterns of British and Irish state- and nation-building are the important external factors, and are not reducible to British imperialism and Irish irredentism.

The second argument advanced below complements the stress on the exogenously derived impact of British and Irish state- and nation-building upon Northern Ireland. The province developed a distinct political system, one of 'hegemonic control' (Lustick 1979, 1987). It was the by-product of British and Irish state- and nation-building failures. It also collapsed as the unintended by-product of developments within the British and Irish states. Before these two arguments are advanced the concepts of particularism and hegemonic control need to be explained.

Particularism and Hegemonic Control

The question 'who should rule the state?', as Aristotle suggested, has three secular answers: the one, the few, and the many. In modern idiom 'the many' are 'the people', and they provide the only permissible answer in the Occident. Yet the thorny question is 'who are the people?' There are four obvious answers. Three are egalitarian, but one is not.

The statist asserts that the people are all adults permanently resident within the state's boundaries; the nationalist claims they are all adults who belong to the nation; whereas the universalist answers that they are the entire human species. These egalitarian answers prescribe the multi-cultural state, the nation-state, and the global-state respectively. Of these options the nation-state has proved the most potent normative ideal.

Yet there are many kinds of state other than nation-states. Indeed there are more states which are not pure nation-states than otherwise. There is of course no global state but there are many imperial states and multicultural states, including some consociational states, which are held together through combinations of coercion and co-option. These states lack 'taken-for-granted' nationalist legitimation, and if we accepted the premiss that the nation-state is the 'natural' outcome of modernization, we might expect them to be precarious and brittle. Indeed states which cannot build one nation seem doomed 'in the last instance', to steal the determinist language of a pattern of thought unable to explain nationalism. But this reasoning is questionable, and not merely because it presupposes that nation-building ends at some definable point, and that all peoples must go through the liberation/torture of nation-building. The fact is that some states which have not built nations seem stable, and capable of survival, despite the presence of pressures to conform to the standards of nation-states competing in inter-'national' markets and in a states-system.

One set of such states are *particularist*, because they provide a fourth and profoundly inegalitarian answer to the question 'who are the people?' In particularist states the people are defined by reference to an Other: another gender, race, ethnicity, religion, or class. Members of the Other are not part of the people, but rather should be subjected to the rule of the people. Rule over the Other, born out of conquest or fear of conquest, must be coercively maintained. Particularists oppose the egalitarian responses given by statists and universalists to the question 'who are the people?', and the democratic egalitarianism implicit in liberal nationalism. They are often frankly anti-nationalist, fearful that they will be a subordinated minority within an Other's national identity. Alternatively, they develop a pathological nationalism in which their nation consists merely of a fraction of the state's population, defined by its opposition to the remainder. In particularist nationalism the match between the nation's population and the state's legitimate territorial extension is severed. The nation rules the state, but the definition of the nation is exclusivist, internally domineering, segmental, and pathological. The pathology is simple. Liberal and socialist nationalists usually seek to equate state boundaries and national communities. Particularists make no such effort. Northern Ireland, between 1920 and 1972, was particularist, although it was not a fully fledged state: the disloyal Catholic population were not regarded as part of the Ulster people by Ulster Protestants.

Particularist regimes should not be seen as archaic survivals, traditional rather than modern, or at most transitional deviations on the road towards a universalist nation-state. They are politically feasible, albeit profoundly unpleasant, reactions to a world in which the construction of nation-states is the dominant paradigm. Particularist regimes can exist and thrive in 'modern' parts of the world, and particularist political forms can be found at the sub-state level within many multicultural states, partly because of the chaotic consequences of nationalist doctrine on the ethnic and territorial raw materials upon which it works. Moreover, particularist states can be stable, rather than brittle. They endure because they are based on what Ian Lustick (1979, 1987) calls rule through hegemonic control.

Hegemonic control has been the most common mode through which ethnically divided societies have been governed in world-history. Imperialist or authoritarian regimes control multiple cultures within their territories through coercive domination and élite co-option. The control capacities of such regimes suppress latent divisions between ethnic groups which might otherwise be manifested in conditions of modernization. The control is hegemonic if it makes an overtly violent segmental contest for state power either 'unthinkable' or 'unworkable' on the part of the subordinated segments. Hegemonic control in imperial or authoritarian regimes need not, although it may, rest on the support of the largest or most powerful segment.[2]

In liberal democracies hegemonic control seems less feasible than in empires or authoritarian regimes, because they permit, indeed facilitate, segmental organization and mobilization, especially after the introduction of universal suffrage; and segmental contests for state power become eminently 'thinkable' and 'workable' in their environments. The extensive mobilization of the Irish 'nation' in favour of home rule in the late nineteenth century was coterminous with the extension of male suffrage and the democratization of the United Kingdom; and this development made traditional modes of British control in Ireland unworkable, and made thinkable other ways of organizing political relationships within the British Isles.

However, hegemonic control is feasible in nominal liberal democracies, even if it appears difficult to maintain. Hegemonic control can be created and persist in a liberal democracy where one ethnic segment (or, perhaps, coalition of segments) can effectively dominate another segment (or segments) through its political, economic, and ideological resources; and where this superordinate segment (or coalition of segments) can extract what it requires from the subordinated (or prevent redistributive demands being made by the subordinated).

Minorities in liberal democracies invariably suggest that such control is exercised over them. Not all such claims are true. However, few external observers deny that Northern Ireland, between 1920 and 1968–9, was an example of a society in which hegemonic control was exercised by Ulster Protestants. The Stormont regime was a textbook illustration of Mill and Tocqueville's fear that democratic rule could be compatible with 'tyranny of the majority'. Political, economic, and cultural domination, discrimination, and monopoly were widespread in the province (Buckland 1979, Cameron Committee 1969, Darby 1976, Farrell 1976). Moreover, nationalist insurrection by the minority, if not unthinkable, certainly proved unworkable before the late 1960s.

The current conflict in Northern Ireland resulted from the breakdown of the system of Unionist hegemonic control. The collapse culminated in the abolition of the Stormont Parliament by the British government in 1972. Ever since, the recreation of such control through the restoration of 'majority rule', as a bulwark against Irish nationalism and British disloyalty, has remained a central objective of some unionists. Examining the structure, genesis, and maintenance of the system which developed in Northern Ireland between 1920 and 1972, and enquiring why it broke down, are imperative if we are to understand the present conflict and the solutions offered in this book. The structural relations between the evolution, maintenance, and collapse of hegemonic control and British and Irish state- and nation-building failures provide some of the answers.

3. HEGEMONIC CONTROL IN NORTHERN IRELAND, 1920–1972

The Constitution of Northern Ireland

Northern Ireland was governed under the Government of Ireland

Act of December 1920, which partitioned the island of Ireland and created home-rule parliaments and executives in Northern and Southern Ireland. The Act never operated in the South, where it was superseded by the Anglo-Irish Treaty (signed between the British government and Irish revolutionary nationalists in December 1921) that created the Irish Free State. The Government of Ireland Act was an attempt to maintain the British state in Ireland while satisfying some of the aspirations of Irish nationalists. The Act preserved British sovereignty by subordinating the two new Dublin and Belfast Parliaments to Westminster. 'Home rule' was granted to both juris-dictions, but both parts of Ireland were to have (reduced) represen-tation in Westminster. Two Parliaments, rather than one, were created in Ireland in an effort to mediate the conflict between Ulster unionists and Irish nationalists. It was thought that home rule for both parts of Ireland would meet the Irish demand for self-govern-ment, whereas home rule for Ulster unionists would enable them to avoid domination by Dublin. Finally, clauses in the Act suggested that the political reunification of the island could take place, albeit under the jurisdiction and sovereignty of the British Crown, pro-vided both Parliaments consented. However, Northern Ireland was given the right to opt out of rule by the Dublin Parliament, both in the Government of Ireland Act of 1920, and in the Anglo-Irish Treaty of 1921, a right which it exercised promptly.

Irish unionists had opposed home rule for any part of Ireland, but Ulster unionists pragmatically accepted home rule for Northern Ireland to ensure they would not be ruled by Dublin. They thereby abandoned Protestants elsewhere in Ireland and in Ulster. They protested that accepting home rule was a sacrifice. They had after all always opposed home rule for Ireland. Their Westminster spokes-men claimed they would have preferred Northern Ireland to be ruled in just the same way as the rest of the United Kingdom and that they did not seek to dominate Catholics. However, they were prepared to accept the 'supreme sacrifice' of home rule because it was being sold by the British government as the first part of a package of home rule throughout the British Isles: a package which never materialized (Murphy 1986). However, Ulster unionist leaders knew that home rule would provide them with an effective bulwark against both the untrustworthy intentions of London governments, and the claims of the Irish Free State (intent on achieving complete independence from Britain and on the political unification of the island of Ireland).

Northern Ireland as a political unit of government thus emerged out of the conflict between Irish nationalism and the British state, and, from 1920 until 1969, was marked by three features. First, sovereignty over the territory was formally contested by two states, the British and the Irish. Second, it was not fully integrated into either of those states. The Irish Free State was excluded from the government of Northern Ireland, and the British deliberately withdrew from exercising coercive state power within the territory, leaving the devolved government with considerable autonomy. Finally, the Stormont regime was a semi-state, rather than a state. It had, *de facto*, some of the key organizational features of a state: an effective monopoly over the means of coercion and law enforcement, law-making authority, and clearly demarcated territorial boundaries. However, the regime lacked and did not seek ultimate sovereignty in foreign affairs, and its fiscal autonomy was sharply circumscribed by its dependence upon the British Treasury (Lawrence 1965). Moreover, much of the important legislation of the Stormont regime consisted of reproducing British laws for Northern Ireland. However, this 'semi-state' was sufficient to guarantee Protestant domination.

Territorial Domination

The creation of the home-rule parliament in Belfast and the territorial demarcation of Northern Ireland as six counties of the historic province of Ulster laid the foundations for the localized system of hegemonic control. In the nine counties of historic Ulster, Protestants precariously outnumbered Catholics (56 per cent to 44 per cent). However, without Cavan, Donegal, and Monaghan, the religious ratio in the rest of Ulster altered dramatically in favour of Protestants (65 per cent to 35 per cent). In the negotiations with British governments the territory of Northern Ireland was self-consciously carved out by unionists. They wanted 'those districts which they could control' (Miller 1978: 122 ff). Indeed, Sir James Craig, the first Prime Minister of Northern Ireland, envisaged the six counties as a new 'impregnable Pale',[3] a rampart behind which the descendants of British settlers in Ireland could defend their civilization.

The territorial definition of Northern Ireland was thus the first act of domination; it guaranteed an in-built Protestant majority, providing Catholic population-growth did not dramatically exceed that of Protestants. It established the conditions under which the Ulster Unionist Party would win all the elections for the Northern Ireland Parliament held between 1920 and 1969, drawing almost all of its support from the Protestant population, irrespective of class or income. The partition was dramatically imperfect for those who sought to legitimize it on national, ethnic, or religious grounds. The Catholic, and largely Irish nationalist, population not only composed over a third of the entire population, but were also a local majority in two of the six counties (Fermanagh and Tyrone), the second city of the territory (Derry/Londonderry), and in almost all of the local-government jurisdictions contiguous with the border. The British negotiators of the Anglo-Irish Treaty, especially Lloyd George, were acutely aware of the injustice of incorporating Fermanagh and Tyrone into Northern Ireland. However, they reassured the Irish negotiators by the promise of a future Boundary Commission and with the thought that the presence of a large minority within Northern Ireland would make the statelet both unworkable and illegitimate (Laffan 1983).

Electoral Domination

The threat posed by the promised Boundary Commission to the territorial integrity of the fledgling regime was taken very seriously. Many nationalist councils were situated on the border and had declared their allegiance to Dáil Éireann, the Irish Parliament. They were therefore visible advertisements for the merits of revising the border of Northern Ireland. Unionists immediately changed the local-government election system, and gerrymandered local-government jurisdictions. They sought to reduce radically the number of local councils held by nationalists (25 out of nearly 80 in 1920). Consequently they abolished proportional representation in local elections in 1922, replacing it with the conventional British plurality-rule method,[4] and simultaneously passed a law requiring all councillors to take an oath of allegiance to the Crown. They then postponed the local elections due in 1923, and appointed Sir John Leech to head a one-man judicial commission to reorganize electoral districts. His speedily executed work resulted in shameless gerrymandering, and after the 1924 local elections nationalists were reduced to holding two councils. (The results of the changed election system and 'Leeching' were exaggerated by nationalist boycotts and abstentionism. When boycotting was abandoned nationalists normally won control of 10 or 11 councils out of 73.) These measures helped Unionists in their efforts to ensure that the Boundary Commission would not cause immense damage.

However, even after the Boundary Commission of 1925 failed to produce any alterations in the border[5] Unionists made no moves to reform the local-government system: plurality-rule and gerrymandering remained constant features of Northern Ireland local government for fifty years. Notoriously the second city of Northern Ireland, Derry/Londonderry, had to be gerrymandered several times to ensure the right results. These measures guaranteeing electoral domination were reinforced by the restriction of the local franchise— which was confined to rate-payers and their wives—and by the retention of company votes (which gave company directors up to six votes, depending upon the rateable valuation of their company). Since Catholics were disproportionately poorer than Protestants this pattern of franchise was seen as sectarian as well as class-based. When the 1945 Labour Government introduced universal suffrage for local government in Britain the Stormont Parliament passed its own Representation of the People Act (1946), which retained most of the old system, but restricted it further by removing the franchise from lodgers who were not rate-payers.[6]

The most spectacular illustration of the combination of gerrymandering and the restricted franchise was in Derry/Londonderry. The adult population of the city was approximately 30,000 in the 1960s, consisting of 20,000 Catholics and 10,000 Protestants, a Catholic:Protestant ratio of 2:1. The restricted franchise reduced Catholic predominance, but still left them with a substantial majority. However, the electoral division of the city into three districts, South, North and Waterside Wards, produced the dramatic results shown in Table 1. Gerrymandering completed the conversion of a Catholic:Protestant adults' ratio of 2:1 into a Unionist:anti-Unionist councillors' ratio of 3:2, by the expedient of concentrating the Catholic (and therefore) anti-Unionist vote in one ward, and creating two smaller wards which could be guaranteed to produce Unionist councillors.

The extent of electoral domination throughout Northern Ireland is evident from one striking statistic: whereas unionists represented at most 66 per cent of the population in the late 1920s they controlled 85 per cent of all local authorities (Buckland 1981: 60). However, electoral domination was not merely exercised at the level of local

14 Brendan O'Leary and Paul Arthur

TABLE 1.1. *Wards and local-government election results, Derry/London-derry, 1967*

Ward	Anti-Unionist			Unionist		
	No. of votes	No. of councillors	Ratio, votes: councillors	No. of votes	No. of councillors	Ratio, votes: councillors
South	10,047	8		1,138	0	
North	2,530	0		3,946	8	
Waterside	1,852	0		3,697	4	
TOTAL	14,429	8	1,803.6	8,781	12	731.7

Source: Cameron Committee (1969, para. 134).

government. In 1929 the election system to the Northern Ireland Parliament was changed: again from proportional representation to plurality rule. Nobody disputes that this measure was designed to cement the hegemony of the Ulster Unionist Party, although there is debate over whether its primary purpose was to weaken labourist political movements which threatened unionist solidarity, to reduce all types of fragmentation within the unionist camp, or to weaken further the position of nationalists (Bew *et al.* 1979; Buckland 1979; Farrell 1976; Osborne 1979; Pringle 1980). Resolution of the debate is not vital since abolition of PR and the redrawing of electoral boundaries achieved all functions equally effectively. The plurality-rule method weakened labourist movements and ultra-loyalist populists (the latter being the real threat to unionist unity) and thereby inhibited unionist fragmentation. This entrenchment of the unionist monolith naturally weakened the strategic position of nationalists, even though their numerical representation was not significantly affected. The UUP were able to ensure that all future Stormont elections were referendums, or 'sectarian head-counts', on the legitimacy of Northern Ireland and the border—just what the Prime Minister Sir James Craig had ordered:

What I want to get in this house and what I believe we will get very much better in this house under the old-fashioned plain and simple system, are men who are for the Union on the one hand, or who are against it and want to go into a Dublin parliament on the other. (*Northern Ireland Parliamentary Debates* (Commons), vol. 8, col. 2276)

The electoral institutionalization of sectarian divisions meant that many Westminster, Stormont, and local-government seats were not even contested as the results were foregone conclusions. Unionist hegemony was established. Nationalists, who regarded the regime as illegitimate, regularly resorted to abstention, and in the fifty years of home rule their opposition had merely a solitary legislative achievement: the Wild Birds Act.

Coercive Domination

Hegemonic control must ultimately be sanctioned by coercive resources. Revolt has to be made unworkable. Unionists' minds were concentrated by the presence of an irredentist neighbour which had won its autonomy through guerrilla war, the existence of traditional legitimations of violence within Irish culture, by an ethnic minority prepared to offer both overt and covert support to armed insurrection against the regime (and supported by an Irish diaspora in the United States prepared to fund armed struggle).

The monopolization of force in reliable hands seemed imperative, and even before the formal establishment of the Northern Ireland government in 1921 key Unionist leaders had built a 'state-in-waiting', an administration backed by a body of armed men. A provisional government, backed by a paramilitary organization supplied through illegal gun-running, had been envisaged before World War I to oppose home rule. A second 'arming of the Protestants' in the Ulster Special Constabulary took place in 1920, under the tutelage of Dawson Bates, who was to become the Minister of Home Affairs in the new Northern Ireland government (Farrell 1983). The core membership, 5,500 full-time A Specials, were recruited from the paramilitary Ulster Volunteer Force, which had been mobilized to resist home rule before World War I, and had fought as a unit in that war. They were backed by 19,000 part-time B specials, and by an uncertain number of C specials. All told 1 in 5 Protestant males were estimated to have been members of the Specials, and together with the armed police, the Royal Ulster Constabulary, they were able effectively to repress IRA incursions into Northern Ireland in the early 1920s. Thereafter the A and C Specials were disbanded and approximately 10,000 B Specials were maintained as a part-time paramilitary police force. Together with the RUC they were subsequently able to control IRA offensives against the regime during World War II, and between 1956 and 1962.

The Specials were nakedly sectarian, Protestant to a man. The police force, by contrast, was not nakedly sectarian. In the beginning it was envisaged that it would be representative of the population as a whole. However, less than a sixth of the new force was Catholic, and this proportion declined to about a tenth in the late 1960s. This implicit sectarianism was reinforced by the development of institutional affiliations with Orange lodges, which mightily reinforced Catholic perceptions of the RUC as armed Protestants. However, since the police were the primary agents in controlling the threat of insurrection from the Catholic minority, sectarian perceptions did not need much encouragement.

Legal Domination

The legal system in Northern Ireland, at least as it affected civil liberties, civic order and security, was entirely geared for the threat of insurrection. The Civil Authorities (Special Powers) Act of 1922, renewed annually until 1928, renewed for five years until 1933, and then made permanent, was one of the most draconian pieces of legislation ever passed in a liberal democracy. Two of its sentences have achieved deserved notoriety in jurisdictions based on English law:

The Civil Authority shall have power, in respect of persons, matters and things within the jurisdiction of the Government of Northern Ireland to take all such steps and issue all such orders as may be necessary for preserving the peace and maintaining order.

If any person does any act of such a nature as to be calculated to be prejudicial to the preservation of the peace or the maintenance of order in Northern Ireland and not specifically provided for in the regulations, he shall be deemed to be guilty of an offence against the regulations.

The Special Powers Act (and subsequent regulations developed under it) provided for other extraordinary state powers, even though they were hardly necessary given the above two clauses. The government had the right to intern people without trial (which it did between 1922 and 1925, between 1938 and 1946, and between 1956 and 1961), to arrest people without warrant, to issue curfews, and to prohibit inquests. The security forces also had the right to compel people to answer questions on pain of being guilty of an offence. Other laws, notably the Public Order Act (1951) and the Flags and Emblems Act (1954), enabled the government to control non-violent forms of political opposition, and effectively outlawed symbolic displays of nationalist allegiance amongst the minority population.

A system of order and a system of law is held together by rules and rule-interpreters as well as rule-enforcers. In the 1960s the Campaign for Social Justice enquired whether discrimination practised by local authorities was reviewable under the Government of Ireland Act—which prohibited religious discrimination—but were told it was not possible (McCloskey 1989, app. 2). In any case supervising the administration of justice was an overwhelmingly Protestant judiciary, integrated into the Ulster Unionist Party, and often into the Orange Order. They closed prospects for using the law as a mechanism for the protection of the civil liberties of the minority— although there is little evidence that the Catholic nationalist minority tried to use the legal system for redress of their grievances. The first Chief Justice of Northern Ireland was a Catholic, but after his death in 1925 no other Catholic was appointed to the Supreme Court until 1949; and as late as 1969 Catholics held a mere 6 out of 68 senior judicial appointments (Corrigan 1969: 28; cited in Whyte 1983a).

Economic Domination

Hegemonic control was cemented by systematic discrimination in employment, both in the public and private sectors, and in the distribution of public consumption benefits, especially public housing. The mechanisms through which segmental inequalities in employment and receipt of public consumption were reproduced included intentional, deliberate, and publicly known discrimination in certain occupations. However, informal or indirect discrimination through recruitment on the basis of school or familial networks and 'unintended' structural effects were also important in sustaining persistent inequalities.

The structural pattern of male occupations within each segment in the 1971 census is shown in Table 1.2. In a detailed analysis of the 1961 and 1971 censuses Aunger (1975: 16–17) demonstrated that three principal forms of stratification existed between Protestants and Catholics. First, there was horizontal, or inter-class stratification: Protestants dominated the upper occupational classes while Catholics were found predominantly in the lower classes. Second, there was horizontal intra-class stratification: Protestants predominated in superior positions within occupations within the same class. Finally, there was vertical stratification: Protestants were concentrated in the higher-status industries and locations, while Catholics were disproportionately represented in the lower status

TABLE 1.2. *Religion and occupational class, economically active men, 1971 (per cent)*

Occupational class	Catholic	Protestant	Total
Professional/managerial	9	16	14
Lower-grade non-manual	12	17	16
Skilled manual	23	27	26
Semi-skilled manual	25	24	24
Unskilled/unemployed	31	16	20
TOTAL	100	100	100

Source: Aunger (1975: 10).

ones. He also showed that on the basis of modal averages the 'typical' Protestant male was a skilled worker, whereas the 'typical' Catholic male was unskilled; that most occupations which were strongly Protestant were 'male', whereas those which were disproportionately Catholic were 'female'; that Protestants were over-represented in positions of authority and influence; that the Catholic middle class were largely a service class, servicing their 'own' community; and that Catholics constituted a majority of the unemployed even though they were less than a third of the economically active population. The last dramatic finding has remained a constant feature of Northern Ireland and the most revealing indicator of the nature of its political economy. Moreover, despite British reform programmes in the 1970s, by the mid-1980s Catholic males were still two-and-a-half times as likely to be unemployed as Protestant males (Smith 1987, table 2.1).

The scale and depth of the segmental stratification in the economy was not simply the product of public policy and overt discrimination. However, the explanatory weight which some analysts (and many apologists) wish to attach to educational differences between Catholics and Protestants, differences in family size between Catholics and Protestants, the differential in the relative size of age cohorts between Catholics and Protestants, or to the geographical location of Catholics and Protestants (Hewitt 1981; Wilson 1989), do not survive objective analysis (SACHR 1987; Smith 1987). Moreover, historians have little difficulty in documenting explicit exhortations by Unionist politicians which encouraged sectarianism in employment (Bew *et al.* 1979; Buckland 1981: 55–81; Farrell 1976: 121–49). Such activities naturally cemented unionist unity. They underlined vested interests across all Protestant classes in the maintenance of hegemonic control. They also encouraged Catholic emigration, which remained disproportionately higher than Protestant emigration throughout the Stormont regime (Barritt and Carter 1972: 107–8)—a structural consequence which served to maintain the system.

Structural economic inequality reinforced the other dimensions of hegemonic control: territorial, electoral, and coercive. The linkages are best illustrated in two spheres of public administration: housing and public employment. The allocation of housing and the organization of electoral districts of Northern Ireland were connected in straightforward ways (Cameron Committee 1969, para. 140). Not surprisingly Unionist local authorities west of the Bann (where Catholics were far more likely to be the local majority of the electorate) were most zealous in using planning controls and allocation systems to maintain their political domination. East of the Bann housing-allocation patterns were less influenced by sectarianism. (It should also be noted that some of the few Nationalist local councils practised reciprocal discrimination in housing.) The use and abuse of housing-allocation procedures was also helpful in maintaining clientelist relations within the Protestant community.

Public employment patterns in policing, in both the normal and 'paramilitary' senses, have already been discussed. They were mostly self-selecting as opposed to being determined by intentional discrimination. The same case could not be made for the employment patterns in the civil service, local authorities, and quasi-governmental agencies. In the higher grades of the civil service Catholics made up a total of 5.8per cent in 1943.[7] In local authorities a government commission of inquiry in 1969 found that Unionist-controlled councils had systematically discriminated in favour of Protestants especially in key administrative posts (Cameron Committee 1969, para. 138). In nationalized industries and public utilities Catholics were grossly under-represented at all levels (Aunger 1975); and in other statutory bodies, such as the judiciary, we have already noted a similar picture.

Summary

This picture, sketched from secondary sources and official government commissions, suggests a systematic story of hegemonic control, rather than the 'not particularly inequitable' system suggested

by critics of the claims of the civil rights movement (Hewitt 1981:
377). This judgement does not imply, of course, that Northern
Ireland was the most, or even one of the most, oppressive regimes in
the world for a minority to live within—the black population of the
southern states of the USA were subject to more brutal and oppressive local hegemonic control. Nor does this picture imply that the
degree of domination explains—let alone justifies—in some simplistic way the subsequent level of republican violence from 1971
onwards. However, there was 'a consistent and irrefutable pattern of
deliberate discrimination against Catholics' (Darby 1976: 77–8); and
there was apparently little effective political, or military, action
which Catholics could take to remedy their lot before the 1960s. They
were effectively disorganized. What was distinctive about this
system of local domination was that it was exercised within a liberal
democracy. Northern Ireland, after all, was a region within the
British democratic order.

4. EXPLAINING THE SECOND STATE- AND NATION-BUILDING FAILURES: WHY HEGEMONIC CONTROL DEVELOPED

What explains the creation and maintenance of this system of
hegemonic control, this British affront to the standards of equal citizenship associated with liberal-democratic regimes? The answer lies
in the internal motivations of the actors who established and maintained the system, the unionists, and the environment which made it
possible.

Unionist Motives for Hegemonic Control

The motivations of Ulster unionists are relatively easy to establish,
although ranking their salience is more controversial. Hegemonic
control was developed and maintained because of their fears of
incorporation into a Gaelic, Catholic Irish nation-state, betrayal by
Britain, insurrection and expropriation by the Catholic minority,
and, not least, disunity and fragmentation within their community.

The Irish Free State and the Irish Republic, as it became in 1949,
seemed to develop in ways which confirmed Ulster Protestants'
predictions of what would happen in an independent Irish parliamentary regime. The speeches and statements of unionist leaders,
faithfully reflected in the unionist press, demonstrate an obsessive
fear of Irish nationalism in the years between 1920 and the formation

of the Irish Republic in 1949 (Kennedy 1988: 6). The major theme of the unionist media was the constitutional evolution of the Irish Free State away from the dominion status negotiated in the Anglo-Irish Treaty of 1921 (Kennedy 1988: 21), towards an autonomous republic, achieved *de facto* in 1937, and *de jure* in 1949. It meant the end of Ireland's participation not only within the United Kingdom, but also within the British Empire, and eventually the British Commonwealth. For most unionists this evolution was calculated treason, disloyalty, and a dishonest breaking of the Treaty. The neutrality of the Irish Free State in World War II 'proved' that Ulster unionists had been right to reject incorporation within the Irish Free State.

The second unionist fear focused on Irish irredentism. The early years of Northern Ireland were profoundly uncertain, as civil war and the prospective Boundary Commission threatened the regime's territorial integrity. The defeat of the republican side in the Irish Civil War of 1922–3, and the absence of major boundary revisions in 1925, briefly lessened unionist anxieties, but not for long. The electoral mobilization of the bulk of the defeated republicans under de Valera's Fianna Fáil kept unionist fears alive. Fianna Fáil were openly 'semi-constitutional' in the late 1920s and early 1930s, hostile to the Treaty, and ambiguous in their relationships with the IRA. They were unambiguous about their desire to obtain a republic and the territorial unification of the island. De Valera's electoral victory in 1932, and the entrenchment of Fianna Fáil as the dominant party in the Irish party system confirmed unionists' anxieties. The re-writing of the Irish Constitution in 1937, under de Valera's personal supervision, permanently entrenched their fears. The Irish Constitution claimed the whole island of Ireland as its territory in Articles 2 and 3, and thus formally repudiated the tacit 1925 Boundary settlement between the Irish Free State and Northern Ireland:

ARTICLE 2: The national territory consists of the whole island of Ireland, its islands and the territorial seas.

ARTICLE 3: Pending the re-integration of the national territory and without prejudice to the right of Parliament and Government established by this Constitution to exercise jurisdiction over the whole of that territory, the laws enacted by that Parliament shall have the like area and extent of application as the laws of Saorstat Éireann and the like extra-territorial effect. (*Bunreacht Na hÉireann* (Constitution of Ireland)).

The Irish Free State also seemed to establish unionist prophecies that Catholicization, Gaelicization, and economic retardation would prevail under a Dublin Parliament. Some atrocities against Protestants in the war of independence, and the rapid fall in the Protestant population between 1911 and 1926, reinforced stereotypical attitudes. Although outsiders argue that the independent Irish state treated its Protestant minority well, both by international and (especially by) Northern Irish standards (Bowen 1983: 324–37), this judgement has never been shared by Ulster Protestants. Catholic social morality, especially in matters of family law, divorce, contraception and abortion, determined the majority's attitudes in the South, and eventually the law and the Constitution. Unionist leaders were able to argue that the Irish state was a Catholic state for a Catholic people, and that 'home rule' had meant 'Rome rule'. Compulsory bilingualism (in English and Gaelic) in education was regarded as cultural genocide of the most primitive kind by most Ulster Protestants. Finally, the merits of their decision to exclude themselves from the Irish Free State were demonstrated for them by the greater scale of the depression in the South, its lack of economic growth between the 1920s and 1958, and the baneful repercussions of de Valera's 'economic war' with Britain in the 1930s.

Fear of the Irish state, and of the consequences of incorporation within it, provided some essential motivations for the establishment and maintenance of hegemonic control by Ulster Protestants, but they were not sufficient. Their criticisms of the Irish state, after all, might suggest that they were, or would be, more sincere advocates of equal citizenship, tolerant of their minority's religious, cultural, and economic liberties, and prepared to make Catholics part of the British nation. Self-evidently they were not. One reason they were not, even if they had wanted to be, was another external fear: the threat that the British state would abandon them, or hand them over to the Dublin Parliament, whenever it seemed expedient. This fear was well grounded. The Home Rule Bills of the 1880s and 1890s and the Home Rule Act of 1914 envisaged a Dublin Parliament with authority over Ulster (Lyons 1973). During the planning of the Government of Ireland Act some British policy-makers at several stages, considered subordinating the prospective Belfast Parliament to the Dublin Parliament. The Council of Ireland proposed in the Act was intended to mollify the implications of partition and to be a means through which partition might one day be reversed. Moreover, British policy-makers were to raise again the idea of subordinating the Belfast to the Dublin Parliament, even after the Northern Ireland Parliament had been established. It was seriously reconsidered in the Anglo-Irish Treaty negotiations (Laffan 1983: 82). The Boundary Commission eventually conceded by Lloyd George in the same Treaty threatened Northern Ireland during its formative years, and firmly wed unionists to the merits of having their own Parliament.

Although unionist anxiety about British commitment to the union briefly receded after 1925, it gradually increased due to the willingness of successive British governments to appease, as they saw it, de Valera's strident nationalism in the 1930s. It was raised to fever pitch following the fall of France. In 1940 Winston Churchill secretly offered to support Irish unification in return for Eire's entry into the war on the side of the British Empire and its allies (Fisk 1983: 186–219). (The offer was turned down by de Valera primarily because of his estimation that Nazi Germany would defeat Britain, and he therefore held out, consistently if unrealistically, for both unification and neutrality.) The offer could not be kept secret from Unionist leaders, who were outraged.[8] Although Britain's eventual victory and Eire's neutrality entrenched post-war British support for Northern Ireland's status as part of the United Kingdom, the episode was not forgotten. The unionists' strategic dilemma had been confirmed: full integration with Britain would make them nominally more British, but such integration, by depriving them of the instruments of hegemonic control, would make them correspondingly more vulnerable to abandonment in future Anglo-Irish negotiations. 'Loyal Ulster', despite its record of support for Britain in two world wars, had been shown to be an expendable, negotiable territory, and its people inessential to the British definition of their nation or their state. Eternal vigilance and the retention of hegemonic control seemed appropriate responses.

A further motivation for control was straightforward. Protestants feared the 'enemy within'. In Protestant eyes Catholic Ireland, whether in revolutionary or parliamentary guise, threatened their 'ascendancy'. For Ulster unionists the 'siege of Derry' never ended. They had always been threatened by Catholic insurrection and atrocity. The new Northern Ireland would inevitably face the threat of rebellion from its Catholic nationalist minority, who would regard the statelet as illegitimate. In the interlude between the

Government of Ireland Act of 1920 and the Irish Civil War of 1922–23 which followed the Anglo-Irish Treaty, the IRA engaged in active combat in Northern Ireland. Moreover, although distracted by and defeated in the Irish Civil War, they continued to oppose the existence of Northern Ireland. The reality of this threat made the case for repressive security seem self-evident to Protestants. Catholics were disloyal so there was no case for equal treatment, or authentic equal citizenship. The equally self-evident fact that Catholics' unequal treatment would reinforce disloyalty did not matter so long as they could be controlled.

Thus the colonial legacy was preserved into the liberal-democratic era. Protestant settlers were loyal and under siege from native Catholics; and being besieged they were justified in crushing rebellion by whatever means. The messages of control were spelled out in formal practices of electoral, coercive, legal, and economic domination. They were also culturally and psychologically expressed in sectarian organizations, like the Orange Order, in triumphalist marches through Catholic areas,[9] in regular acts of 'representative violence' and 'communal deterrence' (Wright 1987: 11–20) against the minority, and accompanied by a vitriolic rhetoric which spelled out the insecurities of those who articulated it.

Successful control of Catholics necessitated Protestant unity. Fear of disunity is pervasive within settler colonial communities. Vulnerable to native insurrection and abandonment by the metropolis they cannot afford much internal dissent. Since hegemonic control in Northern Ireland required a conception of politics as a zero-sum game it was essential to inhibit heretical or dissident Protestant voices, whether socialist or otherwise, to prevent factionalism or accommodation with the enemy. Fear of internal betrayal is one of the most constant elements in the history and culture of Protestant Ulster (Nelson 1984; Stewart 1986). It explains the Lundy fixation.

The unfortunate Governor of Derry whose notoriety is preserved in Protestant mythology [is] the archetype of those who would have truck with the enemy; therefore each crisis [in Northern Ireland] inevitably produces a new Lundy. It is not an archaic survival but a recurrent nightmare [that Protestants will be betrayed from within]. (Stewart 1986: 48)[10]

After 1920 'Lundyism' came in two forms: 'from below' it was manifest in labourist movements which briefly threatened to transcend sectarianism in the 1930s and in the late 1950s and early 1960s. This threat was easily handled by the Ulster Unionist Party. Explicit accusations of disloyalty, reminders of the dangers inherent in splitting the unionist cause, and overt renewals of sectarian appeals elicited the required responses. However, Lundyism 'from above' was another matter. 'Modernizing' Unionist élites eventually undermined hegemonic control.

There is no need to elaborate further the motivations behind Ulster Protestants' enthusiasm for the Stormont system. They were persuaded that the relaxation of any of the elements of control spelled their destruction. Consequently they failed to develop the politics of accommodation essential for the functioning of liberal-democratic norms. These fears are sufficient to explain Protestant motivations, and it is not necessary here to come to a more controversial verdict on the relative salience of economic, religious, or political elements in this matrix (for differing interpretations see Bell 1976; Bruce 1986; Nelson 1984; Stewart 1986). Some would argue, however, that Ulster Protestant motivations were determined by an identity which required hegemonic control for its preservation; i.e. Ulster Protestantism just is an ideology of hegemonic control, and Protestant fears are mere rationalization. This thesis has been advanced by an American political scientist:

Fundamental interests and identities not only lead to [the Northern Ireland] conflict but depend upon it. To be Protestant is to be privileged; to be privileged is to require that Catholics be visibly deprived; and to deprive Catholics is to build the social order on overt as well as covert domination. Thus rather than a liberal society invoking universal 'rights' (whatever the objective inequalities) Northern Ireland is a colonial one based on invidious and abiding privileges . . . (MacDonald 1986: 8)

Whereas the elites of most societies would prefer full to partial legitimacy, Northern Ireland's Protestants are threatened by the mere prospect of extended legitimacy. The point is not that other societies achieve full legitimacy, or even that it is actively pursued, but only that most elites would want full legitimacy were it available at an affordable price. In contrast, Protestants in Northern Ireland justified their political power and social privileges on the grounds of their 'loyalty' and Catholic 'disloyalty' to the established order. The catch is that Protestant 'loyalty' is only meaningful in contradistinction to the 'disloyalty' of Catholics. Thus Protestants, especially the more marginal ones, have developed an enduring stake in sustaining the disloyalty of Catholics, even at the cost of chronic instability and violence. Violence poses less of a danger to some Protestants than does the threat of a social order accepted as legitimate by Catholics. (Ibid.)

This thesis is problematic. In its favour is one important consideration: Northern Ireland was carved out with a substantial Catholic minority, rather than in the more homogeneously Protestant counties of north-east Ulster. This fact suggests that Protestants needed Catholics whom they could dominate in order to bolster their identity as privileged settlers. Yet it might also be argued that the unionists' major concern was to maintain as many Protestants within the union as possible rather than to have a large Catholic minority to feed their identity. There are also other problems with MacDonald's thesis. First, it presupposes a homogeneous Ulster Protestant identity based on domination of Catholics, which is at odds with the persuasive suggestion that there are at least two traditions in Unionist political culture (Todd 1987), and that one of these, Ulster British ideology (as opposed to Ulster loyalist ideology), professes liberal political values which prima facie refute MacDonald's case. Second, it neglects the extent to which British rule in Ireland, both before and after 1920, removed most of the formal institutions of a colonial kind. Finally, MacDonald requires us to discount Ulster Protestants' expressed fears in favour of the observer's reductionist, essentialist, and imputed conception of their core identity.

The Environment Facilitating Hegemonic Control

Unionist fears about the Catholic minority and disunity within their own ranks were based on sound appreciation of the political environment within Northern Ireland. Furthermore, their fears about the independent Irish state and of betrayal by Britain were based on judgements of the two 'external' states which were by no means paranoid. However, it is also essential to see the Stormont system as a by-product of further British and Irish state- and nation-building failures.

The Second British State- and Nation-Building Failure

The British state was constitutionally ill-equipped to deal with Northern Ireland. Indeed Northern Ireland 'provides a case study . . . of the failure of the British tradition of constitutional development on the basis of pragmatic empiricism' (McCrudden 1989). The

British Constitution is said to embody three key principles, parliamentary sovereignty, majoritarian democracy, and constitutional conventions. These principles proved to be compatible with hegemonic control in Northern Ireland. It is true that the Government of Ireland Act provided some safeguards for the minority— the Northern Ireland Parliament was forbidden from discriminating in those spheres where it possessed legislative competence (Section 5); and the executive was prohibited from exercising its discretionary powers on a religious basis (Section 8(6))—but clearly these safeguards proved insufficient. Why?

The . . . formal arrangements . . . were expected to be merely the tip of an iceberg of political and constitutional practice deriving from British constitutional and political conventions. Governments would be constrained by the knowledge that they would not remain in power forever. The civil service would operate as a restraining influence. Opposition parties would be brought into a limited share of government through active participation on the one side, and respect for their views on the other. (McCrudden 1989)

These assumptions were neither sensible at the time, nor confirmed by subsequent practice. Indeed the framers of the Government of Ireland Act operated with contradictory assumptions. Northern Ireland was different, therefore it needed special treatment, but on the other hand its devolved government would develop as a miniature version of the British political system.

Some contemporary unionists regret that Northern Ireland was not fully incorporated into the British political system. A devolved Parliament left them in limbo, both outside and within the British political system. They believe that the presence of British political parties, competing over non-ethnic ideological principles and interests, would have eroded sectarianism within Northern Ireland (see Chapter 4). This regret was shared by a very small minority of unionists in 1920, but today is rapidly becoming the conventional wisdom of liberal unionists (Aughey 1989). However, their regrets beg the question: why did British policy-makers not incorporate Northern Ireland within the British political system, after 1920 or 1925? The obvious answer is that they did not regard Northern Ireland as part of the British nation.

Having decided to partition Ireland in 1920, and having conceded dominion status to the Irish Free State in 1921, British policy-makers were faced with strategic choices over Northern

Ireland—although they preferred to avoid them rather than confront them. On the one hand, in the external interests of the British state, they could improve relations with the new Irish Free State, either by cajoling Ulster unionists into accepting some mode of Irish unification, or by reducing the size of Northern Ireland to remove its Catholic minority. Such policies would have facilitated the retrenchment of the overburdened British imperial state, and enabled it to preserve its geo-political and defence interests in Ireland (even if the Irish state eventually became a republic rather than a dominion). On the other hand, in the internal interests of British nation-building, policy-makers could choose to assimilate *all* the Northern Irish into the British nation. There were also two principal ways to achieve this objective, either by the integration of Northern Ireland (including its Catholic minority) into Britain, or of a territorially reduced (and more homogeneously Protestant) Northern Ireland.[11]

The vigorous pursuit of one strategy, external interests of state or a nation-building policy, might have resolved Britain's 'Irish Question' before World War II. Why were these choices rarely explicitly posed, let alone taken? First, it was widely believed that Lloyd George had solved the major Irish questions through partition and the Treaty. The bloody wars and difficult negotiations of 1919–23 were regarded as final settlements. Lloyd George had reorganized the British archipelago so that Irishmen fought Irishmen rather than against Englishmen.[12] Reopening Irish questions promised the opening of Pandora's boxes. Ireland was best managed with a barge-pole. Stormont was an excellent device for 'screening out' Irish questions from entering British politics. The creation of two Irish Parliaments and the reduction of the number of (Northern) Irish MPs at Westminster removed Irish questions from the centre of the political agenda. After 1923 the major parties accepted the Speaker's convention that Northern Irish questions were matters for the Northern Ireland Parliament which would not be discussed at Westminster, and in consequence the Westminster Parliament spent an average of two hours per year on Northern Ireland between partition and the emergence of renewed troubles in the late 1960s (Lyons 1973: 700).

British party competition, now increasingly focused on economic and class cleavages, was a by-product of the 'solution' of Irish questions between 1920 and 1921. Territorial and religious issues receded in importance. The focus of political competition on bargainable issues of economic welfare took the heat out of the British political system, facilitating its stability. British national development would proceed more smoothly without further interventions in Ireland.[13] It was no longer in the interests of ambitious politicians to raise Irish questions in British politics. Northern Ireland commanded a mere 12 or 13 seats in the House of Commons, by comparison with the 105 seats which Ireland had in the 1918 election. The abolition of the Stormont Parliament would have required increased representation for the province, and whose interests would that have served? Labour had no interest in the revival of internal party debate over the territorial definition of the British state, especially given its electoral heartlands in Scotland and Wales. Northern Ireland was best left alone as 'a place apart'. Contributions from Northern Irish trade unionists were welcomed by the Labour Party, but the party deliberately refused to organize in the province. The Conservatives had been and remained the Conservative and Unionist Party, but felt no need fully to incorporate the Ulster Unionist Party within its ranks. Labour avoided organizing in Northern Ireland to prevent creating possible divisions within its own ranks; whereas the Conservatives felt no need to do so given that the bulk of Northern Ireland's Westminster MPs habitually voted with them. These reasons explain why no moves were made by British policy-makers to integrate Northern Ireland into the British nation. Knowledge of their force encouraged the establishment of local domination by Ulster Protestants. Hegemonic control, provided its uglier manifestations were not too visible, was preferable for British policy-makers to the known historical costs of direct intervention and management of Irish affairs. Northern Ireland was best kept quarantined from 'normal' British politics (Arthur 1985).[14]

There were also reasons of state why British policy-makers persistently avoided making dramatic choices over the status of Northern Ireland after 1921. The integration of Northern Ireland into Britain would guarantee poor relations with the Irish Free State and Irish America; whereas repartition or forced Irish unification might renew the bloody conflicts of the early 1920s. Northern Ireland remained therefore both a problem and an issue for negotiation between the British and Irish states throughout the 1920s and 1930s. The interests of the British state were clear: good relations, especially in defence, with their neighbour in the British archipelago and the maintenance of good relations with all British dominions. However, the British could not or were not prepared to deliver Irish unity, at least until they were threatened by German conquest. Yet they were also not prepared to resolve the status of Northern Ireland in the 1920s and 1930s as long as it might jeopardize Anglo-Irish relations. It was only in 1949, following the declaration of an Irish Republic, and the experience of Irish neutrality during World War II, that the British government clarified the status of Northern Ireland in the Ireland Act (1949):

Northern Ireland remains part of His Majesty's dominions and of the United Kingdom and it is hereby affirmed that in no event will Northern Ireland or any part thereof cease to be part of His Majesty's dominions and of the United Kingdom without the consent of the parliament of Northern Ireland.

British equivocation over the status of Northern Ireland, still present in the above formulation, created a climate in which hegemonic control made sense to Ulster Protestants. The Act of 1949 lifted the threat of repartition (note the reference above to 'any part thereof'), and it also formally consolidated control over Northern Ireland's status in the hands of its own Parliament. However, given that the British Constitution was very flexible, and that every Act of Westminster was as reversible as any other, unionist fears were only marginally eased. They knew that they were not regarded as really British, and that there were always going to be circumstances when their status would be negotiable in Britain's interests.

The Second Irish Nation-Building Failure

Irish nation-building failure also reinforced the milieu which established hegemonic control in Northern Ireland. The Stormont regime owed its existence to the refusal of Ulster Protestants to identify with the Irish nation, a refusal premissed on the assumption that Gaelic, Catholic, and anti-British values excluded them. Protestants perceived independent Ireland as confirming their fears, and as a justification of the political development of Northern Ireland. The lament of Senator W. B. Yeats during the 1925 debate over the illegalization of divorce in the Irish Free State was prophetic:

If you show that [we are] going to be governed by Catholic ideas and Catholic ideas alone, you will never get the North. You will create an impassable barrier between North and South, and you will pass more and more Catholic laws, while the North will, gradually, assimilate its divorce and other laws to England. You will put a wedge into the midst of this nation. (cited in Kennedy 1988: 159–60)

Yeats's analysis and prediction can be generalized if we replace the word Catholic by the omnibus expression 'Gaelic–Catholic–anti–British'.

Irish cultural nationalism offended Protestant sensibilities, and it is now increasingly accepted in revisionist Irish history that Ulster unionism was mirrored, albeit in a less extreme and unjust way, by the exclusivism and sectarianism of Irish nationalism (O'Halloran 1985). The conditions under which the Irish Free State was created and developed had unintended consequences which facilitated the consolidation of hegemonic control in Ulster. The Irish Civil War was fought by Irish nationalists over the terms of the Anglo-Irish Treaty, but not over the terms which referred to Ulster. Both sides assumed that the Ulster question would be satisfied by the Boundary Commission in ways which would make the northern state unworkable. The terms which provoked the Civil War were those which affected the scope and extent of Irish 'statehood', its degree of substantive and ritual subordination to the British Empire. The geographical scope of the state was not an issue. The war was fought between the pro-Treaty forces, who argued that the Treaty gave the Irish Free State the freedom to achieve freedom, and anti-Treaty forces, who argued that it did not. This war of Green against Green (Hopkinson 1988) occluded the Ulster question, and thereby facilitated the consolidation of hegemonic control by the Ulster Unionist Party. The victors of the war in the South were in no mood to renew instability through prosecuting another war for the North, and in effect accepted British money in return for burying the report of the Boundary Commission of 1925, and tacitly accepting partition.

Moreover, although the Civil War was won by the pro-Treaty forces, it established the central axis of competition between the parties which emerged in the new state. The two main Irish parties carried on the Civil War by parliamentary means, competing over which of them would best establish the freedom of the Irish state. Competition focused on which party would best stand up for the Irish against the British. This party competition had three mutually reinforcing effects in the years before 1949. First, the external activities of the Irish Free State were directed towards the repeal, rewriting, and alteration of those terms of the Treaty which affected Anglo-Irish relations, and which were regarded as intolerable violations of Irish sovereignty. Second, the internal activities of the Irish Free State were directed towards achievements made possible by independent Irish statehood: i.e. distinct cultural, social, and economic policies. Finally, both of these external and internal state-building activities, almost inevitably, cut against the logic of contending that Ulster Protestants were parts of the Irish nation, and served to reinforce partition. The less Ireland remained within the symbolic trappings of the British Empire and the more its internal policies reflected the cultural values of its Catholic majority, the greater the likelihood was that hegemonic control would be entrenched north of the border. Irish state-building, logically but unintentionally, took place at the expense of pan-Irish nation-building. The symmetry is evident, since British state interests were also pursued at the expense of pan-British nation-building in Northern Ireland. Hegemonic control in Northern Ireland was the joint by-product of these nation-building failures.

5. THE COLLAPSE OF HEGEMONIC CONTROL, 1963–1972

The status of Northern Ireland was apparently consolidated by the Ireland Act of 1949, and the continuing coercive power at the disposal of the Stormont regime was advertised in its ability to cope with the IRA campaign of 1956–62. Why then, within a decade of a resounding defeat of the IRA, was the system shattered?

There are three obvious answers. First, the 'modernization' of Northern Ireland under the premiership of Terence O'Neill (1963–9) exposed the limits to reforming hegemonic control and unleashed (what in retrospect can be seen as) uncontrollable political developments. Second, social justice and civil rights movements, based primarily on Catholic constituencies, advertised the position of the Catholic minority within and outside Northern Ireland. They used the rhetoric of equal citizenship to undermine hegemonic control. Finally, Catholics' appeal to be treated as British citizens prompted the 'benign' intervention of the embarrassed central state, then managed by Labour and Conservative governments who shared the view that the application of the British social-democratic consensus to Northern Ireland was eminently reasonable.

Lundyism from above: O'Neill's Failed 'Modernization'

The breakdown of hegemonic control in Northern Ireland exemplifies Tocqueville's thesis that when a bad government seeks to reform itself it is in its greatest danger (Arthur 1980: 107). O'Neill's modernizing threatened Unionist/Orange clientelism, raised Catholic expectations, and trapped British policy-makers into believing that the reform of sectarianism in Northern Ireland was under way, thereby helping to precipitate Westminster's intervention (Bew and Patterson 1985: 7–34).

O'Neill sought to modernize political institutions in Northern Ireland to accommodate Keynesian economic, infrastructural and regional programmes. His programme threatened the local-government system because he wanted to centralize key decision-making powers in the hands of either Stormont departments or quasi-governmental agencies. This managerial rationalization, which would have reduced the numbers of councils and their functions, caused grave anxieties to those who ran and benefited from local power bases, especially in western Northern Ireland. Such persons were to become key figures in intra-Unionist opposition to O'Neill. The latter's rhetoric of good feelings alerted militant unionists to the threat of disruption of hegemonic control but at the same time it also raised Catholic expectations. O'Neill's indulgence of symbolic politics—visiting Catholic schools, meeting the Irish Taoiseach, Sean Lemass, and his visible irritation with 'archaic' sectarian discourse—intimated change: too much for some Protestants, too little for many Catholics.

New Catholic Stratagems: Social Justice and Civil Rights

However, Catholic politics had also changed in the years after 1949. Traditional nationalism had failed. Constitutional nationalism, articulated most recently in the Anti-Partition League of 1948–9, had done nothing to alter Northern Ireland's constitutional status or to improve Catholics' position within Northern Ireland. The Ireland Act of 1949 seemed to copper-fasten partition. Voting for Sinn Féin candidates in elections in the 1950s expressed alienation but achieved nothing, apart from encouraging the IRA to believe that insurrection was viable. However, its military nationalism failed more abysmally than constitutional nationalism, and its 1956–62 campaign was a fiasco. 'Volunteers' were interned in both the North and South. They won no sustained international publicity or sympathy, and more importantly so little support from northern Catholics that they dumped their arms. In the wake of this crushing defeat some republicans embarked upon the political rather than military road, eventually becoming more Marxist–Leninist than Catholic. By 1967 the IRA, as a military organization, was close to extinction.

In this milieu reformist, and hitherto disorganized, Catholic voices began to make themselves heard. The Catholic middle class, while not abandoning their nationalist sentiments (McCloskey 1989), began to seek the reform of Northern Ireland as their first goal; and before long for many it became the overriding goal. A succession of groups emerged to advertise minority grievances under the Stormont regime. The British Labour Party, and to a lesser extent the Stormont regime, were the addressees. National Unity (established in 1959), the Campaign for Social Justice (established in 1964), and the Northern Ireland Civil Rights Association (established in 1967), represented successive challenges both to the traditional Nationalist Party and to conventional republicanism. Emphasis was placed upon the demand for 'equal citizenship' and upon disparities between British and Northern Irish standards of democracy.

The Catholic middle class were encouraged both by O'Neill's apparent commitment to vaguely defined change and by his reluctance to undertake any steps which would genuinely redress sectarian inequalities. His moderation 'lay in avoiding bigotry' (Arthur 1974: 17). O'Neill's Government's decisions over the siting of major public projects (new towns and a university) showed up the gap between the rhetoric of reform and reality, enabling Catholics to press home their case. Discrimination, electoral abuses, housing-allocation procedures, the restricted local-government franchise, and the sectarian B Specials were the key issues raised in the new Catholic agenda, targeted at the governing British Labour Party in Westminster and gradually taken to the streets in demonstrations modelled on the American civil rights movement. The appeal addressed to the centre (Westminster, Whitehall, and the mainland parties) was simple: 'We are second-class British citizens. Make us first-class citizens. Enforce your laws and practices in Northern

Ireland.' This challenge echoed that addressed to Washington by the black civil rights movement in the 1960s. The local minority was calling on Westminster and Whitehall to redress their grievances against the local majority.

British Intervention: The Politics of Embarrassment

Why did Westminster and Whitehall listen? They had turned a blind eye in the 1920s, 1930s, late 1940s, and the mid-1950s when Catholic discontent was effectively crushed, so what changed in the 1960s? First, Westminster and Whitehall were being explicitly addressed. Until the 1960s the Catholic minority had articulated their grievances at the Irish government or the Irish diaspora in America. They had hoped for change from without rather than within the British system. Addressing London implied some degree of willingness to accept and work the British Constitution, and accordingly made it more difficult for the centre of government to ignore them.

Contingent developments also forced London to listen. As in the United States national and global television made the exercise of hegemonic control over a local minority embarrassingly visible. The power élites of regimes whose international rhetoric suggested that they were homesteads of Western human rights were confronted by their own backyards. The Labour Government, in office since 1964, also contained active back-benchers. Some of them, led by Paul Rose, were interested in ensuring equal citizenship for Catholics, others were more interested in re-raising the national question. Harold Wilson had continually encouraged O'Neill's 'reformist' rhetoric. Consequently, when the Catholic minority took O'Neill's rhetoric at face value he felt obliged to encourage reform. The relatively 'peaceable militancy' of the civil rights movement, the intransigence and fragmentation within the unionist bloc, the resurgence of extra-parliamentary action by loyalist Protestants, were all taking place in the absence of visible nationalist irredentism (from the IRA or other quarters). Protestants were thereby deprived of one key source of legitimation for hegemonic control: the threat of armed nationalist insurrection.

British intervention occurred against this background. The key instruments of hegemonic control, the local security forces, ran amok. The RUC and the USC (B Specials) were seen to permit (and participate in) naked sectarian attacks against civil rights demonstrations. They were seen to be partial when they attacked Catholics in Derry, who promptly resorted to street battles against the police, and even more so when Loyalists mobilized retaliation attacks on Catholic West Belfast. Unarmed Catholics apparently seeking full British citizenship were seen to be being repressed by armed Protestants who claimed to be more British than the British. Strategically minded Catholic actors played these developments consciously. Reformists sought to expose the 'violence in the system' precisely to encourage the British to dismantle Stormont; and revolutionaries hoped to precipitate a more thoroughgoing crisis for republican or socialist purposes.

The British first intervened on a large scale 'to keep the peace' in 1969. The Army was brought in to regulate conflict. The Westminster government, both under Labour and the Conservatives who succeeded them in 1970, pressured the Unionists into conceding the entire package of demands made by the civil rights movement. The local security forces were to be disarmed, reorganized and reformed. Professional public administration on the mainland model would replace clientelism in local government. The local-government system would be reformed, and its franchise would be based on 'one person one vote'. Discriminatory practices and incitement to sectarian hatred were to be outlawed. Commissions of inquiry were established which reported unfavourably on the Stormont regime.

The impact of British intervention was destabilizing. Unionists were outraged and in disarray. Admonishment from Westminster and the loss of direct control over the local security forces created sharp divisions between reformers and intransigents. The Ulster Unionist Party split, and two new parties formed: Paisley's ultra-loyalist Democratic Unionist Party, and the reforming biconfessional Alliance Party. There were three different Unionist Prime Ministers within three years. Catholics were elated, but also confused. Should they press for reform and power-sharing within Northern Ireland, for the abolition of Stormont, or for full-blown national unification?[15] Constitutional nationalists and social democrats rapidly merged to create the Social Democratic and Labour Party, but remained unclear as to their primary objectives. Republicans split, dividing between Marxists and ultra-nationalists. This split divided the IRA, revived by the attacks on Catholic areas and the absence of any means of defending them. The militantly nationalist and militarily minded Provisional IRA emerged as the more powerful faction, and rapidly went on to the offensive, seeking to bring down the Stormont regime and to end the British presence in Ireland. From February 1971 the level of violence rose sharply, most of it due to republican terrorism (Hewitt 1987). Unionists saw the birth of the Provisionals and their military campaign as proof of their contention that the civil rights movement had been a front for the IRA. They demanded to use the tried and trusted mode of repression, internment without trial. They told the British government that they would continue to reform Northern Ireland provided they were able to repress nationalist insurrection. Without internment they could not command the support of their own community. The Conservative Government, anxious to avoid becoming embroiled in Northern Ireland, granted this request in August 1971.

However, internment proved to be a political and military disaster, the last attempt to reassert hegemonic control. It unified the entire Catholic bloc in civil and armed disobedience, brought a propaganda coup for the Provisional IRA and international embarrassment for the British, and was the catalyst for even greater violence. The wrong people were arrested, some of them were tortured, and the level of violence rose rather than fell in its aftermath. Hegemonic control was over. Revolt was thinkable, although it remained to be seen whether it was workable. The British moved to abolish Stormont in March 1972, prompted by the grave embarrassment of the killing of thirteen unarmed Catholic demonstrators by British troops in Derry in January of that year. In turn the abolition of Stormont precipitated a wave of loyalist paramilitary mobilization and sectarian assassination of Catholic civilians.

The Exogenous Causes of the Collapse of Hegemonic Control

The collapse of hegemonic control had nothing to do with British imperialism and little to do with Irish nationalist irredentism. There was in fact much less of both these 'national character traits' in the 1960s. The limits to the maintenance of hegemonic control were exposed precisely because this was the case. The collapse of control was precipitated by other exogenous consequences of British and Irish state-building, just as it had been created and maintained by such factors.

Developments in the Irish state contributed decisively to the collapse of Stormont in unanticipated ways. The fact that the Irish government actively participated in crushing the IRA campaign of 1956–62 helped break the mould in Northern Irish politics. It deprived unionists of the argument that the Irish state and the IRA were in coalition against their regime, and created the space for O'Neill's rhetoric, which called for 'community reconciliation'. This tendency was reinforced by the major switch in Irish political and economic development strategy which took place in 1958 and has continued, with minor hiccups, ever since. The Irish state decided to develop itself through encouraging international and multinational capitalist investment and through abandoning any form of autarkic nationalism. The resolution of the national question would have to await advanced economic development. Good relations with the UK, Northern Ireland, and the European Community became imperative for the success of this strategy: irredentism was bad for business. Fianna Fáil, the party which managed the transition from protectionism to economic liberalism, came to believe (or claimed to believe) that without advanced economic development Ulster Protestants would continue to find unification an uncompelling prospect. They became 'technocratic anti-partitionists'.[16] The post-1958 strategy was of course primarily driven by political considerations within the Irish Republic but it had significant spillover effects on Northern Ireland.

Fianna Fáil effectively legitimized O'Neill's Government in the historic encounters between Irish and Northern ministers in 1965 and 1966. The impact on Catholic politics within Northern Ireland was decisive. The Nationalist Party, after belated consultations with Dublin, decided to accept, for the first time, the role of official Opposition in 1965. Northern Catholics knew more firmly than ever before that they were on their own. Material and legal improvements would have to come from within Northern Ireland, i.e. within the British political system. Moreover, the behaviour of the Irish government after 1958 improved Anglo-Irish relations. The abandonment of vigorous irredentism after de Valera's departure from active politics made it more difficult for the British government to refuse to accommodate the pressure from the Catholic minority for reform, and made unionists' justifications for hegemonic control seem threadbare and self-serving. The fact that the Irish government did not switch back to full-blooded irredentism when the troubles broke out (despite the temptations and a murky arms-running scandal involving some key government ministers) increased the international pressure upon British policy-makers to reform Northern Ireland.

The development of the British state in the post-war period also had unintended consequences which served to undermine the foundations of hegemonic control. The British welfare state was dramatically extended after World War II, and applied in Northern Ireland. Its universalist principles meant that Catholics began to benefit from the state, in health, social security, and education. Universalism and sectarianism clashed. The material prosperity of the worst off improved. Catholics began to interact more with state institutions and to expect more from them. Their dependence upon their own community organizations and the Church was reduced, hastening the erosion of deference to their traditional clerical and professional service élites, making them more capable of participation in the social protests of the civil rights movements.

As British regional policy and Keynesian interventionism in industrial policy got under way in the early 1960s the Unionist Government was obliged to respond to the challenges of social-democratic modernization. The Protestant working class wanted more economic growth and material rewards, just like their British counterparts. A rising vote for the Northern Ireland Labour Party in 1958 indicated a certain impatience amongst the Protestant proletariat. O'Neill's programme was thus triggered by pressures from the British social-democratic state, pressures for governmental reorganization and new public infrastructure to meet the requirements of modern multinationals. These programmes both raised and dashed Catholic expectations since the prime sites and beneficiaries of the new public expenditure seemed to be located east of the Bann, mostly a Protestant-dominated area.

There is also widespread acceptance amongst analysts of an important unintended consequence of the British welfare state. The civil rights movement was spearheaded by a new Catholic middle class, spawned by participation in British economic growth and the educational benefits derived from the new welfare state, especially the 1947 Education Act (Arthur 1974: 23; Buckland 1981; Farrell 1976). Attempts to challenge the thesis of a new Catholic middle class are not compelling.[17] The civil rights movements and the student-based movement, the People's Democracy, were led by middle-class figures. These organizations, even if their importance has been exaggerated in comparison with local and traditional Catholic organizations, were new in their rhetoric and objectives. The same is true of National Unity which challenged the Nationalist

Party in the early 1960s (McKeown 1986). These leaders led the
organizations which attracted public and British attention and
developed the rhetoric of equal citizenship which destroyed the
reputation of the Stormont regime. Civil rights rhetoric partially
displaced traditional Catholic nationalism, and one reason it did so
was because Catholics had been brought up as citizens in the new
British welfare state. The British state had unintendedly made
Northern Irish Catholics more British. The tragedy of the unionist
reaction was that it failed to realize that this was an opportunity
rather than a threat.

6. THE THIRD WAVE OF STATE- AND NATION-BUILDING FAILURES, 1972–1985

Thus the establishment, maintenance, and collapse of the Stormont
system owed much to forces exogenous to Northern Ireland, to the
unintended consequences of British and Irish state- and nation-
building failures. However, a third wave of state- and nation-
building failure commenced in 1972. The solutions to the conflict
considered and spurned since then are elaborated on by most
authors in the chapters which follow. Moreover, the scale and
patterns of violence and party-political developments are treated in
Appendices 3 and 4. Therefore it is not necessary here to offer a
detailed chronology of events, policies, or institutions which can be
found elsewhere (Arthur and Jeffrey 1988). However, it is essential
to recognize that British and Irish state- and nation-building failure
have continued.

British failure since 1972 is more evident. Only the outbreak of
conflict and violence in Northern Ireland prompted reluctant intervention from Westminster. British policy-makers between 1968 and
1972, by their indecision and willingness to sustain Stormont, albeit
in a reformed mode, showed that they were not prepared to contemplate the integration option. Northern Ireland was to remain a
place apart. Instead from 1972 until 1985 British governments
pursued a twin-track, and primarily internal, strategy: encouraging
the creation of a devolved power-sharing—or consociational—
government within the province, and falling back on direct rule
when that proved a failure. The consociational strategy failed in
1973–4 with the collapse of the Sunningdale experiment; in 1975
when the Constitutional Convention failed to produce agreement; in

1979–80 when cross-party talks produced no results; and again in 1982 when Jim Prior's experiment in 'rolling devolution' was boycotted by nationalists. Successive British governments therefore felt obliged to continue with direct rule. Consequently, the government of Northern Ireland has been primarily executed through the Secretary of State for Northern Ireland, a super-prefect who is in effect the plenipotentiary of central government in the province. Local government has been emasculated and in the absence of a devolved government elected Northern Ireland politicians have no substantive input into Northern Ireland policy-making. The Secretary of State is not beholden to any local interests, is not a member of any Northern Ireland political party, and has the capacity to make laws and policy through Orders in Council and executive action without the express consent of any of the locally elected representatives in the province. This structure of government creates the appearance if not the substance of colonial administration.

Successive Secretaries of State have claimed to be neutral arbiters of the conflict. Their neutrality rests upon the refusal to countenance 'majority rule' in anything resembling its pre-1972 manifestation (the anti-unionist premiss), or to contemplate coercing unionists into a united Ireland (the anti-nationalist premiss). In the absence of a consociational agreement Britain persisted with direct rule as the least bad default option. British governments also committed themselves to reforming Northern Ireland along the lines of the post-war British consensus. Social problems were to be solved through public expenditure, economic growth, and professionalized administration, especially in housing and the operation of the security forces. The idea here was that equal citizenship within the welfare state would enable Northern Ireland to transcend its sectarian conflicts. Successive governments also responded, after some equivocation, to political violence as a problem of 'law and order' rather than as a problem of 'legitimacy'. Violence was 'criminalized'. However, the British government also introduced an array of new repressive legislation, draconian by liberal-democratic standards, which made the mere 'criminalization' of violence less easy to sell abroad let alone in Ireland. The overarching concern of British policy-makers appeared to be to quarantine Northern Ireland (Arthur 1985), to prevent conflict spilling over into Britain, rather than to tackle the fundamental divisions through vigorous pursuit of state- or nation-building strategies.

British policy-making between 1972 and 1985 was not a success. It failed to achieve the establishment of an agreed devolved government. Direct rule was increasingly discredited, both domestically and internationally. It did not appear to be neutral, even if it was meant to be. The British were perceived to rely on sectarian instruments of government—the Protestant-dominated RUC and the Ulster Defence Regiment, which seemed to be merely a new version of the B Specials—and the 'extraordinary' legal system. Tacit integrationist measures—such as increasing the number of Northern Ireland seats at Westminster—were perceived as pro-unionist by the SDLP and encouraged them to return to traditional abstentionist politics. The insufficiency of reform, especially in employment practices, in political participation, and symbolic and cultural recognition of their ethnic identity, encouraged Catholics to return to traditional nationalism. The IRA could not be defeated, and deliberately set out to destabilize the legitimacy of the British presence in Ireland. British security policy unintentionally played into the IRA's hands. In the Catholic ghettos and border areas the policies of internment, screening, emergency legislation, and maltreatment, suspicions of 'shoot-to-kill' practices, and, above all, British management of the hunger strikes of 1980–1 enabled Sinn Féin to mobilize an electoral constituency from 1982 onwards. It did not peak until they had obtained 43 per cent of the nationalist vote in Northern Ireland (see Appendix 4). It was against this background that the British government from 1980–1 set out on the process which culminated in the Anglo-Irish Agreement (Kenny 1986; O'Leary 1987*b*). Since 1985 the British government has formally recognized that there is no 'internal' solution to the stalemate in Northern Ireland and has actively sought to co-operate with the Irish government in the management of Northern Ireland.

From 1972 until the New Ireland Forum of 1983–4 Irish governmental policy-making towards Northern Ireland could also be characterized by the preoccupation with quarantining the conflict and preventing it spilling over into the Republic. Although the Republic supported several British consociational initiatives, notably the Sunningdale Agreement, the Republic's leaders failed to make constitutional, policy, or rhetorical changes which might have made unionists more willing to accommodate their nationalist minority, or to monitor British reform programmes in Northern Ireland with the detail they required. The propensity to concentrate on traditional nationalist shibboleths was most marked under Charles Haughey's Fianna Fáil.

The fear that instability in the North might seriously affect the stability of the Republic finally shifted Irish policy-makers from rhetoric to serious explorations of feasible long-run strategies for solving the conflict in Northern Ireland. The Thatcher–Haughey summit communiqués of 1980–1, which presaged Anglo-Irish studies on the 'totality of relationships' between Britain and Ireland, preceded the New Ireland Forum of 1983–4 established by the Fine Gael–Labour coalition government. The Forum produced a formal revision of traditional Irish nationalist conceptions and enabled Dr FitzGerald's Government to negotiate and sign the Anglo-Irish Agreement in November 1985. The Irish government committed itself to achieving a united Irish nation by consent, recognizing in effect that its history had not been conducive to the attainment of a pan-Irish nation.

CONCLUSION

The chapters which follow take the Anglo-Irish Agreement as their background in evaluating the best ways forward for Northern Ireland, and there is no need to anticipate the authors' arguments here. Some are hostile to the Agreement, others favour it, while others take a more detached view of its significance. However, whatever their differences over creating the best future for Northern Ireland all agree in recognizing Northern Ireland as the site of the most pressing state- and nation-building failures in Western Europe. Their debates centre over which state and which nation, if any, Northern Ireland should belong to, and over how to redress inherited grievances without creating new ones. The arguments matter because as long as they remain unresolved Northern Ireland has no worthwhile future.

Notes

1. Wales had effectively been administratively and politically subordinated to England in pre-modern times.
2. Yugoslavia and the Soviet Union are good examples of countries in which, at least in Tito's and pre-Gorbachev times, segmental contests

for state power were made 'unworkable' under Communist hegemony. However, in the more open regimes which have prevailed since Tito's death, and since Gorbachev's programme of *perestroika*, Communist hegemony has been broken. The Serbs seem intent on replacing Communist by ethnic hegemonic control in Yugoslavia, and in many Soviet republics outside the Russian heartland a series of 'Ulster questions' are emerging.

3. The Pale was the historic boundary which marked English colonial settlement in Ireland. It was situated in the environs of Dublin. The expression 'beyond the pale' still refers to barbarians, those outside the frontiers of (colonial) civilization.

4. Proportional representation had been introduced in the Government of Ireland Act to safeguard minorities in both parts of Ireland (especially the Protestant minority in Southern Ireland). The British government briefly delayed the royal assent to the 1922 Bill abolishing PR, the one and only time they were to delay Northern Ireland legislation for the next half century.

5. An account of the origins of the idea of the Boundary Commission and its critical role in the negotiation of the Anglo-Irish Treaty can be found in Pakenham (1967: 166–82). Accounts of its subsequent failure can be found in Laffan (1983: 91–105) and Gwynn (1950: 202–36). There is little doubt that (1) the Boundary Commission was designed to avoid a break in negotiations over the issue of Ulster because that would have left the British government seriously embarrassed, especially in America, (2) that Lloyd George assured Unionists that the Boundary Commission would lead to very minor changes, whereas he assured Sinn Féin that it would lead to very substantial changes; and (3) that the Irish negotiators paid insufficient attention to the precise wording of the Boundary Commission clauses in the Treaty.

6. The Government Chief Whip declared that the entire measure was necessary to prevent 'Nationalists getting control of the three border counties and Derry City'. He added that 'the best way to prevent the overthrow of the government by people who had no stake in the country and had not the welfare of the people of Ulster at heart was to disenfranchise them' (*Northern Whig*, 11 Jan. 1946, cited in Farrell 1976: 85–6). The Stormont Hansard was incompetently edited to hide this frank remark: it curiously records opposition outrage at a statement absent from the proceedings.

7. This figure is quoted by Buckland (1979: 20) from the records of an inquiry conducted by the Northern Ireland Ministry of Finance to investigate the accusation that Catholics were taking over the service (*sic!*). The petty case of the dismissal of a Catholic gardener at Stormont, because of pressure from the Orange Order, further demonstrates Protestant sectarian surveillance of the civil service (Bew *et al.*, 1979: 97

n. 12). The man in question had a worthy Army record and a reference from the Prince of Wales, but to no avail.

8. Craigavon's telegrams to Chamberlain express this outrage with brutal frankness (Fisk 1983: 207–10). He even suggested that de Valera was a German collaborator, and that the British government should invade Eire (Fisk 1983: 210). Other Unionist leaders were more circumspect, and the biographer of Brookeborough (Prime Minister of Northern Ireland between 1943 and 1963) records his conviction that some Unionists would have felt obliged to accept some Irish unification settlement to maximize support for the British Empire (Barton 1988: 160 ff).

9. The meaning of the desire of Orange marchers to parade through 'their' territory is simple. Continuous reminders of the Protestant ascendancy, hammered out in the terrifying rhythms of Lambeg drums, in their view, are necessary to deter Catholic rebellion. Such marches have been defined as integral components of Protestant culture, but if this is culture, it is like diplomacy, war by other means.

10. 'The most hated character in Orange history is not some fiendish rebel, or devil-worshipping communist agitator, but one Robert Lundy, the Protestant Governor of Londonderry, who in 1689 attempted to surrender the city to the Catholic King James II, rather than wait for the arrival of the glorious Protestant King William III. For the Ulster Protestants the name Lundy has become synonymous with traitors and turncoats. To be a "Lundy" is the capital crime of Ulster loyalism' (Bell 1976: 65).

11. There was another means through which British nation-building was actually followed, and in this case successfully. The Irish in Britain (i.e. in England, Scotland, and Wales) were given full citizenship rights, even after the declaration of the Irish Republic.

12. This insightful cynicism is Alan Beattie's.

13. Thus British national development does not conform to Rokkan's (1975) model of nation-state formation in Western Europe. The model postulates the following developments: (1) the state apparatus is created ('penetration'), (2) a national identity forged ('standardization'), before (3) the masses are turned into citizens ('participation'), and (4) use the state to build a welfare system ('redistribution'). Standardization failed in the British Isles, partly because participation occurred before it had been completed. It is only after the departure of the Irish Free State (after the destruction of British state-penetration) that the British nation-state (except Northern Ireland) conforms to Rokkan's model.

14. British policy-makers were aware of the nature of the UUP's control in Northern Ireland. Sir Henry Batterbee, Assistant Under-Secretary at the Dominions Office in the 1930s, surveyed evidence on discrimination against Catholics in Northern Ireland and concluded that 'the bias of the Northern Ireland authorities is bound to be in favour of those who are

supporters of the present regime: it is everywhere inimicable to good and impartial administration where Government and Party are as closely united in Northern Ireland' (cited in Boyce 1988: 89–90).

15. Hewitt (1981) argues that the civil rights movement was Catholic nationalism in tactical guise. His arguments are ingenious but not compelling. Purdie (1988) shows the extensive range of opinion within the civil rights movement (and thereby implicitly casts doubt upon Hewitt's arguments). Hewitt is correct to show that Catholic nationalism remained important in the 1960s and to contend that simplistic economic or deprivation theses about Catholic behaviour will not do. However, because he relied on older works now discredited by more recent research (Smith 1987), he underestimated the scale of indirect discrimination in Northern Ireland, and the degree of segmentation of its economy and society.

16. The phrase is Tom Lyne's.

17. This plausible thesis has, however, been challenged recently on three grounds (Morgan and Taylor 1988: 6–7). (1) It is objected that the new multinationals were no less discriminatory towards prospective Catholic managers than local Protestant-dominated enterprises. (2) They argue that Catholics were seriously under-represented in the grammar school population (they were only 27 per cent of the grammar school cohort in 1961). More importantly they argue Catholics were also under-represented in higher education. They point out that the expansion in Catholic participation did not come until the mid-1960s, and that Catholic representation amongst the student population at Queen's University Belfast did not reach 33 per cent until 1971–2. (3) They argue that the 1971 census showed a rather small Catholic middle class (2,721 Catholics in social classes A and B, of whom 907 were in the professional and public services).

Morgan and Taylor quote no percentages. However, Aunger (1975: 4) shows that in 1971 12 per cent of economically active Catholics (as opposed to 15 per cent of Protestants) were ranked as members of professional and managerial occupations on the Hall-Jones classification of occupations. The discrepancies were greater between economically active Catholic men (9 per cent) and economically active Protestants (16 per cent). Whatever the merits of the Hall-Jones classification there was a Catholic middle class.

Second, the impact of multinationals may not have affected Catholic middle-class employment prospects but it certainly raised Catholics' expectations, and if one accepts the merits of arguments about relative deprivation the impact of greater economic modernization (multinationals) may well have catalysed discontent amongst the Catholic middle class.

Third, the arguments Morgan and Taylor advance about Catholic proportions in higher education are unpersuasive. It is the growth of Catholic participation in higher education rather than its absolute level which must be critical in evaluating the 'new middle class' thesis, and they do not deny that such growth was occurring.

Finally, what Morgan and Taylor omit to examine is the meaning of 'new' in the 'new middle class' thesis. Whatever the objective indicators on the absolute level or rate of growth of Catholics in higher education and new occupations nobody disputes the subjective 'newness' of the Catholic middle class in the 1960s.

2

A Unitary Irish State

Anthony Coughlan

> In Ireland over the centuries we have tried every possible formula—direct rule, indirect rule, genocide, apartheid, puppet parliaments, real parliaments, martial law, civil law, colonization, land reform and partition. Nothing has worked. The only solution we have not tried is absolute and unconditional withdrawal.
>
> (Paul Johnson, *New Statesman*, 1970)

ALL policy prescriptions express values. The case for a unitary Irish state rests on democratic and internationalist grounds. The democratic ground is that this is the wish of the majority of the Irish people, as expressed by their elected representatives on various occasions this century.[1] From the Irish nationalist standpoint, the unionists who oppose self-determination are a politically alienated minority of the Irish nation possessing minority rights but not entitled to override the political wishes of the majority when majority and minority rights conflict.

The internationalist ground is that friendly and stable relations between nations and nation-states, particularly when neighbours, as in the case of Britain and Ireland, can only exist when they recognize and respect one another's integrity, independence, and sovereignty. From this perspective, internationalism and peace between nations depend upon respect for the principle of self-determination on a world scale. National communities normally have special interests and problems which they are best able to deal with themselves by making their own laws and conducting their domestic affairs and international relations in accordance with the wishes of the majority of their people. The attempt by governments of another nation or group of nations to deny or frustrate such self-determination is in effect imperialism. It is the antithesis therefore of genuine internationalism.

1. MAJORITIES AND MINORITIES

These propositions form a set of coherent and interrelated principles in accordance with which democrats can make political and moral judgements about national problems generally and the Irish problem in particular. It is only by basing policy upon them that the relevant governments, and particularly the government of Britain, can find a way out of the labyrinth of the Irish problem towards a final settlement which would make possible permanent good relations between the peoples of these islands. Contrariwise, unless public policy is so based, one can take it that violence, trouble, and instability will continue indefinitely in Northern Ireland—or if it recedes for a period will recrudesce again—and that any other attempted 'solution' will prove abortive.

Until a united Ireland is achieved, opposition will be expressed in constitutional and extra-constitutional ways. If there is no foreseeable practical way forward towards attaining a united Ireland, embodying the wishes of the Irish majority, by constitutional and peaceful means—either because British policy stands in the way or Irish constitutional politicians fail to give a convincing lead—then it is a fact of life that some of those who wish to see their country united in independence will take up arms to seek to attain that end by violence. Democrats may deplore this, but they should be able to understand it. One may particularly deplore it if one recognizes that the means chosen—a military campaign—shows no likelihood of obtaining the political end desired because of the disparity of strength between the parties, but rather aggravates communal division. But such a recognition should increase the obligation on those opposed to violence to show that there is a more effective way. The root of IRA violence is a resentment and frustration which should be wholly understandable. It is futile as well as hypocritical for critics to moralize about the IRA for seeking to end partition by means of bullets and bombs unless they can show that the constitutional path is more effective and unless they work for it by example. The constitutional politicians so challenged are of course the Irish government and opposition in the Dáil, the SDLP in the

North, and those in the Labour and Liberal Democratic camps in the
British Parliament, from where alone a change in British government
policy on Ireland can realistically be expected to come.

Unitary or Federal–Confederal?

It has never been a matter of principle for Irish nationalists that an
all-Ireland state should be unitary or federal. But such consideration
as has been given to the matter, as for instance in the New Ireland
Forum, has pointed to the superior merit of a unitary state over a
federation or confederation.[2]

The Kilbrandon Commission on the British Constitution, which
examined different possible governmental structures for the United
Kingdom in the early 1970s, concluded that, even at its best, federalism is an awkward system to operate (Kilbrandon Commission
1973: 152 ff). It was a more suitable structure in the nineteenth
century when the functions of central government were much fewer
and the pressures for equal standards of taxes and public services
throughout the state were much less urgent than they are today. The
Kilbrandon Commission noted that, in order to make federalism
work in modern conditions and to ensure greater uniformity, federal
countries have been compelled to take steps which tend to undermine the principle of provincial sovereignty on which the system
itself is based. Thus, for example, the modern United States seems to
be moving away from a nominal federalism to an effectively
decentralized unitary government. Moreover, there seem to be no
examples of a unitary state like the Irish Republic changing to
federalism, with the sole exception of West Germany in the unique
circumstances of the aftermath of World War II.[3]

As a result of its research and deliberations, the Kilbrandon
Commission advocated devolution and radical decentralization
within the United Kingdom. It held that to adopt a fully-fledged
federalism would be going too far, principally because it would
undermine political and economic unity and make the objectives of
the state as a whole more difficult to attain. It concluded: 'Only
within the general ambit of one supreme elected authority is it likely
that there will emerge the degree of unity, cooperation and flexibility
which common sense suggests is desirable.'

The Kilbrandon Commission's defence of a unitary state for the
United Kingdom and its criticism of the appropriateness of federalism for dealing with the different political interests of the English,

Scots, and Welsh within one state, seem apposite when considering what constitutional structure might best help overcome Ireland's politico-religious divisions. Thus a confederation of North and South would scarcely qualify for being a united Ireland at all. Its pre-requisite would seem to be some form of independent North, an arrangement which would entrench the permanent-minority political status of the nationalist community. A two-province federation, as put forward by Fine Gael, would be analogous to a confederation (Fine Gael 1979). A four-province federation, as advocated by Desmond Fennell (Fennell 1978a,b) and others, and by Sinn Féin (Sinn Féin 1971) until they dropped their *Eire Nua* policy in 1982, comes up against the objection that—however desirable a measure of administrative devolution and decentralization might be—there is no popular demand either North or South for the division of sovereignty between central and provincial governments which federalism proper would require. It would be administratively cumbersome, requiring the establishment of a new tier of govern-ment, with four legislatures and four executives, under a federal legislature and executive, in an island of five million people where it is widely felt there is more than enough government already.

More fundamentally, perhaps, a federal–confederal arrangement would tend to perpetuate some of the worst political aspects of partition. A federation–confederation which joined Northern Ireland to the South, would enable northern unionists to continue to exercise effective political power within the former area, at least for a period. It would encourage them to maintain that political Prot-estantism which has been at the root of the anti-Catholic bigotry, political misrule and sectarian discrimination in the allocation of jobs, housing, and public office, from which northern Catholics and nationalists have suffered when under UUP majority rule in the past. Maintaining Northern Ireland as a distinct political unit within a federation would continue to foster the irrational attitudes at the root of such behaviour. It would perpetuate the psychology of the *laager*, give a further injection of political life to those unionist leaders who have built their careers on the exploitation of that psychology, and retard the perception by northern unionists of a shared community of interest and citizenship with their nationalist fellow countrymen. That is why nationalists throughout this island would oppose any constitutional arrangement likely to perpetuate unionist political dominance in the North. For them it is Northern

Ireland itself which is, in the oft-quoted phrase of the present Irish Taoiseach, Charles Haughey, a 'failed political entity'—most obviously because it lacks the normal political consensus between majority and minority which would enable it to work. Federalism–confederalism would be an endeavour to endow with a spuriously sacrosanct character the state boundary drawn by Lloyd George's Government in 1920, which neither geography, historical tradition nor political logic can justify.

The New Ireland Forum pointed out that federalism–confederalism would permit North and South to retain the many separate laws and practices which reflect the different development of both areas since 1920. But for most nationalists an important reason for favouring a unitary state is that it would most expeditiously remove the Orange–Green political lumber from the past which has built up in both parts of divided Ireland under partition, retarding political development South and North. Ireland is virtually unique among developed countries in the weakness of its political labour movement and in the power of political clericalism in both parts of the island. This is mainly due to the division of the country. A prophetic intimation of what the politics of a partitioned Ireland would be like was given in 1914 by the labour leader James Connolly, who was executed following the 1916 Rising, four years before the country was divided by the Government of Ireland Act:

Such a scheme as that agreed to by Redmond and Devlin, the betrayal of the national democracy of industrial Ulster, would mean a carnival of reaction both North and South, would set back the wheels of progress, would destroy the oncoming unity of the Irish Labour movement and paralyse all advanced movement whilst it endured. (Connolly 1973: 275)

The Merits of the Unitary State

In contrast to federalism, which would tend to entrench some of the more undesirable features of partition, a unitary Irish state, with or without devolution for its north-east counties, would most effectively reorient the political energies of the northern Protestant community towards the part they could play in an all-Ireland polity where they would constitute one-fifth of the population, instead of the 2 per cent they amount to in the present United Kingdom. To apply the words of Wolfe Tone, the eighteenth-century Protestant founder of Irish republicanism, a unitary state would provide the optimum framework within which to 'unite the whole people of

Ireland, to abolish the memory of all past dissensions and to sub-stitute the common name of Irishman in place of the denominations of Protestant, Catholic and Dissenter' (Tone 1910: 50). This was the ostensible reason why Sinn Féin dropped its proposal for a nine-county Ulster provincial parliament within a four-province Irish federation.

A unitary state would give most scope for the interplay of the best elements of liberal pluralism on the one hand and of labour on the other. There is an old saying about Irish reunification bringing the forces of national freedom from South to North and the forces of social freedom from North to South. In reality both forces would intermingle in quite a new way in both parts of a united country. So far as the labour movement is concerned, the trade unions in both parts of Ireland are at present affiliated to one national body, the Irish Congress of Trade Unions. Labour is industrially strong in that it organizes over half of Ireland's employees. But it is politically weak in that workers North and South are divided on Orange–Green lines, so that the Irish Congress of Trade Unions must avoid constitutional questions if it is to maintain its organizational unity. In the parliament of a united Ireland political divisions would almost certainly tend in due course to become like those of other advanced industrial societies. A Labour–Republican bloc could be expected to wield a powerful influence in time.

Internationally a unitary Irish state would be likely to be more weighty and influential than a federation–confederation. Its govern-ment would speak to other nations with a more united voice than might be possible for a federation possibly racked by constitutional jurisdictional disputes over the respective rights of federal and provincial governments, which the historical legacy of unionist–nationalist antagonism could well encourage for a period. A unitary state would also be very likely to be more effective in encouraging overall national economic development than a federation–confeder-ation with constitutionally entrenched economic, commercial, and taxation powers at provincial as well as at national level.

In a unitary state minority rights and pluralist democratic values can be adequately protected in ways which would avoid the internal and external political weakness of an all-Ireland state organized on federal lines. One way is through devolution. Devolution is not federation of course, though the two are sometimes confused. Power devolved is power retained. Northern Ireland had devolved government for fifty years until the Stormont Parliament was suspended in 1972, but this did not make the United Kingdom a federation. On a number of occasions Mr Éamon de Valera proposed devolution within a unitary state as a solution of the Northern problem.[4] This would have been an arrangement whereby the reserved and excepted powers retained by London under the Government of Ireland Act 1920 would be transferred to Dublin, with Belfast retaining all or some of the devolved powers it had under that Act. Other mixes of centralized and devolved powers could be envisaged. The Irish Constitution of 1937 is the Constitution of a unitary state with provision for devolution. Its Article 15 states: 'The sole and exclusive power of making laws for the State is vested in the Oireachtas . . . Provision may however be made by law for the creation or recognition of subordinate legislatures and for the powers and functions of these legislatures.'

The special interests of the present unionist population, who would become a political minority in a united Ireland, could be taken account of within the context of a unitary state either through such a devolutionary arrangement as de Valera suggested or through some form of temporary 'power-sharing' at national government level for Ireland as a whole. Mr C. J. Haughey, the present Irish Taoiseach, referred to these possibilities in his statement as leader of the Fianna Fáil Party to the New Ireland Forum in 1983:

The divergent practice which has been followed in many matters, not just matters of a conscientious or moral nature, North and South, mean that complete harmonisation of laws, administrative practices and social structures may only be possible if carried out over a gradual and perhaps extended period. We may have to consider some degree of autonomy for Northern Ireland, be it on the basis of the same area, or a smaller one. We have the example in the state of Great Britain, for instance, of Scotland with its own legal system and its own educational system, an administration in Edinburgh, a cabinet minister, and a Grand Committee of Scottish MPs in Westminster who legislate on Scottish affairs. . . . We would greatly wish to have full Northern participation in an Irish Government and Parliament from the beginning. At present, Northern politicians play no direct role in the government of Northern Ireland. From that frustration there naturally arises a fear among unionists that in a new Ireland they might also be without power or influence and the people they represent discriminated against. A proposal which must be maturely examined is that for a specified transitional period power should be shared in the island as a whole. In an extended and reconstituted government for the whole island, arrangements could be devised to guarantee adequate participation in government by Northern representatives. (New Ireland Forum 1984, No. 1, Public Session, p. 11)

The present Irish Constitution is flexible enough to be adapted to incorporate such changes. For example, a transitional 'power-sharing' arrangement in an all-Ireland state could be provided for by a constitutional amendment, analogous to that which permitted the Republic to join the European Community, whereby such arrangements would have precedence in the event of conflict over every other provision of the Constitution for a period. The alternative would be to draw up an entirely new Constitution for a unitary Irish state, but this would risk putting in jeopardy the many positive aspects of the Republic's present Constitution and open up the possibility of political division over matters quite extraneous to that of devising the best framework for accommodating the erstwhile unionist–nationalist communities in a united Ireland.

The fundamental rights provisions of the Irish Constitution should be sufficient to protect the classical civil liberties for all citizens in a reunified country and prevent any discrimination which northern unionists might fear in the allocation of jobs, housing, or public positions. Indeed, the entrenchment of these rights in a written Constitution, enforceable in the Irish Supreme Court, should in principle provide a stronger defence against improper government encroachment than can be provided under a regime of parliamentary sovereignty such as the United Kingdom. The main areas of difference in civil liberties between North and South relate to abortion and divorce. Legislation permitting both is constitutionally banned in the Republic. These differences could be accommodated in a unitary state by a devolutionary arrangement or by constitutional provision for differential legislation in different administrative areas. At any rate, the differences in social attitudes between North and South with respect to these matters are much exaggerated. While the constitutional provisions on abortion and divorce are frequently cited by people in the North and Britain as evidence of Roman Catholic influence in the Republic, it would be wrong to think that most northern Protestants are liberal in such matters.[5] There is no doubt that the political leaders of the Irish Republic would make strenuous efforts to devise constitutional, legal, and political arrangements which would guarantee Protestant minority rights and assuage all reasonable concerns of the present unionist population in the event of reunification coming practically on to the political agenda.

Practicalities and Obstacles

The main obstacle to Irish reunification, in either a unitary or a federal state, is that it is not British government policy and is unlikely to become so in the immediate future. Britain seeks to maintain sovereignty in Ireland by means of partition. The effect of partition was not, as is usually supposed, to free one part of Ireland while holding the other, or to give each part the form of self-determination its inhabitants wanted, but rather to create a partition system in which England continued to be the overall arbiter of Irish destinies. The Northern troubles are the latest manifestation of England's involvement in her first and oldest colony. It has been axiomatic up to the present that British governments and politicians will seek to stay in Ireland rather than leave. Motivations change with time and doubtless vary with individuals. Inertia, sentiment, and short-term thinking play their part. State boundaries are rarely altered except in a context of general international crisis.

Strategic and military considerations would seem to be the most important single determinant of British policy in relation to Northern Ireland. It touches on sacred matters of national defence. The continuance of the union guarantees bases in Ireland for Britain and for NATO. In a period when states are willing to spend extraordinary resources in preparing for a possible World War III, the cost of maintaining a presence in Ireland, situated astride vital communication lines between Europe and America, might properly be ascribed to the heading of defence expenditure. The *locus classicus* for a statement of Britain's strategic interest in partition is a memorandum in 1949 from Cabinet Secretary Norman Brook to Prime Minister Attlee conveying the views of a working party of top officials:

Now that Eire will shortly cease to owe any allegiance to the Crown, it has become a matter of first-class strategic importance to this country that the North should continue to form part of His Majesty's Dominions. . . . So far as can be foreseen, it will never be to Great Britain's advantage that Northern Ireland should become part of a territory outside His Majesty's jurisdiction. Indeed it seems unlikely that Great Britain would ever be able to agree to it even if the people of Northern Ireland desired it.[6]

There have been many statements from politicians and military people over the past forty years indicating a British interest in facilities in Ireland. For example in 1983 General Farrar-Hockley, former NATO commander in Northern Europe, said:

Ireland would be of considerable value to NATO in the event of a conventional war with the USSR. Irish ports and airfields would be of considerable value in terms of covering the western approaches and the North. There are parts of Ireland which would give considerable range out into the Atlantic for NATO air patrols. That would be of no mean value. Of course it isn't a question of Ireland putting divisions into the field, but there is the question of solidarity with NATO. (*Irish Times*, 18 April 1983)

Whatever the motives, the weight of evidence demonstrates the British government's interest in maintaining the Union, despite occasional wishful thinking to the contrary by the Irish side.[7] Official British policy is embodied in the following formula: 'There shall be no change in the constitutional position of Northern Ireland without the consent of a majority there.' Its latest legal manifestation is in Article 1 of the Anglo-Irish Agreement signed at Hillsborough in 1985. From the nationalist standpoint, this formula is deeply unsatisfactory in that it purports to give democratic legitimacy to an area whose boundaries were so drawn as to constitute unionists into a permanent majority. From the standpoint of retaining British sovereignty a pledge to abide by the wishes of the majority can be safely given because it will never lead to a change without British encouragement. For the British the ideal position would be if Dublin were to co-operate with London to this end, treating the problem as one of security and working to isolate republicans and encourage northern nationalists into 'power-sharing' with unionists—so widening and strengthening the political base of the Union. For recent British governments this seems to be the leitmotif of the so-called 'Anglo-Irish process' and of the Anglo-Irish Agreement. It is unlikely that this British interest in remaining in Ireland will change until there is an era of fundamental *détente* in East–West relations, accompanied by a major shift in internal British politics.

Practically speaking, as long as British policy underpins the unionist position in this way, unionists have no incentive either to contemplate or work towards a common political future with their fellow countrymen in a united Ireland. Any unionist leader prepared to consider that would find himself repudiated as a Lundy[8], and be attacked from his political right.

What then can Irish people do to change British government policy? As the weaker party, the Irish nationalist side must find allies. The most obvious potential allies are, firstly, organized political opinion within Britain itself, especially in Labour and trade union and Liberal Democratic circles, where there is already considerable sympathy for Irish aspirations. Only that is strong enough on its own to alter British government policy and turn the present inchoate popular desire for withdrawal from Ireland into a powerful political force. Secondly, there is international public opinion. And thirdly, as the northern unionist population becomes more disillusioned with the experience of direct rule from London and power-sharing experiments, there should emerge potential allies among them over time who will begin seriously to consider the advantages of Irish unity. Sustained effort by Irish nationalists, and in particular by the Irish government in relation to these three elements, has the potential to alter the balance of political forces on the reunification issue.

In 1981 the British Labour Party adopted a policy of positively favouring the ending of partition 'with consent', reverting thereby to its old policy of the 1920s and 1930s. This was the result of a long campaign of education and agitation on the issue within Labour, conducted by English people who supported majority rule in Ireland and by organizations of the Irish community in Britain (Bell 1982; P. Rose 1982: 178 ff.). But much remains to be done in generalizing support in British Labour and trade union circles for a policy of favouring Irish reunification, until it becomes the policy of Labour in government.[9] The case needs to be argued for altering Britain's 'guarantee' to northern unionists from a 'negative' to a 'positive' form.[10] The Irish government could help significantly if it used its resources to cultivate British labour, trade union, and democratic opinion generally in seeking support for a change in the British government's position on the Union and liaised with the organizations of the near-million-strong Irish community in Britain in so doing. That could inhibit a reversion to Labour–Conservative bipartisanship on the issue. Dublin did considerable lobbying in Conservative circles in the run-up to the Hillsborough agreement and employed individuals full-time for this purpose. A sustained effort directed at Labour and wider democratic opinion in Britain, with a more fundamental aim, should be capable of winning substantial allies for the Irish side. Other sections of nationalist opinion could also help.

In the period following the Agreement it is also open to Dublin to put the British government on the spot, as it were, by inviting it to co-operate with the Irish government in winning unionist consent. This would flush out British policy-makers on whether they would like unionists to consent or not. It has been argued above that they do not; but it may be embarrassing before international opinion to say so.

Nationalists should launch a vigorous propaganda campaign aimed at convincing the British of the merits of constructive disengagement from Ireland. The principal political merit of Britain's adopting a policy of undoing partition is that it would mean that for the first time it was acting justly with reference to the Irish majority. From the moment of its adoption, such a policy end would have the overwhelming support of British and Irish public opinion, including nationalist opinion in Northern Ireland. In time it would bring England's ancient involvement in Ireland to a close and make possible permanent good relations between the two islands without fear of political troubles recurring. The prospect of an eventual end to subsidization of Northern Ireland should be welcome to British taxpayers. Escaping from the Irish imbroglio would raise Britain's standing internationally. It is unfortunate that the standard of Britain's civil liberties, the behaviour of her security forces, and the appearance of impartiality of her courts and legal system have all been adversely affected by her Irish involvement. A whole series of reports (Bennett Committee 1979; Cameron Committee 1969; Compton Committee 1971; Diplock Committee 1972; Gardiner Committee 1975; Hunt Committee 1969; Stalker 1988; Widgery Committee 1972) provide evidence of this.

Irish governments should continue to indicate their willingness to meet Britain's legitimate security and defence interests in the event of a withdrawal from Ireland. The government of a United Ireland would undoubtedly be willing to give Britain satisfactory guarantees that it would not help Britain's enemies in wartime and that facilities on the island would be denied to an aggressor.

The Logistics of Reunification

Assuming that Irish reunification became an end of British policy, how could it be brought about? Adopting a policy end does not mean it can be achieved overnight or even quickly. Entering the Common

Market and making the substantial concession of sovereignty which that entailed was an end of British government policy for twelve years before it was accomplished. It took some years to bring about the partition of Ireland. Similarly, ending it will take time, especially if it is to be done with maximum consent and minimum trouble.

No one can possibly forecast the length of time or details of a disengagement process which would begin with the adoption of reunification as a policy end and terminate presumably with the passage through Parliament of a Renunciation Act or some such instrument and its administrative implementation. If constructive withdrawal by Britain from Ireland were the policy intention—and this would surely be in Britain's interest if it wished for friendly relations with its Irish successor—then the co-operation and agreement of the Irish government regarding the timetable and *modus operandi* of the policy would be needed throughout.

One way a British government which had adopted a reunification policy might proceed would be for it to ask Parliament to legislate a Bill of Rights for Northern Ireland which would at once guarantee equal treatment for Protestants and Catholics and empower a locally elected assembly to develop closer administrative and political links with the Republic—and merge with the rest of Ireland if desired. This would restrict the power of such a body to permit anti-Catholic discrimination, as happened under the old Stormont, while encouraging it to develop in an all-Ireland direction. If devolution on such lines were accompanied by a clear expression of British policy to work towards ending the Union, it might establish a suitable political framework for winning unionist consent over time.

If the two sovereign governments encouraged the establishment of all-Ireland boards, covering one function or another, or all-Ireland industries or state companies paying generous salaries to managers of unionist background, it would help the process of reunification and divide and isolate its opponents. An imaginative measure might be the endowment of a Chair of Reconciliation at Queen's University or the University of Ulster. There academics could be encouraged to sieve through Ireland's past, studying and highlighting the instances of shared endeavour rather than conflict between Protestants and Catholics. If such a policy change occurred and appropriate steps were taken, there are good grounds for believing that a united Ireland could be brought about over a period of time in a relatively painless fashion, without bloodshed and with the consent and

agreement of all the interested parties, including a large element—
possibly the great majority—of the present unionist population of
the north-east.

The first effect of such a change in British policy towards supporting Irish reunification would be to divide unionists among themselves about their future. Once Britain had declared its intent to end
the Union, unionism as such would no longer have a *raison d'être*. For
many ex-unionists, it would become a question of the terms on
which they could coexist with nationalists on the island of Ireland. A
reunification policy concerted between the two sovereign governments would seek to play on such divisions, with the aim of
increasing the numbers supporting the policy and minimizing the
number of its opponents.

The political challenge of winning unionist consent would depend
crucially on the constitutional, political, and financial deal that
erstwhile unionists could be offered in an all-Ireland state and on
Britain's willingness to spend adequate resources to encourage an
amicable settlement.

The resistance of many unionists to a united Ireland centres on
their fear of economic loss. This is understandable when one
considers that the British subvention to the North amounts to one-
third of the area's GDP. At present over half the adult population of
the North depend on the British Exchequer for their incomes. This
includes the third of the labour force in public employment and
those dependent on public pensions and unemployment benefits as
well as their spouses.[11] Such a degree of financial dependence
provides any British government with a powerful instrument for
securing compliance with its policy wishes. The main concern of
most of those dependent on the British subsidy would be their
financial future in an all-Ireland state, which would depend in turn
on the financial terms of a final Anglo-Irish settlement. Such a settlement would have to deal with the transference of responsibility for
British subsidies to Northern Ireland from the United Kingdom
Treasury to an all-Ireland exchequer. The subsidies would have to be
phased out over a period. It would obviously be in the Irish interest
that the period should be an extended one. This would also be the
view of any British government committed to a constructive disengagement policy which aimed to secure maximum consent from
the present Northern Ireland population. From the standpoint of
British taxpayers a burden which continued even for a considerable

period should be preferable to the indefinite commitment to subsidy entailed by the North continuing within the United Kingdom.

The probable, though admittedly speculative, economic advantages resulting from unification should appeal to thinking members of the unionist community. It is difficult to speculate about what kind of economy might now exist in Ireland if it had not been divided in 1920, but there is little doubt that partition held back the economic development of both parts. There were economic losses from having two separate governments and administrations in one country. The mainly agricultural South had to develop without the help of the resources of the mainly industrial North (New Ireland Forum 1983*b*). In the event, what the South has achieved is remarkable. Since 1920 the areas on both sides of the border have suffered particularly by being separated from their natural economic hinterlands. The Isles Report of 1957, which was commissioned by the Northern Ireland Government, hinted that the North's economic problems were insoluble in the absence of the fiscal and monetary powers of a sovereign state. Because of the area's full incorporation in the monetary and economic union of the United Kingdom, differential unemployment rates and high levels of emigration between the North and Britain were the balancing factor keeping its regional balance of payments in equilibrium, rather than changes in exchange rates or real earnings (Isles and Cuthbert 1957: 307 ff.). On this argument, an all-Ireland polity should provide a more appropriate setting for the North's general economic development than continuing membership of the United Kingdom. An all-Ireland administration which encouraged complementary development North and South could also be expected to foster public and private enterprise in areas which are now ignored or where it is impossible to do so in present circumstances. A united Ireland would have obvious advantages in marketing and establishing consular relations abroad, which should help particularly with northern products. The peace that unification would bring would have obvious economic advantages, given that the present economic malaise in the province can be attributed in major part to the 'troubles'. There should be economic benefit from the enthusiasm of people, especially young people, in building a new Ireland free of the Orange–Green divisions of the past. Such an economically prosperous country, united in independence and conducting its relations with Britain on the basis of friendly co-operation, would be in the best interests of both Britain and Ireland.[12]

What of violent unionist reaction? Dr Conor Cruise O'Brien and others have forecast appalling bloodshed, manifold and nameless horrors. But how does one react against the adoption of a policy, especially if it were made clear, as it should be, that there was no question of suddenness or simultaneity of change?

Violent unionist reaction would be unlikely. For how, concretely, does one assert a supposed unilateral right to union if the other party is bent on divorce? The bulk of northern Protestants are law-abiding citizens. In 1972 the half-century-old Stormont Parliament was suspended, to the accompaniment merely of a few street riots. Harold Wilson's vacillation before the Ulster Workers' Council strike of 1974 brought down the power-sharing executive established under the Sunningdale agreement; but a more resolute Prime Minister, like the present one, would not have been defeated. The attempt by Ian Paisley and the United Unionist Action Council to repeat the exercise in May 1977 in order to obtain the return of Stormont with security powers was a humiliating failure. Unionist opposition to the Anglo-Irish Agreement and the Intergovernmental Conference Centre in Maryfield, Belfast, has been largely a matter of political huffing and puffing. One might even suggest that this succession of what were 'betrayals' in unionist eyes has unintentionally helped to condition them for what many would regard as the final 'betrayal' of an explicit British statement of intent to seek to end the Union.

None the less, constructive disengagement would obviously have a security aspect. As the IRA campaign, deprived of its *raison d'être*, would almost certainly cease, the British would be free to concentrate their resources on recalcitrant loyalists. Elements which might threaten violence would have to be disarmed. There is a fallacy in the naïve 'Troops Out' position put forward sometimes by anti-partitionists in Britain. Troops and other security forces are only one expression of sovereignty. Constructive disengagement requires that troops be last to go, not first. The Ulster Defence Regiment, which is a predominantly loyalist force staffed by local people, is a full regiment of the British Army. There is no question of withdrawing it, whatever about disbanding it, or disarming any who might be disinclined to obey orders.

2. ALTERNATIVE COURSES

What of possible alternative policies? All alternatives must, by definition, be based on the continuing denial of Irish majority rights. As a consequence they must generate a reaction, further violence, and a continuation of periodic instability into the future.

Repartition would be an attempt to do a better job than Lloyd George did in 1920. Nationalist leaders in the past have looked for the cession to the South of Counties Fermanagh and Tyrone and Derry City, areas where there is a nationalist majority. It would be regarded as an instalment of national unity with more to come. There is no conceivable altering of boundaries, however, which could wholly separate Catholics and Protestants. All practical proposals for repartition would leave the nationalist stronghold of West Belfast outside the Republic. Exchanges of population are not a practical proposition without such bloodshed and loss of life as would make the troubles of the past twenty years pale into insignificance. That would destroy Britain's relations with the Irish Republic and cause consternation to the international community. For these reasons it is hard to imagine repartition serving Britain's interest.

Similar considerations rule out an independent Northern state. That would require Westminster to transfer sovereignty to a government in Belfast instead of Dublin. It could hardly be done in practice without a repartition and mass population movements. The Irish government and the Northern nationalist community would probably have the support of the United States and the rest of the international community in opposing it. Britain's fellow EEC members would scarcely welcome a new state whose establishment was bitterly opposed by the Irish government, and without Dublin's approval the new state could not join the Community. Nor would British public opinion be likely to tolerate northern Catholics being put under what must in practice become an Orange junta. An independent North would not be economically viable without massive British subsidy. Its independence would be illusory. What would be the principle of cohesion of such a state? Hardly nationality, for the Protestant unionist population of Northern Ireland do not claim such. Unionists are Irish people, mostly Protestant, who give allegiance, along with the English, Welsh, and Scots, to the multinational British state. They do not claim rights of national self-determination. The only modern precedent for a state set up to cater for a particular religious group, Pakistan, is not encouraging. Since Pakistan was first established it has divided. There are vigorous separatist movements within it which may well divide it further. Religion has proved inadequate as ideological cement for the state, and lacking the cohesion of nationality, it is held together for much of the time by military dictatorship. So is its erstwhile other element, Bangladesh.

If alternative policies are ruled out, 'direct rule' must continue. Integration with Britain, without devolution, is what has existed for most of the time since 1972. It is a logical demand for unionists, who believe their interests are identical with those of the rest of the United Kingdom. But it denies expression to the national rights of nationalists. The reluctance of many unionists to welcome it is a recognition, perhaps unconscious, that their interests too are different as Irish people. The British do not want it to continue either, for it brings the problem of Northern Ireland too close to their domestic politics. They know well that the unionists are Irish, despite their unresolved political identity problem, and that the issues of Northern Ireland politics are quite different from those of Britain. Hence the search for successive devolutionary schemes—the Sunningdale Executive, the Prior Assembly, 'power-sharing' under the Hillsborough agreement—which are all attempts to make the union work better than under the old Stormont Parliament. 'Power-sharing' may satisfy for a time those middle-class Catholics who may hope to gain something from such an arrangement. It does not satisfy republicans. Unionists object because it gives equality of representation to majority and minority, in effect enshrining the sectarian division, and being inconsistent with the democratic principle of majority rule.

3. CONCLUSION

The approach advocated in this paper may not bring quick results, and politicians with short life-spans in office rarely think long-term. But if popular British perceptions could be changed so that people saw that it was not the IRA but their own government's insistence on maintaining sovereignty which was the real root of the problem, it would be a major step towards a united Ireland. It is suggested that action on these lines would be a worthwhile task for politicians of statesmanship and vision. For it would be directed at achieving an end which is in the best interests of the people of Britain as well as of Ireland and would advance the cause of democracy and internationalism in both.

Notes

1. The claim of the Irish people to rule the whole of their national territory as a Republic was first embodied this century in the proclamation of the leaders of the 1916 Rising. This was given democratic legitimacy in the 1918 United Kingdom general election, when those pledged to establish an All-Ireland Republic won 73 out of the 105 seats in the whole country. It was subsequently expressed in the Declaration of Independence adopted by the First Dáil on 21 January 1919 and repeated in the Irish Constitution adopted by popular referendum in the 26 counties of Southern Ireland in 1937. Article 2 of this Constitution defines the national territory as the whole of Ireland, its islands, and territorial seas. Article 3 expresses the claim of the Irish Parliament and government to rightful jurisdiction over this territory. This is the counterpart of the British claim to sovereignty in Ireland expressed in the Government of Ireland Act 1920 and the Northern Ireland Constitution Act 1973. On 10 May 1949 the Irish Dáil unanimously adopted a declaration which repudiated Westminster's claim to enact legislation in Ireland, protested against the British Parliament's endorsement of partition in the Ireland Act of that year, and called upon the British people to end it. In 1984 the New Ireland Forum, comprised of representatives of the Fianna Fáil, Fine Gael, Labour, and SDLP Parties, representing most Irish constitutional nationalists, stated that 'The particular structure of political unity which the Forum would wish to see established is a unitary state, achieved by agreement and consent, embracing the whole island of Ireland and providing irrevocable guarantees for the protection and preservation of both the Unionist and Nationalist identities' (New Ireland Forum 1984, para. 5.7). So far as the Irish labour and trade union movement is concerned, unions representing the majority of organized workers in the country have gone on record as opposing partition and desiring the British government to base its policy on working to end it.
2. For various points in this section, the author is indebted to a paper on the New Ireland Forum kindly given him by Dr Martin Mansergh, currently special adviser to the Taoiseach, which was read at the Ulster People's College in November 1984.

3. Editors' note: It might be argued that Belgium has switched from being a unitary to a federal state in recent years, and that Austria reactivated its federal constitution after its experience of membership of a unitary German state under the Nazis. Moreover, Spain after Franco is in some respects such a radically decentralized unitary state that many commentators call it federal or quasi-federal.

4. For a detailed account of de Valera's attitude to the problem of partition, see Bowman (1982).

5. In an interesting submission on behalf of the Belfast Bible Study Group to the New Ireland Forum, Dr G. Dallas, a northern Presbyterian who advocated a unitary state as the best political framework for encouraging a wholehearted reconciliation between Protestants and Catholics, said that it would be wrong to see this as necessarily or only taking place in a secular, irreligious society populated by ex-Catholics and ex-Protestants (New Ireland Forum 1984, No. 10, Public Session, 39 ff.). Nationalist and unionist MPs from Northern Ireland had no difficulties in agreeing to support a Conservative amendment to Britain's abortion law during the present session of the British Parliament.

6. Public Record Office, *Cabinet Papers,* 7. Jan. 1949; cf. the discussion of this aspect of Anglo-Irish relations in Bell (1982) and Cronin (1987).

7. Irish wishful thinking was strikingly shown in the divergent interpretations of the 1985 Anglo-Irish Agreement. The Taoiseach at the time, Dr FitzGerald, told the Dáil in November of that year that Article 1 of the Agreement demonstrated that 'Britain has no interest in the continuing division of this island and that its presence in this island, undertaking the responsibility of government in Northern Ireland, continues solely because this is the wish of a majority of the people in that area' (*Dáil Debates,* 19 Nov. 1985, vol. 361, no. 11, col. 2570). A week later, Prime Minister Thatcher said the opposite in the House of Commons: 'Far from representing any threat to the union of Northern Ireland with the United Kingdom, the Agreement reinforces the union' (*Parliamentary Debates* (Commons), 26 Nov. 1985, vol. 87, col. 751). The Northern Ireland Secretary, Tom King, told the Commons: 'May I make it absolutely clear that the government wish Northern Ireland to be part of the United Kingdom' (*Parliamentary Debates* (Commons), 27 Nov. 1985, vol. 87, col. 885).

8. Editors' note: See ch. 1, n. 10.

9. Editors' note: Labour's latest and most comprehensive strategic statement on how to attain unification by consent is contained in McNamara *et al.* (1988).

10. As John Hume put it: 'The whole thrust of the guarantee is that it is a sectarian guarantee, a unilateral guarantee and an unconditional guarantee. When the state came into being it was set up on the basis of a sectarian head-count. That having been done, the British Government

then said, "We guarantee you can stay with us as long as the majority want to." By doing that they trapped the unionist population into perpetual sectarianism, because what in effect they were saying is, "In order to maintain your power and your privilege you must behave as a sectarian bloc." And that is exactly how unionism has behaved. . . . If one is to break down sectarianism one has to remove that guarantee. . . . British policy should be: "There are no guarantees for any section of this community any more. Our policy, the reasons we are there, is to promote the coming together of the people of this island in a manner and form they can both agree to." The British should join the ranks of the persuaders' (quoted in O'Malley 1983: 100).

11. Data on the two economies may be obtained in the study of the New Ireland Forum (1983*a*).

12. Teague (1987*b*) argues for the economic integration of Ireland and, while he claims that this does not require any particular political framework, it would clearly be easier to achieve in a unitary structure. See also Rowthorn and Wayne (1988), where the authors argue for Irish reunification and deal with its possible economic consequences.

3

Towards a Federal or Confederal Irish State?

Claire Palley

THE concepts of federalism and confederalism could assist the development of institutional arrangements to accommodate the differing interests, aspirations, and fears of Irish nationalists and unionists. This argument is developed in three parts. First, the distinctions between unitary, federal, and confederal states are clarified; secondly, emergent federalizing trends in Ireland, past and present, are examined; and finally the merits and defects of con/federal government are examined before suggesting its development in Ireland.

However, some preliminary remarks about the assumptions behind this essay are essential. Constitutions can only marginally shape human attitudes and behaviour, but they are not insignificant. Constitutional limits and checks and balances can constrain governmental action, but they do not guarantee success, and too much 'constitutional engineering' can be attempted. The Republic of Cyprus, established in 1960 and described by Friedrich (1968: 126–7) as 'federal', could not ensure co-operation between the Greek and Turkish Cypriot communities. The Constitution's complexity and inbuilt *immobilisme* exacerbated tensions, so that neither community could constitutionally obtain decisions it considered just, and governmental institutions could only continue to function by illegalities or contrivances.

Realism about the capacity and attitudes of political élites and their constituencies is the best guide to governmental functionality. It is frequently said of federations (but should be said of all governmental institutions) that there must be political will and cultural attitudes to create and maintain the system. As Dicey (1939: 141–3) said:

absolutely essential to the founding of a federal system is the existence of a very peculiar state of sentiment among the inhabitants of the countries which it is proposed to unite. They must desire union, and must not desire unity . . . The aim of federalism is to give effect as far as possible to both these sentiments.

These sentiments require the demand for both 'self-rule' and 'shared rule' (Elazar 1979*b*: 2–3). Neither federation nor confederation can work successfully if there are majoritarian or triumphalist attitudes. Conversely, frequent reliance on the 'vetoes' built into any federal system will destroy it. There must be willingness to achieve consensus and employ conflict-regulating practices (Nordlinger 1972). Federation, unless it becomes a dictatorship, requires not only constitutionalism, but co-operativeness. Until such a political culture evolves in Ireland it will be pointless to embark on federal arrangements. However, greater discussion might encourage a federalist ideology, which may in turn create popular sentiment in favour of institutions allowing both diversity and unity in Ireland.

Groups are not monolithic but I shall refer to two communities in Ireland, nationalist and unionist, treating them as bound by inherited religious, political, cultural, and ethnic ties. The unionist identity and attitudes were analysed by the New Ireland Forum. Their political aims were identified as being to preserve Britishness, Protestantism, and the economic advantages of the British link (New Ireland Forum 1984: 20–1). The nationalist identity was analysed as requiring separation from and opposition to British domination of Ireland, and promoting a positive Irish 'society that transcends religious differences and that can accommodate all traditions in a sovereign independent Ireland united by agreement' (New Ireland Forum 1984: 19).

The beliefs of nationalists and unionists about themselves and the impact of such beliefs on the possibility of agreed constitutional arrangements are crucial. They cannot be persuaded that they are not what they think themselves to be. The unionists believe themselves to be 'a people' entitled to exercise 'self-determination'. They have not seen themselves as an internal 'minority', part of 'the Irish people' of the island of Ireland. Irish nationalists, by contrast, have until very recently denied that unionists constitute 'British people':

unionists were not entitled to identify with Great Britain, but were duty bound to accept Ireland's secession and the all Ireland independent state desired by the all-Ireland Irish majority. Nor, on this view, are unionists entitled to choose independence outside the United Kingdom, merely because since 1920 they have formed the majority in Northern Ireland as defined by the Government of Ireland Act.

Whether or not unionists constitute 'a people' with the right to 'self-determination', the unionist community has the right to have its singularity reflected in the governmental institutions under which it lives. Once a state contains a large territorially based group, conscious of and wishing to maintain its culturally distinct identity, such a group is entitled, in accordance with the law of self-determination, to collective rights, not necessarily to statehood or to secession, but at least to maintain its identity and to some form of autonomy (Brownlie 1988). An imaginative leap is required of nationalists to understand that, just as they have claimed human rights and self-determination, unionists have seen themselves as entitled to similar rights. Even if nationalists cannot accept full self-determination for unionists, if they bring themselves to accept the unionist community's right to autonomy, they may find their inability to create a unitary Ireland without unionist consent more tolerable. Fortunately, such thinking is emerging. Although not accepting that the unionist community had a right of self-determination, the Forum Report recognized that 'the political arrangements for a new and sovereign Ireland would have to be freely negotiated and agreed to by the people of the North and by the people of the South' (p. 27).

The new concept of 'the people of the North' was formally given effect by Article 1 of the Anglo-Irish Agreement 1985, which recognized the 'people of Northern Ireland'.[1] The Agreement is very significant: it means that although Articles 2 and 3 and the 1937 Irish Constitution declare Northern Ireland to be part of the national territory of the Republic,[2] the Irish and United Kingdom Governments have, by an international treaty, recognized that the principle of self-determination in international law applies in respect of 'the people of Northern Ireland', if not to the unionist community. It is in this context that we must assess the meaning, feasibility, and desirability of con/federal options for Ireland.

1. FEDERATIONS, UNITARY STATES, AND CONFEDERATIONS

Debate over the merits of confederal, federal, and unitary states is confused partly because federalism has so many meanings. In the early 1950s political scientists saw federalism as a social phenomenon and used the term to describe situations where religious, ethnic, cultural, or social groups form the components of an emerging larger community and are to a considerable extent territorially concentrated. Federalism was also used to refer to the political phenomenon which is found if communal development is accompanied by moves towards establishment of a political entity. This political phenomenon emerges from a dynamic federalizing process as groups enter into arrangements for adopting joint policies and for making joint decisions. The federalizing process is supported by an evolving federalist ideology, a political philosophy of 'diversity-in-unity', allowing for variable responses to opposed demands for centralization and decentralization of power, and is characterized by advocacy of balance. This federalist ideology can also be described as federalism. Accordingly, federalism can refer to a particular philosophy of social organization, a social phenomenon, a political phenomenon, or an ideology of a pluralist kind (King 1982: 20, 19, 74–5; see also Burgess 1985b).

Definitions of the concepts of 'federation', 'confederation', and 'a unitary state' vary radically. The uninitiated will find conflicting and frequently imprecise definitions and models. Vile (1982: 216) has rightly pointed to the danger in vaguely using terms such as 'confederal' or 'federal' to create a climate of opinion favouring agreement: this will be followed by disillusionment. Advocates and the public must know precisely what is being sought or is on offer. Ignorant rhetoric does not result in 'creative ambiguity', the paternalistic idea that dialogue gives time to create constructive solutions (Ben Dor 1979: 72–6, 86). Rather there will be polemic and missed opportunities if people are imprecise, especially if 'sovereignty' issues are obscured.

There has been such extensive debate about the nature of a 'confederation' (*Staatenbund*), 'federation' (*Bundesstaat*), a 'federal' union of states (*Bund*), and the doctrine of 'sovereignty' that cautionary words are necessary, especially because 'sovereignty' leads to emotional as well as metaphysical debate in the rhetoric of

European nationalism. Classical theory assumes that in every system there is a sovereign consisting of some one indivisible agent exercising overriding power and always to the exclusion of other agents. Originating on the Continent, the doctrine was expanded by Hobbes and turned into the orthodox view of the English Constitution by John Austin. Constitutional lawyers familiar with the American tradition, however, realized that in a federation power was constitutionally divided between the central federal government and the states. Some said sovereignty was divided between Congress, President, courts, and the states; others that it resided in the Constitution; while others found it in the people. The Civil War was fought over whether indivisible sovereignty resided in the Union as a whole or whether it remained in the states, temporarily qualified, but capable of reverting to them. The general opinion today is that legal sovereignty is in the collective organs operating in accordance with the Constitution, while political sovereignty is in the American people.

Similar controversy occurred in Europe, but most French and German thinkers still think sovereignty is indivisible. Bryce (1901: 552) thought that, except in the case of German philosophers from Kant to Hegel, 'These controversies have been at bottom political rather than philosophical; each theory having been prompted by the wish to get in a speculative base for practical propaganda.' None the less the generalization can be made, when comparing the internal constitutional law of states, that political sovereignty is in the people, i.e. the electorate, while legal sovereignty is vested in the appropriate organs designated in the Constitution and acting in accordance with it.

In a federation constitutional change requires that the appropriate amending process must be followed and that central federal and provincial (member state) governmental organs with different powers and functions must observe their limits as constitutionally defined. It is fruitless to argue where the precise location of sovereignty is: whether in the federal legislature or in the member states. The state as a whole enjoys sovereignty when acting in the constitutionally prescribed fashion. In contrast, in a unitary state legislative power is not generally limited by the Constitution. But there is no reason why its legislature cannot be subject to procedural requirements or so defined that several organs have to act in a particular combination or pattern.

Thus far analysis has been confined to sovereignty in internal constitutional law. In international law the position is different. International law recognizes states as persons who must be internationally responsible to other states. Each state is sovereign, having unlimited power, and cannot avoid responsibility for internal acts or omissions, even if its Constitution divides power in creating a federation. International law therefore still has difficulties with the concept of federation.

In contrast, the earlier concept of confederation was well understood. The Swiss Confederation lasted from 1291 to 1798 and from 1815 to 1848; the United Provinces of The Netherlands lasted from 1580 to 1795; the German *Bund* from 1815 to 1866; and there were arguably two phases of Confederation of the USA, from 1781 to 1789 and from then until the outbreak of the Civil War in 1861. International lawyers agreed that in a confederation, or *Staatenbund*, the confederating states remained sovereign and that a new state was not brought into existence. This was so even though the *Staatenbund* (as in the case of the United Provinces) had undisputed possession of the most important international rights, namely the right to send and receive ambassadors, to make war, and to make treaties, while the Provinces' rights to embassies and to make treaties were much more restricted. European international-law publicists, immersed in classical assumptions, saw sovereignty as indivisible in confederations and as still vested in the states, who by treaty created a union of states (*Staatenbund*). They believed that only when a federation (*Bundesstaat*) is created does sovereignty go to the new state. Theirs is an either/or position. More recent theorists see the location of sovereignty as an existential question and concentrate on the creation of a federal union of states (*Bund*), a broader category comprehending both a *Staatenbund* and a *Bundesstaat*.

The federalizing process and ideology, operating on a communally diversified society, may result in a set of institutions for organizing the government of the relevant political entity. These political institutions are a federation if the entity created is a single composite state, having both central governmental organs and territorial-unit governmental organs, each set of institutions being constitutionally independent of the other in certain governmental activities. Furthermore, the units' permanency is secured by constitutionally entrenched representation in at least some central governmental organs. In Anglo-American federations functions are vertically divided between the federal government and the member states/provinces/regions. Thus both legislation for and execution in respect of, say, health matters will be federal, while both legislation for and execution in respect of, say, social welfare will be provincial. Each set of authorities has scope for independent action within its sphere although, as Vile (1961: 198–9) has pointed out, in practice in working federal systems governments become interdependent and work co-operatively. In the German and Austrian federations, and to some extent in Switzerland, the principle of division is horizontal, with the federal legislature having the bulk of the legislative powers, either exclusively or concurrently with the *Länder* or cantons, which are responsible for the bulk of administration, i.e. execution of laws and direct provision of services to the public.

If there is no constitutional permanence to governmental units within a single state, or to central representation accorded to them, it will be a unitary state, however extensive may be the power that is devolved to regional governments or to decentralized authorities. Sovereignty rests with the central legislature, from which subordinate governments derive their power. These subordinate authorities may be legislatively overruled or legislated out of existence.

Yet another result of the federalizing process may be a confederation. Here the process will have led not to the creation of a single new state, but to a permanent union of states with governmental organs formed by a treaty operating both internationally and as a constitution for certain limited purposes.[3] Because there has not been a merger of the uniting states' personalities the states will retain their international identities and internal power apart from those activities which, by virtue of the treaty, they have surrendered to the confederal union. Of course a new international person, a supra-state organization, but not a single new state, will have been created.

From the perspective of constitutional law, a single state with an institutional structure will have been established. German *Bund* theorists such as E. R. Huber make this point, distinguishing a confederation as an overall state with organs which are exclusively federative in structure (i.e. they consist of the member states' delegates) from a federal state, an overall state in which federative and unitary organs work together. Unitary organs are those where the people elect representatives, rather than the states sending delegates (Forsyth 1981: 138).[4]

Political scientists, and politicians, have made play of the differences between and relative advantages of federation and confederation. Many of their often conflicting views were first propounded while federations were at an early stage of development or in ignorance of federations elsewhere in the world. In the following fifteen points I attempt to summarize the relevant (and alleged) differences and similarities.

1. Although in a confederation no single state in international law emerges, the confederated states have created a new autonomous governmental body, a permanent confederacy of supreme governments, and this new entity (*Bund*) will have a degree of personality in international law and will be the subject of rights and duties, enjoying power to enter treaties and to send Ambassadors. In a federation a new state is created and the member states are no longer regarded as internationally sovereign, but, depending upon the provisions of the constitution and recognition by other states, they can enjoy aspects of international personality, treaty rights, diplomatic representation, etc. So the differences here between confederations and federations are ones of degree, depending upon the drafting of the particular constitution.

2. Sovereignty is vested in the relevant bodies of the confederation (*Bund*) or member states depending on the terms of the treaty creating the confederation. In a federation there is a division of power, with sovereignty formally being in the appropriate constitutional organs as a whole. Usually the states are incorporated through representation into the amending process or upper house of the federal legislature. Again these are differences of degree.

3. Both confederations and federations are permanent and secession is in theory impossible.[5] In reality, of course, secession is a political question. Law cannot determine such matters: in the USA the Civil War was waged over the southern states' claim to secede.

4. Constitutional amendments in a confederation are to the treaty and must be unanimous. In a federation the amendment procedure can vary in flexibility. It may range from requiring a specified majority of states to approve, to a referendum, or to weighted voting in the legislature. In a two-unit federation there would have to be the approval of both states for amendment, i.e. the equivalent of unanimity.

5. Legally speaking, powers in a confederation are not delegated and capable of being withdrawn.Treaty amendments, unanimously

agreed, are required to reverse delegation. The position that powers cannot be withdrawn at will is paralleled by enumeration of powers in a federation: the Constitution requires formal amendment for change.

6. Confederations usually do not have judicial bodies to enforce their decisions. But they can use the courts of the member states and sometimes themselves set up small administrations. They can also pass laws directly acting upon the population. Federations also vary in respect of methods of enforcement.[6] Again differences are questions of degree.

7. Foreign-policy matters are usually partly transferred to the confederal organs in a confederation. So are military powers. In a federation the same applies. Again these are questions of degree.

8. Citizenship in a confederation is usually that of the relevant member state, although dual or multiple nationality is sometimes possible. In a federation there can be dual citizenship of the federation and the relevant member state, but there is always federal citizenship. Some federations have continuing citizenship of member states, because, prior to creation of the federation, such citizenships were of long standing, e.g. in Germany and Switzerland, or because when they became federations the Constitution made provision for this. Others do not have member-state citizenship.

9. Confederations have generally had limited taxation powers, for example in relation to customs, excise and postal dues. Federations have more extensive taxing power. Again these are questions of degree and depend on the particular treaty arrangements made.

10. In confederations residuary power (i.e. that not transferred to the confederation) remains with the member states. In some federations (USA, Australia, Switzerland, West Germany) residuary power is with the member states, but in others with the federal government. Location of residuary power is a question for the particular constitution and is less relevant the more carefully the lists of powers are defined. Residuary power may be made concurrent to avoid litigation as in India.

11. In both federations and confederations it need not be the case that confederal or federal laws take precedence over state laws. It all depends upon the provisions of the relevant treaty or constitution.

12. Confederations need only require unanimity in certain significant decision areas, elsewhere majority rule is possible. In federations unanimity of states is seldom required.

13. The methods of implementation of confederal and federal laws vary: sometimes the states have sole responsibility for implementation, sometimes powers of implementation are concurrent, and sometimes the confederation or federation have independent capacities for implementation.

14. It is not true that in confederations the representatives of member states are merely delegates and have no right to decide, but must have their decisions subsequently ratified. In so far as power has been delegated to a confederal institution its members can take decisions, otherwise the confederation would be a mere league of states.

15. In confederations and federations member states can send delegates to participate in the central governmental organs. In the Federal Republic of Germany (and before that in the German Empire) the *Bundesrat* (upper chamber) is formed of delegates from each *Land*'s cabinet, and such delegates vote *en bloc* upon *Land* instructions, and change with changing composition of the *Land* cabinet.

These fifteen points of clarification demonstrate that twilight shadings confound the pedant (Maddox 1941). Indeed Kelsen (1945) finally concluded that the differences between confederations, federations and unitary states (other than 'the unanimity principle' which characterizes confederations) were ones of degree of decentralization.

None the less, both in practice and in law five differences between confederations, federations, and unitary states can be of crucial significance. (1) In a unitary state with devolution a local legislature can be abolished, as occurred with the Parliament of Northern Ireland in 1972, and autonomy or power-sharing could equally be legislated away in a unitary Ireland. (2) In a confederation, despite European theory that secession is impossible, the union being permanent (Forsyth 1981: 151, 157), secession is more likely because the confederal states retain greater power-bases. (3) Since in confederations unanimity is required for decisions on major matters, decision-making is more difficult than in a federation. However, in a deeply divided society this difficulty may also be a virtue. (4) In confederations the member states retain international personality and they are regarded internationally as sovereign and as responsible for acts and omissions within their territorial jurisdiction. (5) In a confederation, citizenship will be that of each individual citizen's state and not that of the confederation, which might be particularly significant in the Irish context.

Above all, it should be remembered that those who establish federations as opposed to confederations have differing political objectives. Although both sets of founders want union, those wishing to safeguard their separate identity choose confederation. Those who want to organize an effective unity and become one enlarged state (or to stay one, as Belgium is now doing) choose federation. The political thrusts of the two comparable institutions differ: in confederations consensus is essential; in federations, although consensus is sought and democracy has limits imposed on it by the composition of decision-making organs, in the last resort there are usually mechanisms to allow the majority to prevail.

2. THE EMERGENT FEDERALIZING PROCESS IN IRELAND

Although differences between federation and confederation as institutions exist, it is their appropriateness for Irish society which is important here. Furthermore, both organizational forms, since they involve union, fall within the tradition of Irish nationalism. In an Irish context the most unfortunate aspect of the need to evaluate confederation and federation is the intellectual baggage they carry: theological disputation is inevitable; and those who wish to make propaganda about 'sovereignty' will find a surfeit of quotations to their tastes. Yet conceptualism must not be overdone. Legalistic debate about the location of sovereignty and the nature of the proposed state can displace the necessary examination of whether social forces exist which are conducive to con/federalism. Although Friedrich (1968: 177) caused some intellectual apoplexy (King, 1982) when he declared 'a federation is a union of groups, united by one or more objectives, rooted in common values, interests or beliefs but retaining their distinctive character for other purposes', his definitionally lax approach is useful in assessing whether or not federalizing trends exist. If applied to events and circumstances in Ireland, it enables one to see that the social phenomenon of federalism is present; that the ideology of federalism is present; that there are already some institutional arrangements which are 'federal' in character; and that a dynamic but very slow federalizing process is in train. If such factors were not present, neither a federation nor a confederation could emerge as modes of governmental organization for Ireland.

Any interpretation of what a 'united' Ireland means will find its detractors, but some propositions appear reasonable. (1) Ireland should be governed by the people (who form the communities) of Ireland. (2) On the Forum view, two traditions in Ireland are to be respected, and there is now a dual or composite, rather than a compound, 'Irish' identity. (3) No specific kind of governmental arrangement is dictated by aspirations for a united Ireland. (4) A 'unity' in Ireland may be desirable, but should not be dictated. (5) Finally, the most contentious proposition is that as long as Irishmen are reunited in a union there is no necessity that they be reunited in one state, rather than in a union of states. If the last proposition is rejected on ideological grounds then nationalism excludes the arrangement of a confederation. If, in contrast, Irish nationalists accept that an Ireland united by a federal union of states, a *Bundesstaat*, would satisfy their aspirations, federalist processes appear feasible. It is to be hoped that Irish nationalists will be convinced by *Bund* theory, rather than place undue weight on an interpretation of 'sovereignty' which, although of Continental origin, came to them through England.

Each country's circumstances, historical, political, social, and cultural, are unique in combination, so that parallels with evolving federalism elsewhere must be cautiously drawn. The most significant variables affecting political development are the timing and sequences of currency of ideas, formation of attitudes, the role of socio-economic factors, and patterns of institutional development (Nordlinger 1968). Federal ideas have long been one Irish tradition. A federation between Ireland and other parts of Great Britain or 'home rule all round', rather than for Ireland only, was advocated in the late nineteenth century and up till 1918 (Burgess 1985*a*; Kendle 1968, 1971).[7] Federation was promoted by de Valera, first in 1919 and consistently until his death (Bowman 1982: 15–16, 58–60, 186–8, 247, 262, 282, 294, 309–12). Amongst others who have advocated federation or confederation (alternatives which became official Fine Gael policy in 1979) are Erskine Childers, who realized that Ulster would, if it were ever to agree, insist on federation; Alfred O'Rahilly, who immediately after the Treaty drew up a draft constitution on the Swiss model;[8] Sean MacBride (from at least 1948 to his death);[9] Jack

Lynch (as Prime Minister and Fianna Fáil leader);[10] and, above all, Garret FitzGerald. Although traditional 'nationalist' ideas were also prominent at the New Ireland Forum, particularly in the questioning, the thrust of much of the evidence and the reasoning of the Forum Report was federal. Arguably those ideas have since grown in stature (O'Halloran 1985: 206–8).

At one time even the IRA, in *Eire Nua* (Sinn Féin 1971), took up the suggestion, first made by de Valera in 1920, of a federation of Ireland's four ancient provinces of Connaught, Munster, Leinster and Ulster. Ulster would consist of its nine historic counties (the six in Northern Ireland together with Cavan, Monaghan, and Donegal in the Republic). Such a proposal was disingenuous as a mode of protecting unionist interests, as they would, at best, have had a bare majority in Ulster and would have always been subject to outvoting in the federal legislature. This artificial device would have been equally unacceptable to the three Ulster counties which since 1922 have been part of the Republic. In any event, the IRA, under the prompting of its new Northern leadership, abandoned the policy in 1982.

Federalist institutions (i.e. ones tending towards a federation) have also been established in Irish history. The Government of Ireland Act 1920, Section 1, established two home-rule Parliaments in Ireland even though the Southern Parliament never became operative. Section 2 of the Act established a Council of Ireland, equally composed of southern and northern parliamentarians elected by their respective Houses. The Council was to promote mutual intercourse and uniformity in matters affecting the whole of Ireland. It was given immediate exclusive jurisdiction over railways, fisheries, and animal diseases. Section 3 gave the two Irish Parliaments power to establish a Parliament for the whole of Ireland and to transfer some or all of their powers to the Irish Parliament either initially or by stages. For the British Cabinet, partition was a temporary expedient and the majority expressly recorded their view that 'the unity of Ireland was the long-term aim' (Mansergh 1978: 41). Although Northern Ireland members were elected, the Council never functioned, and it was extinguished by Article 5 of the Ireland (Confirmation of Agreement) Act 1925 (Palley 1972: 378–9).

There has been and is a considerable amount of functional cross-border co-operation between the Republic and Northern Ireland, with joint committees operating in respect of drainage, fisheries, conservation, electricity supply, highways and railways, a new impetus being given in the early 1950s. Functional co-operation and combination on matters of common concern were advocated by both Sean Lemass and de Valera, and by Brian Faulkner.

A second attempt at establishing a Council of Ireland, agreed at Sunningdale in 1973, proved equally unsuccessful, ending with the 1974 collapse of the Northern Ireland power-sharing Executive. The attempt was unlucky because the February 1974 United Kingdom general election gave an opportunity for unionist politicians and electors to repudiate the arrangements before they had time to work; and unwise because both power-sharing and the establishment of a Council of Ireland should not have been simultaneously imposed on unionists.

Co-operation has continued under direct rule. In 1985 a wider framework for co-operation was established by an international treaty between the United Kingdom and Republic of Ireland. Article 2 of the 1985 Anglo-Irish Agreement provides that an Intergovernmental Conference shall on a regular basis promote cross-border co-operation. Article 10 effectively makes the Conference the framework for promoting co-operation. A special programme of work is to be put in hand under Article 9, which provides for enhancing police co-operation.

The Anglo-Irish Agreement is a federalist institution, allowing for evolution to a *sui generis* confederation between the Republic and part of the United Kingdom (Northern Ireland), with confederal authority being exercised by Irish and United Kingdom ministers. Some see the Agreement as merely *de facto* joint authority. This is contradicted by the institutional framework of the Intergovernmental Conference, involving both regular and specially convened meetings at ministerial or at official level, and the establishment of a joint secretariat (Article 3). The Conference deals with the whole gamut of governmental matters (Articles 2 to 10) in relation to Northern Ireland and relations between the two parts of the island. Although there is a reaffirmation of each government's sovereignty and retention of responsibility for decisions and administration of government within its own jurisdiction, the Agreement provides that there shall be 'determined efforts . . . to resolve any differences' (Article 2(b)). Several Articles also envisage application of proposals in the Republic (Articles 2(b), 5(b), and 7(b) on human rights, measures fostering the two traditions' cultural heritage etc., and security matters). Mixed courts in both jurisdictions are to be considered (Article 8). Article 12 envisages a parliamentary decision in Westminster and Dublin to establish an Anglo-Irish parliamentary body, and the establishment of such a body was prefigured early in 1989. In sum, the arrangements amount to a confederation concerned with cross-border aspects of security, economic, social, and cultural matters in relation to which the Secretary of State exercises authority until devolution. If this occurs, Article 10(c) requires new machinery to be established to ensure practical co-operation on cross-border aspects of those matters devolved.

Much has been made of EC membership as a factor facilitating political as well as economic convergence and long-term all-Ireland integration. Many Europhiles hope that the North will appreciate that in an EC context its economic interests may be better served by Dublin than by London (Fine Gael 1979; Moxon-Browne 1978; O'Cleireacain 1983, 1985). Bitter memories of earlier Republican protectionism are fast fading. The significance of joint EC membership is even greater now that the EC is becoming a federation— earlier it was a hybrid between a federation and a confederation. After 1992 the EC will evolve rapidly. Economic developments, a common currency, a central bank, and a genuine common market will lead to the assumption of even greater economic powers, not least through the European Court's rulings over time. Development of EC social policy and ultimately reinforcement of its political institutions must follow. The United Kingdom, and through it Northern Ireland, will, together with the Republic, then be subject to full-blown federal government from Brussels. 'Regional' government matters for Northern Ireland which are not common to the EC will be controlled by United Kingdom governmental action, in accordance with the framework of the Anglo Irish Agreement. The Republic's government will continue to exercise influence in non-EC matters through its input into the Intergovernmental Conference.

Once the ideology of European federal democracy takes root in the 'Western European islands' and the full implications are appreciated of all parts of Ireland belonging to a greater federation (the EC), and also to a smaller confederation (the institutions of the Anglo-Irish Agreement), further federalization is likely to follow. The process will be slow until its irreversibility is appreciated. Impatience is not in order: the Agreement has been in place for less than four of the more than 800-year-long Anglo-Irish relationship.

Economic Factors

Economic factors in Ireland are linked to bicommunal conflict and competitiveness, and are a factor impeding federalization, despite the positive EC factors, *de facto* cross-border business links, and the existence of all-Ireland companies (Whyte 1983*b*: 300). Not only was the economic structure of the Plantation counties stronger than that of the rest of Ireland and dominated by the unionists, but after independence a generally state-led economy in the South and protectionism from the early 1930s led to two distinct economies in the Republic and in Northern Ireland. The Republic's economy rapidly began catching up after 1959 and accelerated in the early 1970s. However, its gains from joining the EC were temporary, and the Republic's government from 1980 undertook external debt requiring huge interest repayments. At the same time unemployment rose (now 18 per cent) and the rate of growth of GNP fell, despite a greatly improving trade balance (Kennedy *et al.* 1988). Hopes that the Republic could catch up with the northern economy have proved unrealistic.[11] The northern economy, never strong, went into further decline due to the troubles, and per capita GDP is now roughly the same in both economies. However, because of massive transfer payments from the United Kingdom Treasury, slightly higher living standards, better welfare payments, and lower taxes prevail in Northern Ireland than do in the Republic. Part of the transfers arise from the presence of the Army, but by far the greater part comes from application of the 'parity' principle, the policy agreed since the late 1930s that no part of the United Kingdom should have services greatly worse than the average, or state welfare benefits of a smaller amount. The scale of United Kingdom Treasury transfers to Northern Ireland's Exchequer is enormous. Transfers amounted in 1982–3 to £(sterling) 1,313 million, 29 per cent of the northern GDP and 13.8 per cent of that of the Republic. This is the equivalent of 29 per cent of the Republic's publicly levied revenue, and 69 per cent of that raised in the North (New Ireland Forum 1983*a*, Sections 3.12 and 4). Maintenance of northern living standards, in the event of the ending of the United Kingdom subvention, would mean an even greater tax burden on the Republic's taxpayers—already among the highest taxed in Europe.

These economic factors are crucial to further federalization. As Sir Charles Carter told the Forum:

If there was a simple change of sovereignty you would expect the British Government to apply to this the general principles of foreign aid . . . The extent of the obligation which it would feel would depend on its views about its internal circumstances, foreign aid being a rather poor relation which gets cut whenever cuts are necessary. What I am really trying to put over is that the function which is performed in the Republic by fairly massive borrowing is performed for Northern Ireland by the transfers which are natural within the unitary state and the problem is essentially that the Republic could not expect to provide a similar level of transfer by additional borrowing. Nor is it realistic to suppose that they could get it by a guarantee of transfer from a British Government which had renounced its sovereignty. I am dropping various hints that one has to look at more complicated solutions and that it is up to you. (New Ireland Forum, *Report of Proceedings*, No. 2, 21 September 1983, p. 30)

To avoid turning a grave economic problem into an almost insoluble one, it was essential to 'leave good ground for a continuing British economic responsibility for the welfare of those who are and wish to remain British subjects' (p. 7). Clearly, even if it is agreed that transfers should continue after secession of Northern Ireland from the United Kingdom in order to join all-Irish institutions, faith in long-term transfers (or in long-run replacement United States aid) is misplaced. Nor, unless the EC evolves rapidly and differently, are transfers from its Social Fund likely to replace the massive United Kingdom transfers.

It also seems misguided to believe transfers will cease while Northern Ireland is part of the United Kingdom. Transfers, from being approximately one-quarter of total public expenditure in Northern Ireland in 1972–3, rose to approximately 50 per cent in 1979–80, although they dropped to about 34 per cent in 1982–3. With privatization policies, reduced public expenditure, and altered social-welfare support systems, a further reduction in public expenditure and in transfers may occur. Yet it is inconceivable that future United Kingdom governments will adopt the policy towards United Kingdom citizens implicit in Harold Wilson's 1974 reference to 'spongers'.[12]

Economic factors leave only two alternatives for further federalization in Ireland. The first is a 'British Isles federation', a utopian scheme which might one day be advocated to accommodate Scottish, Welsh, and Cornish (and even Yorkshire) nationalism, but is politically highly unlikely because of the geographical distribution of political support for the United Kingdom's major parties. The second is a confederation between the United Kingdom, in respect of Northern Ireland, and the Republic, thereby retaining United Kingdom economic responsibility and, of course, sovereignty. The Anglo-Irish Agreement is an early prototype, but without as yet the necessary democratic support in Northern Ireland for such a confederation. If the federalizing process is to continue, the Agreement will, whatever the window-dressing permitting modification and adaptation, be the appropriate institutional framework.

Demographic Factors

Both communities have kept a close watch on the respective birth-rates of Roman Catholics and Protestants. Both sides have thought that the passage of time and natural forces might ultimately lead to an ending of partition (Bowman 1982: 313).[13] Yet the dynamics of population-growth are slow, and, even when Catholics form a majority of the Northern Ireland population, this will not result in an immediate plebiscite (Border Poll) favouring reunification. Because of the age composition of the electorate, Protestants will remain a voting majority for a further fifteen to twenty years. Furthermore, many Catholics either abstain or vote for parties favouring the Union (Compton 1981: 89–91).

None the less, because demographic factors affect both the thinking of the two communities and the composition of the Northern Ireland electorate, birth-rate projections are significant. The denominational rates of natural increase, with a rapidly falling Protestant birth-rate and a much higher, although slightly falling, Catholic birth-rate, mean that, before adjustment for emigration is made, there is (on the 1977 fertility and mortality estimates) likely to be a Catholic population majority in Northern Ireland by 2010 to 2020, and an electoral majority of Catholic voters in Northern Ireland by 2025 to 2035. If emigration rates (at 1977–79 levels) continue and Catholic fertility rates come down to levels prevailing in other European countries, then a majority of Catholic voters can be expected in Northern Ireland in the middle of the twenty-first century (Compton 1981: 88). The demographer making these projections in 1980 took a similar attitude two years later, although noting that Catholic emigration rates had been falling since 1971 (Compton 1982: 96–9). In 1979 Catholics were about 37.6 per cent of the Northern Ireland population (Compton 1981: 87). In short, there might well be a Catholic population majority by 2015 and, taking age distribution into account, an electoral majority by 2030. When these possibilities begin to impact on the minds of unionists, attitudinal reassessment and reconsideration is likely.

Attitudes of the Irish Communities and the British Government

Traditional Irish nationalism has sought an entirely independent Irish Ireland, proud of its Gaelic and Catholic culture, believing in Republican values and neutrality, free of British domination, and open to minimal British influence. This approach was institutionalized in the 1937 Constitution. The Forum in 1984 propounded a positive approach of a new Ireland in which Irish identity would be broadened to permit all Irish persons, both those with a nationalist and those with a unionist identity, to find equally satisfactory and secure places and symbolic expression in new all-Ireland structures. If nationalism can equally accommodate other traditions, and, if it allows for a composite ideology, then it will no longer be the exclusivist ideology of the past.[14]

Whether unionists will ever accept the Forum's view of nationalism and of the Republic's aspirations, or treat the Report as sheep's clothing leading to their absorption into a traditional Ireland, is an open question. If unionist perceptions become more favourable, there could be federalizing moves. Equally, confederation or federation could well be seen as devious devices, just as Greek Cypriots have characterized Turkish Cypriot calls for federation as intended to lead to partition, whereas Turkish Cypriots have called Greek Cypriot suggestions for federation attempts to bring about a unitary state and Hellenistic domination. Much will depend on whether the Republic continues to be perceived as a base for terrorists and as unwilling to act against them.

The unionists are generally perceived as British, Protestant, and as conscious of the economic advantages of the United Kingdom link. The unionist community is resentful of the way in which it has been disempowered since March 1972 with the suspension of the Parliament of Northern Ireland. Furthermore, since 1973, Northern Ireland has been without adequate local-government institutions and has, not unlike a colony, been directly governed by the Northern Ireland Office. Unionists consoled themselves with a sense of security that they had it in their hands to keep themselves permanently part of the United Kingdom. In 1920 the Northern Ireland Parliament had had the right to decide whether or not to create an all-Ireland Parliament. In 1922, when the Irish Free State was created or recognized (depending upon your preference) United Kingdom Acts permitted the Northern Ireland Parliament to petition to remain under the 1920 Act and not to be part of 'Ireland' (Palley 1972: 379). Since 1949, when Eire left the Commonwealth, successive guarantees have been incorporated in Acts of Parliament dealing with the constitutional position of Northern Ireland (1949, 1972, 1973).

The 1949 guarantee affirmed that in no event would Northern Ireland cease to be part of the United Kingdom without the consent of the Parliament. The 1972 Northern Ireland (Temporary Provisions) Act reaffirmed the status of Northern Ireland as part of the United Kingdom, while the Northern Ireland Constitution Act of 1973, Section 1, declared that in no event would Northern Ireland cease to be part of the United Kingdom and of HM dominions 'without the consent of the majority of the people of Northern Ireland voting in a poll'. (This reformulation was necessary in view of the suspension, followed by abolition, of the Parliament of Northern Ireland.) But it should not be forgotten that the symbolically Green Paper of 1972 on Northern Ireland, which first made the phrase 'the Irish dimension' fashionable, also indicated indirectly that HMG had no interest in maintaining partition and would welcome a reunited Ireland were that agreed. The December 1973 Sunningdale communiqué expressly stated that 'if in future, the majority of the people of Northern Ireland should indicate a wish to become part of a united Ireland the British Government would support that wish'. On 15 November 1985, while affirming that change in Northern Ireland's status would only come about with the consent of a majority of the people of Northern Ireland and recognizing the present wish that there be no change, Article 1 of the AIA declared that 'if in the future a majority of the people of Northern Ireland clearly wish for and formally consent to the establishment of a United Ireland, the two governments will introduce and support in the respective Parliaments legislation giving effect to that wish'.

Here was a solemn international treaty obligation to legislate a united Ireland if the people (1) 'clearly wish for', and (2) 'formally consent' to, a united Ireland. Formal consent would presumably occur by way of a Border Poll (supposed to be held at not less than ten-yearly intervals). What 'clearly wish for' means leaves margin for interpretation. The uncertainty of this situation has intensified unionist anger towards Britain, the British government, and British parliamentarians. There are now two guarantees: the legislative guarantee is in the 1972 and 1973 Acts that Northern Ireland has a status as, and will remain, part of the United Kingdom and of HM dominions (unless the consent of the people of Northern Ireland to its ceasing to be part of the dominions and of the United Kingdom is given); and the international guarantee is that in the international treaty, the Anglo-Irish Agreement, which undertakes that the United Kingdom will, under certain conditions, reunite Ireland.

In consequence unionists must rely on their own will and their relative population strength. They do not have the right to govern themselves (or the Northern Ireland nationalist community either), but they do have the right, so long as their population strength remains, to block a united Ireland. Indeed, they have the power and the right to produce a stalemate, both in relation to internal power-sharing and to reunification for at least another twenty years. Even when Protestants lose their electoral majority (say, after 2030) any reunited Irish state will be unstable if a large number of unionists are not part of the majority supporting reunification. I believe, and hope, that unionists will come to realize that they can secure guarantees which will be in their own hands, if they negotiate now for an Irish confederation or federation. It is an essential aspect of such institutional arrangements to accord permanent guarantees to the constitutional units.

Violence debilitates society, but unless it amounts to civil war or causes international conflict, although it can damage and embitter, it cannot result in outright victory. Although violence shakes United Kingdom governmental and parliamentary attitudes it will not, in my view, succeed in coercing unionists to accept a united Ireland. Intermittent violence over seventy years, with the last twenty being virtually continuous, has not had that effect. Leaving aside the obvious point that unionists could, if they wished, cause even more disruption than does the IRA, it should be realized that states are generally only violently reunited or turned into confederations or federations if there is a war (international or civil) which one side has lost.[15] After a Northern Ireland civil war, were there to be one, it is doubtful if anything other than a smaller but more concentrated Northern Irish state would be created.

So far as the United Kingdom government and Parliament is concerned, successive governments have, since settlement of their disputes with Ireland in 1938, been convinced that reunification of Ireland is the best outcome (Bowman 1982: 165–6, 181, 201, 229 ff.). For a short period during World War II and in NATO's early days there was a re-evaluation of Northern Ireland's defence potential and hostility to Irish neutrality. Hence it is easy to find quotations in that period contending that Ireland was strategically significant, but whatever opinions any retired military man may express,[16] it has usually been firm bipartisan British policy since 1973, at latest, to encourage a reunited Ireland and to take the preliminary institutional steps which will lead to that outcome. Going to the other extreme, the possibility of imposition of unification is, as indicated, a Gaelic hallucination. Since 1914 coercion of Ulster has been 'out', although indirect pressure by deprivation of self-government has been 'in' since 1972, while since 1985 there has been further pressure by way of London–Dublin consultation in respect of United Kingdom government decisions concerning Northern Ireland, and the example of what, in the long run, co-operation may achieve.

3. THE ADVANTAGES AND DEFECTS OF FEDERATION AND CONFEDERATION IN IRELAND

The prevalence of federal ideas, the working of federalist institutions (the EC and the Anglo-Irish Agreement), economic needs (the two relatively weak economies and the necessity for continuing subventions which can only follow if Great Britain is linked to Northern Ireland), and demographic probabilities are all tending to promote the consideration of unity of the two parts of Ireland in some form of association. Such consideration is the more likely with the growth of the new brand of nationalism, the desire for and conditional commitment of United Kingdom governments to Irish reunification, and the relative weakness of unionists, who in the short to medium run can stalemate processes of federalization, but who in the long run are losing the power to retain their unionist political identity. They can however, take steps to maintain their Protestant and British identity in a federal/confederal Ireland.

Any settlement of the Northern Ireland and Irish problems has advantages: by way of diminished violence, leading possibly to peace; opportunities for economic development; possibilities of introducing regional institutions and of decentralizing, with the reintroduction of genuine local government in Northern Ireland; possibilities of protecting human rights by new machinery; and, eventually, attitudinal changes, ultimately leading to political integration and the development of 'normal' right/left politics with a spectrum of parties unaffected by traditional divisions and past historical associations. Everything positive that other authors in this book have said on these scores regarding a unitary state and joint authority applies equally to federation and to confederation.

What requires explaining are two categories of benefit from federation or confederation.[17] First, there are those specific to such institutional arrangements. Secondly, the special circumstances of Irish history may make these arrangements pragmatically more likely and advantageous.

Specific Advantages of Federation or Confederation

Both federation and confederation preserve diversity, but introduce a measure of unity in government. This facilitates co-operation, but, since the common area is not too extensive, reduces the risk of clashes. Both institutions are pluralistic, allowing the accommodation of social and political diversities by recognizing them in the formal institutional structure of the state and member states. Where diversities already exist, as they have done for a very long period in Ireland, the existing reality is accepted, rather than pushing rapidly towards change, which occasions loss of confidence and suspicion. The way this is done is to create territorial (state-located in the case of confederation) governmental systems which enjoy a large degree of autonomy. Such autonomy would be entrenched (not removable except by constitutional amendment requiring compliance with an inflexible procedure). Within the territorial member state/unit there would be democracy, subject in Northern Ireland to power-sharing. This would be required by Article 4(c) of the Anglo-Irish Agreement (see Appendix 1), and would be a necessary precondition were con/ federal arrangements to be agreed by the Republic. Thus those not in the northern 'majority' would be safeguarded and presumably a Bill of Rights would also be enacted. In a federation the groups in the territorial unit could promote their interests as against the group controlling the central federal institutions. The preservation of the distinctive cultural identity of the groups concentrated in the territorial units would be facilitated. Gaelic language preference and

Catholic social philosophy in the Republic's legal system could be preserved without running into human-rights problems about discrimination, denial of privacy, and the connected implied rights to personal choice in developing one's personality and to private and family life.[18] Such distinctive policy would be legally more secure in a confederation than in a federation in which identical standards of human rights must prevail and where there cannot be discrimination in according rights to citizens.

At the same time the units and territorial groups can participate at the federal central governmental level at which such units are represented, either by way of elected representatives (general in federations) or by nominees of the legislature or executive (confederation). At that central level member-state representatives can work in the common interest, thereby encouraging state integration, the development of common values, a common 'national' ideology, and allegiance to the 'national' centre. Just as the 1866 and 1871 German confederation and federation led to growth in shared consciousness of German groups recently at war, the communities of Ireland, living in a Western European democratic ethos, will expand their sense of common Irishness.

Federation can speed the channelling away of conflict and facilitate consensus in the state-building process. It can be used to hold together diverse cultural groups, especially in a post-colonial situation as in India. It is also being used for this purpose in Belgium, which would otherwise be subject to partition, especially as linguistic borders, apart from in Brussels, are so clearly drawn.[19]

Perhaps the most significant features are the 'good government' aspects of federalism. An institutional base is created which makes autocracy and majoritarianism more difficult. Those in a federal system are less easily overridden by the largest group. Furthermore, the system provides a ready platform for opposition, making it easier to draw attention to any local party abuses. Even more important, because there are constraints on the composition of the legislature and executive, a spirit of compromise is encouraged: otherwise government decisions could not be taken or would be much delayed. Of course, such need for consensus can lead to inability to take decisions and even to deadlocks, but in a federation, as opposed to a confederation, it is normal for there to be constitutional deadlock machinery permitting majority decisions to go through after some delay.

Adverse effects have also been ascribed to federations although, depending on the commentator's standpoint, he or she may characterize their effects differently. Clearly in one sense federations are undemocratic. Units of different size are usually equally represented in the upper house of the legislature, which has blocking power. Such equality of the units cuts against the right of individual citizens that their votes should have equal weight. The answer given is that there should be both a national majority and a majority of the entities: one person one vote and co-operation between political entities (Bogdanor 1986: 58). Additionally, the will of the majority may be frustrated on matters agreed in advance under the constitution to be of special importance to a regionally grouped minority. But then protection of human rights, power-sharing, and STV PR are equally limits on absolute majoritarian democracy and it is not usual to label these institutions as undemocratic.

Federation has been described as slow, time-consuming, complex, and cumbersome. It is more expensive, but costs and slowness are as nothing to the costs of forcing through measures against the will of a large section of the population. Delaying precipitate action and requiring negotiation is better in a divided society. Interestingly, in Switzerland the fact that there is no political 'mobilization' is ascribed to federalism. Were things more 'dynamic', the federation might not hold.

Federations do tend to legalism and result in more constitutional litigation. However, this can be mitigated by drafting techniques (more concurrent powers should be given) and by co-operative federalism with close consultation and co-operation between central and provincial governments.

All these arguments against federalism were touched on by the Kilbrandon Commission,[20] in defence of the existing and reasonably working unitary state of the United Kingdom against Scottish and Welsh nationalism. Such arguments have much less relevance to creating a new federal, rather than a new unitary, state in Ireland, especially when the latter is not a viable possibility.

A Two-Unit Federation?

Vile has succinctly attacked suggestions for a two-unit federation. He pointed to the likelihood of head-on clashes, when two units were each dominated by different communal majorities; to the fact that bargaining partners to balance and ensure working arrangements were unavailable, to the problems created when one unit was much larger than the other (the southern province's population would be twice that of the northern province); to the likelihood of immobility; and to the absence of mitigating factors, such as cross-cutting cleavages and a developed party system (Vile 1982).

In Czechoslovakia, only the 'democratic centralism' of the Communist Party has enabled the two-unit federation, created in 1968, to function. Possibly Pakistan's failure to operate a federation between West and East Pakistan can be discounted because the units were widely separated by Indian territory, were constitutionally unequal, and were socio-economically and culturally at quite different levels. Other bicephalous federations in underdeveloped countries have been unworkable. In practice they have either made for domination of one part and degradation of the other (as in Ethiopia and Cameroon), or for immobilism and political paralysis by the employment of a parity formula (as in Mali) (Neuberger 1979). This dilemma of choosing between constitutional formulas for ultimate majority decision-making or for absolute equality (even to the extent of separate decision-making) in a two-unit federation explains why agreement on a Cypriot federation has not yet proved possible, apart from the 'tall order' of getting together after years of hostility (Elazar 1979a,b).[21] These experiences indicate that only at a stage when hostilities have abated, and after a long period of successful cooperation, when Northern Ireland would not see the Republic as a threat, should federation be attempted.

A recent and persuasive examination of thirteen bicommunal polities concludes:

The evidence . . . seems to point to either a confederal framework or federalism with confederal ingredients as appropriate for managing conflict and cooperation in bi-communal societies and polities. Despite its obvious deficiencies, the confederal–consociational modification of federalism is more acceptable to two asymmetric and antagonistic communities than a concept of a federal overarching cultural-political union with its promise of majoritarian decision-making. Despite a constant threat of veto and thus potential immobilism, both basic and current issues have to be negotiated and renegotiated time and again. Our understandably reserved reaction to the confederal non-majoritarian formula and its piecemeal and very slow implementation by compromise and consensus is necessarily tempered by the quite disarming and familiar query: 'If not that, what else?' (Duchacek 1988: 31).

CONCLUSION

It is evident that I believe that on rational grounds the unionists should consider a bargain with the Republic and the United Kingdom to cut short their trauma and to secure guarantees at a time when they are relatively still powerful in blocking change. This bargain should be acceptance of a confederation, initially under the Anglo-Irish Agreement with the introduction of internal power-sharing, followed by negotiations for modification to the Agreement to permit Northern Ireland representatives to act in lieu of British ministers in the framework of the Intergovernmental Conference. This framework could be, always with agreement, subject to further development.[22] Northern Ireland could ultimately become an 'associated state' in relation to the United Kingdom (like the relations between the Åland Islands and Finland) and also part of an Irish confederation.

The reasons for suggesting a confederation are that it is far more likely to be acceptable to unionists than a federation. It will ensure that socio-political changes made by executive and legislature occur at a pace unionists feel they can tolerate. In confederation the unanimity rule ensures their consent and that they will not be subject to majority rule.

Ultimately, a federation would be a possibility but, as that prospect is remote, discussion of possible constitutional details seems relatively pointless. What must be said, however, is that complex discussions would be needed to reach agreement on a *sui generis* federation. Among the points at issue would be methods of constitutional amendment; the allocation of powers to federal and provincial governments; the creation of fiscal equivalence between units; the composition of, election to, and procedure of one or two legislative chambers; the composition and nature of the executive; whether a dual leadership or rotating system is appropriate; whether there should be federal executive power-sharing; what checks and balances (separation and composition of powers) should apply; the securing of the independence and composition of the judiciary; the contents of a new Bill of Rights; and how provincial constitutions safeguard the interests of the different communities.[23] However, so vast an exercise and overall bargain is many years in the future and would encompass so many variables that now it is only appropriate to discuss a general outline of federation and confederation. The Anglo-Irish Agreement, subject to modifications and increasing confederalization, and federalization is the most likely and most constructive means towards these ends.[24]

Notes

1. Editors' note: See App. 1.
2. Editors' note: See ch. 1, sect. 4.
3. If the treaty is not intended as permanent a League or Alliance is created. The goals of an Alliance are limited (usually to defence). If it sets up a central organization, it does not represent the totality of states and the organization cannot bind members. The members must meet, reach agreement, and thereafter the member states of the League must enact the appropriate measures.
4. For Forsyth the confederation is not a union of individuals but a union of states in a body politic. Subsequently a social union of individuals may emerge. There is then a state.
5. However, the USSR Constitution, Article 35, gave the right of secession (the attempt to remove it in 1988 proved controversial). The power of the UK Parliament to provide for secession was discussed in respect of the now defunct Federation of Rhodesia and Nyasaland by the Monckton Commission, and given effect, but that was explicable because Parliament retained power to amend the (Constitution) Order in Council.
6. Switzerland does not use its constitutional Court to enforce the Constitution in case of interjurisdictional disputes. In some Commonwealth post-colonial federations the courts of member states were used to enforce federal law. Horizontal federalism (Germany, Austria and Switzerland) leaves much execution of federal law to the member states.
7. Editors' note: The interested reader will find in the pamphlet published by Eamon Dyas (1988) an account of the linkage of federalist ideas to the creation of Northern Ireland.
8. New Ireland Forum, *Report of Proceedings*, No. 3, 4 Oct. 1983, p. 5, Sean MacBride.
   Editors' note: MacBride also pointed out that 'strangely enough' O'Rahilly's constitution 'has vanished'.
9. MacBride, Foreign Minister in Costello's multi-party coalition government of 1948–51, offered the unionists any reasonable constitutional guarantee if they would accept a federal (or a unitary) Ireland, but Brooke, like Craigavon, answered that 'they may bid as high as they please ... Ulster is not for sale.' MacBride much later submitted a

memorandum and gave evidence to the Forum suggesting a federation even less centralized than the Swiss model. He argued that central-government functions might be confined to foreign affairs, central finance, security, and health.

10. There is such an implicit plea in his suggestion for a new Ireland with an entirely different constitution from that of the Republic's Constitution of 1937 (Lynch 1972: 615–6). On 28 Aug. 1969, after British forces had been called in to restore order in Belfast and Londonderry, Prime Minister Lynch suggested a federal union was the way forward with two pro-vincial legislatures and a new Council as the federal parliament.

11. Editors' note: See Rowthorn and Wayne (1988: 70–125) for an up-to-date analysis of the Northern Ireland economy. Whatever its political deficiencies Rowthorne and Wayne's economic analysis is instructive.

12. An ending of British 'economic support for Partition' was sought as long ago as 1938 from Neville Chamberlain's Government (Bowman 1982: 303). From time to time, although not publicly, some northern national-ists suggest it as a method of coercion.

13. Unionists also feared Irish migrant workers would ultimately become Northern Ireland voters or that there would be peaceful penetration by settlement. A parallel fear has arisen in Cyprus since Turkey's 1974 invasions, where settlers have augmented the Turkish Cypriot popu-lation.

14. Anthony Coughlan (see ch. 2) contends that unionists are Irish with an unresolved political identity problem, and do not have rights to union or even a right to negotiate the terms of their absorption in a successor all-Irish state. If this reflects the official nationalist view, then there has been a reversion to the one-nation myth.

15. The Swiss Confederation of 1848 followed the 1847 Sonderbund War; the 1871 German Empire followed the 1866 Austro-Prussian and the 1870 Franco-Prussian Wars; the USA Confederation of 1789 followed the War of Independence; the United States was reunited when it won the Civil War which erupted in 1861, converting itself from confeder-ation into federation; if there is a Cyprus federation, it will be because of Turkey's 1974 invasions; Nigeria's new reformed federalism is because of the Biafra war; and the victorious allies forced federation upon West Germany in 1948. The EEC came into existence only after two world wars had made it clear to Europeans that bargaining their way towards European federalism was the best way of preventing future competition and hostilities. Alternatively, fear of threatening neighbours contributes to formation of federations, e. g. Switzerland, Australia, and Canada, but in the last two cases there were also decolonizing processes involved. Although an outgoing colonial power can bring about feder-ations, and, despite the historical truth that Ireland was England's first over-the-water colony, the time for that kind of imperial imposition (or

pressure) passed between 1919 and 1922, and could only come again if there were war between the Republic and the United Kingdom in respect of Northern Ireland. Riker (1964: 11–12) believes that the existence of some threat is a prior condition to federalizing and argues that US federation arose by way of a 'bargain' for purposes of aggregating territory and to meet a threat. Both an 'expansion condition' and a 'military condition' are required to be present. On Riker's empirical analysis of the appropriate prerequisites, conditions would appear right for federalizing Ireland.

16. Editors' note: see ch. 2, pp. 56–7.
17. These advantages are a summary of points made in the Forum Report (New Ireland Forum 1984), Fine Gael (1979), Elazar (1979*a,b*), Bryce (1901: 216–62), Duchacek (1970), and Ostrom (1973).
18. These rights, judicially developed by the European Court of Human Rights, will in the long term impact on the Constitution and law of the Republic.
19. Just as states unite to form federations, unitary states have been federalized. A recent example is Belgium, which in an attempt to hold francophone and Flemish communities and regions together had by 1989 created the most diversified set of governmental institutions in the world. Austria from 1920 is another example of a federalizing unitary state. There are also three socialist federations and three Latin American ones formed from unitary states. The Cypriot communities since 1975 have been attempting to reach agreement on a federation, converting the unitary Republic of Cyprus (now *de facto* divided by Turkish occupation) into a federal Republic.
20. They are also made by Coughlan (see ch. 2 of this volume).
21. Referring to Israel and the West Bank, Elazar notes that to jump from active hostility into federalism is a tall order indeed. This comment is *a fortiori* applicable to jumping to a unitary state or centralized federation.
22. All constitutions evolve, including federations which at different times veer between centralization and peripheralization, e.g. Switzerland and the USA. To imply long-term continuance by describing arrangements as 'durable' is somewhat disingenuous. This has been done regarding joint authority.
23. Fine Gael (1979: 35) mentioned a long list of powers. By contrast the Forum list was short (New Ireland Forum 1984: 35). I believe that the essential federal powers are: foreign affairs, although these need not be exclusively federal; defence and federal security; powers necessary for co-ordination and co-operation; advisory powers on harmonization and general standard-setting; customs and excise; federal budget; central banking and currency; public-sector borrowing controls; federal officers, and federal judiciary (in so far as there is a federal court system). Such a 'loose' federation may be too centrifugal, as was the not dissimilar and

now defunct West Indies Federation. But the prospects of successful federation of widely scattered islands were remote in view of conflicting interests, political rivalries, and the artificiality of constructing a federation as part of the decolonization process.

24. I have not set out the objections, except in passing, to other alternatives. Clearly joint authority is a possible alternative as a preliminary to a fuller confederation, provided there is unionist agreement. However, it is doubtful whether unionists would accept the *bona fides* of the referee (chairman) under joint authority. Nor would acceptance of repartition by the Republic be regarded as anything except treachery, as Mr Curran told the Forum about Catholic concentration west of the River Bann. Compton (1981) makes similar points about repartition. The various other options, including independence and repartition, are criticized in my articles (Palley 1981, 1972). See also Boyle and Hadden (1985: 19–41).

4

Sound Stupidity: The British Party System and the Northern Ireland Question*

Hugh Roberts

All suppressed truths become poisonous.

(Nietzsche, *Thus Spoke Zarathustra*)

THE purpose of this article is to examine a fact about the situation in Northern Ireland which, until very recently, has been almost universally overlooked or misunderstood, where, that is, it has not been deliberately concealed, and to draw out its principal implications. This is the fact that the people of Northern Ireland are excluded from the party-political system which determines the government of the United Kingdom (the state of which Northern Ireland nominally forms part), that they have not chosen to exclude themselves but have been excluded by the actions of the major British political parties, and that their continuing exclusion is today sustained by deliberate decision of the leaders of these parties.[1]

This aspect of the Northern Ireland question has been the subject of intense public debate in the province in recent years, as a result of the effective agitation launched by the Campaign for Equal Citizenship for Northern Ireland (CEC), in the wake of the signing of the Anglo-Irish Agreement in November 1985.[2] But the CEC has been ignored by the mainland British media and the point which it has been making has remained entirely unknown, until very recently, to the overwhelming majority of the population of Great Britain, whose impatience with the intractability of the Northern Ireland problem

* This chapter is a revised and updated version of an article first published in *Government and Opposition*, 22(3) (Summer 1987), 315–35.

has been so regularly invoked by successive British governments in support of their Northern Ireland policy. It also appears to have been unknown to or, at any rate, unappreciated by academic observers of Northern Ireland politics.

1. A MYSTERY DESCRIBED BUT NOT EXPLAINED

In their authoritative study *The Government of the United Kingdom,* Max Beloff and Gillian Peele introduce their account of the political parties in Northern Ireland by noting that 'Northern Irish party politics differ radically from politics elsewhere in Britain. In Northern Ireland the sectarian divisions between Protestant and Roman Catholic—which interlock with the divisions over the constitutional status of Ulster—are the most important factors shaping electoral choice' (Beloff and Peele 1985: 211).

Beloff and Peele initially appear to suggest that it is because 'the community is so polarized' by religious affiliation that 'Northern Irish politics . . . tend to be isolated from those in the rest of the country' (p. 212), but they later cite other factors, entirely independent of the sectarian division, which clearly have also contributed to this isolation. Of the period of devolved government at Stormont from 1921 to 1972, they observe that

The relationship between Northern Ireland and the rest of the United Kingdom was . . . an extremely unusual one, both constitutionally and politically. For although there was theoretical subordination to Westminster and although there were twelve Northern Ireland representatives at Westminster (increased to seventeen in 1983), the two political systems in many ways hardly interacted. This was partly because London was unwilling to be drawn back into Irish politics and partly because the constitutional settlement of 1920 had been quasi-federal in character (p. 331).

And having thus introduced 'London' into the scheme of things as an explanatory factor, Beloff and Peele further insist that

The virtual insulation of the internal political system of Northern Ireland from Westminster's scrutiny between 1921 and 1969 was perhaps the most eloquent testimony to London's weariness with Irish affairs. . . . few questions were ever asked about the nature of Ulster's domestic government between 1920 and 1966. Indeed, it was a convention that Northern Irish affairs were not proper subjects for Westminster's attention; from 1923 the Speaker refused to allow parliamentary questions dealing with matters devolved to Stormont (p. 334).

Between the first and the last of these excerpts a fundamental shift in explanatory perspective has occurred. The first perspective tends to attribute the isolation of Northern Ireland's politics to its different character. But the later perspective tends to attribute this isolation to the attitude of 'London', its distaste for 'Irish' affairs, and the procedural conventions which it established at Westminster to ensure that it was not 'drawn back into' them. From this second perspective it is but a short step to the inference that the different character of Northern Irish politics has been a consequence of its isolation from the politics of Great Britain rather than vice versa, an isolation which, as Beloff and Peele have shown, has been sought and secured by 'London'.

Beloff and Peele do not actually take this step, however. They mention all the essential elements of the Northern Irish conundrum without ever quite managing to put them together in a manner capable of explaining it. In describing how 'London' has contributed to the lack of interaction between the two political systems, indeed to the fact that it has been possible to speak of two distinct political systems at all, Beloff and Peele concentrate entirely upon such secondary matters as procedural conventions at Westminster. They completely fail to explore the significance of the fact that the parties which have dominated the British political system and the Westminster Parliament have consistently refused to contest elections in Northern Ireland since 1920, if not earlier. Yet they are not unaware of this fact. It receives a passing mention in the somewhat imprecise remark that 'none of the United Kingdom parties campaign or organize there' (p. 328).

Had Beloff and Peele undertaken to elaborate upon this observation, they might perhaps have come to appreciate that their initial suggestion that in Northern Ireland 'the sectarian divisions . . . are the most important factors shaping electoral choice' is the exact reverse of the truth and that it has been the lack of electoral choice in Northern Ireland since 1920 which has ensured the perpetuation and permanent politicization of the sectarian division.

The fact that the people of Northern Ireland are excluded from the party-political system which determines the government of the United Kingdom is alluded to by Richard Rose (1982: 125):

Westminster has been anxious to establish a *cordon sanitaire* within the United Kingdom. In violation of the integrity of the United Kingdom as a state, Northern Ireland has been treated as a place apart. The segregation is complete politically, for the British Labour Party does not wish to sponsor candidates for Parliament in Northern Ireland constituencies, notwithstanding the desire of the Northern Ireland Labour Party, its former affiliate, for this to be done. Nor do the Conservatives contest seats in collaboration with one or another fragment of their old Unionist alliance.

Unfortunately, this is only a passing remark which is quickly lost sight of in the flow of Rose's argument. Yet Rose here touches upon the single most important fact about the Northern Ireland question. In order to explain why this fact is so very—indeed, uniquely—important, it is essential to improve upon Rose's very incomplete presentation of it. Let us therefore examine this 'segregation'—which is exactly the right word for it—in the terms which are appropriate to it.

2. PARTY POLITICAL SEGREGATION

The British Labour Party

The British Labour Party (BLP) has never contested a single parliamentary or local election in Northern Ireland. It maintains no party branches there and not only refrains from recruiting members there but actually goes so far as to reject membership applications from Northern Ireland residents.[3] This boycott of Northern Ireland residents not only violates the party's own constitution (namely Clause 2, Section 4; Clause 4, Section 1; and Clause 9, Section 2(a)) but also has been found to amount to 'racial discrimination' within the meaning of the 1976 Race Relations Act, passed by the last Labour Government.[4] It is maintained by the BLP despite the fact that about 90 per cent of trade union members in the highly unionized Northern Ireland workforce belong to British trade unions, that the majority of these trade unions are represented at BLP annual conferences, and despite even the fact that some 60,000 Northern Irish trade unionists *opt in* to pay the political levy[5] to the BLP, a party they may neither join nor support at the polls.

All kinds of absurd anomalies follow from this state of affairs. For instance, for many years the BLP's spokesman on Northern Irish affairs in the House of Lords was Lord Blease, formerly Billy Blease, a leading figure in Northern Ireland trade unionism, who throughout his trade union career was excluded from membership of the party.

In addition, let us note the implications of this boycott when combined with the terms of the 1949 Government of Ireland Act, which
allows for Southern Irish nationals resident in Great Britain to enjoy
all the rights of British citizenship: Eire nationals resident in England,
Scotland, and Wales may vote for the BLP, join it, work for it, take
part in formulating its policies (including its policy on Northern
Ireland!), and stand for election to Parliament or local-government
councils as official Labour candidates, while British citizens resident
in Northern Ireland are not permitted to do any of these things. The
sole exception to this concerns Northern Ireland members of British
trade union delegations at British Labour Party annual conferences,
who have this one, very limited, opportunity to participate in
formulating the policies of a party to which they do not and may not
belong. This anomaly has to be provided for in the party's constitution (Clause 8, Section 1).

This singular state of affairs is not even alluded to in the recently
published memoir of the Labour Secretary of State for Northern
Ireland, 1974–6, Merlyn Rees (1985). And one will search in vain
for any reference to it in an extended review of Rees's book by an
academic specialist on Northern Ireland affairs, Paul Arthur.
Arthur's silence on this matter is especially remarkable, for his
article is entitled 'Labour and Ireland' (Arthur 1986), and discusses
not only the Rees memoir but also Graham Walker's *The Politics of
Frustration: Harry Midgley and the Failure of Labour in Northern Ireland*
(Walker 1985).[6] That an academic specialist can discuss the 'failure of
Labour' in Northern Ireland without once even mentioning the fact
that the BLP has never, at any time, made any attempt to develop its
politics in the province is surely symptomatic of the scale of public
and academic ignorance of Northern Ireland's political history. It
would be explicable were it the case that, as Rose suggests, the old
Northern Ireland Labour Party (NILP), which Harry Midgley worked
for, was indeed at one time an affiliate of the BLP and thus a proper
local surrogate for it. Were this the case, the failure of the NILP could
reasonably be said to be the 'failure of Labour' in Northern Ireland.
But it is not the case.

The NILP has *never* been an affiliate of the BLP.[7] The latter's
refusal to organize in Northern Ireland on its own account may not,
therefore, be regarded as irrelevant to the 'failure of Labour' in
Northern Ireland and accordingly passed over in silence. The NILP
actively sought affiliation in 1942 and again in 1970 but, on both

occasions, its proposal was turned down by the National Executive Committee (NEC) of the BLP without wider discussion in the party (CLR 1986a: 16, 19). The incorporation of the NILP as a Region of the BLP was also mooted in 1949, after the reinforcement of Partition by the proclamation of the Republic in the South in 1948 and the subsequent passing of the Government of Ireland Act at Westminster, and again in 1970. It too was vetoed on both occasions by the BLP NEC in the same way, without any discussion in the party at large (CLR 1986a: 18–19). Instead, a small annual payment was made to it from 1952 to 1975 (CLR 1986a: 11–15),[8] but in other respects its status was identical to that of socialist parties in France, West Germany, and elsewhere, not that of the old Independent Labour Party (ILP) or the Co-operative Party, both of which were real affiliates of the BLP.

Had the NILP been allowed to affiliate to the BLP, it would have been entitled to send delegates instead of mere observers to the annual conferences of the BLP and to be represented on the latter's NEC. In other words, Northern Irish socialists would have been able to participate in the formation of Labour policy, including Labour policy on Northern Ireland. Since Scottish and Welsh delegates to annual conferences have traditionally exerted a considerable influence on Labour policy towards Scotland and Wales, it cannot be doubted that Northern Irish delegates, had there been any, would have come to exert a comparable influence on Labour policy towards Northern Ireland. This has never been allowed to happen. Above all, affiliation would have enabled the NILP to contest local and parliamentary elections in Northern Ireland on behalf of the BLP, just as Co-op and ILP candidates have contested elections in certain constituencies in Great Britain, that is, as genuine surrogates for the BLP. There can be no doubt that the NILP would have been able to secure a substantially increased vote in such conditions. But the NILP has never been able to contest elections as a genuine surrogate for the BLP, for this is something which the latter—or, rather, its leadership, deliberating in camera—has never been willing to countenance.

The NILP disintegrated fast after the BLP leadership's refusal to affiliate or incorporate it in 1970. It had obtained no fewer than 98,193 votes (12.6 per cent of the total vote cast in Northern Ireland)[9] in the 1970 general election, despite the disabilities it laboured under and the three years of sectarian polarization since late 1967, but the

BLP's refusal to support it in the rapidly deteriorating situation in Northern Ireland was the last straw for the NILP leadership. In October 1974, the NILP contested only three of Northern Ireland's twelve constituencies and its aggregate vote fell to 11,539 (1.6 per cent of the total vote cast).

Since the NILP's collapse, the BLP has been continuously canvassed by Northern Irish socialists and trade unionists who wish it to organize in Northern Ireland and admit Northern Ireland residents to party membership. The Campaign for Labour Representation for Northern Ireland (CLR) was founded in Belfast in 1977 and quickly gained an audience both in Northern Ireland trade union circles and in the BLP itself.[10] A detailed paper, 'Labour Party Organisation in Northern Ireland: Observations by the National Agent', was considered by the NEC on 23 November 1977. This paper identified four possible scenarios for Labour Party organization in the province: (1) 'Retention of the Northern Ireland Labour Party'; (2) 'Affiliation of the Northern Ireland Labour Party'; (3) 'Establishment of a New Labour Party in Northern Ireland', and (4) 'Integration with the British Labour Party'. The paper pointed out the major drawbacks to the first three proposals but remarked of the fourth (by which was clearly meant the extension of the BLP's organization and membership to Northern Ireland), 'This is a new approach which should be given serious consideration. It would seem that this course would receive the support of the NILP which would then cease to exist if it was adopted' (CLR 1986*a*: 20).[11] The NEC took no decision at that meeting, but in May 1978 a special meeting of the Organisation Committee of the NEC was held to discuss the National Agent's paper, among other reports and proposals, and resolved 'That the Organisation Committee does not support the proposal that the Labour Party should extend its organisation to Northern Ireland' (p. 20).

This was not the end of the matter, however. A new NEC Study Group on Northern Ireland was set up in January 1980. Partly as a result of its deliberations, the NEC Policy Statement on Northern Ireland submitted to the 1981 annual conference of the BLP included (in its final paragraph) the statement that:

We recognise the need for a class-based party of Labour in Northern Ireland, in order to give a clear political lead to the social and economic issues which unite Catholic and Protestant workers. The foundation of such a Labour Party must be rooted in the trade unions in Northern Ireland. We therefore believe that interested trade unions, trades councils . . . and various other Labour Movement organisations should discuss whether it would be possible to form such a Labour Party (British Labour Party 1981).

This statement did not specifically advocate the extension of BLP organization and membership to Northern Ireland but it did not rule it out either. It left all options open. A Northern Ireland Liaison Committee was set up by the NEC to take soundings in Northern Ireland concerning the proposed discussions, and reported in favour of calling a conference of labour organizations in Northern Ireland to decide between the various options. This report was shelved by the NEC. No such conference was ever called.

In 1983, resolutions from three Constituency Labour Parties (CLPs) calling on the party to organize in Northern Ireland were on the agenda of the annual conference. The movers of the eventual composite resolution agreed to remit it (instead of pressing it to a vote) at the NEC's request, in exchange for a public promise by the NEC that it would look into the question of Labour Party organization in the province and, in particular, into that of holding a trade union-based conference there to discuss the matter. This promise was never honoured. In 1984, four CLPs submitted resolutions in the same vein to the annual conference. But, unlike the previous year, these resolutions were not placed in the 'Northern Ireland' section of the conference agenda, but in the 'Party Organisation' section instead, and were not debated. Similar resolutions in every year since 1984 have met a similar fate.

It would be tedious to document all the numerous other ways in which the BLP's leadership and party managers have acted since 1983 to stifle debate on this issue. But the way in which the leadership's position has evolved in recent years is worth noting. The refusal to admit Northern Ireland residents into membership of the party (in violation of the party constitution, as it happens) was explained in purely pragmatic terms until very recently. Disappointed applicants from Northern Ireland were told that the party could not afford to organize in the province for lack of funds. This excuse was dropped in 1986, in the context of the turmoil provoked by the Anglo-Irish Agreement, and official BLP spokesmen on Northern Ireland began to cite the existence of John Hume's Social Democratic and Labour Party (SDLP) as the reason why it was neither necessary nor desirable for the BLP to admit members or contest elections in the province.[12]

According to Beloff and Peele, 'the formation of the Social Democratic and Labour Party in 1970 was the first attempt to transcend the old and rather sterile pattern of Ulster politics in which all other issues were subordinated to nationalist concerns' (Beloff and Peele 1985: 335). This interpretation (which overlooks fifty years of dedicated, if ultimately futile, NILP activity) is entirely erroneous. At every critical juncture since its foundation the SDLP has subordinated all other issues, including even that of power-sharing within Northern Ireland,[13] to nationalist concerns. By the late 1970s, if not earlier, it was clear that the SDLP was merely a new and more effective version of the old Nationalist Party, under a different and highly misleading name (by virtue of which it was able to secure admission to the Socialist International). The element of ambiguity in the SDLP, arising out of the formal coexistence within it of nationalist and socialist perspectives, was definitively resolved in favour of the former when its founder and first leader, Gerry Fitt MP (now Lord Fitt), resigned from the party in November 1979, on the grounds that the party had become merely nationalist. In fact, however, the party had been merely nationalist all along, under Fitt's leadership. The only other prominent socialist in the SDLP, Paddy Devlin, had resigned more than a year beforehand. And the subordination of socialist to nationalist concerns was never more vividly demonstrated than in Fitt's own decision to abstain in the House of Commons in March 1979 on the motion of 'no confidence' which brought down the last Labour Government. Fitt withheld his support because the Labour Government had agreed to raise Northern Ireland's representation in Parliament from 12 to 17 seats, and thereby bring it into line with the ratio of seats to population in the rest of the United Kingdom. It was no part of the SDLP's purpose that Northern Ireland should be properly represented at Westminster. The 'no confidence' motion was passed by a majority of one vote.

The decision of the BLP leadership to consider the SDLP as a 'sister party' has been an entirely informal affair. In view of the SDLP's responsibility in bringing down the last Labour Government, it is perhaps understandable that this decision has never been submitted for ratification to an annual conference. That this attitude towards the SDLP has been little more than a debating point for use in justifying the leadership's refusal to consider the CLR's proposals (or to honour its own commitments made at the 1981 and 1983 annual conferences) is suggested by the fact that the current Labour spokesman on Northern Ireland, Kevin McNamara MP, has repeatedly stated, with unprecedented frankness, that there is no question of the Labour Party organizing in Northern Ireland since to do so would be inconsistent with the party's 'belief in a United Ireland' (CLR 1987: 3).

The Conservative Party

The Conservative Party has never contested any elections in Northern Ireland nor has it ever accepted Northern Ireland residents into membership or maintained constituency associations in the province. Like the British Labour Party, it has actually rejected applications for membership from Northern Ireland residents when it has received them.[14] Unlike the BLP, it has maintained a definite and formal relationship with a Northern Ireland party, the Ulster Unionist Party, such that Ulster Unionist MPs used to sit and vote with Conservative MPs in the House of Commons.

This relationship began to wither following the suspension of Stormont in 1972 and the subsequent fragmentation of Ulster Unionism into a number of distinct and competing parties, but elements of it were preserved until recently with respect to the 'Official' Ulster Unionist Party (OUP). Members of the OUP youth wing, the Young Unionists, were able, for instance, to belong to the Federation of Conservative Students (FCS) right up until the dissolution of the FCS by decision of Conservative Central Office in late 1986.[15] But, on leaving the FCS, they could not join the Conservative Party. The substantive demise of the old relationship between the two parties was made manifest in 1979, when two OUP MPs supported James Callaghan's Labour Government in the vote of confidence, and was explicitly consecrated by the decision of the OUP leadership, in the wake of the Anglo-Irish Agreement of November 1985, to dissolve the last formal connection between the OUP and the Conservative National Union.

But, even in its heyday, prior to 1968–9, this relationship was anomalous in the extreme. It was not a relationship between essentially similar parties, but an alliance between parties which were very different from one another in most ways. For the Ulster Unionist Party was never the Northern Ireland Region of the Conservative Party. It represented and enjoyed the support of all social classes within the Protestant community on the basis of support for the Union, not on the basis of support for Conservative economic and social philosophy or policies. Unionist governments at Stormont from 1922 to 1972 re-enacted the economic and social legislation passed at Westminster, including that of Labour governments, notably all the socialistic welfare state legislation of the 1945–51 and 1964–70 periods, even though they were constitutionally free to choose not to. The Unionists did not govern Northern Ireland as the Conservative Party, and the fact that Ulster Unionist MPs at Westminster voted with the Conservative Party there up until the early 1970s did not mean that the Conservative Party maintained any kind of political presence in the province. And the collapse of this old relationship over the last fifteen years has not prompted the Conservative Party to establish an independent presence there.[16]

The Conservative Party is very different from the Labour Party in its inner life and organization and it cannot be canvassed in the same way. The proposition that the good government of Northern Ireland would be greatly facilitated, and the prospects for social peace there correspondingly enhanced, were the party to establish its presence and contest elections there has, none the less, been energetically canvassed within it in recent years, at several levels. These include those of the Federation of Conservative Students, the Young Conservatives, the Northern Ireland Committee of the Parliamentary Party, Conservative Central Office, and that of the party leader herself. Its failure to accept or act on the case for its organizing in Northern Ireland cannot therefore be put down to ignorance of this case, nor to a lack of sympathy for it within the party's membership at large. This became clear in the course of 1988, when a group of Conservative sympathizers in Northern Ireland set up an unofficial or 'model' Conservative Constituency Association in the overwhelmingly Protestant and middle-class constituency of North Down and then applied to Conservative Central Office in London for official recognition.

This grouping was an offshoot from the cross-party Campaign for Equal Citizenship (CEC)[17] and was acting on advice from certain British Conservatives that the way to persuade the Conservative Party to organize in Northern Ireland was to establish unofficial constituency associations and thereby demonstrate the existence of support for the party in the province, which demonstration (it was suggested) would be enough to persuade Conservative Central Office to recognize the constituency associations in question. This strategy was premised on the assumption (which had originally been rejected by the CEC[18] that the absence of the Conservative Party from Northern Ireland was essentially an organizational question, not a matter of conscious policy. It meant abandoning the CEC's fundamental argument, that the Conservative Party was bound by democratic principle to seek a mandate to govern in Northern Ireland, for the more superficial and much less defensible demand that the Conservative leadership admit a particular group of individuals to the party on the mere grounds that they were bona fide Tories. This line of argument made it possible for the Conservative leadership to dismiss the demand on the grounds that, among other things, the North Down 'Tories' were not, in fact, bona fide Conservatives since they did not support Government (and therefore Conservative) policy on Northern Ireland, notably in relation to the Anglo-Irish Agreement.[19] The application of the North Down 'model constituency association' to affiliate to the party was rejected by the Conservative National Union Executive Committee at its meeting in London on 10 November 1988.

None the less, the canvassing of the Conservative Party both by the remnants of the CEC and by the North Down grouping at the party's annual conference at Brighton in October 1988 elicited the first ever editorial support for this idea from the British Press[20] and has had a discernible impact on grass-roots Conservative opinion. In February 1989, the annual conference of the Young Conservatives held in Scarborough passed a resolution urging 'the Conservative Party to organise in Northern Ireland and to begin this process by recognising the North Down constituency association' on an overwhelming show of hands. Five weeks later, when the Conservative Central Council met (also in Scarborough, as it happens) on 18 March, no fewer than nine resolutions favouring the party's organizing in Northern Ireland had been submitted (*Cork Examiner*, 18 March 1989). None of them were selected by the party managers for debate, but in deference to grass-roots opinion the Chairman of the National Union Executive Committee, Sir Peter Lane, announced that the question would be discussed at the party's annual conference in Blackpool in October (*Irish Times*, 20 and 22 March 1989).

Whatever form the discussion will take, Sir Peter's announcement does not necessarily indicate a change in the thinking of the party leadership on the substantive issue of principle. For even if the leadership did eventually agree to admit the North Down 'Tories' and their counterparts in East Belfast (where a second 'model' constituency association was formed in January 1989), this decision would not necessarily imply a commitment to organize throughout Northern Ireland and to contest elections on a province-wide basis. And in the absence of such a commitment, publicly proclaimed and honoured in practice, the fledgling associations in North Down and East Belfast could not seriously be expected to make electoral headway and would be liable to wither on the vine.

In the meantime, the Conservative Party's public position *vis-à-vis* its frustrated sympathizers in Northern Ireland remains that it advises them to vote for the Official Unionist Party.

The Liberal Party

The Liberal Party was the dominant political party in what is now Northern Ireland up until Gladstone's first Home Rule Bill in 1886. Gladstone's policy was strongly criticized by the Ulster Liberals, but in vain, and the majority of them were absorbed into the Ulster Unionist alliance formed to oppose the Bill. In other words, the Home Rule controversy effectively destroyed Ulster Liberalism.

However, the Liberal Party maintained a notional presence in Northern Ireland following the revival of the party by local supporters in the mid-1950s. But this presence was notional in the extreme, notwithstanding the (very) occasional contested election. Its adherence to Gladstonean anti-partitionism ensured that it had no audience among Protestants while being insufficient to attract substantial Catholic support. (Why vote for Liberal anti-partitionism if you can vote for Catholic anti-partitionism, if you are a Catholic anti-partitionist? And those Catholics who were not particularly anti-partitionist in their political outlook would have had even less reason to forsake the specifically Catholic parties for the Liberal Party than those who were nationalists first and Catholics second.) One may surmise that, had the Liberal Party adopted a strictly neutral position on the border after 1922 (or at least 1949) and contested elections in Northern Ireland on the same basis and the same policies as it did everywhere else in the United Kingdom, it would have been in a position eventually—and particularly after the suspension of Stormont in 1972—to attract support from Catholics frustrated by the political cul-de-sac of permanent opposition nationalism and also from Protestants uneasy about the sectarian character of the Unionist parties. But the Liberal Party never adopted this stance. And, even had it done so, this would probably have made little difference, because of the very marginal place of the Liberal Party in British national politics for most of the period in question.

Most, if not all, political parties have a core of followers who vote for them through thick and thin for sentimental or ideological reasons, irrespective of other considerations. But most people vote for a given party in expectation or, at least, a reasonable hope of material benefit in some form or other. A party which is permanently out of office has very little with which to attract new voters, however sympathetic they may be to its principles. This was the problem which confronted the NILP throughout its entire history; the surprising thing is that it attracted as much support as it did. The same problem confronted the Liberal Party in Northern Ireland. From the 1930s right up until the emergence of the Social Democratic Party (SDP) and its alliance with it in the early 1980s, the Liberal Party was never remotely in contention for power at Westminster. It was accordingly in no position to exert a gravitational pull upon those elements, in either of the two religious voting blocs in Northern Ireland, who might otherwise have been subjectively susceptible to the appeal of a non-sectarian and mildly progressive brand of politics. In this respect, of course, the Liberal Party was quite different from both the British Labour Party and the Conservative Party. It has thus been an irrelevance twice over, both in practical terms and from the point of view of the argument being developed here. Its failure to act as the focus for the development of non-sectarian politics in Northern Ireland is entirely explained by its own behaviour and standing, and therefore has no wider implications.

The Social Democratic Party

The SDP has clearly failed in its aim of 'breaking the mould of British politics'. The mould of British politics is not easily broken. But there are grounds for thinking that the SDP could have made a strategic contribution to breaking the mould of Northern Ireland politics and that, when its leaders realized this, they chose to do no such thing.

The fact that the SDP actually recruited members in Northern Ireland upon its formation in 1981 is probably to be put down to an oversight on its part. For it subsequently behaved towards the young, enthusiastic, and dynamic membership it rapidly if unintentionally acquired in Northern Ireland in a way which suggested that it was acutely embarrassed by their very existence. From 1981 to 1986, it refused to allow them to 'constitute an 'Area Party', the standard form of SDP grass-roots organization and the organizational pre-condition of engaging in electoral activity. Instead, the SDP members in the province were allowed to maintain only a very vague collective existence in what was known as 'the SDP Northern Ireland Forum'. The attitude of the SDP leadership towards its Northern Ireland members was defined by Dr David Owen at the first ever meeting of the Northern Ireland SDP, held in the Stormont Hotel in Belfast on 1 October 1981, where he made it clear that there was no question of the SDP contesting elections in the province. The efforts of the Northern Ireland members to persuade the party leadership to change its mind on this question proved unsuccessful and a significant number of activists who were initially attracted to the party in 1981 left it thereafter, since they were precluded by the policy of the party leadership from engaging in any purposeful activity.

In late 1986 a slight change in policy appeared to occur, with the decision of the national leadership to upgrade the 'SDP Northern Ireland Forum' to the status of an 'unrecognized Area Party'. The implication of this was that, should the SDP membership in Northern Ireland attain the requisite number, it would thereafter be recognized as a full 'Area Party', entitled as such to stand candidates in elections. The way might therefore have appeared to be open towards the contesting of elections in Northern Ireland by a substantial British political party. In fact, however, there was little real prospect of this. The initial enthusiasm and public interest which the Northern Ireland SDP could have counted on in its recruiting efforts in 1981–82 had long since evaporated. It could have been rekindled in 1986 only if the SDP leadership had publicly announced its willingness in principle to contest elections in Northern Ireland should the required membership target be achieved. No such announcement was made.

In any case, of course, whether or not such a development was in prospect, it has probably been precluded by the split in the SDP over the issue of merging with the Liberal Party in the aftermath of the 1987 general election, and the ensuing reduction of the SDP to a small group of Owen loyalists.

The Social and Liberal Democratic Party
The formation of the SLD through the absorption of the majority of

the SDP into the old Liberal Party has only recently occurred, and it might therefore be thought premature to describe its policy towards Northern Ireland. In fact, however, there is every reason to expect it to follow a substantially identical policy to that which was being pursued by the Liberal Party prior to the merger. This policy is to support the Alliance Party of Northern Ireland (APNI) as the provincial counterpart or 'sister party' of the SLD, and ignores to all intents and purposes the former members of the old Liberal Party in Northern Ireland. Much more to the point, it also ignores the particular nature of the APNI, which is, in reality, by no means a counterpart of the SLD.

The APNI certainly contains within its ranks people of broadly social-democratic and liberal beliefs. But it also contains people who would be much more at home in the Conservative Party and yet others who would belong to the Labour Party if they could. The 'middle ground' which the APNI occupies has nothing to do with the 'centre ground' which the SLD aspires to occupy in British politics. It is the middle ground between sectarian parties, between political Protestantism and political Catholicism, not that between left and right. The principle which the APNI represents is thus a negative one—the refusal to engage in sectarian politics. The very basis of the APNI's appeal precludes it from advancing any positive principles concerning the conduct of government at the national level; it must abstain from doing so if it is to maintain unity within its own ranks. It therefore cannot exert any gravitational pull on the supporters of the sectarian parties, because it has nothing positive to offer them. In so far as the APNI has tended to represent a positive principle over and above the purely negative principle of fastidious non-sectarianism, it has tended to represent the principle of ecumenicalism, that is, an alternative *religious* position.

The APNI accordingly remains firmly imprisoned in the structure of provincial politics in Northern Ireland, in which party-political differences are essentially the electoral expression of religious differences. The APNI is constitutionally inhibited from transcending this structure, although this was the avowed ambition of its founders in the early 1970s, and has instead evolved within this structure and even acquired a vested interest in it. In recent years it has become a vigorous champion of the restoration of devolved government in the province and an even more determined opponent of the proposal that the major political parties of Great Britain should organize and contest elections in Northern Ireland. It is true that this proposal, if

put into effect, would very probably make the APNI obsolete overnight, as its members disappeared into more purposeful forms of
non-sectarian politics.

This policy, which the SLD has so far given every sign of
following, therefore boils down to using the APNI as a pretext for
refusing to recruit potential SLD supporters in Northern Ireland into
party membership and for refusing to canvass Social and Liberal
Democratic politics in the province, despite the failure of the APNI
to win a single parliamentary seat since its foundation and the
virtual certainty that it will not do so in future. This policy is therefore identical, in substance if not in form, to the policies of the
Labour and Conservative Parties.

3. ABNORMAL AND IRREGULAR GOVERNANCE

No sincerity of purpose ever excludes the possibility of conduct for which no
excuse can seriously be made.

(Harold Laski, *The Dangers of Obedience*)

In these ways has it been made impossible for the people of
Northern Ireland to engage in normal, purposeful, non-sectarian
party politics.

The leaders of the major British parties have often expressed their
impatience that Northern Ireland does not settle down into the comparatively peaceful routine of British politics. And they have
apparently succeeded in communicating this impatience to the
people of Great Britain. But they never tell the British public that
they have deprived the people of Northern Ireland of the means of
settling down into normal politics, let alone that it is their policy to
continue to withhold these means from them.

It was not always so. As Richard Rose has noted, the initial
reaction of British politicians to the disturbances in Northern Ireland
in the late 1960s was the opposite of the view which prevailed in
1920 and which has once more prevailed in British political circles
since the early 1970s. As he reminds us, 'the evident abnormality of
conditions in Northern Ireland was taken by the media and by MPs
to show the need to "normalise" Northern Ireland, that is, to make it
meet the standards applied elsewhere in the United Kingdom'. But
this perspective was not entertained for long, for 'subsequent to
internment in 1971, the opposite conclusion was drawn: abnormal

conditions justified using abnormal or irregular means of governance' (Rose 1982: 111).

The decision to suspend Stormont in 1972 did not involve a reversion to the 'normalization' perspective, although it may be thought to have offered a favourable context for this. On the contrary, it was the preliminary merely to attempts to reconstruct in Northern Ireland a form of devolved government acceptable to Westminster, attempts predicated upon the assumption that, in Reginald Maudling's words, 'the Westminster pattern of democracy, which suits us so well, is not easily exportable'. And, as the word 'exportable' implies, this assumption itself rested on the unspoken and therefore unexamined axiom that 'Northern Ireland is an "alien" land and not an integral part of the United Kingdom' (Rose 1982: 115). So the policy of 'normalizing' Northern Ireland's political life was no sooner mooted than it was abandoned, without ever being put into practice and, 'instead of removing practices anomalous by Westminster standards, the government sought to introduce new anomalies' (Rose 1982: 115). This has been the essence of the British government's approach to the Northern Ireland problem for the last seventeen years. This approach can hardly be said to have justified itself by its results.

Now, a policy of 'abnormal and irregular governance' is liable to be self-sustaining, for it has built into it a profound imperviousness to criticism. If a policy is an affair of anomalies, by what yardstick is it to be judged? A policy of anomalous governance is inherently proof against all criticism based upon 'the standards applied elsewhere in the United Kingdom', for the policy itself is predicated upon the assumed irrelevance of these standards. Where and when these standards are applied, a policy which fails to attain its notional objectives is vigorously criticized and pressure is brought to bear to ensure that it is not persisted in. But all this immediately becomes impossible once these standards are dismissed and no substitutes found for them.

A policy which was manifestly failing to attain its notional objectives in Northern Ireland more than a decade ago has not been abandoned. It has been doggedly persisted in. And its continuing failure to secure its notional objectives, with all that this has meant and continues to mean for life and limb in Northern Ireland, has not been held against it. The notion that Northern Ireland is a place apart for which anomalous arrangements must be made is one of the few things on which the British political parties are unreservedly agreed. That it remains the keystone of government policy is clear from the peculiar terms of the Anglo-Irish Agreement (Clifford 1985, 1986*a*,*b*; Roberts 1986: 11–15) and was reaffirmed with uninhibited frankness by the Parliamentary Under-Secretary for Northern Ireland, Nicholas Scott MP,[21] in the very title of his article in the *Daily Telegraph* (14 July 1986), 'Northern Ireland is Different and must be Governed Differently'.

The ability of the British political parties to agree upon this so far spectacularly unsuccessful policy of abnormal, irregular, and anomalous governance, the inability of the electors of Northern Ireland to induce the British government, of whatever party, to countenance a different policy, and the 'abnormal conditions' which are invoked in justification of this policy have one and the same cause: the fact that the electors of Northern Ireland are excluded from the British party-political system, which is to say, disfranchised.

4. A DISFRANCHISED ELECTORATE

The people of Northern Ireland are not governed democratically. They are not governed by the parties which represent them and they are not represented by the parties which govern them. Northern Ireland is part of the United Kingdom and the United Kingdom is governed from Westminster. England, Scotland, and Wales all have representative government at Westminster. But Northern Ireland does not have representative government.

The people of Northern Ireland are governed by virtue of the workings of a political system in which they may not participate. The government of the United Kingdom is determined by the functioning of a party system of which the principal protagonists for most of the time since 1920 have been two in number, the Labour and Conservative Parties. And even if the SLD or what is left of the SDP should ever succeed in transforming this two-party system into what would amount in effect to a three-party system, the people of Northern Ireland will continue to be excluded from this.

It is a characteristic of every state that it possesses a political system. It is through the operation of the political system that the government is constituted, interests represented, policies debated, laws made, and consent for them secured. The proper functioning of the political system is indispensable to the legitimacy of the government and it is through the ramifications of the political system that the subjective unity of the sovereign political community which is the state is continuously expressed and thereby sustained. All this the electors of Northern Ireland are excluded from. Their situation has no contemporary parallel.

It may be argued that the 'quasi-federal' character of the constitutional settlement of 1920, of which Beloff and Peele speak, is adequate explanation of this extraordinary state of affairs. But the 'quasi-federal' character of the constitutional arrangements in question cannot be said to have persisted beyond 1972, when the measure of self-government which Northern Ireland had known under Stormont came to an end.

In fact, however, it is by no means a corollary of the federal principle—let alone the 'quasi-federal' principle, if there is such a thing—that a self-governing constituent part of a federation or union of states is excluded from the political system by which the federation or union as a whole is governed. The people of Georgia are not excluded from the party-political system of the United States any more than the people of the other Georgia are excluded from the political system of the Soviet Union. A Georgian Democrat has been elected to the White House and a Georgian Communist has occupied the Kremlin. The electors of both Atlanta and Tbilisi are represented politically at the level of the federal state as a whole on exactly the same basis as their fellow citizens in New York and Leningrad, because they have access to the same political institutions which matter, the parties which form, or are in electoral contention to form, or provide the principal personnel of, the government. But the electors of Belfast and Derry are not represented politically on the same basis as their fellow citizens in Birmingham, Glasgow, and Swansea. They can join and vote for only small provincial parties which can never form, or even expect to be part of, the government of the state and which, therefore, count for little or nothing at Westminster. The right to vote for and belong to political parties capable of forming governments and so too of exerting influence when in opposition—a right enjoyed and taken entirely for granted the length and breadth of Great Britain—is denied them.

It is this disfranchisement of the electors of Northern Ireland which allows the British government, whichever party is in office, to persist in a misconceived and self-evidently unworkable policy towards the province. The party in government has no seats at risk there and the principal opposition parties similarly have no electoral inducement to oppose the government's Northern Ireland policy or even to subject it to serious scrutiny. Indeed, they have every incentive to allow Northern Ireland business to be transacted as summarily as possible, so that it does not waste valuable time which would otherwise be available for the consideration of matters in respect of which these parties have representational obligations to discharge and electoral interests to defend.

This is the explanation of the remarkable convention known as 'bipartisanship', the agreement amongst the British political parties to support whatever the government has in mind to do about Northern Ireland, whichever party is in government. It is *an agreement to agree* or, at any rate, an agreement not to disagree to any effect. No such convention operates with respect to any other sphere of public policy. The party conflict is not suspended in respect of foreign policy or defence or anything else. It is suspended only in relation to Northern Ireland. Not even in time of war has any aspect of government policy—including its defence policy—been subject to such superficial consideration in Parliament as has been given to government policy towards Northern Ireland.

It is often suggested that the convention of bipartisanship is all to the good, that it ensures that the Northern Ireland problem does not become, as the cliché has it, 'a party-political football'. The implication, or underlying assumption, of this, which is never stated openly, is that the normal routines of party-political competition and debate inhibit the effective formation of policy. In fact, they are the *sine qua non* of effective policy formation in the British political system.

A convention which permits, if not condemns, an unworkable policy to be persisted in indefinitely is invariably presented in public as an unparalleled self-denying ordinance which the British parties have agreed to impose upon themselves out of a high-minded seriousness of purpose in the face of a problem of exceptional gravity. In reality, it expresses nothing so much as their comprehensive indifference to Northern Ireland and their freedom of any obligation to think about the place because they are none of them accountable to its electorate.

It is also often suggested that the convention of bipartisanship is informed by the purpose of mitigating sectarian antagonisms in

Northern Ireland. By agreeing to remain above, or at any rate outside, the mêlée, the British political parties are commendably
refusing to take sides in a sectarian conflict. The opposite is the
truth. The united boycott of Northern Ireland by the British parties
makes sectarian conflict unavoidable there, by precluding any feasible
alternative to it. But the British parties go further than this: the
Labour Party actively supports one side in the sectarian conflict, the
Catholic nationalist side, through its encouragement and endorsement of the SDLP, while the Conservative Party, as we have seen,
continues to call on its notional sympathizers in Northern Ireland to
support the Ulster Unionist Party.

The disfranchised electors of Northern Ireland would not suffer
from becoming a political football of the British political parties, they
suffer from not being one. The electors of Great Britain do not
consider themselves to be mere footballs because the major parties
are forever after their votes; on the contrary, it is because the parties
are obliged to court public opinion that the people of Great Britain
cannot be kicked about politically. The people of Northern Ireland
are already a football of the British parties in the sense of being an
impotent object of their contempt. They have everything to gain
from becoming a much disputed object of their desire.

5. THE *SINE QUA NON* OF CONSENT

The substantive enfranchisement of the people of Northern Ireland
through their admission to the party-political system of the state is
the pre-condition of effective policy formation in London and of the
development of non-sectarian politics in the province. It is also the
pre-condition of any lasting constitutional settlement based upon
consent.

The development of non-sectarian politics in which ordinary
Catholics and Protestants can come together—and divide—politically upon the basis of interests which transcend the religious—
communal division is impossible for as long as the indispensable
medium for this development—the major parties of government and
opposition within the state—is withheld. Not one of the British
national parties is associated with a particular religious faith. They
each of them contain and represent people of widely different
religious beliefs, and enable their members and supporters to sink

their religious differences in the political pursuit of common interests and purposes.

It is an article of faith with British politicians and commentators that the people of Northern Ireland are obsessed with their religious differences and the communal politics which express them, and that they cannot be induced to set aside these preoccupations. Not only is this belief groundless, it has actually been demonstrated to be groundless. But this demonstration has had no effect.

During the 1987 general election, a major opinion poll was carried out for Ulster Television and Channel 4 by the consultant firm Coopers and Lybrand Associates.[22] 1,100 adults, selected reasonably proportionally for age, sex, and religion, and drawn from all twenty-six district council areas in Northern Ireland, were interviewed. One of the questions they were asked was 'which factor do you consider to be of greater importance as an electoral issue . . . the Anglo-Irish Agreement or the state of the economy?' The Anglo-Irish Agreement had been in force for eighteen months by May 1987, the controversy surrounding it had not begun to abate, and it was the central issue in the electoral contest in all seventeen of the province's constituencies. One might therefore have expected the respondents to identify it as the 'factor . . . of greater importance as an electoral issue'. Only 24 per cent did so (31 per cent of Protestants and a mere 14 per cent of Catholics). Seventy-one per cent in all (64 per cent of Protestants and 80 per cent of Catholics) regarded the state of the economy as the more important issue, despite the fact that this was not being addressed by any of the provincial parties they could vote for. Nearly three-quarters of the Northern Irish electorate were more interested in what was at stake in the general election in England, Scotland, and Wales than in what was at stake in the only election they were allowed to vote in.

The ground of non-sectarian politics already exists in an un-developed state in Northern Ireland. The apparent political polarization of the population along sectarian lines reflects the absence of plausible non-sectarian alternatives to the existing provincial parties, not a popular rejection of these alternatives. And further evidence, of much longer standing, of the underlying common ground between the two communities is provided by the remarkable success of the trade union movement in preserving its non-sectarian character throughout the period since 1920. This common ground can be built on only if the opportunity to sink religious differences in common political activity within the British national parties is made available to the people of Northern Ireland. And until this happens, there can be no solution of the Northern Ireland question based on the consent of the people concerned.

The canvassing of Irish unity by Catholic parties since 1920 has manifestly failed to secure Protestant consent to unification. The British Labour Party is in favour of Irish unity but is devoid of any particular religious associations. Unless it undertakes to canvass a non-sectarian case for Irish unification amongst the Protestant population, it can safely be said that unification by consent will never occur. The active presence of the British Labour Party in Northern Ireland may not be sufficient to achieve it, but the BLP's continued absence makes its achievement inconceivable.

Equally, the championing of the Union by Protestant parties over the last sixty-nine years has conspicuously failed to elicit a sufficient degree of general Catholic consent to Northern Ireland's position within the United Kingdom. This is not because of widespread Catholic dissatisfaction with this position in itself. It is because the sectarian character of the unionist parties has precluded Catholic participation in them, such that, in the absence of other options, Catholic political energies have had no outlet but that provided by the nationalist parties (the SDLP and Provisional Sinn Féin). It is taken for granted in Great Britain that all Northern Ireland Catholics are nationalists. The equation: Catholic—Nationalist is actually written into the terms of the Anglo-Irish Agreement,[23] and it is, of course, the assumption which underlies the random assassination of Catholics by Protestant paramilitaries. This assumption is false, it has been known to be false for many years, and it was conclusively demonstrated to be false by the Coopers and Lybrand poll in May 1987, which found that only 9 per cent of the total population of Northern Ireland prefer the nationalist solution, Irish unity, to the other options, and only 22 per cent of the Catholic population do so.[24] A clear majority, 57 per cent, of Catholic respondents favoured one or another political solution within the framework of the Union with Great Britain. In other words, the actual political outlook of the majority of the Catholic community in Northern Ireland is being systematically misrepresented at the level of party politics.

Only through access to and participation in the non-sectarian parties of Great Britain could the substantial *de facto* consent to the Union which already exists within the Catholic community be

consolidated in the political life of this community. The presence of
the British parties would not prevent Catholics from continuing to
register nationalist sympathies by voting for explicitly nationalist
parties if they wished. But in the continued absence of the British
parties, the decline of interest among Catholics in the old Republican
ideal and the development of interest in other issues have no
politically effective means of registering themselves.

Essential if ever Protestant consent to Irish unification is to be
achieved, essential if Catholic consent for the Union is to be consolidated, the presence of the British parties is also essential if a stable
and generally accepted form of devolved government is to be
established in the province. The proposal that the British parties
accept members and contest elections in Northern Ireland is not an
'integrationist' proposal except in electoral terms. It is perfectly compatible with the various forms of 'integration' which have been canvassed, and is necessary if these forms are to have any effect. But it is
equally compatible with administrative, judicial, and even legislative
devolution in Northern Ireland (Davidson 1986a,b), as it is in
Scotland and Wales. Indeed, far from precluding the devolutionist
option, the presence of the British parties would greatly facilitate it,
by transforming the party-political arena in Northern Ireland in a
manner which would break down sectarian barriers and so enhance
the prospect of a genuine system of power-sharing involving
Catholics and Protestants on an equal basis. The only kind of
devolved government which would satisfy the SDLP's traditional
demand for 'power-sharing' and the Unionists' traditional demand
for 'democratic majority rule' at one and the same time is that based
upon electoral integration and the concomitant supersession of
sectarian by non-sectarian party politics. Unless the religious difference is transcended in party politics, devolved government can only
institutionalize and perpetuate sectarian politics and thereby
regularly generate the very impulses to challenge or undermine the
constitutional framework that it is its notional purpose to pre-empt.
It is the absence of the British non-sectarian parties which makes a
stable, equitable, and functional system of devolved government an
impossibility.

The obvious question which arises at this point is this: if the
presence of the British parties is all-important, why do the people of
Northern Ireland not recognize this fact and demand admission to
the British party system? The answer is that they do recognize this

fact, but their demand for the necessary change is virtually inaudible.

By the time Coopers and Lybrand conducted their opinion poll in May 1987, the Campaign for Equal Citizenship had been in existence for a little over a year. The CEC's principal demand was that the British parties organize and seek a mandate to govern by contesting elections in Northern Ireland, and this demand and the CEC's campaigning activities received extensive media coverage in Northern Ireland. Coopers and Lybrand accordingly included in their poll the question 'Should the British political parties field candidates in Northern Ireland?', the first time this question had ever been asked in any of the numerous opinion polls and surveys conducted in the province. Sixty-two per cent of all respondents said 'Yes'; 27 per cent said 'No'; and 11 per cent said 'Don't know'. A clear majority of the population of Northern Ireland had taken the CEC's point. Moreover, what was really striking about the poll's findings was that support for this proposition was almost the same in the two communities: 65 per cent of Protestants and 59 per cent of Catholics. Nearly three times as many Catholics wanted the British parties to organize in Northern Ireland as wanted a United Ireland.[25]

Nor were these findings a mere flash in the pan. In February 1989 a new survey was carried out by Ulster Marketing Surveys Ltd. on behalf of the Belfast newspaper *Sunday Life*.[26] In answer to the much more demanding question 'Would you vote for British parties in Northern Ireland?', 53 per cent of all respondents said 'Yes' (57 per cent of Protestants, 45 per cent of Catholics); 45 per cent said 'No' (41 per cent of Protestants, 52 per cent of Catholics); and 2 per cent said 'Don't know'. These figures do not represent a significant decline in public support for the CEC's demand since May 1987. Had the broader and less demanding question asked by Coopers and Lybrand in 1987 been asked by Ulster Marketing Surveys Ltd. in its February 1989 poll, it is entirely possible that substantially the same responses as in 1987 would have been forthcoming.

Public opinion in Northern Ireland has recognized that the presence of the British political parties is all-important. But the demand which expresses this recognition is virtually inaudible, for two reasons. In the absence of the British parties, the existing provincial parties enjoy a collective electoral monopoly, and they are all opposed to a demand which spells their own obsolescence. That they do indeed have a collective vested interest in the continued absence of the British parties emerged very clearly from the February 1989 opinion poll. Ulster Marketing Surveys Ltd. provided a break-down of potential electoral support for the British parties in Northern Ireland in terms of existing party allegiances; these find-ings are summarized in Table 4.1. It reveals that the presence of the British political parties as an electoral option in Northern Ireland would practically wipe out the APNI's support and deprive the OUP of nearly 60 per cent of its vote, while virtually halving the current support of the DUP and the SDLP. Only Sinn Féin would retain its vote substantially (78 per cent) intact, but even it stands to lose a fifth of its support to British parties. That the leaders of all the existing Northern Ireland parties have an interest in discouraging the British parties from organizing in Northern Ireland is clear. And that the support for sectarian parties in Northern Ireland is anything but immutable is also clear. The idea that the electors of Northern Ireland are irredeemably wedded to sectarian political allegiances is a demonstrable myth.

But it is the sectarian parties which, together with the British parties themselves, have sustained access to the media of Great Britain and thereby largely determine British media coverage of Northern Ireland affairs. The supporters of the proposition that the British parties should organize in Northern Ireland have—with the

TABLE 4.1. *Willingness to vote for British parties in Northern Ireland by present party allegiance*

Present party allegiance		Yes, would vote		No, wouldn't vote		No reply	
Party	No.	No.	%	No.	%	No.	%
APNI	94	72	76.6	22	23.4	—	—
DUP	98	45	45.9	51	52.0	2	2.0
OUP	272	157	57.7	110	40.4	5	1.8
Other Unionist	20	12	60.0	7	35.0	1	5.0
Sinn Féin	50	11	22.0	39	78.0	—	—
SDLP	148	70	47.3	73	49.3	5	3.4
Workers' Party	23	15	65.2	7	30.4	1	4.3
Other	3	2	66.7	1	33.3	—	—
Wouldn't vote	40	17	42.5	22	55.0	1	2.5
Undecided/refused	54	22	40.7	26	48.1	6	11.1
TOTAL	802	423	52.7	358	44.6	21	2.6

Source: Ulster Marketing Surveys Ltd., *Inter Party Talks, Northern Ireland Opinion Poll,* Feb. 1989.

sole exception of the North Down 'Tories'—received no coverage
from the British media. The CEC was ignored by the British media
from its inception in March 1986 to its final break-up in 1988, and the
Campaign for Labour Representation (CLR), which was founded in
Belfast in 1977 and is as active as ever, has been ignored for the
entire twelve years of its existence.[27] The socialist supporters of
British politics in Northern Ireland have therefore been unable to get
their point across to British public opinion in general, which accordingly remains almost entirely unaware of the point at issue.

In other words, it would appear that the exclusion of the electors
of Northern Ireland from the British political system—and its
principal consequence, the impossibilty of mobilizing consent for
any conceivable solution to the Northern Ireland question—are self-
perpetuating.

6. ABSENCE OF MALICE

So far the disfranchisement of the electors of Northern Ireland has
been described and its principal implications have been explored. No
attempt has been made to explain the genesis of this state of affairs
and in this article none will be. But it is worth our while to consider
in more depth why this state of affairs has endured for so long,
especially since 1969, when 'London' was at last obliged to concern
itself directly with Northern Ireland's affairs once more.

The exclusion of Northern Ireland from the British political system
was an accomplished fact by mid-1920. Until the balloon went up in
August 1969, this exclusion was sustained by the force of inertia as
much as anything else. The decisions of the British Labour Party not
to affiliate or incorporate the NILP in 1942 and 1949, however much
they may have been influenced by pro-nationalist sympathies and
anti-unionist prejudices, can be taken as essentially conservative in
their subjective content, that is, as decisions not to upset an existing
state of affairs rather than as decisions to establish a new state of
affairs for some purpose or other. The decision of 1970 in the same
sense can also be put down in large part to inertia and conservatism,
in so far as the system of devolved government at Stormont still
existed and with it a kind of provincial political system, into which
the British Labour Party was understandably reluctant to be drawn.
For its part, the Conservative Party, as we have seen, had up until
the early 1970s a formal alliance with the Ulster Unionist Party,

which yielded it useful votes in the House of Commons and which it was understandably reluctant to jettison for the uncertain dividends of an independent presence in the province.

None of these considerations have applied since the early 1970s. The provincial political system ceased to exist to most intents and purposes with the proroguing of Stormont in 1972. The failure of the Sunningdale agreement of 1973 and of the Convention in 1975–6 demonstrated the impossibility of re-establishing a provincial political system on the basis of power-sharing between sectarian parties. Yet the years which have elapsed since then have not seen a fundamental change in British policy. Indeed, every initiative which has been taken since 1976, including the talks set in motion by Humphrey Atkins in 1979–80, James Prior's 'rolling devolution' via a Northern Ireland Parliamentary Assembly in 1982, and now the Intergovernmental Conference set up under the terms of the Anglo-Irish Agreement in 1985, has been predicated upon the assumption or, rather, the dogma that Northern Ireland must, *volens nolens*, be reconstituted as a distinct (though not sovereign) political unit. Of all the senior actors in this drama (apart from the Provisional IRA), only the Irish Taoiseach, Charles Haughey, has drawn the lesson of experience, that Northern Ireland is, in his words, 'a failed political entity'.

So British policy since 1972 has not been simply conservative. It has not sought to preserve existing political arrangements within the province. It has sought to re-establish a set of political arrangements which have disappeared. There have been elements of determination and voluntarism in British policy since 1972 which seem to bear no resemblance whatever to the force of inertia. The exclusion of the electors of Northern Ireland from the British political system, which could previously be explained as an accidental by-product of circumstances and events of several generations ago, has unquestionably become a matter of conscious policy where the leaderships of the British political parties are concerned.[28]

Attempts have been made to explain this voluntarism as being the refraction in British policy of an external political will. Enoch Powell, for instance, has explained it as the refracted will of the United States government to secure the incorporation of the Irish Republic into NATO by holding out and, indeed, enhancing the prospect of the eventual incorporation of Northern Ireland into the Republic, in exchange for the latter's abandonment of neutrality. One might also explain this voluntarism as the product of, on the one hand, Dublin's irredentist will, refracted via the British Foreign Office and the Northern Ireland Office and, on the other hand, the Northern Catholic nationalist will, articulated by the SDLP and the Provisional IRA–Sinn Féin and refracted via their respective sympathizers in the British Labour Party.

Since I propose to discount both of these theories, it may appear to the reader that I am, in effect, suggesting that British policy towards Northern Ireland is actuated in large part by malice towards the people of the province. I must therefore emphasize that I am not suggesting anything of the kind. Ill will cannot seriously be held to explain British policy towards Northern Ireland any more than good-will can be. Both may well be present in the situation but neither matter very much. Malice is entirely absent from the explanation which I intend to put forward, as is transatlantic conspiracy, Foreign Office scheming, and the influence of nationalist sympathizers in the British Labour Party. The point about all of these explanations is not that they are false; on the contrary, they may very well contain a great deal of truth. But this is entirely beside the point. None of these theories is necessary and all of them are superficial. They, or at least one or another of them, would be necessary and correspondingly more plausible than any of them actually is if the voluntarism which they undertake to explain were a substantial thing. These theories all assume that it is a substantial thing and have accordingly set out to account for it. But the voluntaristic search for a formula for reconstituting Northern Ireland as a distinct political unit has not been a substantial affair in its positive aspect, which has consisted of a succession of different political initiatives and schemes. Continuity and therefore substance have been confined to its negative side.

Every initiative taken since 1973 (if not much earlier) has been predicated upon the unspoken or, at any rate, conspicuously un-argued assumption that the one option which is 'not on' is the admission of the people of Northern Ireland to the political system by which they are in fact governed. The substance of British policy has not been a proposal, but a refusal. The successive proposals which have been made by British governments since 1973 have been merely variant surface expressions of the one, constant, underlying refusal. It is this which needs to be explained. It is, of course, the common denominator, the fundamental presupposition, of all the different positive proposals emanating from the various lobbies identified by the theories referred to above. But what remains to be explained is why these various lobbies should have been able collectively to exercise such a determining influence, if only a negative one, on successive British governments when the effect of this influence has been the adoption of policies which have had in common the manifest and demonstrable failure over some twenty years to achieve the good government of Northern Ireland, government to which people consent.

The explanation lies in the fact that successive British governments have approached the Northern Ireland problem *both* in the same general spirit as that in which they approach all other issues *and* in radically different conditions from those which normally determine the process of policy formation. British governments have taken the Northern Ireland question, like every other question, as they have found it, and have tried to deal with it within its established parameters. But the single most important aspect of these parameters is the fact that the formation of government policy on Northern Ireland, unlike any other question, is radically disconnected from the operation of the party system at Westminster, such that its positive content is inevitably determined by extraneous influences because systematically insulated from all the complex pressures which emanate from the operation of the party-political system and which ensure that policies adopted are workable.

In other words, the apparent voluntarism of British policy towards Northern Ireland is an entirely superficial affair. It is essentially the expression of something else. And this other thing is precisely a great and long-standing force of inertia. But it is a far more fundamental force of inertia than, for example, that which determined the decisions of the Labour leadership in 1942 or 1949. It is not the relatively minor force of inertia in a particular policy position at a particular period. It is the profound force of inertia which is inherent in the British political system as a whole and which generally constitutes one of its surest safeguards. It is the nature of this force of inertia and the manner in which it has precluded a solution to the Northern Ireland question which must therefore be explained and reckoned with.

7. THE QUESTION AND THE CHALLENGE

I fear you will laugh when I tell you what I conceive to be about the most essential mental quality for a free people, whose liberty is to be progressive, permanent, and on a large scale; it is much *stupidity* . . . I need not say that, in real sound stupidity, the English are unrivalled . . . . In fact, what we opprobriously call stupidity, though not an enlivening quality in common society, is Nature's favourite resource for preserving steadiness of conduct and consistency of opinion. It enforces concentration; people who learn slowly, learn only what they must. The best security for people's doing their duty is, that they should not know anything else to do; the best security for fixedness of opinion is, that people should be incapable of comprehending what is to be said on the other side.

(Walter Bagehot, *Letters on the French* Coup d'État *of 1851*)

The question of what is to become of Northern Ireland and its inhabitants presents a fundamental and unique challenge to the British political system. This challenge is, in the first instance, a challenge to the major British parties themselves and, in particular, to their several and collective capacities to recognize a policy dead-end when it is pointed out to them and to envisage and jointly embark upon an entirely new approach to the Northern Ireland question, an approach firmly grounded in the only political standards with which they are familiar and by reference to which they are competent to discharge their functions of representation, of government and of opposition, namely those applied everywhere else in the United Kingdom.

In his brilliant reflections on French political life, on the occasion of Louis Bonaparte's *coup d'état* in 1851, Walter Bagehot contrasted the penchant of French politicians for deriving their policies by logical deduction from first principles with what he provocatively called, as we have seen, the 'real sound stupidity' of the English and which we may, perhaps, paraphrase as their unimaginative, plodding, but also steady, purposeful, and, normally, effective empiricism. But, if English politicians and, at least nowadays, British politicians in general are effective empiricists, this is not because empiricism has been taught them as a doctrine, but because the operation of the party-political system itself obliges them to be empiricists. Theorists by and large get nowhere in British politics because it is not in the nature of the British political system to allow for policy to be developed theoretically. Effective British politicians operate by means of reflexes rather than theories and the only principles which are really required of them—and then only of those who aspire to positions of party and national leadership—are not so much principles as qualities: probity and purposefulness, backbone and bottom.

What obliges a British politician to develop the requisite reflexes is the fact that he is continuously assailed by pressures on all sides, from his constituents, his constituency party or association, his seniors and juniors—and, for that matter, his colleagues and rivals— within his own party and, of course, his opposite numbers in the other parties. He is continuously submerged within the party-political system through which all these pressures are channelled, he is necessarily absorbed in it and is correspondingly uninterested in and impatient of all matters which arise outside it.

The drama of Northern Ireland is precisely such a matter, and it is precisely this necessary preoccupation with matters which arise within the party system and this determined indifference to every-thing which does not that constitutes the foundation of the force of inertia to which I have referred. It is the basis of the outlook of the vast majority of British MPs on Northern Ireland, and the parameters within which party leaders act are defined by the outlook of the majority of MPs in their respective parties.

British politicians have insulated themselves from Northern Ireland by excluding it from their political system and are accord-ingly incapable of understanding it or dealing with it. It follows that it is necessary that they somehow find the mental and moral strength to do the one thing which their own experience of political life has not trained them to do. This is to think coherently about the question, and to derive policy from thought. They need to stand back from their own political system for a moment and reflect upon the principles embodied in it, principles which are rarely if ever made explicit for the simple reason that the system has been in existence for so long that its constitutive principles can be, and therefore are, taken entirely for granted.

Once they do this, once they recognize that these principles, of party government, of government with opposition, of party organization based on economic interest and social philosophy, not religious or cultural identity, are precisely what Northern Ireland lacks and that it lacks them because it has been perversely excluded from the political system which embodies them—once, in short, they recognize that the party boycott of Northern Ireland is 'a constitu-tional atrocity' (Clifford 1985: 2), and the fundamental reason for the continuing conflict in the province, all they need do is resolve to end this boycott and admit the people of Northern Ireland to their political system.

They need behave like good Frenchmen only once. Once the thinking has been done and the policy of enfranchising the electors of Northern Ireland resolved upon and carried out, they can safely resort to their excellent reflexes, their splendid 'stupidity', once more. The question and the challenge are therefore this: do British politicians or, at least, the leading figures in the major parties, have it in them to act—just once—out of character?

Notes

1. Editors' note: Since Roberts's chapter was written the British Conservative Party voted in its Oct. 1989 annual conference to recognize constituency associations in Northern Ireland. Four associations (North Down, East Belfast, East Derry, Lagan Valley) were officially recognized by decision of the National Executive of the Conservative National Union on 11 Nov. 1989.
2. The CEC was founded in Belfast in Mar. 1986 but its central demand had been pioneered by the Campaign for Labour Representation in Northern Ireland (CLR), founded in Belfast in 1977, and CLR activists were prominent in the CEC's leadership. The CEC grew rapidly in 1986-7 but broke up in mid-1988 as fundamental disagreements surfaced within it. This split gave rise to the North Down 'model' Conservative Association (see above) on the one hand and the Institute for Representative Government on the other, the latter being founded by elements of the original nucleus of the CEC.
3. Private communications from Mr Joseph Keenan of Belfast and Mr John Cobain, also of Belfast, whose applications to join the Labour Party were rejected in 1982 and 1986 respectively.
4. Judgement of the Industrial Tribunal in Case No. 24364/85/LS (*H. McAlister* v. *The Labour Party*), London (South), 1 Nov. 1985.
5. Unlike their counterparts in Great Britain, trade unionists in Northern Ireland have to 'opt in' to, rather than 'opt out' of, paying the political levy. The payment of this levy, most of which goes to a party which refuses them membership and refuses to represent them politically, is thus a most remarkable act of solidarity. The figure of 60,000 is an estimate; a figure of 70,000 was given in 'Labour Party Organisation in Northern Ireland: Observations by the National Agent', a paper prepared by the National Agent of the BLP in late 1977, since when the figure appears to have declined. This paper was not published but is cited in 'The Labour Party and Northern Ireland: An Historical Account of the Relations

between the Labour Party and the Northern Ireland Labour Party', a paper produced by the BLP's Research Department in Feb. 1984. This too was not published by the BLP but has been published in full by the Campaign for Labour Representation in Northern Ireland (CLR 1986*a*).

6. This omission is all the more striking for the fact that Walker's book cannot be faulted on this score.

7. This fact has been persistently mystified by front-bench Labour Party spokesmen on Northern Ireland. Thus Stuart Bell MP, in his evidence on behalf of the BLP to the Northern Ireland Parliamentary Assembly on 7 Jan. 1986, claimed that the BLP had contested Northern Ireland seats in the general elections of 1959, 1964, and 1966 (*Northern Ireland Assembly: Committee on the Government of Northern Ireland: Tuesday January 7, 1986, Minutes of Evidence*, p. 8). In fact, only the NILP did so, but Bell referred to the NILP as 'we', a permissible usage in respect of an affiliated party, but indefensible in respect of an entirely separate party, such as the NILP always was.

8. This payment was £300 in 1952 and had risen to £2,000 p.a. by 1975, when it was suspended definitively in the context of deteriorating relations between the two parties. These modest subventions must be set against the far greater sums accruing to the BLP from the political levy paid by Northern Ireland trade unionists. Following the BLP's decision in 1920 not to organize in the province, the NILP claimed these payments for itself, but the BLP resisted this claim and it remained a dead letter thereafter (CLR 1986*a*: 11–12), the NILP being consequently short of funds throughout its existence.

9. The NILP did not contest West Belfast or Londonderry in 1970, giving a free run to the 'Republican Labour' and 'Derry Labour' candidates, who obtained 30,649 and 7,565 votes respectively. If the NILP had fought these seats its total vote in the province would probably have exceeded 100,000 by a clear margin.

10. One of the CLR's founder members is a prominent trade unionist from Northern Ireland, Eamonn O'Kane, President of the National Association of Schoolmasters/Union of Women Teachers in 1986–7. The CLR's Honorary President is the well-known left-wing former Labour MP, Frank Allaun.

11. Despite its collapse after 1970 the NILP remained formally in being, although it contested only one seat in the 1979 general election.

12. Speech of Stuart Bell MP (then deputy front-bench spokesman on Northern Ireland) to CLR fringe meeting at BLP annual conference, Blackpool, 1986. A transcript of this remarkable speech has been published by the CLR together with extracts from the ensuing discussion in CLR 1986*b*.

13. Notably during the much misrepresented events of 1974, in which the

power-sharing executive elected in late 1973 following the Sunningdale agreement fell, not over the issue of power-sharing (as has been widely alleged), but over the issue of a Council of Ireland, upon which its SDLP members insisted at all costs.

14. Letters from Conservative Central Office to Miss J. Trewsdale of Newtownards, 2 Feb. 1984, and to Miss O. Stewart of Belfast, 2 July 1986.

15. The FCS was militantly opposed to the Conservative leadership's Northern Ireland policy in general and the Anglo-Irish Agreement in particular, but its opposition, unlike that of the Friends of the Union grouping led by Ian Gow MP, was not based on support for the Ulster Unionist parties. Instead, the FCS supported the CEC's proposal that the Conservative Party should organize in Northern Ireland and actively canvassed this position at the Conservative Party's annual conference in Bournemouth in Oct. 1986. The dissolution of the FCS was announced by Party Chairman Norman Tebbit MP shortly afterwards.

16. Editors' note: See n. 1.

17. The North Down 'model Conservative Constituency Association' has been led by Dr Laurence Kennedy, who was previously Chairman of the CEC in 1987–8.

18. I owe this information to Mr David Morrison, who was Secretary of the CEC from its inception to late 1987, when he resigned in protest at the way in which the CEC Executive Committee was allowing the Campaign to depart from its original perspectives.

19. Letter of Sir Peter Lane, Chairman of the National Executive of the National Union of the Conservative Party, to Conservative MPs and party officials, 10 Nov. 1988 (Conservative Party News Service release).

20. *The Times*, 15 Oct. 1988; *Today*, 11 Oct. 1988; *Independent*, 29 Aug., 14 Nov. 1988; *Daily Telegraph*, 11 Nov. 1988; *Spectator*, 3 Sept., 10 Dec. 1988. See also signed articles in support of the principle of party organization in Northern Ireland in the *Sunday Times*, 16 Oct., 4 Dec. 1988, *Spectator*, 22 Oct., 12 and 19 Nov. 1988, and *Independent*, 22 Mar. 1989.

21. Mr Scott was promoted Minister of State for Northern Ireland Affairs in the autumn of 1986. He has since been moved to another department.

22. Coopers and Lybrand, *Ulster Television PLC Political Opinion Poll*, Belfast, May 1987.

23. There is an interesting evolution in the terminology employed in the Anglo-Irish Agreement. The preamble refers in different places to 'the two major traditions', 'unionists and nationalists', and 'the two communities'; the phrase 'the rights and identities of the two traditions' appears in Article 4, Clause (a), and Art. 5(a); the phrase 'the minority community' is used in Art. 4(b) and Art. 5(c). (Nowhere are the terms 'Catholic' and 'Protestant' employed.) All of these distinct notions are

finally brought together in Art. 7(c), which speaks for the first time of 'the nationalist community', and thereby consecrates, as a matter of state policy enshrined in a treaty, the equation of 'minority'—that is, Catholic—with 'nationalist'.

24. Coopers and Lybrand, *Ulster Television PLC Political Opinion Poll*, para. 328.
25. Ibid. paras. 302, 304, and accompanying tables.
26. Ulster Marketing Surveys Ltd., *Inter Party Talks: Northern Ireland Opinion Poll*, Feb. 1989.
27. The CLR has held fringe meetings at the BLP's annual conferences every year since 1977 and anyone attending the 1987, 1988, and 1989 conferences could not fail to notice the large and permanent CLR picket outside the main entrance of the conference centre. It has also published numerous informative pamphlets. This persistent activity has gone almost entirely unreported by the British media and has never received the editorial support of any national newspaper.
28. This is perhaps clearer in the case of the BLP, whose leadership has been put under relentless pressure by the CLR to make its attitude explicit.

5

Repartition

Liam Kennedy*

THERE is no solution to the Ulster Question. The grounds for this negative assessment are simple. Despite at least a century of searching, from the first Home Rule debates of the mid-1880s to the recent signing of the Anglo-Irish Agreement, *no* proposal has emerged which has commanded widespread support in *both* the Catholic nationalist and Protestant unionist communities. Nor is one in prospect, especially after twenty years of intercommunal violence. Short of an ideological earthquake, there is no reason to suppose that almost one million unionists are likely to experience belated conversion to Irish nationalism. Similarly, northern nationalists show few signs of reconciling themselves to a unionist future, however much they may be endowed with rights within the British state. It follows that the maximum achievable is a settlement rather than a solution, that is, rough rather than ideal forms of political change. But a critical problem arises immediately one entertains notions of compromise or settlement. The political aspirations of nationalists and unionists are not only conflicting but mutually exclusive. One way out of this dilemma is to offer nationalists and unionists quite separate packages of constitutional arrangements. Repartition offers the greatest scope for such a dual approach, though variants like internal autonomy or cantonization are also highly relevant.

Partition, it may be objected, has been tried and has failed, or has been proposed and found wanting. The concept of partition, how-ever, embraces not a single but a family of possibilities. Some constructions of the partitionist case are obviously crude and

---

* This essay is derived from Kennedy (1986). Some of the arguments and much of the supporting data have, of necessity, been either compressed or omitted. For a discussion of the dangers of a slide into forcible repartition see the larger study.

unworkable. What is explored here is a sensitive use of the partition principle, guided by the desire to satisfy the separate national aspirations of as many Catholics and Protestants as is practically possible. The end result would mean that the majority of northern nationalists would be part of a unitary Irish state—the collective aspiration defined in the New Ireland Forum Report—and most unionists would be securely and permanently integrated into the UK. There would be both a new Ireland and a new United Kingdom (New Ireland Forum 1984).

1. SOME ALTERNATIVES REVIEWED

Before offering a historical and contemporary perspective on partition, it may be helpful to review briefly some of the major competing proposals. One of the most anachronistic involves demands for the return of an old-style Stormont regime. Such notions, quite apart from being anathema to Irish nationalists, are probably unacceptable to many unionists as well. An opinion survey conducted in 1982, for example, found that a mere 18 per cent of Protestants favoured a revived Stormont.[1] A variation on the Stormont theme is the notion of an independent Ulster. This is not inconceivable under the crisis conditions of British abandonment and continuing Irish irredentism. An independent state in east Ulster would be Orange, sectarian, and economically impoverished. In any case the idea enjoys only fringe unionist support as yet, would be resisted by nationalists, and is probably unacceptable to Britain for security reasons.

Some have urged full integration of the six counties into the UK, that is, treating Northern Ireland like any other region of the state. This might have worked in 1920—there was no inevitable road from Partition to Provisional violence (still less from 1690 to 1969)—but the time has passed. Integration fails to accommodate conflicting national loyalties, except under heroic assumptions regarding long-term prospects for assimilation of the northern minority within British society. British public opinion is indifferent or hostile to the notion. It is significant also that no British government has seriously contemplated such a move. A number of policy measures, in fact, seem designed to distance Britain as far as possible from Ulster politics and violence. One thinks of the creation of Stormont in the first instance, and, in more recent years, support for a power-sharing local administration as well as the 'Ulsterization' of the security problem.

Direct rule is a type of integration settlement in the short term, but with the added disadvantage of built-in uncertainty regarding the future shape of political and constitutional structures. It is certainly preferable to anything on offer at the moment; it stands in the way of dangerous adventurism such as calls for a British withdrawal; but it offers little prospect of generating cross-community support for a more permanent settlement. Perversely, the addition of a faint green tinge to direct rule since 1985, following the institution of an Anglo-Irish Conference with advisory powers in relation to Northern Ireland, has had the effect of reducing some of the stabilizing benefits of direct rule.

A power-sharing administration in Northern Ireland, with perhaps some form of Council of Ireland or British–Irish Council as the icing on the cake, is a frequently canvassed proposal. While appealing to moderates, it necessarily threatens hard-line unionists and nationalists. The one brief experiment in the 1970s *just* might have worked for a number of years had it withstood the Ulster loyalist workers' strike of 1974. But it is doubtful if the Sunningdale agreement could have survived the continuing stress of Provisional IRA violence. The latter preceded, accompanied, and outlived the power-sharing interlude. More than a decade after Sunningdale the prospects for co-operation between unionist and nationalist politicians seem even less promising. There is a greater legacy of oppression and suffering—however conceived and apportioned—to be overcome. Paramilitary violence still flourishes. The two political communities are deeply alienated from each other. The forces of accommodation remain weakly developed. Apart from these inauspicious circumstances, power-sharing possesses a deep structural weakness which, while not making it impossible, certainly reduces its likelihood of successful operation. The political representatives of the northern minority proclaim that, come what may, a united Ireland is their ultimate objective. Thus participation in a power-sharing administration would be at best only a temporary accommodation on the road to Dublin.

Joint sovereignty might seem to go some way towards reconciling the basic contradictions in the Northern Ireland conflict. But attempts to impose such a settlement could well have the perverse effect of deepening the crisis. For instance, while giving partial institutional expression to the nationalism of the minority, it would, in see-saw fashion, diminish the national and constitutional position of unionists. There is no doubt that unionist reaction would be intensely hostile, as the fall-out from the Anglo-Irish Agreement amply demonstrates. The prospect of joint sovereignty is rejected by the largest political party in the Irish Republic, Fianna Fáil, and would be unacceptable to northern ultra-nationalists. In relation to security it is possible that the level of nationalist violence would be reduced, but this would almost certainly be counterbalanced by an upsurge of activity on the part of the loyalist paramilitaries. At the level of Anglo-Irish relations one could foresee joint sovereignty opening up limitless possibilities for friction over administrative and security matters. In the context of Irish politics Northern Ireland could become a multi-coloured political football offering dangerous possibilities of play for narrow party ends. In short, the notion of joint sovereignty over Northern Ireland by London and Dublin gives too little to both communities, and offers an unstable recipe for harmonious relations between the two.

At the other extreme from the restoration of Stormont lies the mirage of a united Ireland. Ironically, one of the few issues on which northern nationalists and unionists agree is the belief that the Irish Republic is strongly committed to achieving 'unity'. There appears to be little appreciation of the lukewarm and conditional character of this aspiration, a factor in itself virtually sufficient to make the idea unrealizable.[2] On top of this, the unionist population of Northern Ireland has no wish to be absorbed into an Irish Republic. A large, embittered minority would introduce major instabilities into the politics of the new all-island state. On the security front a united Ireland would seem simply to substitute one set of security problems for another, replacing the killing fields of south Armagh with theatres of war in east Ulster. In the economic sphere, linking the most depressed region in the UK with one of the weakest economies in Western Europe makes little sense. Historically the two economies have lacked complementarity. North-east Ireland experienced intense industrialization in the nineteenth century; its industries were highly dependent on imported raw materials and much of its produce destined for foreign markets. Outside of Ulster, industry was weakly developed. While economic structures north and south have changed greatly by the late twentieth century the extent and potential for complementarity has changed little if at all. Finally, standards of living in Northern Ireland are boosted by transfer payments (subsidies) of the order of £2 billion annually.[3] To fail to match these payments would be to condemn the poorest sections of northern society to greater poverty; to do so would wreck the Irish public finances.

Finally, a federal Ireland, *mutatis mutandis*, suffers from disabilities similar to those associated with the unitary-state model. Neither fits easily with the history of conflict between the peoples of Ireland.

2. PARTITIONIST LOGIC

The division of the island of Ireland occurred, not because of some conjuring trick on the part of a wily Welshman (Lloyd George), as the popular mythology has it, but because of the conflicting political and constitutional demands of Ulster unionists and Irish nationalists. Quite simply, 'the border' of 1920 was a rough recognition of contemporary realities. The historical depth to partition and partitionist mentalities also needs to be recognized. By the second quarter of the nineteenth century two great political blocs, a Catholic nationalist and a Protestant unionist one, were beginning to take shape on the island. Though the divisions were still blurred, the fault lines along which Ireland would eventually subdivide were becoming apparent to some contemporaries. Thomas Macaulay, speaking in the House of Commons in 1833, observed that

every argument which has been urged for the purpose of showing that Great Britain and Ireland ought to have two distinct parliaments may be urged with far greater force for the purpose of showing that the north of Ireland and the south of Ireland ought to have two distinct parliaments. . . . It is indeed certain that, in blood, religion, language, habits, character, the population of some of the northern counties of Ireland has much more in common with the population of England and Scotland than with the population of Munster and Connaught. (6 February 1833, quoted in O'Ferrall 1985: 280)

But it was the challenge to the Union represented by the Home Rule movement of the 1880s which finally crystallized the Ulster dimension to the Irish Question. Once Irish self-government entered the realm of practical politics, virtually all Ulster Protestants were resolved to resist incorporation into a separate Irish state. Attachment to the Empire and the Union with Britain became more strident, particularly among the Protestant working class in the North. The creation of an Ulster Unionist Council in 1905 prefigured the emergence of a Northern Irish state. By the eve of the Great War, following the enactment of a Home Rule bill, Ireland was poised on the edge of a civil war involving two huge private armies of North and South, the Ulster Volunteer Force and the Irish Volunteers. Divisions widened during the political and military crises of 1919–21, though the Treaty debates of Dáil Éireann, with their scant reference to Ulster, confirmed that a realistic appreciation of the Ulster question had yet to penetrate the militant nationalist consciousness (Murphy 1975: 42).

Partitionist tendencies operated not just at the level of high politics but were, and still are, rooted in more basic levels of behaviour. Children in this and the previous century have been rigidly segregated along sectarian lines, both at school and at play. Residential segregation in the northern towns and countryside place further restrictions on cross-communal contact. Significantly, much of the spatial segregation seems to have been desired by both nationalists and unionists. One of the ugly corollaries has been political and sectarian rioting, the first fatal confrontation in Belfast between Orangemen and Catholics dating back to 1813 (Buckland 1973: 36). Hostility to interdenominational marriage reinforced ethnic exclusiveness. The papal *Ne Temere* decree of 1907 underlined existing dogmatic ideas regarding alliances between Catholics and non-Catholics. Orange lodges expelled members for 'dishonouring the Institution' by marrying non-Protestants.[4] Other manifestations of exclusive or partitionist attitudes abounded: the ban on 'foreign' games enforced by the Gaelic Athletic Association (founded in 1884), which had the effect of excluding Protestants and unionists; the expulsion of Catholic workers from the Belfast shipyards in 1920; the hitching of the Gaelic language restoration movement to Catholic nationalism as early as 1915, with a consequent outflow of Protestant supporters; the reflection of Catholic social teaching in the laws of the Irish state, particularly in relation to social issues such as health care, contraception, and divorce; and in Northern Ireland various forms of sectarian exclusiveness and discrimination against Catholics in the housing and job markets (de Paor 1970: 90–124; Lyons 1973: 226–7; Miller 1973; Patterson 1980: 115–42; Titley 1983: 126–30).

More generally, there is the Catholic face of northern nationalism and the Protestant face of Ulster unionism. Faith and fatherland intertwine and serve to exclude. Or, as one study referring to the contemporary problem puts it:

Above all, the Northern crisis has highlighted the limitations of Catholic nationalism as a unifying culture for the whole of Ireland, and the weakness of Protestant unionism as a basis for social consensus in Northern Ireland. (Curtin *et al.* 1984: p. vii)

Partition, therefore, is in tune with the attitudes and behaviour, if not always the rhetoric, of nationalists and unionists. 'The real partition of Ireland'—to repeat the sentiments of an eminent Irish historian—'is not on the map but in the minds of men' (quoted in Two Traditions Group 1984: 14). It follows that the tragedy was not partition *per se* but the clumsy manner in which it was executed.

The six-county boundary was originally defined by the Government of Ireland Act (1920) under circumstances of intense political and sectarian conflict (see Irish Boundary Commission 1969). Had the border been designed to reflect as far as possible the spatial distribution of nationalists and unionists, then a smaller but politically more homogeneous Northern Ireland statelet could have been brought into being. In fact unionists, by neglecting the national rights of northern Catholics, and Irish nationalists, by opposing the right to self-determination of Ulster Protestants, succeeded jointly in producing one of the worst possible outcomes: a state which contained a large, dissident, and sometimes threatening minority (Boal and Douglas 1982: 336). Thus, because of a poorly conceived partition scheme, the conditions for political instability—mutual fear, a sense of betrayal, national and sectarian antagonisms—were built into the very foundations of the state.

The relative size of the Catholic minority increased slightly from 34 per cent in 1926 to 37 per cent in 1971, and still further to 39 per cent in 1981. None the less, on current demographic trends there seems little likelihood of a Catholic majority until well into the next century, if ever (Compton 1985: 22). The most remarkable demographic changes in recent times relate, however, to the changing distribution of population within Northern Ireland. Between 1971 and 1981 districts in the south and west of the province have become more Catholic and nationalist (see Map 5.1 and also Table 5.1, which show the relative rates of population change, by religion, for the

twenty-six council districts into which Northern Ireland is subdivided for purposes of local administration). In most instances the
Protestant decline was relative rather than absolute but in the
council districts of Newry and Mourne, Fermanagh, and London-
derry/Derry there was an absolute fall in Protestant numbers. The
case of Derry/Londonderry is particularly striking. There the Protestant and, by implication, the unionist population fell from 30,000,
to 26,000 between 1971 and 1981. By contrast, Catholic numbers rose
from 54,000 to 67,000 (Kennedy 1986: 52). The emerging pattern in
east Ulster is more complex. Belfast city is somewhat anomalous. For
every 5 inhabitants in 1971 there were only 4 in 1981. Surrounding
areas gained at the expense of the declining city. The Catholic share

TABLE 5.1. *Proportionate change in population by religion in the district
council areas of Northern Ireland, 1971–1981 (%)*

District council area	Roman Catholic	Other denominations	Overall change
Antrim	50	29	35
Ards	11	25	23
Armagh	16	0	8
Ballymena	32	8	12
Ballymoney	5	4	5
Banbridge	10	2	4
Belfast	−12	−25	−20
Carrickfergus	−38	13	5
Castlereagh	−37	−1	−5
Coleraine	12	4	5
Cookstown*	18	8	13
Craigavon	25	−3	8
Derry*	24	−14	11
Down*	22	4	14
Dungannon*	6	9	7
Fermanagh*	10	−7	2
Larne	−3	−2	−2
Limavady	11	23	17
Lisburn	37	19	23
Magherafelt*	9	5	7
Moyle*	16	−11	2
Newry & Mourne*	15	−4	9
Newtownabbey	−30	17	9
North Down	5	27	26
Omagh*	21	0	14
Strabane*	11	2	7
N. IRELAND	8.7	−1.5	2.3

* Districts with a Roman Catholic majority in 1981.

Source: Calculated from Compton (1978) and Eversley and Herr (1985).

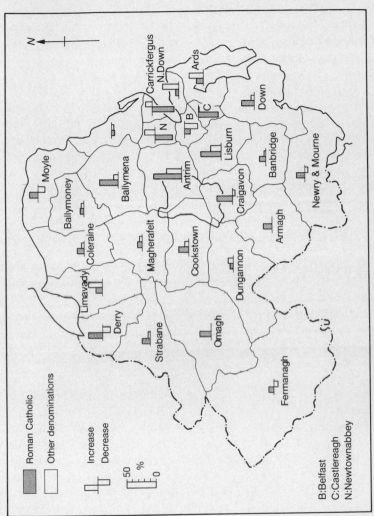

MAP 5.1. Proportionate change in population by religion, 1971–1981, in the district council areas of Northern Ireland

of Belfast's population rose from 34 per cent to 38 per cent. However, in many of the neighbouring districts—Newtownabbey, Carrick-fergus, Castlereagh, Lisburn (minus Collin Ward, which is an extension of West Belfast), North Down—Catholics experienced both an absolute and relative decline. And in North Down and the Ards district Protestant growth rates greatly exceeded those of the Catholic population. With the exception of the district of Antrim, therefore, the core of densely populated areas adjoining Belfast is becoming more Protestant and unionist (Kennedy 1986: 30–1).

These changes are in part a function of different marriage and fertility patterns and possibly also of distinctive cultural values (including attitudes to unemployment and migration). But they are also related intimately to the experience of living in a strife-torn society. Rioting, petrol-bomb attacks on homes, intimidation, and fear of assassination have all contributed to population movement and a compacting of the two political communities in different areas of the province. While the conflict continues it may be assumed that spatial as well as political polarization will persist and possibly intensify.[5]

These changes, which have an important bearing on the feasibility of repartition, may be summarized as follows. East Ulster remains predominantly Protestant, a position which is not seriously threatened by the rise in the Catholic share of the overall population. Significantly, the Protestant position is being consolidated in some eastern districts adjoining Belfast Lough. Belfast itself has become more rigidly segregated along politico-sectarian lines. South and west Ulster are becoming more homogeneously Catholic and nationalist. In effect Protestants are withdrawing as the *de facto* border advances northwards towards Newry, Armagh and Enniskillen and eastwards across the Sperrin Mountains. The end result of these differential changes in demography and settlement patterns is that the two political communities occupy substantially different territorial spaces. It is as if the process of repartition has been initiated at grass-roots level. However regrettable this is as a comment on intercommunal relations, it does point to the increased relevance of the repartition option.

Proposals

The objective of a new partition must be to give most people in Northern Ireland what they want in terms of expressing their national aspirations, thereby resolving the central political problem: the existence in one region of these islands of two political communities, each with a strong but separate sense of national and cultural identity. This involves establishing a boundary, or set of boundaries, that broadly reflect constitutional preferences as between the two states. Such a redefinition of political relationships necessarily implies spatial considerations. The latter, however, should be viewed as of secondary significance, being by-products of the attempt to resolve the central political problem. But geographical factors, even if subsidiary, are important. It may reasonably be wondered if the two communities are so closely intermingled as to rule out the possibility of any effective redrawing of boundaries, thus thwarting the object of the exercise. That this seems not to be the case is due to a variety of historical circumstances, including self-segregation and forced population movements since 1969.

For purposes of illustration a number of specific proposals regarding the spatial basis of a new Ireland and, by implication, a new United Kingdom, are set out. In Map 5.2 four options are presented and the religious composition of each of these 'two Ulsters' is indicated in Table 5.2. It should be emphasized that these are simply some examples chosen from a family of possibilities. The more politically sensitive the settlement sought, the more complex becomes the geography (though the trade-off is not perhaps as severe as some might imagine). The basis of the calculations is the 1981 census of Northern Ireland, as revised in the light of problems surrounding its compilation (Compton and Power 1986; Eversley and Herr 1985). Trends towards increased spatial polarization, strongly evident in the 1970s, are likely to have continued into the 1980s. Thus, use of the 1981 census probably introduces some bias

TABLE 5.2. *Repartition: The relative size of minorities under alternative sets of proposals (%)*

Option	British Ulster minority	Irish Ulster minority
Status quo	39.1	0
Option 1	20.2	16.2
Option 2	20.0	17.4
Option 3	19.6	19.2
Option 4	26.2	21.4

Source: Kennedy (1986: 57).

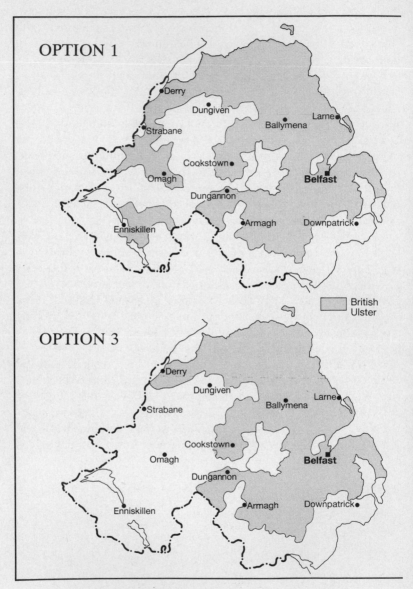

MAP 5.2. Four repartition options

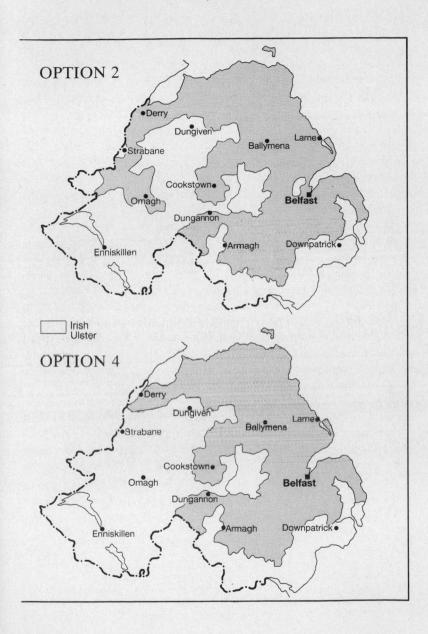

OPTION 2

Derry
Dungiven
Larne
Strabane
Ballymena
Cookstown
Omagh
Belfast
Dungannon
Enniskillen
Armagh
Downpatrick

Irish
Ulster

OPTION 4

Derry
Dungiven
Larne
Strabane
Ballymena
Cookstown
Omagh
Belfast
Dungannon
Enniskillen
Armagh
Downpatrick

against the repartition case. Clearly more up-to-date studies and local plebiscites throughout Northern Ireland would be a precondition for an effective repartition policy.

All of the options assume a small voluntary movement of population (of slightly under 5 per cent in relation to both the Catholic and Protestant communities). Options 1 to 3 break with traditional conceptions of repartition by envisaging, not just transfers of territory in border regions, but also the creation of a new nationalist West Belfast that is linked politically and constitutionally to the Irish Republic. The final option is the most conservative of the four. It is Option 3 but without any territorial change involving the Belfast area. It represents essentially a tightening of the existing border around east Ulster.

Under these proposals Northern Ireland would be divided into two entities, each of which would have a high degree of political homogeneity. But it is not simply the size but the location and political character of the respective minorities that are important. Taking Option 1, for example, the great majority of Protestants, more than 90 per cent of the Protestant population of Northern Ireland in fact, would be retained within the British state (see Table 5.3). There would be some 75,000 Protestants in the new territories of the Irish state. These may be presumed to be virtually all unionist, given the consistent failure of the Irish state and, more generally, of Irish nationalism to attract Northern Irish Protestants to the cause of Irish unity. However, this small and quiescent minority of unionists, located in south and west Ulster where there has been little recent experience of Protestant terrorism, should pose no threat to the Irish state. Southern society is almost exclusively Catholic—only 5 per cent of the population have other religious affiliations—so the

TABLE 5.3. *Roman Catholics and other denominations after a repartitioned Northern Ireland: Option 1*

	British Ulster	Irish Ulster
No. of Catholics	222,000	388,000
No. of other denominations	876,000	75,000
Total population	1,098,000	463,000
Relative size of minority (%)	20	16

Source: Kennedy (1986: 54–7).

political impact of this minority of displaced Protestants should be marginal. Furthermore, should southern society prove sufficiently uncongenial to the new minority, generous resettlement grants could provide a ready means of exit.

British Ulster with a population of 1.1 million would contain a 20 per cent minority of Roman Catholics. This is half the existing ratio of Catholics to Protestants in Northern Ireland but still an appreciable minority. However, the largest grouping of Catholics would be in the Greater Belfast region and the Coleraine–north Antrim area. The latter does not have a tradition of political violence and intercommunal relations are fairly good. The position in relation to Belfast and its environs is more variable. Certainly there would remain within the city some staunchly nationalist enclaves such as the Markets and the Short Strand but the most populous and militant areas would have been hived off into the new West Belfast. It is important to realize also that in east Ulster the fit between Catholicism and Irish nationalism is less than complete. Support for the unionist Alliance Party within the Catholic community—of the order of 7 to 8 per cent of the Catholic vote at the 1985 local elections, and larger in the past[6]—suggests that a section of the Catholic population openly favours the Union. In addition, various opinion polls reveal that a substantial minority of Catholics, while not voting for unionist parties, none the less prefer the Union to other constitutional alternatives, including a united Ireland.[7] One may conclude, therefore, that the *political* as distinct from the *religious* minority in British Ulster would in practice be lower than 20 per cent, and more like 15 per cent or possibly even less. With the constitutional question put beyond doubt one might look forward to the development of 'normal' politics and the progressive erosion of ethnic and sectarian differences as occurred in Liverpool, Glasgow, and other British cities earlier in this century.

There is a set of associated possibilities, a fifth option involving forms of 'internal autonomy', that also deserves serious consideration.[8] Briefly, this means creating a mosaic of local self-governing areas that are almost exclusively nationalist or unionist, but within the existing constitutional framework of Britain and Northern Ireland. How extensive the powers devolved to these local councils might be is a matter for political negotiation, as is the extent to which they might co-operate formally with each other. These could, in principle, form the basis of a federal power-sharing government at regional level. Indeed the best prospects for cross-community co-operation at a provincial level (and on the island generally) would seem to be under the conditions of ethnic reassurance and confidence afforded by largely homogeneous political units. A strong version of internal autonomy might also confer on nationalist areas, not only the right to substantial material and symbolic expression of an Irish identity, but also the ultimate right of secession to the Irish Republic.[9] In practice Dublin and London might prefer to limit rights of secession to districts contiguous with the existing Irish border, thus leaving open a voluntary pathway into the form of repartition outlined in Option 4 above. Forms of internal self-government with only weak powers are also possible but run the risk of not securing sufficient nationalist backing and thus having little real impact on the continuing crisis.

The internal-autonomy approach would permit an even closer fit between people and political framework than in the case of repartition. Smaller, more homogeneous areas could be used in building up local-government districts while the constraints implied in attempting to produce manageable international boundaries would be absent from the task of creating boundaries internal to Northern Ireland. An examination of the political composition of the ninety-eight electoral divisions into which Northern Ireland is subdivided gives some idea of the potential. In 1985 over two-thirds of these had minority voting proportions of under 30 per cent (in many instances less than 10 per cent), further testimony to the steep majority–minority patterns which characterize the province (Kennedy 1986: 33; Kennedy *et al.* 1988: 106–14). So, for example, a division of Fermanagh, Derry, or Belfast into twin political entities, on the basis of detailed ward-level information on religious affiliation, would produce populations of an overwhelmingly unionist or nationalist composition. Overall, about a dozen cantons—roughly half the existing number of district councils—could serve the entire province.

It may be noted that the internal-autonomy approach, while less radical than any of the repartition options, holds important features in common. Firstly, it recognizes explicitly the unpalatable realities of political and spatial polarization within Northern Ireland. Secondly, it employs a muted form of the partition principle—seeking to create areas of politically homogeneous populations—with the aim of accommodating these fundamental problems.

Thirdly, it is an attempt to undo the mistakes of 1920, which derived from insufficient attention to the relationship between territory and political affiliation.

3. COMPLEMENTARY POLICIES

A repartition settlement would call for a high degree of co-operation between the Irish and British states, particularly on economic, public administration, and security matters. Safeguarding and promoting joint interest in relation to Northern Ireland would almost certainly require some institutionalized framework. An Irish–British Commission, composed of equal numbers of representatives nominated by the two sovereign powers, could provide the forum for continuous contact and consultation. To avoid the danger of Northern Irish issues being used as political footballs for party-political gains, it is probably desirable that the membership be composed of top civil servants and administrators. The Commission would act in a policy-advisory role and as a co-ordinating centre, possibly with certain delegated powers, in relation to the issues outlined below. Its first task might well be to identify the basis for a repartition settlement, bring forward concrete proposals, and supervise their implementation.

Mass unemployment, heavy reliance on state income supports, and a seriously weakened industrial sector are among the unenviable features of the Northern Ireland economy (Northern Ireland Economic Council 1984). What is needed is a Marshall Aid-type programme of economic and social reconstruction. The indications are that, given a durable settlement underwritten by Dublin and London, aid on this massive scale would be forthcoming from the international community, in particular from the United States. Such a programme of reconstruction would involve the creation of new industrial bases in Belfast (East and West) as well as in Derry and other regional growth centres. In line with EEC regulations there would be free mobility of labour across national boundaries. It would also be necessary to develop a new institutional and administrative apparatus in nationalist Ulster, and this obviously has resource implications. It would not, however, be as costly as might first appear. In nationalist areas of Ulster there already exists an extensive infrastructure of public buildings and facilities (council chambers, local-government offices, court-houses, police barracks, hospitals, and health and social security offices). These could be the subject of direct transfer in most instances. Furthermore, because there are major economies of scale in the provision of certain types of public service, the rational use of public resources would imply various types of co-operative approaches involving the two states. Such co-operation already exists in relation to transport, drainage, and other infrastructural schemes. Finally, it is highly desirable that living standards in all of Northern Ireland, that is in British and Irish Ulster, should be held at British levels for a transitional period of a decade or so. These transfer payments are currently being funded by British taxpayers in any case. To the extent that outside aid was forthcoming, the British tax burden would be lightened.

The process of reshuffling and compacting the population of Northern Ireland along national lines, particularly evident in urban Ulster since 1969, could be taken a stage further by attractive resettlement grants. Two factors in particular suggest that relocation could assume significant dimensions. The first is the existence of active markets for private houses, especially in urban Ulster and in commuter-belt areas such as North and mid Down. Secondly, in a fragmented Northern Ireland the distances involved would be small. In Belfast city, for example, some relocation distances would not be much in excess of those involved in some of the more conventional rehousing schemes. Grants should compensate for housing and small-business transfers as well as allowing for individual disturbance and resettlement costs. Clearly the supply of attractive housing alternatives on both sides of the new national boundary, in itself an integral part of the programme of reconstruction outlined earlier, is central to the resettlement process. This applies to both public- and private-sector housing. In addition, the direct exchange of accommodation and property, particularly in relation to public housing, should be feasible. Finally, it might be desirable to offer special compensation to workers where movement involved higher costs of travelling to and from work.

Options 1 to 3 involve a twin city of Belfast and West Belfast. This is an unfamiliar idea. Although there are difficulties with the notion, it may be observed that, in practice, the division already exists. 'Peace lines', security barriers, party symbols, and distinctive cultural worlds mark off the west of the city. Social intercourse between Protestant East Belfast and Catholic West Belfast is virtually non-existent. But in terms of these scenarios West Belfast would also be cut off physically from the rest of the national territory. This raises problems of access, mainly of an economic and security nature. A number of international precedents exist in this regard. With the emergence of a Polish state after the Treaty of Versailles in 1919, a 'corridor' was created which linked this otherwise land-locked country to the sea (Pound 1964; Smogorzewski, 1934). The strip of land stretched across German territories, culminating ultimately in Danzig on the Baltic. A less familiar and more enduring example is that of Llivia, a part of Spain situated in the Cerdagne region of south-west France and *totally enclosed* by French territory (Gomez-Ibanez 1975). This dates from the Treaty of the Pyrenees in 1659, which partitioned the Pyrenees and established the modern boundary between France and Spain. The case of Alaska is also pertinent. This US state juts out of the side of Canada and is separated by Canadian territory from the main land area of the United States. None the less, no real problems of access, either by land or sea, present themselves. In the Northern Irish case it may be noted that West Belfast is less than 70 kilometres from Newry on the Irish border. The largely completed dual carriageway from Newry to its point of intersection with the M1 motorway near Lisburn could have an international status, with free movement for all kinds of traffic, including security personnel. The M1 itself, which connects with West Belfast at two points, and also links the east and west of the province, could have a similar status, thus joining West Belfast to nationalist areas in west as well as south Ulster. Industrial and other goods produced in West Belfast, in line with provision for the free movement of goods within the EC, could be shipped out through the ports of Larne and Belfast. No change in existing trading and communication relationships are required.

Under repartition there would be extensive border areas adjoining the lines of division between the two states. These would not create problems of security unfamiliar to Dublin or Westminster but they could in the medium term intensify the importance of cross-border co-operation on the security front. It is in these contexts that an earlier Irish suggestion of an all-Ireland judicial and policing system merits serious reconsideration (Fitzgerald 1982: 17). The essential idea, however, is probably best modified so as to relate to the Northern Ireland area only. Thus a joint police force, with powers to operate throughout the province but not beyond the existing boundaries of Northern Ireland, would facilitate anti-terrorist

activity. Basically, though, such a force should supplement rather
than substitute for purely British or Irish security forces within
Northern Ireland.

Policing raises issues of economics as well as security. The cost to
the Irish Republic of combating terrorism is greater, proportionately
speaking, than in the UK.[10] It would not be unreasonable, as part
of the general programme of social reconstruction in the post-
repartition period, if the Republic was given special aid to develop its
security resources over the expanded area which would then constitute the territory of the state. Presumably an early task would be
recruiting and training local men and women from West Belfast,
Derry, and other nationalist areas of Ulster as members of the Irish
police and Army. As terrorism was finally reduced to insignificant
levels the security bill would fall, but an immediate decline in
security costs should not be anticipated. Hence the desirability of
financial aid for a transitional period as the institutions of the Irish
state were firmly implanted in northern territory.

4. ASSESSING REPARTITION

The Northern Ireland question may by analysed in terms of seven
interrelated problems. These provide a useful checklist against
which the strengths and weaknesses of repartition, or indeed of any
of the competing proposals, may be tested.

1. The first problem is the existence of two mutually exclusive sets
of national aspirations, Irish and British, within Northern Ireland.
Most settlement proposals pursue the impossible task of seeking to
accommodate these national contradictions within the same state.
The creation of a British Ulster and an Irish Ulster, both fully integrated into their respective states, would surmount this problem.
The effect of repartition is to confer full national rights on the
majority of nationalists and unionists within their preferred states.

2. What we have in Northern Ireland is not simply a case of two
very different collective identities but the further complication that
contact between the two political communities in the 'narrow
ground' of Ulster has frequently been mutually deforming.[11] This is
so both at the level of ideology and political praxis. Repartition could
call a stop to this malign encounter, and offer also the prospect of an
eventual *rapprochement* between the Irish and British communities in

Ireland on the more secure basis of mutual agreement, shared benefits, and equal national status.

3. There is the issue of the legitimacy of the security forces. This is central to any return to peaceful conditions and normally functioning democratic institutions. This problem is at its most severe in nationalist areas of Northern Ireland. Among unionists, the RUC, the UDR, and the legal apparatus of the state still enjoy high levels of acceptance. The insertion of Irish security forces and the Irish judicial system into nationalist areas accommodates directly one of the thorniest problems thrown up by the Northern Ireland conflict.

4. There is the continuing existence of paramilitary violence, especially that of the IRA and its supporters. For many Ulster people, Catholic and Protestant, existing constitutional arrangements cannot guarantee the most basic right of all, that is the right to life. Extreme nationalism has, however, a real basis: it is rooted in conflicting national aspirations and question marks over the legitimacy of state institutions. By endowing Irish Ulster with the full constitutional and security apparatus of the Irish state the political basis of the Provisionals' campaign would be heavily undermined. Furthermore, a largely homogeneous British Ulster would be less susceptible to infiltration and armed attack. It would also be much more difficult to justify attacks on a largely British as compared to a divided society. As O'Malley observes in *The Uncivil Wars*, 'both the South's assertion of territorial right and the IRA's campaign owe whatever legitimacy they claim solely to the presence of Catholics in Northern Ireland' (O'Malley 1983: 297). Almost certainly there would be some confrontation between the IRA and the Irish security forces. This is regrettable, but any conceivable settlement (or continuing non-settlement as at present) implies confrontation with extreme nationalism. But just as the RUC have proved much more effective against loyalist paramilitaries, so the Irish security forces would have definite advantages in coping with Catholic paramilitaries.[12]

5. The existence of acute intra-community divisions, in addition to the fundamental cleavage between nationalists and unionists, means that the local political system is virtually immobilized. The unionist vote is deeply split between the Democratic Unionist Party and the Official Unionist party. On the nationalist side, the Social Democratic and Labour Party enjoys majority support but the IRA's political front, Sinn Féin, still controls a substantial 30 per cent of the

nationalist vote. The existence of a major competing party *within* each political community effectively vetoes any radical initiatives or compromise proposals. Though not the only means of doing so, repartition would render the existing party divisions obsolete.

6. There is the problem of economic and social deprivation, which is both cause and effect of the current troubles. Economic regeneration is dependent on a durable settlement being achieved. This does not of course guarantee economic development but it does at least remove a fundamental barrier to investment, especially inward investment, and consequent job expansion.

7. Finally, there is the issue of the legitimacy of the Northern Ireland entity, as perceived internationally. The province is widely regarded as a failed political entity. However, the chief concern of interested members of the international community—North Americans and Europeans primarily—appears to relate to political restabilization rather than to a specific form of settlement. Repartition eliminates the Northern Ireland entity and brings into being a new Ireland and a new United Kingdom.

There are, none the less, a number of serious objections to this form of settlement. Some practical difficulties of implementation have already been alluded to. One might add that it would be necessary to saturate the province with troops to prevent any forced population movements during the period of transition to 'two Ulsters'. In addition, the adoption of such a policy presents special problems. It would mark a decisive step away from the gradualist (and less than successful) approach that has been in vogue for twenty years. Low-risk strategies have their attractions, particularly as viewed from London. It may also be objected that there is little popular demand for repartition. The first preference of nationalists and unionists remains outright victory. It is of course true that there is no truly popular, as distinct from sectional, support for *any* of the major political alternatives, but in the case of repartition it is unlikely that any Northern Irish party could espouse openly such a course. This would be to betray the illusion of eventual victory. Like measures such as the Anglo-Irish Agreement, the initiative would have to come from outside the frozen structures of the Northern Ireland political system. This would require political will and determination in London and ideally also in Dublin. The Dublin government has long claimed a special role in safeguarding the interest of the northern nationalist minority. By virtue of the transfer of most nationalist areas, and their peoples, to the Irish Republic it would have succeeded beyond measure in realizing that particular objective. But, like aspirations to unity, is this largely at the level of rhetoric? Does Dublin want to assume real responsibility, with the attendant costs, in relation to Northern Ireland? One suspects that the major architect of repartition would have to be Britain. Finally, there are some question marks over the extent to which nationalists, particularly in east Ulster, actually want to be part of the Irish state. However, offering real choice, and carrying through the consequences of such choice, would confer a unique legitimacy on the new constitutional settlement.[13]

Subjecting the internal-autonomy proposals to the test of the seven problems outlined above yields, subject to a number of qualifications, a broadly satisfactory outcome. Problems (1) and (2), as well as (5) to (7) inclusive, could be partially met. However, the limited resolution of the national question might have only weakly beneficial effects on the legitimacy of the British security forces and the effectiveness of the counter-terrorist campaign.[14] Much would depend on how significant the powers of autonomy conferred on local legislatures would be. While grappling with the key problems less thoroughly than does repartition, internal autonomy does have some advantages at the level of Anglo-Irish relations. It would pose fewer difficulties of ideological adjustment for Dublin, as such a settlement need not rule out, in principle at any rate, an eventual united Ireland. And, from the viewpoint of London, there would be less dependence on the co-operation and goodwill of the Dublin government. The political will and resources demanded would also be less.

5. CONCLUSION

It is high time to acknowledge the irreconcilable conflicts at the centre of the Northern Ireland problem and to depart from constitutional formulas that serve well in relation to homogeneous political units such as Britain or the Irish Republic, but do not work in the case of complex societies such as Switzerland or Cyprus. The repartition idea emerges as quite robust when matched against the harsh realities of Northern Ireland. It would produce two Ulsters, each largely homogeneous in terms of political composition, each attuned to the constitutional preferences of its inhabitants, and each policed by its own security forces. The settlement would possess legitimacy in that the Northern Irish inhabitants of the two states would have chosen deliberately and freely between the Irish and British constitutional packages available. This could offer the prospect of a lasting settlement, of self-determination without domination. Repartition is congruent with specific elements in the historical development of Ulster, and, more importantly perhaps, with hardening political positions in recent decades. Use of the partition principle in the muted form of internal autonomy possesses broadly similar advantages and drawbacks, though the weighting of these between the two approaches differs. Both types of settlement, it is worth emphasizing, do not involve heroic assumptions regarding attitudes and political behaviour. The proposals outlined here take existing configurations of sentiment and opinion as given, and work broadly within these constraints.

Notes

1. National Opinion Polls' survey as reported in the *Irish News*, 13 Feb. 1982.
2. The trend in opinion also seems to be against unity. According to the Market Research Bureau of Ireland, in 1983 some three-quarters of the people of the Republic favoured unity. This level of support had fallen to two-thirds by 1987. Significantly, when it was put to respondents in the 1987 poll that unity might involve some increase in taxes, the proportion aspiring to it fell away from 67% to 39%. Thus, under any realistic assumptions relating to a future United Ireland, it appears that only a *minority* of people in the Republic would actually support such a move. See extensive report on the MRBI surveys in the *Irish Times*, 1 Sept. 1987. Indeed during the general election campaign of the same year another opinion poll showed that a mere 5% of respondents considered Northern Ireland issues sufficiently important to influence their voting behaviour (*Irish Times*, 12 Feb. 1987).
3. The northern economy has become even more dependent on the British subvention and consequently a unitary, federal, or confederal Irish state would be increasingly difficult to achieve without enormous economic sacrifices on the part of both the South and the North, unless the subvention and/or other external transfers were maintained on a very large scale for many years. See Gibson and McAleese (1984: 14). The size

of the subvention in 1988–9 was £2 billion. See *Parliamentary Debates* (Lords), vol. 510, cols. 407–8.

4. Copies of late 19th-cent. Orange records for County Monaghan in the possession of the author.

5. The largest forced population movements occurred in the period 1969–72 when more than 30,000 Catholics and Protestants fled their homes. See Farrell (1980). Subsequent movements have been less visible, though in the year following the Anglo-Irish Agreement of Nov. 1985 several hundred families were driven out of their homes (report in *Irish Times*, 19 Aug. 1986).

6. In the local elections of 1977 the Alliance Party secured 14.4% of the vote, mainly in the Belfast Urban Area. See Osborne (1982: 162).

7. A survey commissioned by the BBC 'Spotlight' programme in May 1985 found that one-third of Roman Catholics supported the link with Britain (*Belfast Telegraph*, 14 May 1985). While such surveys are subject to various limitations there can be little doubt that a significant minority of Catholics would vote themselves into a fully integrated United Kingdom.

8. In his review of possible settlements Lijphart (1975) places special emphasis on the positive features of internal devolution.

9. This would open up some quite revealing possibilities both locally and at the level of Anglo-Irish relations, with the pursuit of political aspirations now carrying real consequences. Thus, responsibility and power would become more closely aligned.

10. According to the New Ireland Forum (1984: 15–16), the direct cost to the Irish Republic of paramilitary and related violence since 1969 has been £900 million. The indirect costs are estimated as being close to £1 billion (£983 million).

11. This malign dialectic affects not only the nationalist and unionist communities of Northern Ireland but also distorts North–South relations. The effect in each instance is to limit progressive political developments while selecting out and nourishing some of the most reactionary elements in nationalism and unionism.

12. The argument is developed further in Kennedy (1986: 69–70).

13. This point is well made by McKeown (1984).

14. While the northern crisis is clearly much more than a security problem, it would be naïve to ignore the permanent veto on political development exercised by the Provisional IRA. All settlement proposals must face up to the twin challenge of the political and paramilitary problem.

6

Co-determination

Charles Graham with John McGarry*

IF an agreement is to be reached between the Catholics and Protestants in Northern Ireland, it must recognize two fundamental realities. First, Protestants will not accept any formal involvement by the government of the Republic of Ireland in the affairs of the province or agree to any scheme which they believe will lead them towards a united Ireland. Secondly, Catholics will not accept any settlement which excludes them from playing a full role in the affairs of Northern Ireland, whether a return to the majoritarian system which existed from 1921 to 1972 or some variant of direct rule from Westminster. *Common Sense,* the document released by the Ulster Political Research Group (UPRG) in January of 1987, is based upon a recognition of these realities. In it, the UPRG suggests a process which could lead to an overall constitutional settlement acceptable to both communities in Ulster and gives details of the form such a settlement might take. It is aimed, therefore, at breaking the political impasse which has existed in the province not just since the signing of the Anglo-Irish Agreement in November 1985 but since the formation of the state of Northern Ireland in 1921.

1. THE PROCESS

The first step in the process would be for the Secretary of State for Northern Ireland to invite all the political parties there to discuss the

---

* This chapter is based largely on proposals put forward by the Ulster Political Research Group (1987). John McMichael, the Chairman of the UPRG and main author of these proposals, had agreed to write the chapter but was assassinated on 22 Dec. 1987 before he had started it. Rather than allowing his important and positive views to be left out of the collection, one of the editors, John McGarry, co-operated with Charles Graham, a member of the UPRG and a co-author of its 1987 proposals, to produce this paper.

principle of creating a written constitution for Northern Ireland
which would be firmly based upon the two realities described above.
If the various parties agree in principle to that, the Secretary of State
would then call an election for the parties to seek a mandate for a
constitutional conference. With a chairman appointed by the Secretary of State and ratified by the conference, and with expert
assistance from the Commonwealth, the European Economic Community, and the United States, the conference would draw up and
ratify a constitution. The constitution would then be put to the
people of Northern Ireland for acceptance by referendum and, to
ensure that it would be acceptable to both Protestants and Catholics,
would not come into effect unless approved by a two-thirds majority
of those voting. If the constitution was approved, the conference
would dissolve and elections would be held for representatives to
those institutions of government agreed by the conference and
stipulated in the constitution. If the various factions in Ulster could
agree to embark on this endeavour, an opportunity would be created
which would allow Ulster's Catholics and Protestants to co-deter-
mine the nature of their society.

2. THE PREREQUISITES FOR A SETTLEMENT

The prerequisites for a just settlement in Northern Ireland are that
Protestants have to be convinced that it is not an interim step
towards forcing them into a united Ireland while, simultaneously,
Catholics have to be assured that they will be given a full role in
governing the province.

The vast majority of Protestants have been unwilling to share
power with Catholics not because of their religion but because they
consider them to be Irish nationalists intent on the destruction of
Northern Ireland in pursuit of a united and overwhelmingly Catholic
Ireland. Catholics are seen as fifth-columnists from the foreign state
which has irredentist claims on Northern Ireland entrenched in its
Constitution, claims which bestow a degree of sanctity on IRA
violence. Protestants fear that if Catholics are allowed any authority
or position of influence within the political framework of Northern
Ireland, they will use it to undermine Northern Ireland's position
within the United Kingdom. They fear that Catholic politicians,
while paying lip-service to the need for majority 'consent', would

use cabinet positions to put pressure on the British government to induce that 'consent' by creating forms of dependency between the two parts of Ireland and, ultimately, to declare its intention to withdraw from the province. These Protestant fears are accentuated by their belief that the British government is somewhat less than committed to maintaining the Union, a fear greatly increased by the Anglo-Irish Agreement. The resulting 'siege mentality' has been adequately described by John Hume, the leader of the Catholic Social Democratic and Labour Party (SDLP):

The unionists are a majority in Northern Ireland, but their political behaviour there can only be understood if they are seen, as they feel themselves to be, as a threatened minority in the island of Ireland. Theirs are the politics of the besieged. Hence their stubborn refusal to share power with the minority in Northern Ireland, whom they fear as the Trojan Horse of the real majority in Ireland, the Catholics. (Quoted in Ulster Political Research Group 1987).

If the siege on Ulster's Protestants is to be lifted and they are to consider power-sharing with Catholics, a settlement will have to contain provisions which remove any ambiguity about Northern Ireland's current status as a part of the United Kingdom. If this can be achieved, Protestants will no longer feel compelled to defend the frontier.

The two main British initiatives in Northern Ireland since the outbreak of the 'Troubles', the Sunningdale agreement of 1973 and the Hillsborough agreement of 1985, have failed to bring about compromise in Northern Ireland because, rather than reassuring the Protestant community that their future within the United Kingdom was secure, both resulted in a marked increase in insecurity. Any Protestant leader prepared to consider power-sharing under these circumstances, without obtaining the necessary assurances about Northern Ireland's status within the Union, has quickly been out-flanked by other Protestant politicians who were more closely in touch with the fears of the Protestant electorate. Brian Faulkner after 1974 and Bill Craig after 1976, both respected leaders at the time, were relegated to political oblivion because they underestimated the siege mentality of Ulster's Protestants. Paisley and Molyneaux almost suffered the same fate when they seemed prepared to accept the continuation of the Anglo-Irish Agreement after a meeting with the Prime Minister in February of 1986. Only a swift recantation on their part prevented serious revolts by their followers. These experiences explain why no Protestant politician is prepared to share power with Catholics under the terms of the Agreement or any similar arrangement. Even if the unionist leadership was willing to, it could not hope to retain the support of its followers if it agreed to such a deal.

If adequate safeguards for Northern Ireland's position within the UK could be provided, however, and Catholics were prepared to recognize the legitimacy of this position, the vast majority of Protestants would be prepared to accept power-sharing with them.

While such recognition will not be given by those Catholics who are Republicans and who are determined to achieve nothing less than a united Ireland, there does not seem to be any compelling reason why it could not be given by a majority of the Catholic community. In an opinion poll conducted in February of 1988, for example, when presented with a choice of options, only 32 per cent of Catholics chose a united Ireland while 43 per cent chose options which would operate within a UK context.[1] In the border poll of 1973, despite its boycott by all leading Catholic politicians, one academic source has estimated that the huge majority that voted to remain within the United Kingdom 'must' have contained a large Catholic component, up to 25 per cent of the Catholic electorate (Compton 1981: 91). Objective indicators point in the same direction. The Catholic proportion of the population in Northern Ireland has increased significantly since partition in stark contrast to the decline of the Protestant proportion of the population in the Republic.[2] When they have chosen to emigrate, Catholics from Northern Ireland and the Irish Republic routinely pick Britain as their preferred destination.

A very large part of the alienation which currently exists among members of the minority community is derived not from their desire for a united Ireland but from their exclusion from a significant role in the government of the province. This is exacerbated by a belief that the Protestant majority is intent on preserving an ascendancy over them. While motivated to some extent by their nationalist aspirations, the desire of Catholic politicians for power-sharing and a role for the Dublin government in Northern Ireland can also be explained by their fear that their minority position would not be sufficiently protected within a British framework and could be subsequently overturned.[3] Understandably, Catholics resented their subordinate position within Northern Ireland under the Stormont regime and they gradually demonstrated that resentment. If the loyalty of Ulster's Catholics to a constitutional settlement is to be assured, therefore, they must be allowed a full role in government and must have no grounds for fearing the resurrection of a new Protestant ascendancy at some point in the future.

In return for receiving this protection, it seems fair that Catholics be asked to support the regime and give a basic commitment to the constitution which they would help to draw up. In addition to removing the only fundamental objection which Protestants have about offering them a place in government, this commitment is also an essential prerequisite if the settlement is to be durable. There is not a single instance in the literature of a power-sharing arrangement succeeding when this condition is lacking. In the successful power-sharing systems in Switzerland, Belgium, and The Netherlands, described by Arend Lijphart, while there are fundamental divisions involving language, culture, and religion, there is also an overarching loyalty to the integrity of the regime (Lijphart 1977: 81–3). None of these countries has a group in office that wants to secede or be incorporated into a neighbouring state. The German Swiss have consistently opposed the concept of a Greater Germany, even during the era of Nazi expansionism; the Walloons of Belgium and French-speaking Swiss do not want to be part of France; and the Dutch Catholics have shown no desire to unite with their Flemish Catholic counterparts in Belgium. When this basic commitment has been lacking on the other hand, power-sharing has failed. Greek and Turkish Cypriots could not co-operate with each other at least partly because the Greek majority wanted union (Enosis) with Greece and the Turkish minority opposed that.[4] Similarly, in Northern Ireland itself, Protestants were not prepared to support the power-sharing settlement of 1974 because the minority's representatives would not recognize the legitimacy of Northern Ireland's position within the United Kingdom.

Even if a power-sharing government could be successfully negotiated while the current ambiguity about Northern Ireland's constitutional position remains, that settlement would be unworkable as it would merely reinforce sectarian divisions in the province and prolong their existence through institutional entrenchment. Catholic politicians would continue to search for a way of ending the Union and Protestant politicians would be unwilling to co-operate because of this. As Hugh Roberts argues (Chapter 4), it would regularly generate the very impulses to challenge or undermine the constitutional framework that it is its notional purpose to pre-empt.

3. THE OUTLINE OF AN AGREEMENT

While the constitutional convention could agree on any one of a number of different formulas, below we offer details of a constitution which we think would satisfy the British government's requirement of meeting widespread acceptance in both communities. The settlement would include the following elements:

1. A devolved legislature in Northern Ireland elected by proportional representation and an executive branch drawn on a proportional basis from the parties in the legislature.
2. A Bill of Rights.
3. A Supreme Court with the power to enforce the Bill of Rights.
4. A written constitution which would entrench all of the above features and which could only be implemented or amended by a two-thirds majority of the Northern Ireland electorate voting in a referendum. The Supreme Court would be the guardian of this constitution and would ensure that the legislative and executive branches acted in accordance with it.

The Legislature and Executive

Elections to the legislative assembly would be held every four years using proportional representation in multi-member constituencies, the system currently employed for provincial elections in Northern Ireland. The use of the electoral device of proportional representation would also be suitable for choosing the executive. The approach illustrated below shows how this would work.

We have assumed that there will be ten seats in the executive and that it will reflect the current civil service departmental organization. The departments are therefore assumed to be Economic Development, Agriculture, Environment, Health and Social Services, Education, and Finance and Personnel. In addition, we have assumed that there will be a Chief Executive, a Deputy Chief Executive, a Minister of Justice, and a Minister without Portfolio (perhaps to scrutinize any matters which would be reserved by the Westminster government).

For the purposes of illustrating this form of government, the party representation in the legislature and share of the vote is assumed to be that which followed from the Assembly elections of 1982. There were 26 Official Unionists, 21 Democratic Unionists, 14 from the SDLP, 10 from Alliance, 5 from Sinn Féin, 1 Ulster Popular Unionist, and 1 Independent Unionist. Using the d'Hondt method of proportional representation, the number of seats each party holds is divided successively by 1, 2, 3, 4, etc., and then put in a table (see Table 6.1). According to Table 6.1, if this method was employed, the party composition of the executive would be 4 Official Unionists, 3 Democratic Unionists, 2 from the SDLP, and 1 from the Alliance Party. The choice of seats on the executive could then be allocated in order of the largest numbers as shown in Table 6.2. This method of proportional representation not only ensures that all significant parties are included in government, it gives the electorate a crucial

TABLE 6.1. *Seats on the Executive of a possible Assembly*

Party	Divisor			
	1	2	3	4
Official Unionist	26*	13.0*	8.7*	6.5*
Democratic Unionist	21*	10.5*	7.0*	5.3
SDLP	14*	7.0*	4.7	3.5
Alliance	10*	5.0	3.3	2.5
Sinn Féin	5	2.5	1.7	1.3
Ulster Popular Unionist	1	0.5	0.3	0.3
Independent Unionist	1	0.5	0.3	0.3

* Seat on the executive.

TABLE 6.2. *Allocation of Executive portfolios by a possible Assembly*

Choice	Result	Party	Executive portfolio
1	26.0	Official Unionist	Chief Executive
2	21.0	Democratic Unionist	Deputy Chief Executive
3	14.0	SDLP	Minister of Justice
4	13.0	Official Unionist	Economic Development
5	10.5	Democratic Unionist	Agriculture
6	10.0	Alliance	Environment
7	8.7	Official Unionist	Health and Social Services
8	7.0	Democratic Unionist	Education
9	7.0	SDLP	Finance and Personnel
10	6.5	Official Unionist	Minister without Portfolio

role in deciding how many and what type of cabinet seats each party gets. It has obvious democratic advantages over the method employed by the Secretary of State in 1973–4, which was to restrict executive appointments to parties of his choice. Whereas the Secretary of State only had to ensure that his executive commanded a bare majority in the legislature, the method outlined in Table 6.1 would ensure that the government would be broadly based. The 1973–4 arrangement had little chance of succeeding not least because of the stark asymmetry in the make-up of the governing coalition, which contained only a minority of the majority community's representatives.

Seats on each of the legislative committees in the Assembly could be apportioned in such a way that each committee would directly reflect the proportional strength of the parties within the Assembly. Committee chairmen could be elected using the same method employed to elect members of the executive.

A Bill of Rights and a Supreme Court

A Bill of Rights would be an essential part of the constitution and has already been accepted, at least in principle, by all of Northern Ireland's political parties except Sinn Féin. The constitutional conference could decide to formulate its own set of articles taking into account the communal rights of the two communities or it could simply agree to entrench the European Convention of Human Rights in the constitution, a step which would make those rights more justiciable than they are at present. Because it would involve a step away from the British principle of parliamentary sovereignty, which allows a legislature untrammelled powers to pass unacceptable measures such as imprisonment without trial, the Anglo-Irish Agreement, or the abolition of jury trials, a Bill of Rights would have real advantages for both communities within Northern Ireland.[5]

The surrender of some of the legislature's powers to the courts is also appropriate for a divided society like Northern Ireland because the latter body when interpreting rights does not distinguish between majorities and minorities but makes decisions based on the equality of plaintiff and defendant, and on the quality of the arguments presented to it. It is the strength of the case, and not the numerical size of the parties to it, that is meant to decide the outcome.[6]

The Constitution

A written constitution based on the agreement of the representatives of both communities would have obvious benefits. The fact that Northern Ireland's position within the United Kingdom could not be changed without the consent of at least two-thirds of those voting in a referendum would raise the siege on Ulster's Protestants and create a new atmosphere of security and stability conducive to reconciliation and political development. A Northern Ireland existing by the consent of both communities would remove the need for unionists to defend constantly the psychological border.[7]

The fact that the new political structure, including the power-sharing executive, the proportional electoral system, and the new Bill of Rights, could not be changed or revoked without the support of at least two-thirds of those voting in a referendum would dispel the fear of exclusion felt by the Ulster Catholic community and allow them to play a full and productive role in society. As John McMichael writes in *Common Sense*: 'For perhaps the first time in the history of Northern Ireland, the same protective measure could be made to work for both Protestant and Catholic alike' (Ulster Political Research Group 1987).

Agreement on these proposals would do more than create a settlement under which two warring camps could live in peaceful co-existence, though that in itself would be a considerable achievement. By removing the issue of the border from Northern Ireland politics, it would also, in the long term, help to break down the sectarian divisions in the province and replace them with the more placid socio-economic politics prevalent in Great Britain. The negative peace of coexistence would gradually evolve into the positive peace of assimilation. Northern Ireland's people would be able to confront the serious problems of social deprivation, economic recession, unemployment, and the need for more housing with a coalition of all the talents and resources available within the province.

There has always been a base for class politics in the province but it has remained largely undeveloped because of the uncertainty surrounding Northern Ireland's constitutional position. It was the ambiguity of the province's status in the period after partition, fuelled both by Lloyd George's express intention that the arrangement should only be temporary and by the South's continuing

irredentism, that created an opportunity for the unionist establishment and their Nationalist Party counterparts to ensure that every
election became a plebiscite on the border. Along with the abolition
of proportional representation for Stormont elections, this ambiguity
prevented the small Labour Party in Northern Ireland from
mirroring the successes of its British counterpart and ensured that
the middle and working classes continued to be divided along
sectarian lines.

Only when the constitutional question was, temporarily at least,
away from the forefront of politics in the 1950s and early 1960s,
could a basis for class politics be detected in the province. Northern
Ireland Labour Party (NILP) and Independent Labour candidates
polled 24 per cent of the vote in 1953, 29 per cent in 1958, 33 per cent
in 1962, and 22 per cent in 1965. Those who wanted class politics
suffered a severe setback when in 1965 unionists who had moved
towards the labour movement retreated into tribal politics after
O'Neill's meeting with Lemass aroused their fears about Ulster's
future. An increase in this uncertainty, as a result of the outbreak of
the 'troubles' in 1969, caused a further drop in the Labour vote to 10
per cent at the election of that year (McMichael 1987). In the increasingly polarized atmosphere of the early 1970s, the NILP's base
contracted further until it received only 1.6 per cent of the poll at the
general election of October 1974. It ceased to be a political force at
this time.

If, in addition to the proposed constitution, the British parties
decided to organize in Northern Ireland, it would further facilitate
the emergence of non-sectarian politics in the province. With
Northern Ireland's constitutional status secure, the organizational
capacities of the large British parties would quicken the transition
from the existing communalism. Ulster people find it strange that
these parties suggest that the people of the province turn away from
sectarianism, yet refuse to provide organized alternatives for the
electorate there.[8]

In addition to its likely beneficial effect on sectarianism, the
organization of the British parties in Northern Ireland is also
desirable because, even under devolution, important areas of jurisdiction, such as foreign affairs, defence, and fiscal and monetary
matters would remain the responsibility of Westminster. Without
input into the only parties realistically capable of forming the

government at Westminster, the ability of Northern Ireland's electorate to fight against policies it opposes would be severely restricted.

4. CO-DETERMINATION AND ITS ALTERNATIVES

One of the most important obstacles to co-determination is the unwillingness of unionist leaders to grasp the opportunities offered by it. Although *Common Sense* (Ulster Political Research Group 1987) was welcomed by the governments of the Republic of Ireland and the United Kingdom, and by the SDLP, they have been free to refuse it serious consideration because it has not been endorsed by the political representatives of the Protestant community. However, as the proposals in *Common Sense* would remove the threat to Northern Ireland's future most expeditiously, there are no good reasons why unionist leaders should continue to adopt this position.

Despite its advantages, co-determination has been attacked in principle, both implicitly and explicitly, by three other unionist groups. First, the DUP, proponents of the Westminster model of government in which the party or parties winning a majority of seats in the legislature take all of the cabinet positions, claim that power-sharing is un-British and less democratic because it lacks the formal government/opposition dichotomy present in their preferred model (DUP 1984; Unionist Joint Working Party 1987). Because all significant groups are in office together, there is no group, they claim, to perform the important task of criticizing government policies or to act as an alternative government.

These objections are easily countered. The principle of coalition government, while unusual at Westminster, is certainly not unheard of. During times of crisis in the past, such as during both world wars, majority governments in Britain have been very willing to share the responsibility of government with opposition groups. As Northern Ireland is also in a state of crisis, the same policy could be followed here.

More fundamentally, however, the concept of democracy is at least as well suited to the system proposed here, where all groups share power in proportion to the seats they receive, as to a system in which a party winning only a majority of seats, no matter how slim, gains exclusive right to governmental power. It does not seem especially 'democratic' that citizens unfortunate enough to have elected opposition members are denied any representation at the top levels of decision-making, as happens under the Westminster model of government.[9] In addition, majoritarian democracy only works well when two conditions are present: first, when the exclusion of the minority will be temporary and where there will be regular alternations in government; second, when the issues dividing the majority and minority are not fundamental and, as a consequence, the minority believe that their interests will be reasonably well served by the government's policies.

However much these conditions exist in homogeneous societies like Great Britain, they clearly do not hold in divided societies like Northern Ireland. Because voting patterns are rigidly sectarian in these societies, barring major demographic changes, the application of the majoritarian system produces permanent minorities. Far from being democratic, therefore, the application of majority rule under these conditions produces majority dictatorships and is profoundly undemocratic. A minority in this system could certainly not be expected to play the role of responsible opposition associated with the DUP's Westminster model of government. Northern Ireland's own experience, during the period of control by the UUP establishment from 1921 to 1972, when there was no formal opposition for practically all of the period, provides sufficient evidence of this.[10]

Nor is it the case that a partnership executive as outlined in *Common Sense* would necessarily be deprived of all opposition. After the settlement has been in place for a time, some groups may well decide to forfeit their places on the executive. This would not be fatal to the regime as long as there was still consensus on the constitution. In addition, as long as there is a legislature to which the executive is responsible, criticism can be directed not only against the whole government by back-benchers but even more so against individual members of the government by supporters of the other parties. This latter type of opposition worked exceedingly well in Austria during its successful experiment in coalition government from 1945 to 1966 (Lijphart 1977: 48). If at some point in the future a sufficient consensus is established in both communities, the government/ opposition dichotomy of the Westminster model could be reverted to, if that was the general desire. However, this consensus is unlikely in the short term, and it is only liable to appear at all after a period of successful coalition government. Supporters of the Westminster form of majority rule should also be made aware that, even in homogeneous societies, their preferred model of government with its plurality-based electoral system does not necessarily result in a strong opposition (and in extreme cases, as in the Canadian province of New Brunswick where in 1987 the Liberal Party won every seat in the legislature, can result in no opposition at all).

Apart from these objections to majority rule in principle, there is not even a remote possibility that the British government would permit such a form of government in Northern Ireland. Even if London was favourably disposed towards majority rule, inter-national pressure from the EEC, the USA, and the Republic of Ireland would pose a tremendous obstacle to its implementation. The resurrection of majority rule would also produce a tremendous upsurge in support for republican terrorism and the resulting instability would play into the hands of those who seek a British withdrawal from the province and who claim that Protestants are only intent on regaining their ascendancy here. Even the authors of the report of the recent unionist task force 'expressed incredulity' when this option was put forward at their hearings (Joint Unionist Task Force 1987).

The second basic objection to coalition government comes from the 'integrationists', who constitute a large proportion of the OUP. They reject any type of devolved legislature, whether it is based on majority rule or a partnership with Catholics, and demand that Northern Ireland be governed from Westminster in the same way as other parts of the United Kingdom. A devolved legislature in Belfast would, they claim, maintain a distinction between the British main-land and Northern Ireland and would encourage nationalist insurgency by contributing to the uncertainty surrounding the constitutional future of the province. Integrationists call for a range of measures, including the organization of the British parties in Northern Ireland, the passing of legislation relating to Northern Ireland by normal parliamentary means rather than by the present system of Order in Council, and the reinstatement of a standard British form of local government in the province. Only if integration into the United Kingdom took place, they argue, would Northern Ireland's future as a part of the United Kingdom be guaranteed.[11]

However, if 'integration' into the British political system occurred under present circumstances, the future of Northern Ireland would continue to depend on the constitutional 'guarantee' contained in the Northern Ireland Constitution Act of 1973, the same 'guarantee' which allowed the British government to give the Republic of Ireland a role in Ulster's affairs and which does not preclude future extensions in that role up to and including joint authority. Moreover, there is no possibility of agreement within Northern Ireland on integration for the simple reason that it does not offer anything to the representatives of the minority community. It is only by reaching internal agreement on Northern Ireland's position within the United Kingdom that the province's future can be secured, and co-determination has a much better chance of achieving that than integration.

Furthermore, as with majority rule, there is no possibility of the British government accepting integration or wanting closer ties with the province while it remains divided. It has made it clear on numerous occasions that integration is not on offer, partly because it would be unacceptable to the minority in Northern Ireland and the Republic of Ireland but also, and more importantly, because it has no wish to become more closely involved in the difficult task of governing the province.

Even if integrationists had their way, it would place control over the affairs of Northern Ireland in a legislature where it has only 17 MPs out of a total of 650. Northern Ireland, with less than half the number of MPs that Wales has and less than one-quarter of the number Scotland has, would have difficulty having all its interests furthered, social, economic, and otherwise, in a parliament which is becoming increasingly dominated by representatives from the densely populated southern half of England.

The third objection to coalition government in present circumstances comes from unionists concentrated in the Campaign for Equal Citizenship (CEC) and Campaign for Responsible Government (CRG).[12] At the root of their arguments is the fundamental belief that sectarianism in Northern Ireland has been caused exclusively by the fact that the province's electorate has never had the opportunity to vote for the large British class-based parties.[13] They therefore see the organization of the British class-based parties in Northern Ireland as the panacea for the province's problems and a sufficient tool for ending sectarianism there. Only after the British parties have eroded sectarian politics, they claim, should devolution be attempted (see Chapter 4). This analysis of the Northern Ireland problem is fundamentally and dangerously flawed. While the absence of the British parties may partially explain the success of sectarian parties in Northern Ireland, it is wrong to claim that this is the only, or even the most important, factor. Protestants vote unionist not simply because they cannot vote Labour or Conservative, but because they are profoundly concerned about the possibility of a united Ireland, a concern accentuated by the signing of the Hillsborough agreement. A large proportion of Catholics, those who are not die-hard republicans, vote for nationalist parties because they have been consistently denied any say in their government since the establishment of Northern Ireland in 1921.

Unless these questions are resolved before, or at least simultaneously with, the introduction of British parties into Northern Ireland, support for these parties will almost certainly be marginal or will be related to their position on sectarian issues and not on class questions. Thus, Catholic voters under present circumstances could be expected to support Labour, because of its policy of favouring a united Ireland by 'consent', whereas any Protestants who would abandon unionist parties could be expected to gravitate towards the Conservatives, the more pro-union of the British parties. Such a result would not erode sectarianism but would merely convert what are class parties in Britain into sectarian parties in Northern Ireland.

Internal agreement on the lines described in this paper is not only a prerequisite for the removal of sectarianism. By taking the constitutional issue from centre stage it would also remove the main reason why the class parties do not organize here. It could rapidly achieve, therefore, what the CEC and other similar groups have been unable to achieve despite many years of trying. Realistically, even if agreement is reached on co-determination, the sectarian parties could not be expected to disappear overnight but a successful period of coalition government would undermine their *raison d'être*, as it did in the Netherlands, for example (Lijphart 1977: 52). The prospects for the British parties making a breakthrough here would be enhanced by the proportional-representation electoral system which exists at the provincial level and which favours new parties. If they enter Northern Ireland politics before agreement on devolution, they will be faced with the much more difficult task of making a political breakthrough under the outdated plurality electoral system employed for Westminster elections. As the SDP/Liberal Alliance discovered in Great Britain at the elections of 1983 and 1987, it is extremely difficult for a new party to break an established political mould under these conditions.

Co-determination is a fair option which has substantial benefits for both communities and which gives their political representatives significant control over their own affairs. It is surely mere wishful thinking to assume that unionist options which ignore the existence of the large disgruntled minority subculture, and which make no attempt to address its concerns, will lead to its disappearance. If the Union is to be secured, it is much more likely to occur if the divisions in the society are confronted and the minority is given a share in the responsibility of governing the province.

Opinion polls have consistently shown that the partnership formula which lies at the core of co-determination is the *only* option currently under consideration which attracts reasonable levels of support from both Catholics and Protestants (see Table 6.3). In addition, substantial majorities in both communities support the principle of power-sharing (see Table 6.4). If put to a referendum by the proposed constitutional conference, the accommodation outlined in this paper would have an excellent chance of meeting the London government's crucial stipulation that any settlement must secure 'widespread acceptance throughout the community'.[14]

TABLE 6.3. *Two polls on the best form of government for Northern Ireland (%)*

1986: 'Over the next five years, what do you think would be the best form of government for Northern Ireland?'
1988: 'Looking at this list which of these forms of government do you personally think would be the best for Northern Ireland?'

Form of government	Protestants		Catholic		All	
	1986	1988	1986	1988	1986	1988
Complete integration with Great Britain	35	47	6	9	23	32
Direct rule	12	4	6	2	10	3
Devolution with power-sharing	21	17	28	31	24	23
Devolution with majority rule	17	14	2	1	11	9
Independent Northern Ireland	6	7	5	4	6	6
Joint authority between London and Dublin	2	1	16	12	8	5
Federal Ireland	1	1	5	7	3	3
United Ireland	0	1	21	25	9	10
Don't know	5	8	10	10	7	9

Sources: 1986 poll from *Belfast Telegraph*, 15 Jan. 1986. 1988 poll from *Fortnight*, Apr. 1988.

TABLE 6.4. *Three polls on power-sharing (%)*

'Thinking now about power-sharing between the political parties in Northern
Ireland would you say that you agree or disagree with this principle?'*

Community	January 1986		April 1988		October 1988	
	Agree	Disagree	Agree	Disagree	Agree	Disagree
Protestants	61	33	56	42	62	30
Catholics	79	13	84	15	76	14
TOTAL	68	25	68	30	67	24

* This question is from the Feb. 1988 poll. A slightly different question was asked in
Jan. 1986 and Oct. 1988 i.e. 'Do you (a) agree in principle with power-sharing between
the political parties in Northern Ireland or (b) disagree in principle with power-sharing
between the political parties in Northern Ireland?'

*Sources: Belfast Telegraph, 15 Jan. 1986; Fortnight, Apr. 1988; Belfast Telegraph, 5 Oct.
1988.*

5. CONCLUSION

This paper has shown that the arguments of the various unionist
factions about the dangers of co-determination are clearly wrong.
Co-determination would not weaken Northern Ireland's position
within the union but would strengthen it. It would not be undemocratic but would be more democratic* than the Westminster
form of government. It would not entrench and institutionalize
sectarianism but would provide the means to transcend it.

The refusal of the unionist leadership to grasp the opportunities
presented by co-determination indicates a considerable lack of
political sophistication on its part. A more capable leadership would
realize that it could not lose by taking such a step. While the
obstacles to agreement should never be underestimated, a unionist
bloc united behind co-determination would put the present SDLP
leadership on the spot and force it to choose for the first time
between guaranteed power-sharing in Northern Ireland and a role
for the Dublin government in Northern Ireland's affairs. It would
open up the clear fissures which exist within the minority population
and the SDLP leadership between those prepared to accept a
protected future within the United Kingdom and those who insist on
a united Ireland. The minority bloc has appeared relatively monolithic in the past two decades only because they have never had to
choose between these two options. Given the failure of the Dublin

government to effect any significant improvement in the lives of the minority through the Hillsborough agreement, there is a strong possibility that a consensus could emerge in favour of co-determination in both communities.[15]

If agreement could be secured between the two communities in Northern Ireland, there can be little doubt that both the Dublin and London governments would be willing, or would be put under irresistible pressure, to recognize the settlement. Like many Catholics in Northern Ireland, the politicians in the Republic have little interest in a united Ireland. Indeed, with the co-operation of the Republic's electorate, they have spent much of the period since the partition of the country consolidating the sectarian nature of their state and doing little to make it more attractive to Ulster's Protestants.[16] That the Republic's people do not 'hunger and thirst' after unification has been known by all Irish politicians for some time now, though few other than Dr Conor Cruise O'Brien have had the courage to say it (Cox 1985: 41; O'Halloran 1985). As the settlement would meet the British government's long-held criterion that it must be acceptable throughout the community in Northern Ireland, they could hardly oppose it either.

In the unlikely scenario of a substantial proportion of the minority population rejecting the package, loyalists would still gain by supporting co-determination. It would for the first time give them the moral offensive in their struggle against republicanism and go a long way towards improving their image internationally.

If the unionist leadership fail to grasp the opportunities presented by co-determination and instead continue to wait for the accord to collapse because of disagreements between London and Dublin, it risks serious dangers. The accord is becoming entrenched with time and could be radically extended in its scope by new governments in Britain or the Republic.[17] Even the collapse of the Agreement would merely restore the deadlock which existed prior to November 1985, a situation which could result in an exasperated British government deciding to withdraw and a partitioning of the province.

If agreement could be reached on co-determination, the benefits would be far-reaching. It would provide an example to those politicians in Britain who are already questioning their own outdated electoral system and the notion that only simple majorities should form governments.[18] In Northern Ireland, it would release those in political life from the treadmill of sectarian politics and allow them to use their various talents to tackle the real enemies of social deprivation and economic recession, which confront the whole community. To overcome such formidable obstacles, Northern Ireland will need a coalition of all the talents and resources that her people can provide. What is proposed here may be criticized as idealistic and ambitious, but it is surely worth attempting.

Notes

1. This poll showed that only 13% of *all* respondents wanted a united Ireland while 67% wanted a settlement within the framework of the United Kingdom. See *Fortnight*, Apr. 1988.
2. The Catholic proportion of the population of the six counties increased from 34.4% in 1911 to 38.3% in 1981. The Protestant proportion of the population of the 26 counties declined from 10% in 1911 to 3.5% in 1981. Figures from Rowthorn and Wayne (1988: 159, 203).
3. See John Hume's comments on this, *Irish Times*, 24 Dec. 1984.
4. In Austria, too, after World War I, divergent territorial allegiances were important obstacles in the way of accommodation between the Socialists, who were pan-German, and the Catholics, who were more distinctively Austrian. It was only after this division was removed, partly as a result of the negative experience of Anschluss, that the two groups were able to enter a very successful power-sharing arrangement between 1945 and 1966.
5. Several of Britain's top constitutional authorities, concerned about the dangers of parliamentary sovereignty, have argued for a Bill of Rights for the United Kingdom as a whole. See Dearlove and Saunders (1984, ch. 4).
6. For an excellent account of how the black minority in the USA used the courts there to protect and enhance their position, see Rose (1976*a*). Rose also advocates a Bill of Rights for Northern Ireland.
7. This two-thirds requirement would not rule out a united Ireland completely but would merely ensure that it could only be brought about if there was a large degree of support for it in *both* communities. This would be a necessary prerequisite for a stable united Ireland anyway and should be acceptable therefore to all moderate nationalists. As John Hume says: 'If you had a 51 percent–49 percent situation [in favour of a united Ireland] there would still be strong resistance. Therefore, you have to get the broad consent of the Protestant people' (quoted in O'Malley 1983: 111).

8. See Roberts's contribution to this volume (ch. 4) for more details on the British parties' refusal to participate in elections within Northern Ireland.
9. The classic critique of majoritarian democracy from this perspective is given by Nobel Laureate W. A. Lewis in Lewis (1965).
10. For details on the refusal of nationalists to accept the role of official opposition for much of this period, see McAllister (1977).
11. For a good summary of integrationists' arguments, see McCartney (1986).
12. For this perspective, see Roberts's contribution to this volume (ch. 4). Also see Langhammer and Young (1987).
13. Thus, as Roberts argues (ch. 4) it has been the lack of electoral choice in Northern Ireland which has ensured the perpetuation and permanent politicization of the sectarian division.
14. It should be noted that this criterion is not met by the government's own present policy as represented by the Anglo-Irish Agreement. A poll conducted by the *Irish Times* in Feb. 1986 revealed that 81% of Protestants opposed the Agreement while only 8% supported it, *Irish Times*, 12 Feb. 1986.
15. In a poll conducted in Feb. 1988, over two years after the signing of the Agreement, Catholics were asked if the accord had 'benefited the nationalist community': 81% said 'no'. *Fortnight*, Apr. 1988, p. 7.
16. Garret FitzGerald, the former Taoiseach, has often stated that the Irish Republic is dominated by a Roman Catholic and Gaelic ethos which offers little to Protestants (Fitzgerald 1972: 34).
17. The Labour Party, for example, in a front-bench policy statement (McNamara *et al.* 1988) promises a significant extension in the role of the Maryfield Secretariat established by the Agreement.
18. In the 1970s, leading constitutionalist S. E. Finer called for the introduction of a proportional electoral system and coalition governments for the United Kingdom as a whole, in order to end 'the discontinuities, the reversals, the extremisms of the existing system and its contribution to our national decline'.

7

Restoring the Momentum of the Anglo-Irish Agreement

Kevin Boyle and Tom Hadden

THE Anglo-Irish Agreement signed by the governments of the United Kingdom of Great Britain and Northern Ireland and Ireland on 15 November 1985 is potentially the most significant development in the relationship between Britain and Ireland since the partition settlement of the 1920s. The essential objective of the Agreement is to lay to rest the conflicting claims of the two countries to Northern Ireland by recognizing and accommodating both the British and the Irish traditions in Northern Ireland and thus in Ireland as a whole. Its principal provisions can be simply stated: first, to entrench the status of Northern Ireland as part of the United Kingdom until a majority of voters in Northern Ireland decide otherwise; second, to recognize the equal validity and esteem of both traditions within Northern Ireland; third, to provide in the Anglo-Irish Conference a mechanism through which the Irish government may represent the interests of the nationalist minority in Northern Ireland until such time as an agreement on devolution permits elected representatives of that community to carry out that role for themselves; fourth, to provide for cross-border co-operation on security and other matters, initially through the Conference and eventually between a devolved government in Northern Ireland and the Irish government; and finally to ensure that there is no conflict of sovereignty between the United Kingdom and Ireland in the sense that ultimate responsibility for decision-making on either side of the border will remain with the United Kingdom and Irish governments.

It is clear that the underlying objectives and formal provisions of the Agreement rule out as either impractical or undesirable most of the radical solutions proposed in the other chapters of this collection, notably unification, federation, joint authority, integration, partition, and independence. The purpose of this chapter is to explain the reasons why this particular strategy was adopted and to show why it provides the best prospect of achieving long-term peace and stability in Ireland. To do so it is necessary first to set the Agreement in the context of the developing relationship between the United Kingdom and Ireland, and then to justify the political and constitutional strategy it embodies. But if the underlying strategy of the Agreement is right, why then has progress towards peace and stability during its first three years been so disappointing? In the concluding sections some of the reasons for this will be explained and some tentative suggestions will be made for restoring the momentum of the Agreement. For none of the circumstances and arguments which made the Anglo-Irish Agreement the correct solution in 1985 have since altered.

1. THE BACKGROUND TO THE AGREEMENT

Conflicting Claims

Following the partition settlement of the 1920s the relationship between the United Kingdom and Ireland was severely strained for several decades by their conflicting claims to Northern Ireland. In the 1930s the two countries became involved in a trade war. In 1937 Ireland adopted a new constitution (Bunreacht na hÉireann) which asserted a form of jurisdiction over the whole island of Ireland. In 1948 under the Republic of Ireland Act it declared itself to be a republic and left the British Commonwealth. The United Kingdom responded by enacting the Ireland Act 1949, which asserted exclusive British jurisdiction over Northern Ireland.

These conflicting constitutional claims were progressively set aside as economic relations were redeveloped in the post-war years. By 1965 full freedom of trade had been re-established under the Free Trade Area Agreement (Cmnd. 2858). In 1973 both countries joined the European Community. But the outbreak of the 'troubles' in

Northern Ireland in 1968 caused renewed strains in the developing comity. The initial reaction of the British Government was to treat the problem of Northern Ireland as an exclusively internal matter and to reject as improper interference any concerns expressed by Ireland and other countries. Despite this the Irish Government continued to assert its concern. For instance in August 1969 the Taoiseach, Jack Lynch, publicly stated that 'the Irish Government can no longer stand by and see innocent people injured, and perhaps worse' and requested the British Government to apply immediately to the United Nations for the urgent despatch of a peace-keeping force to the six counties of Northern Ireland (*Belfast Telegraph*, 14 August 1969); the British Government responded in the United Nations by asserting that events in Northern Ireland were an internal matter for the United Kingdom government (*Keesing's Contemporary Archives*, 1969, 23584 A).

The Sunningdale Conference

After the suspension of the devolved Northern Ireland government in 1972 and the introduction of 'direct rule' from London, the importance of the Irish dimension in dealing with Northern Ireland was eventually accepted by the British Government. At the Sunningdale Conference in December 1973 an attempt was made to build a settlement on a joint British–Irish basis. Agreement was reached there by both the British and Irish Governments and by representatives of both unionist and nationalist parties in Northern Ireland on a package of measures covering not only the internal government of Northern Ireland but also relations between Northern Ireland and Ireland. Many of the provisions of the Sunningdale agreement, though it was never adopted as a formal international treaty as had been intended, may be seen as direct precedents for those of the 1985 Agreement.

The first significant element in the Sunningdale communiqué was a series of statements by all those involved on the status of Northern Ireland. The Unionist and Alliance Parties asserted their desire to remain part of the United Kingdom; the SDLP and the Irish Government asserted their aspiration for a united Ireland to be achieved by consent; and the British and Irish Governments made the following parallel declarations:

The Irish Government fully accepted and solemnly declared that there could be no change in the status of Northern Ireland until a majority of the people in Northern Ireland desired a change in that status.

The British Government solemnly declared that it was, and would remain, their policy to support the wishes of the majority of the people in Northern Ireland. The present status of Northern Ireland is that it is part of the United Kingdom. If in the future the majority of the people of Northern Ireland should indicate a wish to become part of a united Ireland, the British Government would accept that wish.

It may be noted that the Irish Government made no declaration on what the current status of Northern Ireland was, and that the British Government, while asserting clearly what that status was, indicated its support for Irish unification if a majority of the people of Northern Ireland so wished.

The second element in the Sunningdale agreement was the creation of a Council of Ireland to deal with some matters on a joint basis between the two parts of Ireland. This was also provided for under the Government of Ireland Act 1920 (Section 2(1)), but had not been brought into operation since different arrangements for the government of Southern Ireland were made under the Anglo-Irish Treaty of 1921. Under the Sunningdale agreement the Council was to comprise a Council of Ministers with seven members each from the Northern Ireland Executive and the Irish government, a Secretariat, and a Consultative Assembly with 30 members each from the Northern Ireland Assembly and Dáil Éireann. The Council was to have both harmonizing and executive functions, and a specific role in relation to human rights and the appointment of police authorities for both parts of Ireland. The cost of the Secretariat was to be shared equally by Northern Ireland and Ireland and the cost of other joint services in proportion to the benefit enjoyed. In contrast to the provisions of the 1985 Agreement for a joint British–Irish ministerial conference the Council of Ireland was envisaged as an exclusively North–South body with reciprocal powers and duties in both parts of Ireland and that the British government was to be involved only in so far as it might be necessary to protect its financial interests while it continued to pay a subsidy to Northern Ireland.

The third major element in the Sunningdale agreement was the understanding that Northern Ireland was to be governed by a 'power-sharing' Executive on which agreement had already been reached in discussions between the Secretary of State for Northern Ireland, William Whitelaw, and some but not all of the political parties in Northern Ireland. Those involved attended the Sunningdale Conference in their capacity as members designate of the proposed Northern Ireland Executive.

The final element in the Sunningdale agreement was the recognition that terrorism should be dealt with on an all-Ireland basis. The detailed discussion of the possibilities for creating a common law-enforcement area and an all-Ireland court and of new arrangements for extradition or extra-territorial jurisdiction was left to a commission of legal experts which reported the following year.

Very little of this elaborate package was implemented. No formal international treaty was entered into by the United Kingdom and Ireland, as had been envisaged, since the constitutionality of the declaration by the Irish Government on the status of Northern Ireland was immediately contested by opponents of the Agreement in Ireland. Though the Irish Supreme Court ruled that the declaration amounted at most to a statement of policy, some of the judges indicated that a formal agreement recognizing that Northern Ireland was part of the United Kingdom might be repugnant to Articles 2 and 3 of the Irish Constitution (*Boland* v. *An Taoiseach* [1974] Irish Reports 338). Nor was any progress made in establishing a Council of Ireland, which opponents of the package in Northern Ireland portrayed as a major step towards Irish unification. In the British general election of February 1974 parties which rejected the Sunningdale agreement won 11 of the 12 seats in Northern Ireland and the power-sharing Executive was eventually brought down in May 1974 by a political strike against the creation of a Council of Ireland in any form. The only lasting achievement of the Sunningdale Conference resulted from the report of the Law Enforcement Commission on extradition and related matters (Cmnd. 5627; Prl. 3832). Though the senior British and Irish judges involved could not agree on new rules for the extradition of political offenders, which the Irish members argued would be contrary to international law and therefore unconstitutional, they did agree on new procedures for the exercise of extra-territorial jurisdiction which were enacted in the United Kingdom under the Criminal Jurisdiction Act 1975 and in Ireland under the Criminal Law (Jurisdiction) Act 1976.

The Anglo-Irish Joint Studies of 1981

From 1974 until 1980 a number of attempts were made to promote an internal political settlement within Northern Ireland. But little progress was made, due largely to the continuing differences between the major unionist and nationalist parties over the issue of power-sharing and the 'Irish dimension'. The possibility of making greater progress at an inter-state level re-emerged at a summit meeting between Mrs Thatcher and Mr Haughey on 21 May 1980, at which agreement was recorded on the importance of the 'unique relationship between the peoples of the United Kingdom of Great Britain and Northern Ireland and the Republic and on the need to further this relationship in the interests of peace and reconciliation'. At a further summit meeting on 8 December 1980 it was agreed that special consideration should be given during 1981 to 'the totality of relationships within these islands' and a number of Joint Studies covering possible new institutional relationships, citizenship rights, security matters, economic co-operation, and measures to encourage mutual understanding were commissioned. It was these studies that laid the basis for the Agreement which was eventually signed in 1985.

Final reports of the Joint Studies were published in November 1981 (Westminster, Cmnd. 8414; Dublin, Pl. 299). The study on *Possible New Institutional Structures* explored possible forms for new Anglo-Irish institutions at various levels. The first suggestion was for the formalization of existing patterns of contact at ministerial and official level in an Anglo-Irish Intergovernmental Council. It was also suggested that an Anglo-Irish Ministerial Council might be established without the need for legislation, perhaps by a formal intergovernmental agreement. It was suggested that a Secretariat for any new body might be composed of designated officials from each government and that it might be appropriate for a complementary interparliamentary body to be developed. Finally, it was suggested that it might be appropriate to create an Advisory Committee on economic, social, and cultural co-operation, which would be associated with the proposed Council but independent of governments or parliaments; as an interim measure wider economic, social, and cultural exchanges might be promoted by a body to be called Anglo-Irish Encounter modelled on the Anglo-German Koenigswinter Conference. Detailed studies were also published on *Citizenship*

Rights, Economic Co-operation, and *Measures to Encourage Mutual Understanding.* It was agreed that the work of the new institutional structures must take place within a constitutional framework in which the factual position of Northern Ireland could not be changed without the consent of the majority of the people of Northern Ireland and the agreement of the Parliament at Westminster.

Formal ministerial agreement to the creation of the Anglo-Irish Intergovernmental Council was recorded at the summit meeting between Mrs Thatcher and Dr FitzGerald on 6 November 1981. Despite the suggestion in the Joint Studies this was not recorded in a formal interstate treaty, but was merely reported to the British Parliament (11 November 1981, *Parliamentary Debates* (Commons), vol. 6, cols. 422 ff.) and the Oireachtas (11 November 1981, *Dáil Debates*, vol. 361, cols. 1572 ff.). As a result there do not appear to be any formal constitution and rules of procedure for meetings of the Council, which in one sense is merely a name for the continuing series of intergovernmental contacts at various levels. It was reported in the Joint Report of the Steering Committee of the Council that between January 1982, when the first ministerial and official meetings were held, and November 1983 twenty bilateral meetings had been held within the framework of the Council.

During this period the non-governmental body proposed in the Joint Studies was also established. The formation of Anglo-Irish Encounter was formally announced at a meeting between the British Foreign Secretary, the Northern Ireland Secretary and the Irish Minister for Foreign Affairs on 27 July 1983. Since then Anglo-Irish Encounter has organized a series of half-yearly conferences on a wide range of topics of mutual British and Irish interest.

The New Ireland Forum

While these initiatives were being pursued by the two governments a renewed attempt was made by nationalists in both parts of Ireland to redefine their attitudes to Irish unity. At the Sunningdale Conference and at succeeding summit meetings the leaders of all the main parties in Ireland had committed themselves to the pursuit of unification only with the consent of the majority of people in Northern Ireland. It was obvious that this could not be achieved without some reassessment of the Catholic and Gaelic tradition upon which the Irish state had long been based. There was also some concern in the aftermath of the IRA hunger strikes of 1980 and

1981 that the SDLP, which was also committed to the pursuit of unification by consent, might be overtaken as effective represent-atives of the majority of nationalists in Northern Ireland by Pro-visional Sinn Féin, the political wing of the IRA. It was eventually agreed by the leaders of the three main Irish parties, Fianna Fáil, Fine Gael, and the Irish Labour Party, and of the SDLP that a New Ireland Forum should be established with the express purpose of finding a way in which 'lasting peace and stability could be achieved in a New Ireland through the democratic process'. The main unionist parties were invited but declined to attend.

The final report of the New Ireland Forum in May 1984 stated that 'a united Ireland in the form of a sovereign independent Irish state to be achieved peacefully and by consent' was 'the most durable basis for peace and stability' (New Ireland Forum 1984, paras. 5.4, 5.5). The preferred form of unity, in Mr Haughey's interpretation of the Report, was a unitary state which would 'embrace the whole island of Ireland governed as a single unit under one government and one parliament elected by all the people of the island' (para. 6.1). But other leading participants laid equal stress on the two other options explored in detail, a federal or confederal state and a system of joint authority under which the governments in London and Dublin would share responsibility for the government of Northern Ireland. The Report also included the offer to consider other ways in which the 'realities and requirements' identified in the Report might be met. Two of the most important of these were that both traditions in Northern Ireland would have to be recognized and accommodated and that 'the political arrangements for a new and sovereign Ireland would have to be freely negotiated and agreed to by the people of the North and by the people of the South' (para. 5.2).

The immediate response of the British Government to the New Ireland Forum Report was to reject the three main forum options as unrealistic given the clearly expressed wishes of the people of Northern Ireland (2 July 1984, *Parliamentary Debates* (Commons), vol. 63 (64), col. 23. In the press conference following the summit meeting with Dr FitzGerald on 18–19 November 1984 Mrs Thatcher used even harsher words: 'The unified Ireland was one solution—that is out. A second solution was a confederation of the two states—that is out. A third solution was joint authority—that is out.' The joint communiqué of the summit, however, used less emotive words and merely restated the positions of the two governments as agreed at previous summits, with some significant additions drawn from the New Ireland Forum Report, notably that the 'identities of both the majority and the minority communities in Northern Ireland should be recognised and respected and reflected in the structures and processes of Northern Ireland in ways acceptable to both communities'.

The Completion of the Agreement

The drafting of the Anglo-Irish Agreement began in earnest soon after the summit meeting of November 1984. Most of the work was carried out by a small group of officials and diplomats at the highest levels on both the British and Irish sides, including in both cases the Secretary to the Cabinet. The work was completed in the late summer of 1985. The choice of Hillsborough Castle in County Down, the former residence of the Governor-General of Northern Ireland, as the location for the signing of the Agreement on 15 November 1985 and the presence in Northern Ireland of the British Prime Minister and the Irish Taoiseach, each accompanied by a team of senior ministers, was clearly intended to emphasize the new co-operative relationship between the United Kingdom and Ireland over the government of Northern Ireland. But it is equally clear from the wording of the provisions eventually adopted that the Agreement was not devised in 1985 but was a careful development of the institutional structures suggested in the Joint Studies of 1981 and of the realities and requirements identified in the New Ireland Forum Report.

2. THE STRATEGY OF THE AGREEMENT

The underlying strategy of the Agreement, as outlined above, is to recognize and accommodate the two traditions within Northern Ireland as an established unit of government within the United Kingdom rather than to embark on any radical constitutional change. By making express provision for Irish unification only by consent of the majority of the people in Northern Ireland the Agreement effectively rules out any form of unification as an immediate option. By providing expressly for the retention of British sovereignty over decision-making in Northern Ireland it rules out any kind of formal joint authority. By providing expressly for devolution on a basis acceptable to both communities in Northern Ireland and for consultation with the Irish government pending agreement on devolution it effectively rules out the integration of Northern Ireland with the rest of the United Kingdom. By restricting self-determination for the people of Northern Ireland to a choice between remaining part of the United Kingdom or joining a united Ireland, it effectively rules out any form of independence. And by making no provision for any revision of the existing boundaries of Northern Ireland it effectively rules out repartition.

This strategy appears to have been chosen partly because it was thought to offer the best chance of achieving long-term stability without risking the increased tension and violence which would inevitably accompany any radical constitutional change, and partly because all the other options were thought to be either inherently impracticable or likely to make matters worse in the short term without offering any better hope of long-term stability. The justification for rejecting the more radical options discussed in other contributions can be simply summarized. The positive justification of the Agreement itself, in so far as that is different, is less immediately obvious but is no less compelling.

The Other Options

There are five alternative but unworkable options for policy-makers.

1. It is clear that the unification of Ireland in present circumstances is unrealistic. Everyone accepts that almost all Protestants in Northern Ireland are adamantly opposed to unification and that a substantial proportion of Catholics are content to remain part of the United Kingdom if their identity and interests are adequately protected.

2. The major objection to the integration of Northern Ireland with the rest of the United Kingdom is that the elimination of the Irish dimension that this strategy would bring about is unacceptable to most nationalists in Northern Ireland and would be unlikely to secure the support of any Irish government. It would be as much a denial of the existence of two traditions and communities in Northern Ireland as would Irish unification without the consent of unionists.

3. While repartition of Northern Ireland could be justified on demographic grounds it could not resolve the underlying problem without a very substantial movement of population, notably from West Belfast, which virtually no one is prepared to contemplate.

4. Continued government of Northern Ireland on a long-term basis by a form of joint authority is likely to prove inherently unstable, in that both sides would naturally seek to put pressure on the British and Irish governments to seek or concede further constitutional changes; such a regime would also be inherently undemocratic in that politicians within Northern Ireland would have little effective influence on the course of events.

5. The principal arguments against any form of independence for Northern Ireland are that it is only favoured by unionists as a last resort if a British withdrawal becomes a serious threat, that it is opposed by almost all nationalists, and that it would be financially impracticable without continuing large-scale subventions from Britain or the European Community.

The Justification of the Agreement

It seems likely that the strategy of recognizing and accommodating the two communities within a British Northern Ireland which is embodied in the Anglo-Irish Agreement was adopted largely because all the other possibilities were considered to be less likely to produce lasting peace and stability. But there are some significant positive arguments in its favour.

In the first place the right of ethnic and religious minorities to recognition and accommodation rather than integration or absorption is now accepted in international human-rights law, notably in Article 27 of the United Nations International Covenant on Civil and Political Rights:

In those states in which ethnic, religious or linguistic minorities exist, persons belonging to such minorities shall not be denied the right, in community with the other members of their group, to enjoy their own culture, to profess and practice their own religion, or to use their own language.

The desirability of systems of government which make special provision for the participation of minorities in the processes of government in divided or multicultural societies is also recognized by most political scientists, even if there is less than total consensus on precisely how this should be achieved. The objectives of the Anglo-Irish Agreement are fully in accord with these principles.

In the second place the underlying objective of the Agreement to promote co-operation between the United Kingdom and Ireland over a problematic border region is fully in accord with their obligations as members of the European Community. The prospects of a gradual increase in social and economic integration within the Community and a corresponding lessening of the importance of internal boundaries also underlines the advantage of avoiding any major upheaval in the current constitutional status of Northern Ireland.

Finally, the evidence of successive opinion polls in Northern Ireland is that a settlement which incorporates provision for devolved government with some form of power-sharing and recognition of the rights of members of both communities to equal treatment and equality of esteem along the lines of that embodied in the Agreement is likely to gain more popular support than any other option.

3. THE LIMITED PROGRESS OF THE AGREEMENT

If the underlying objectives of the Anglo-Irish Agreement are correct and if the strategy it embodies is preferable to all other practicable options, why then has progress towards peace and stability during the first three years of its existence been so disappointing?

One of the main problems has been the refusal of almost all unionists to co-operate in any way in promoting the objectives of the Agreement and their insistence on its suspension or abandonment as a precondition to serious talks on devolution. Though the signing of the Agreement was received with almost universal acclaim in Britain, Ireland, and the rest of the world, the reaction of unionists has been almost universally hostile and has been expressed with a vehemence and persistence that must have surprised those who sought in the Agreement to recognize and protect the interests of unionists as well as of nationalists. At a rally at the Belfast City Hall on 23 November 1985 attended by an estimated 100,000 to 200,000 people the leader of the Democratic Unionist Party, Dr Ian Paisley, stated that unionists would 'never, never, never' accept the Agreement. Shortly after, in the Westminster debate on the Agreement, the leader of the Official Unionist Party, James Molyneaux, stressed that it could not bring either peace, stability, or reconciliation (*Parliamentary Debates* (Commons), 26 November, col. 763). Following the debate the Official and Democratic Unionist MPs withdrew from the House of Commons and resigned their seats to ensure a kind of referendum on the Agreement. At the subsequent by-elections held on 23 January 1986 anti-Agreement candidates polled 418,230 votes, representing almost 40 per cent of the entire electorate.

Successive opinion polls have mirrored this result. A poll carried out by MORI for the *Sunday Times* in November 1985 suggested that 75 per cent of Protestants would vote against it in a referendum (*Sunday Times*, 24 November 1985). A poll for the BBC in January 1986 similarly indicated that 76 per cent of Protestants were opposed to the Agreement and that only 8 per cent supported it (see *Fortnight*, 10 February 1986). More recent polls have indicated that Protestant disenchantment has not dissipated. A poll carried out for *Fortnight* by Coopers and Lybrand in February 1988 indicated that 94 per cent of Protestants thought that they had not benefited from the accord (*Fortnight*, 7 April 1988). A *Belfast Telegraph* poll in September 1988 indicated that 62 per cent of Protestants were just as opposed to the Agreement as they had been initially and that only 5 per cent were less opposed (*Belfast Telegraph*, 4 October 1988).

The main focus of unionist opposition has been to the involvement of Irish ministers in the administration of Northern Ireland affairs through the Intergovernmental Conference and to the existence of its joint Secretariat at Maryfield in Belfast. But general unionist opposition to the Agreement as a whole has made any progress towards devolution as one of its essential components impractical. Though the unionist leaders wavered for a period during the spring of 1986, they were prevented by their 'followers' from entering into talks about the Agreement. Subsequent attempts to involve unionist leaders in serious discussion with the British or Irish Governments have proved equally fruitless. The British and Irish Governments have refused to agree to the unionist precondition of a suspension of the working of the Agreement and the closure of the Secretariat at Maryfield and there has been a similar impasse over talks between the unionists and the SDLP.

The British Government has responded to this sustained unionist opposition to the Agreement by adopting an extremely cautious position over action to improve the situation of nationalists for fear of increasing the level of unionist disenchantment. In particular, it has been reluctant to act quickly and effectively to improve equality of opportunity and esteem for members of the nationalist community or to introduce the kind of reforms in security policy and in the administration of justice that would increase the confidence of nationalists.

This slow progress may be illustrated in each of the principal areas of concern to nationalists which were to be addressed under the Agreement. The British Government has taken belated action on some matters specifically referred to in the Agreement, such as the repeal of the Flags and Emblems Display Act (Northern Ireland) and the enfranchisement of certain Irish citizens who were debarred from voting in local-government and Assembly elections under the Electoral Law (Northern Ireland) Act 1962. But little or nothing has been done to give substance to the recognition and accommodation of the rights and identities of both traditions within Northern Ireland as provided for under Article 5 of the Agreement. No consideration appears to have been given to the introduction of general consti- tutional provisions which might help to guarantee equality of treat- ment for members of the two traditions. No positive action has been taken to recognize the rights of those who assert their Irish nationality or who wish to use the Irish language in official papers or for other purposes. No formal measures have been taken to promote Irish or Gaelic culture in officially supported or recognized media, such as radio and television. Similarly there has been no effective action under the provision of Article 5, which required the Con- ference to consider the advantages and disadvantages of a Bill of Rights in some form for Northern Ireland. The only proposal in this sphere has been the idea discussed at a meeting of the Conference in October 1986 for a joint declaration of rights by the British and Irish Governments. But it was not pursued, not least because any such declaration would be legally irrelevant. The British Government has been persuaded to introduce more effective legislation to outlaw religious discrimination and to encourage equality of opportunity in employment. But this action was as much due to pressure from the supporters of the McBride Principles in the United States and the report of the Standing Advisory Commission on Human Rights on discrimination in employment (SACHR 1987) as to action within the Intergovernmental Conference.

Progress on legal and security matters of concern to nationalists under Articles 7 to 9 has been equally unimpressive. There has been no significant improvement in the level of confidence among nationalists in the administration of justice. The apparent influence of the Conference on such matters as the abandonment of super- grass trials has been offset by its lack of influence on such matters as the decision not to prosecute anyone following the Stalker/Sampson inquiry. Nor have any major steps been taken to harmonize the criminal law in both parts of Ireland or to develop structures for mixed courts or extra-territorial jurisdiction. Some progress has been made in improving operational contacts and co-operation between the police forces on either side of the border. But little has been done to secure greater support among nationalists for the security forces within Northern Ireland. Even where there has been some positive action, such as the introduction of more acceptable ground rules for the routing of marches and the promulgation of a new Police Code, it has not been publicly identified with the work of the Conference. There has been a tacit agreement between the two governments not to emphasize the role of the Conference on such matters so as to permit the British Government to emphasize the independent development of its own policies.

It is hardly surprising in this light that there has been increasing disenchantment with the Agreement among nationalists. Though 65 per cent of Catholics indicated their support for the Agreement in a *Sunday Times* opinion poll immediately after it was signed, the opinion poll in *Fortnight* in February 1988 indicated that 81 per cent of Catholics thought that the Agreement had not benefited the nationalist community. The *Belfast Telegraph* poll in October 1988 similarly indicated that 26 per cent of Catholics were less in favour of the Agreement than they had been initially.

The Irish Government has contributed to this lack of progress. Since the signing of the Agreement and particularly since the replacement of Dr FitzGerald's coalition by Mr Haughey's Fianna Fáil Government early in 1987 it has focused almost exclusively on nationalist concerns. By failing to take any action to reassure unionists, for instance by emphasizing or strengthening the constitutional guarantee under Article 1 or by giving positive support to devolution, it has made it more difficult for the British Government to take bold action to improve the position of nationalists.

Opponents of the Agreement on either side, both political and paramilitary, have taken advantage of this general lack of momentum and have been able to ensure that the agenda of successive meetings of the Conference has been dominated by matters of public order and security. The Conference has thus been seen largely as a forum for crisis management of the kind so rightly condemned by the New Ireland Forum Report. It has been correspondingly difficult for ministers to lead public opinion towards the acceptance and implementation of the objectives of the Agreement. In one sense the main achievement of the Conference in its initial years has been in not breaking down altogether in the face of successive confrontations on security and related matters, such as the routing of Orange marches in 1986, the continuing controversy over the Stalker/Sampson inquiry into alleged 'shoot to kill' incidents, and successive disputes over extradition.

4. RESTORING THE MOMENTUM OF THE AGREEMENT

If this deadlock is to be broken, and the positive momentum of the Agreement restored, some action will have to be taken. Public confidence in Britain, Ireland, and Northern Ireland in the value of the Agreement as more than a formal procedure for intergovernmental consultation will require more cogent evidence of the commitment of the two Governments to achieving its stated objectives.

The principal objective must be to secure the consent of the unionist community in Northern Ireland to the broad objectives of the Agreement, since they cannot in practice be achieved without unionist co-operation. This suggests that two levels of action may need to be identified: first, some relatively minor changes in the procedures and possibly in the wording of the Agreement to help to ensure that its objectives can be more effectively pursued in advance of full unionist participation; and secondly, some more fundamental amendments to the Agreement designed to accommodate full unionist participation. These will be considered in turn.

It must be stressed in this context that the view which has sometimes been put forward in official and other quarters that the Agreement as an internationally binding treaty is unchangeable is legally inaccurate. In international law, as codified in the Vienna Convention on the Law of Treaties, the Agreement may be clarified or amended at any time by means of a protocol provided both parties agree. And its operations may be suspended or abandoned at any time if both parties agree. These provisions apply as much to the allegedly entrenched guarantee on the status of Northern Ireland in Article 1 as to the other articles in the Agreement.

Interim Changes

Even if there is no immediate prospect of securing active unionist participation in the working of the new relationships established

under the Agreement, there are a number of changes in practice and
procedure which might help improve the working of the Conference
and a number of ways in which the meaning of the current Agreement might be clarified. Some formal amendments or additions to
the terms of the Agreement, by way of a protocol or otherwise,
would in itself be no bad thing since it would alert unionists to the
fact that both Governments recognize that the provisions adopted in
1985 are neither perfect nor fixed for all time.

1. One of the main drawbacks of the current practices and procedures of the Conference has been the atmosphere of secrecy and
intrigue which has surrounded its operations. This has increased the
opportunities for misrepresentation by the opponents of the Agreement and done little for the public reputation of the Conference as a
vehicle for progress. It would be desirable for the agenda of the
Conference on major issues to be made public well in advance of its
regular ministerial meetings and for views and proposals from other
interested parties to be invited. It would also be desirable for
working papers and joint studies to be published, both to
demonstrate the positive work carried out by the Conference and its
Secretariat and to assist in gaining public support for the underlying
objectives of the Agreement. The Anglo-Irish Joint Studies of 1981
were published in full as parliamentary papers in both jurisdictions.
There is no good reason why many of the working papers of the
Conference should not be similarly dealt with, even if agreement
cannot be reached on every item in them. The fact that some issues,
notably those involving operational decisions on security, must
remain confidential should not be taken as a reason for confidentiality on all other matters. Publication of such documents as the
programme of work for co-operation between the two police forces
provided for under Article 7 and studies by experts on the development of procedures for mixed courts, extra-territorial jurisdiction,
and extradition as provided for under Article 8 should be seriously
considered. Similar studies might be made and published on many
of the issues covered in Article 5, such as ways of recognizing and
accommodating the rights and interests of the two communities in
Northern Ireland and the protection of human rights.

2. There is a good deal of confusion on the precise role of the
Conference in respect of co-operative and reciprocal action in Ireland
and Great Britain under Articles 2, 5, and 8. It would be desirable to
clarify the terms of the relevant provisions in Article 2 so that the

jurisdiction and role of the Conference on such matters as the rights and interests of minorities in Ireland and of people of Irish origin in Britain, for example in respect of concern over the outcome of some terrorist trials in Britain, would be specified. This would assist in emphasizing that while the primary concern of the Conference is in respect of Northern Ireland it is also concerned with the totality of relationships between Britain and Ireland, and particularly those which arise out of the conflict in Northern Ireland.

3. Some of the provisions of the current Agreement make reference to matters of particular concern in 1985 which have now been dealt with, such as changes in electoral arrangements and the use of flags and emblems under Article 5. It would be appropriate to remove these references and to insert some other issues of more current concern, such as the use of the Irish language and provisions for the funding of educational provision in Northern Ireland, which will meet the wishes not only of both communities separately but also those who wish to join in integrated schools.

4. It would be desirable to make express provision for the form and functions of an Anglo-Irish parliamentary body. Pending final agreement on current proposals it would not be appropriate to suggest a precise formulation of its composition here. But it would be desirable to make express provision for such a body to scrutinize the implementation of the Agreement and the working of the Conference on a continuing basis and for the two governments to commit themselves to co-operate with any such interparliamentary scrutiny.

Accommodating Full Unionist Participation

If there is to be a prospect of more active unionist participation in the working of the new Anglo-Irish structures then some more far-reaching changes in the Agreement are likely to be necessary. It would not be appropriate in advance of the negotiations which would be involved in any such recasting of the Agreement to make specific suggestions. But it would probably be desirable to develop the Agreement in four broad areas: (1) the legitimacy of Northern Ireland; (2) arrangements for the government of Northern Ireland; (3) the role of the Conference in Anglo-Irish relations; (4) the expansion of the Secretariat.

1. One of the primary concerns of unionists is that Article 1 of the Agreement does not adequately protect their position within the

United Kingdom. In the drafting of this article there was a conscious effort by both sides to avoid dispute on the definition of a *current* status for Northern Ireland. As was said at the time the two states came to the negotiations with 'different title deeds'. As a result the emphasis in Article 1 is laid on the agreed conditions for any *future change* in the status of Northern Ireland. The intention was to reassure unionists that their right to remain in the United Kingdom, as declared in Section 1 of the Northern Ireland Constitution Act 1973, was formally recognized by the Irish Government, while at the same time assuring nationalists that if they secured the consent of unionists for a united Ireland the British Government would implement it. This joint purpose was to be further emphasized by excluding the article from the review process under Article 11. But it is questionable whether any of these purposes was satisfactorily achieved.

In the first place the concern of those who drafted the article was to avoid any potential conflict with Articles 2 and 3 of the Irish Constitution, and thus the possibility of a damaging legal challenge of the kind which followed the Sunningdale communiqué. These articles read as follows:

Article 2. The national territory consists of the whole island of Ireland, its islands and territorial seas.

Article 3. Pending the reintegration of the national territory, and without prejudice to the right of the Parliament and Government established by this Constitution to exercise jurisdiction over the whole of that territory, the laws enacted by that Parliament shall have the like area and extent of application as the laws of Saorstát Éireann [i.e. the 26 counties of the Irish Free State] and the like extra-territorial effect.

This resulted in a weaker rather than a stronger form of guarantee for unionists than they had been given by the British Government in the Sunningdale communiqué (see above). Two significant changes were made in Article 1 of the Anglo-Irish Agreement compared with the Sunningdale formulation: first, the declaration was a joint one by both governments as opposed to the separate and parallel declarations made at Sunningdale; and second, the word 'would' was substituted for 'could' in relation to any change in the status of Northern Ireland. The result of the first change was that no declaration at all was made as to what the status of Northern Ireland is, even by the British Government; the result of the latter was that the declaration ceased to have any possible legal as opposed to factual significance. Article 1 of the Agreement may thus be viewed as expressing the best guarantee to unionists that was compatible with Articles 2 and 3 of the Irish Constitution. Since it is precisely the continuing presence of the claim in Articles 2 and 3 that is of concern to unionists, it is hardly surprising that few unionists were impressed by the argument that the Agreement represented a new and stronger recognition by Ireland of the status of Northern Ireland.

In the second place, the exclusion of Article 1 from the review procedure provided for in Article 11 gives little if any additional guarantee that the declarations by the two governments will not be altered. As already explained, in international law any provisions of a bilateral treaty may at any time be altered, suspended, or abandoned with the consent of both parties. As a guarantee to unionists, who were not and in international law perhaps could not have been a party to the Agreement as a treaty, Article 1 is therefore less than convincing since the British and Irish Governments might at any time agree to alter or abandon the principle of consent as it is expressed in Article 1. Though the Irish Government may perhaps be regarded as a satisfactory long-term guarantor for nationalists in Northern Ireland, the British Government is not generally regarded as sufficiently committed to the interests of unionists to be a satisfactory long-term guarantor for them.

One possible approach to resolving this difficulty in providing a satisfactory long-term guarantee on the status of Northern Ireland may be to include, as a party to a future agreement or treaty, a representative or guarantor of the unionist as opposed to the general British interest. The absence of an elected government of Northern Ireland, however, and the fact that any such government would not be an independent state party would make this difficult to achieve. The involvement in a treaty of an independent body such as the European Commission might provide better protection against a decision by future British and Irish governments to abandon any guarantee. It would also be desirable, if unionists are to be persuaded to participate fully in any new structures, to make more explicit recognition of the current status of Northern Ireland as part of the United Kingdom. This would in turn require a change in the terms of Articles 2 and 3 of the Irish Constitution to reflect an aspiration for Irish unity by consent rather than a claim to jurisdiction over Northern Ireland. The most appropriate short-term development would perhaps be to add a provision to Article 1 of the Agreement binding both states to adopt in their internal constitutional legislation a parallel statement as to the current status of Northern Ireland as a part of the United Kingdom of Great Britain and Northern Ireland and the principle of formal consent to any change.

It should be noted in this context that it has already been proposed in the Republic on a number of occasions that Articles 2 and 3 of the Irish Constitution should be amended to express an aspiration for eventual unification by consent rather than a claim, whether in the political or legal realm. In formal terms the claim to sovereignty over Northern Ireland has long been completely ignored by the successive Irish governments in its international relations, including its bilateral relations with Britain. The issue of Northern Ireland was not raised when the Republic joined the United Nations in 1955. Nor did Ireland object, when it joined the European Community in 1973, that Northern Ireland also joined as part of the United Kingdom. In more practical terms a number of recent opinion polls in Ireland have indicated clearly that a majority of respondents in practice regard Irish unity as a long-term aspiration rather than a realistic claim. A MRBI poll for the *Irish Times* in May and June of 1987, for example, indicated that while 67 per cent of respondents regarded unification as something to hope for, 49 per cent thought it would never happen, and only 16 per cent thought it would happen within 25 years (*Irish Times*, 1 September 1987). These findings indicate that in the right political climate, such as an agreed reformulation of the Anglo-Irish Agreement with unionist participation, there would be clear majority support for the reformulation of Articles 2 and 3 of the Irish Constitution.

Recognition in this way of the legitimacy of the unionist position would remove one of the major barriers to their co-operation in the Anglo-Irish process. By easing unionist opposition to the Agreement, it would facilitate the adoption by the Conference of a series of measures designed to permit nationalists in Northern Ireland to express their Irish identity in ways that do not conflict with the status of the province as a part of the United Kingdom. It would also help to create a new relationship between the two communities in Northern Ireland and might facilitate the acceptance by both sides of a form of local administration in which both communities could play a part. Until the legitimacy of their position is recognized, unionists will continue to fear that any all-Ireland arrangements and any concessions to the minority in Northern Ireland will merely be the first in a series of steps towards Irish unification.

2. Unionist consent to a revised Agreement is also likely to be dependent on the provision of more satisfactory and stable arrangements for the government of Northern Ireland, whether under direct rule or in the event of devolution, than are currently included in the Agreement. The current method of legislating for Northern Ireland by way of Orders in Council is clearly unsatisfactory. Though draft proposals for Orders are usually circulated for comment, once they have been formally laid before Parliament they cannot be amended in any way. Northern Ireland MPs therefore have very little effective influence on the form of legislation that applies only to Northern Ireland.

It would not be impossible, pending agreement on devolution or for Orders on matters which have not yet been devolved, for special provisions to be made for the consideration and possible amendment of Northern Ireland Orders by a select committee prior to their final approval or rejection by motions in both Houses. The provisions for devolution under the Northern Ireland Constitution Act 1973 and the Northern Ireland Act 1982 may also require some amendment since they provide no guarantee that members representing the majority or minority community may not at any time and on wholly unjustifiable grounds decide to withdraw from a power-sharing administration and thus threaten the whole structure for devolution. It would make for greater stability if formal protections and guarantees on matters of special concern to the minority, such as education and the location of major industrial development, were provided by way of weighted majority requirements or entrenched constitutional rights. This would provide greater scope for the development of informal conventions on power-sharing within government without requiring continuing agreement on all matters as a condition of the continuance of devolved government.

3. It would also be desirable to spell out more clearly the role of the Conference in respect of the three main dimensions of Anglo-Irish relations: the internal Northern Ireland dimension, the North–South dimension (relationships between the two parts of Ireland), and the East–West dimension (relationships between Ireland and the United Kingdom as a whole).

Under the existing Agreement the general relationships between the United Kingdom and Ireland are notionally covered under the auspices of the Anglo-Irish Intergovernmental Council established in 1981, while those relating specifically to Northern Ireland and to North–South relations are covered by the Anglo-Irish Intergovernmental Conference established under the Agreement in 1985. But there are no formal or detailed provisions setting out the precise jurisdiction and role of the Council. Rather than attempt to create a new and detailed agreement to govern the East–West dimension, it would be simpler to retain the general structure of the Conference, as set out in Articles 2 and 3 of the Agreement, but to extend its jurisdiction to cover prescribed matters in respect of Anglo-Irish relations. This could readily be achieved by extending potential membership of the Conference to all British and Irish ministers as appropriate and adding a new article or set of articles to govern the jurisdiction of the expanded Conference in respect of matters of concern to the United Kingdom as a whole and Ireland but without a specific Northern Ireland connection. For example, provision might be made for the discussion of arrangements for the free travel area and the control of aliens, and for the development of a common approach to the protection of human rights by establishing appropriate agencies in each jurisdiction. The creation of an interparliamentary body of the kind envisaged in Article 12 of the current Agreement would also fit readily into an expanded Agreement of this kind.

In this way the role of the Conference would be expanded to cover the totality of relationships between Britain and Ireland, as was envisaged in the summit meeting between Mrs Thatcher and Mr Haughey in 1981, without abandoning the more specific objectives in respect of Northern Ireland which were agreed in 1985. In one sense this would amount to little more than the formalization of the existing close relationships between the British and Irish Governments on many matters of shared concern. But a development of the Agreement along these lines would make it easier for unionists to agree to participate fully in the new institutions, since a number of their leaders, notably Mr Molyneaux, have suggested that an approach based on the Anglo-Irish Intergovernmental Council could be acceptable.

4. In this context it would be desirable to provide for the expansion and possible relocation of the Conference Secretariat to cover all three dimensions of Anglo-Irish relations. A permanent joint

Secretariat could thus be maintained in London and Dublin as well as in Belfast. This too would help to meet unionist concerns about the location of the existing Secretariat at Maryfield without abandoning the real benefits to both governments of maintaining a joint office to deal informally with matters of actual or potential political conflict and to exchange information on particular incidents or issues of immediate concern.

5. CONCLUSION

A recasting of the Agreement along these broader lines would help to remind all the people of Britain and Ireland that the enterprise initiated in 1981 by Mr Haughey and Mrs Thatcher was intended to provide for the totality of relationships between Britain and Ireland.[1] It would assist greatly in securing the full participation of unionists in the new institutions. In so doing it would provide a renewed opportunity to achieve peace, stability, and reconciliation in and over Northern Ireland as a unique frontier zone between two member states of the European Community. And as in the case of the European Community it would not be necessary to prescribe in advance how the new relationships and institutions would develop in the future.

Notes

1. Editors' note: The Review of the Anglo-Irish Intergovernmental Conference was made public on 24 May 1989 (see Appendix 2). Kevin Boyle and Tom Hadden had submitted their contribution a few weeks earlier. See also Hadden and Boyle (1989).

8

Scenarios for Progress in Northern Ireland

Paul Bew and Henry Patterson

OVER three years after the signing of the Anglo-Irish Agreement, the actual short term result of the initiative which had aroused so much optimism in London and Dublin was plain enough. *Fortnight* magazine, Northern Ireland's independent review, commented:

The Agreement was meant to isolate terrorism and squeeze it through security co-operation.
FACT: The Provos demonstrated last year their consummate ability to up the ante.
It was meant to marginalize Sinn Féin.
FACT: Its vote indeed fell between 1985 and 1987—from 11.8 per cent to 11.4 per cent.
It was assumed Protestant opinion would eventually moderate towards the deal.
FACT: The *Belfast Telegraph* poll in the autumn found that opinion, if anything, had *hardened* against it.
The accord was meant to deliver reform of the administration of justice.
FACT: In 1988 the government presided over a more draconian package of 'security' measures than anything since internment.
It was meant to produce devolution.
FACT: Protestant opinion has moved away from devolution, while the SDLP now insists unionists must talk to Dublin about how they 'share this island.'
Oh, and the Agreement was meant to end 'megaphone diplomacy' between Ireland and Britain. Mrs Thatcher has certainly put the megaphone away—she's brought out a 1000-watt loudspeaker instead. The reality is this—and it's neither a unionist nor a nationalist 'reality': the set of relationships condensed in the northern crisis is far more complex than the crass political simplicities of the Agreement ever allowed. It was ludicrously naive of Dublin governments of either hue to assume that Thatcherism could be

persuaded, just through engaging it in dialogue, to pursue a reformist programme in the north when every bone in its political body is *contra-reformist*. And if there was one thing that was guaranteed to unify unionism behind its most reactionary elements, it was the linking of reform of the north to an alleged Dublin role within it—however insignificant in practice—and all done over their heads. (*Fortnight*, January 1989)

But something else was also clear. In the short term the Agreement might have failed to achieve its objectives. (Probably the grandiose aims of 'peace' and 'reconciliation' were always unobtainable but it had failed also to provide a form of direct rule as stable as that of the 1984–5 period.) Direct rule with a green tinge was almost twice as violent as that without.[1] But it was none the less evident that the Unionist 'campaign' against the Agreement was dead.

What follows is an attempt to work out the implications of these political realities: as such it builds upon previous arguments we have developed elsewhere (Bew and Patterson 1987, 1988). At this point it is necessary to make an injunction against dogmatism; this is more than a piety. As John Redmond, the nationalist leader, somewhat flatly put it in 1906, 'mistakes have been made upon our side, as well as upon the other' (Bew 1987: 123). No one 'side' in the Northern Ireland conflict can claim a monopoly of political virtue. Neither mainstream unionism nor mainstream nationalism has come to terms with its poor record in the handling of minority rights. If there is to be a benign resolution of the Northern Ireland crisis it will depend upon the significance of factors which we have not yet been able to detect. What follows is a review of realities—unpalatable as many of these are to the authors. We profoundly hope that one or more of the key players will display an imaginative and flexible disposition and thus transform the overall context of conflict.

1. THE ULSTER UNIONIST PERSPECTIVE

Let us turn first to the likely development of local Ulster Unionist policy. Here there has been much unrealistic projection by writers unfamiliar with trends within Northern Ireland. Many fail to perceive the degree to which the history of Northern Ireland has imprinted unionism (and sadly also nationalism) with many features of sectarianism, rigidity, and immobilism. The broad trends in unionist opinion since the signing of the Anglo-Irish Agreement were clear enough: the *Fortnight* poll of April 1988 showed that only

4 per cent of Protestants felt the Agreement had been of value to them. Two-thirds of those polled saw no hope for the future. There was still widespread support for the principle of power-sharing—as Table 8.1 shows—but 72 per cent of Protestants wanted a form of suspension of the Anglo-Irish Agreement before the opening of any talks on an internal settlement.

TABLE 8.1.   *Poll on power-sharing, April 1988 (%)*

'Thinking now about power-sharing between the political parties in Northern Ireland would you say that you agree or disagree with this principle?'

Community	Agree	Disagree	Don't know
Protestants	56	42	2
Catholics	84	15	1
TOTAL	68	30	2

Source: Fortnight, Apr. 1988.

There was another significant development. As Robin Wilson, the Editor of *Fortnight,* has pointed out,

As in previous polls in recent years, integration with Great Britain came out clearly on top, with 32% support. But, as before, this was heavily skewed, with 9% of Catholics endorsing this straightforwardly Unionist option. The 47% Protestant support for integration, however, indicates a marked 12% shift from the Coopers and Lybrand poll directly after the Agreement was signed. These Protestants, disproportionately middle-class, have turned away from direct rule, and to a lesser extent from the options of power-sharing devolution and Stormont majority rule—an indication perhaps of the insecurity instilled by the Agreement and of alienation from the local political process. (*Fortnight,* April 1988)

These are the unpalatable implications which may be drawn from Table 8.2.

In early October 1988 the *Belfast Telegraph*'s opinion poll broadly confirmed the findings of the April poll. As the newspaper's leader concluded,

The picture has altered significantly since January 1986, when a poll taken in the wake of the Agreement put devolution at the top of the list, with 24%, followed by integration, with 23%. Today integration has roared ahead, approved by 30% and the runner-up is devolved power-sharing, on 25%.

TABLE 8.2. *Poll on the best form of government for Northern Ireland, April 1988 (%)*

'Looking at this list, which of these forms of government do you personally think would be the best for Northern Ireland?'

Form of government	Protestant	Catholic	All
Complete integration with Great Britain	47	9	32
Direct rule	4	2	3
Devolution with power-sharing	17	31	23
Devolution with majority rule	14	1	9
Independent Northern Ireland	7	4	6
Joint Authority between London and Dublin	1	12	5
Federal Ireland	1	7	3
United Ireland	1	25	10
Don't know	8	10	9

Source: Fortnight, Apr. 1988.

Protestants account for the increased support for integration, reflecting not only their frustration with the present form of direct rule, linked to the Anglo-Irish Agreement, but, to some extent, the higher profile of the equal-citizenship campaigners.[2] Integrationists have won nearly half the Protestant voters to their cause—up 12% in three years—but have yet to make any impression on the Catholics or, it has to be added, the British parties themselves. While Protestants cling closer to Britain to escape the implications of the Anglo-Irish Agreement, there is evidence that Catholics are drawing away from Dublin. In 1986, 43% of Catholics opted for a united Ireland and a direct role in government for the Republic; the comparable figure today is 35%. (*Belfast Telegraph,* 6 October 1988)

The other remarkable feature of the poll was the degree of support for the notion that mainland British parties (Conservative, Labour, and SDP) should organize in Northern Ireland. While polls had regularly shown a higher degree of support for the general principle, the *Belfast Telegraph* poll found that many voters claimed that they would actually vote for a 'British party'; in particular, the poll implied that the Conservatives would become the second largest party in the province. (This prospect, far from enticing him, alarmed Secretary of State Tom King, who threw his weight against it in a series of incoherent interventions.)

But in terms of short-term relevance the most important implications of the poll concerned the prospects for power-sharing devolution within the framework of the Anglo-Irish Agreement, which was, after all, the government's official policy.

Thus it was significant that only 18 per cent of Protestants saw power-sharing devolution as the best way forward—and of these we may confidently assume a significant proportion would have been opposed to the simultaneous continuance of the Anglo-Irish Agreement upon which the two governments unalterably insist. The point is a simple one, though it is often ignored by commentators: given the lack of enthusiastic commitment to the principle of power-sharing devolution by Protestants, is it likely that enough Protestants would have been prepared to make painful concessions in the area of the Irish dimension to bring about something which they are not especially keen on in the first place? Let us not lose sight of the fact that 4 per cent of Protestants favoured direct rule, 47 per cent integration, while 14 per cent favoured the total non-runner of majority-rule devolution. In general terms, there is widespread acceptance of the principle of power-sharing. It is also true to say that devolution is an acceptable second choice for many people. But it is clear that the current complex of public opinion militates seriously against the likelihood of devolution taking place within the framework of the Agreement (the only context which is likely to be on offer). Such a development will not therefore take place unless public opinion shifts substantially.

In such a context, what then is Official Unionist strategy? Here it is interesting to look at the ideas of Enoch Powell, former South Down Unionist MP, and Jim Molyneaux, leader of the Official Unionist Party. The Powell–Molyneaux thesis is a fairly coherent one: even if it is open to question on a number of historical points. In their view, British policy has for a long time—perhaps since 1920—been directed at keeping Northern Ireland at arm's length in order to facilitate its eventual merger into the Irish state. Certainly Powell believes that this policy pre-dates the 'current troubles'. He argues that American pressure exercised through the Foreign Office has been in favour of uniting Ireland and thereby bringing it into NATO. The international dimensions of this argument inevitably contain many questionable assumptions, as does Powell's thesis that a changing international scene in the late 1980s (initiated by Gorbachev) is reducing UK sensitivity to US pressure. But if we leave aside the uncertain international superstructure of this argument its more narrowly domestic content is clear. The Anglo-Irish Agreement insists symbolically that Northern Ireland is different from the rest of the UK: the acceptance of a *legislative* power-sharing devolved government *within* that framework would further accentuate that difference. Therefore, it is the strategy of most Official Unionists to argue that Northern Irish MPs should have the same input into the legislative process as other MPs. This means the end of the Order in Council system which has operated since direct rule and which has curtailed the possible contribution of MPs elected in Northern Ireland.

The defence of the Order in Council system has, of course, been that eventually Northern Ireland should have its own legislative assembly to debate fully these matters. Reform of the Order in Council system would imply, at the least, that the government realistically assumed that such a Northern Ireland legislative assembly was a non-starter in current conditions. Hence the weight Molyneaux has placed on the establishment of an Ulster Grand Committee at Westminster, which could probably be combined with a low-level form of administrative devolution on implicit if not explicit 'power-sharing' lines in Ulster itself. The guiding notion here is that such a step would symbolically halt the drift of UK policy in favour of disengagement. It also does not require the abrogation of the Anglo-Irish Agreement (though Molyneaux would prefer it to be symbolically altered) and indeed SDLP MPs would also benefit from the improvement of their position in the House of Commons. It seems probable therefore that Molyneaux (and perhaps a successor such as John Taylor) would be able to keep the Official Unionist Party united around such a perspective. It eschews the full-blooded integrationism of Robert McCartney QC (now expelled from the Official Unionists after a serious leadership bid failed), and it eschews also the full-blooded power-sharing concepts of Ken Maginess, the Fermanagh MP, who leads what is currently a small minority of power-sharing devolutionists within the Official Unionist Party. Thus the Official Unionists are aiming for a pragmatic 'centrism'—setting objectives which are not obviously tainted with 'impossibilism'.

To a remarkable degree, though with occasional difference of emphasis, the Paisleyite DUP has gone along with these perspectives. In part this reflects the serious intellectual bankruptcy of Paisleyism; as a party the DUP's electoral surge peaked in 1981 and since then (despite Paisley's huge personal vote in the 1985 Euro election) it has failed to dent the hegemony of Official Unionism;[3] indeed, the Anglo-Irish Agreement has, perhaps surprisingly, merely accentuated this development. It is now necessary to turn to the development of nationalist strategy since 1985.

2. THE NATIONALIST DEBATE

The development of nationalist politics since the signing of the Agreement has shown signs of some movement and subtlety. There has clearly been a continuing reappraisal of strategy on the part of both the SDLP and Sinn Féin. In the early phase—from November 1985 to mid-1987—John Hume, the SDLP leader, appears to have believed that Unionists would accept power-sharing devolution within the framework of the Anglo-Irish Agreement. This was in line with his long-stated viewpoint that Britain had to confront unionist obduracy in a decisive way. Hume's insistence on the role of Britain here had always concealed an avoidance of one key question: what if unionist obduracy was due less to British irresolution and more to the unappealing (sectarian, violent, economically problematical) offer of nationalism? This lacuna in Hume's thought proved to be decisive: despite his prediction that unionists would negotiate with him by the end of 1986, no such negotiations took place.

Hume's interest in devolution within the framework of the Agreement declined for two other reasons. The change of government and the re-election of Charles Haughey (as opposed to the pro-devolution Garret FitzGerald) as *Taoiseach* substantially reduced Dublin's support for the principle of devolution. Also Sinn Féin's electoral resilience in the 1987 Westminster general election made it clear that the much-predicted Republican electoral melt-down had not taken place. Significantly in this context, only 1 in 6 Catholics (according to the *Fortnight* poll) felt the Agreement had helped the minority community.

The combination of these three developments pointed Hume in one direction: a seven-month-long dialogue with Sinn Féin. This was facilitated by Sinn Féin's well-established desire to avoid political isolation and marginalization—a marginalization which was the objective of the Anglo-Irish Agreement. As early as 1977, the new northern leadership which had taken control of the IRA and Sinn Féin had warned their supporters of the need to face up to a 'long war' of attrition against the 'British presence'. This demanded a new strategy of politicizing the movement, developing Sinn Féin into a political party of substance, and expanding the 'struggle' into the political system in the Irish Republic.

The new approach was massively assisted by the hunger strikes which created the conditions for the political breakthrough of 1982 and 1983. However, Gerry Adams recognizes that as long as the Sinn Féin vote is contained at around 30–40 per cent of the Catholic electorate—as seems likely—the impetus of the 1982 electoral surge may well dissipate. To deal with this and also with the narrow limits of Sinn Féin support in the Republic, the Sinn Féin leadership has been keen to create conditions for a broader 'nationalist coalition', including Fianna Fáil and the SDLP, aimed at mobilizing opinion, domestically and internationally, against the 'British presence'. Clearly there are major problems with, and obstacles to, the realization of this strategy. One obstacle is what Adams has called an 'ultra-leftism' amongst sections of the Republican movement (Adams 1988). This defines Fianna Fáil and the SDLP as 'bourgeois' parties which will sell out the struggle for national liberation. For Adams and the mainstream leadership such leftism merely serves to marginalize Sinn Féin in the Catholic community. Clearly influenced by the 1930s debate in the Republic Congress, the leadership objective is to create a united front with the SDLP, a 'constructive' and 'intimate' dialogue, and hope that by Sinn Féin's more energetic and committed role in such a united front it can demonstrate to SDLP supporters that Sinn Féin are the 'real' nationalists. Whether the SDLP is willing to let itself be put in such a position is, of course, another question—following the elections of the summer of 1989, with a substantial gap now opening up between SDLP and Sinn Féin electoral performance (even though Sinn Féin was more than holding on to its urban-ghetto core) it seemed that the political differences between the two nationalist groupings were widening rather than narrowing.

The Sinn Féin/SDLP meetings were abruptly terminated by Hume after the accidental killing by the IRA of two of his Catholic constituents. Then the two parties made public a series of lengthy and illuminating documents.[4] These touched on all the most salient points of modern Anglo-Irish politics. The most moving moment in these papers is undoubtedly the SDLP's quotation of Parnell's great Belfast speech of 1891: 'until . . .the prejudices of the [Protestant] minority, whether reasonable or unreasonable, are conciliated . . . Ireland can never enjoy perfect freedom, Ireland can never be united'.⁵ In fact, despite this attractive notion, the SDLP text falls short of acknowledging a unionist right to say 'no' to Irish unity.

Commentators generally felt there were two obvious weaknesses in the presentation of the two sides. For Sinn Féin the weakness was an insistence (based on a text by the unrepresentative figure of Sir Patrick Macrory, a strong friend of Ulster Unionism) that Britain had a continuing strategic interest in Irish division. For the SDLP the weakness was an insistence that the text of the Anglo-Irish Agreement had, in effect, rendered Britain 'neutral' on the question of partition. Whilst this interpretation was supported by influential journalists such as John Lloyd of the *Financial Times* but apparently disputed somewhat by Tom King, the Secretary of State for Northern Ireland, in a speech to the Institute of Directors in Belfast, it seems clear that had the SDLP contented itself with the observation that Britain was 'ambivalent' on partition it would have won wider assent for its position.

Since the breakdown of the talks, Hume has accentuated his attack on Sinn Féin's unwillingness to call a ceasefire. At the SDLP party conference in the autumn of 1988, Hume denounced the Provisionals as 'Fascists' and he maintained this hostile tone in an interview with former prominent Unionist Frank Millar in the *Irish Times* in January 1989. In part this was merely Hume's pre-election mode; in the 1984 European election he had swollen his excellent harvest of votes by surrendering hard-line nationalist territory to Sinn Féin and by winning over moderate Alliance-inclined Catholics. In 1989 he obviously (and in political terms reasonably) intended to do the same thing. Nevertheless, Hume's new-found insistence that no British government could ever do business with an active terrorist organization seemed to be deep-rooted.

It also seemed to have impressed the Sinn Féin leadership—which, however, faced the difficulty that from their point of view without violence the Northern Irish situation would merely co-agulate and set in a rut. Adams, however, was keenly aware that certain indiscriminate actions of terrorism had weakened the credibility of the IRA both internationally and domestically. His move to disarm one Donegal-based grouping allegedly responsible for such actions in January 1989 was widely dismissed as a publicity stunt. In fact, it may presage a more subtle Republican approach. Secure in the knowledge that large stock of Libyan supplies of Semtex allow the organization to retain the initiative, the Republican leadership might like to see a less persistent but more dramatic and equally drawn-out campaign focused more explicitly on 'military' targets. But this can only be speculation—what is clear is that there is considerable movement within nationalist politics. It can only be hoped that such movement will allow an accommodation with a demoralized Unionism rather than reduce that possibility.

3. PROSPECTIVE BRITISH GOVERNMENT POLICY

The difficulty about British policy is a profound one. One has to have sympathy for any British politician or official landed with the intractable problems of Ireland—but the fact remains that the UK government's ability to communicate with large sections of relatively 'reasonable' opinion in both communities seems to have broken down. Technically, there are a number of options open to a British government which wanted to open up lines of communication with the unionist community. None of them should be fetishized and there are drawbacks in all of them. The British government could reintroduce the border poll—as a way of attempting to separate questions of internal reform from creeping unification. It could improve the handling of Northern Ireland business at Westminster. The Conservative Party could agree to organize in Northern Ireland—in response to a relatively articulate and well-organized campaign. The critical point is that the British government abandons not the Agreement, but the elements of its mid-1980s intellectual baggage which are now entirely redundant. For the nationalist community, it is essential that the Agreement be kept in place. It must be made to function as a symbol of minority rights: a useful bargaining chip. It is also essential that the material deprivation in nationalist areas be challenged—if necessary by departures from strict Thatcherite orthodoxy.

In the conclusion to *The British State and the Ulster Crisis* (Bew and Patterson 1985), we argued for an active, reformist role for the British state in fields like the economy, structural inequality, and security. Such proposals were made before the Hillsborough agreement. One important question raised by the developments since Hillsborough is just how radically it has narrowed the possibilities of the type of reforms we envisaged then.

It is not being cynical to suggest that it was Thatcherism's bleak implications for a peripheral area of the United Kingdom with a weakening industrial base that provided one of the attractions of the approach to managing the conflict embodied in the Agreement. The depressing realities of significantly higher rates of unemployment among Catholics and multiple forms of deprivation in the ghettos of Belfast and Derry which pre-dated Thatcher's arrival in office have inevitably worsened under governments which prioritize 'market forces' and have been so fundamentally averse to the public sector— the area where it has been easiest to create employment and deal with inequality in employment.

The institutionalization of the 'Irish dimension' such as the Agreement has entailed could provide little effective compensation for such material realities unless the British government was seriously committed to dealing with the crucial economic dimensions of Catholic grievance. In fact it could eventually prove counter-productive as the talk of cherishing and protecting the 'Two Traditions' is exposed as an emollient façade. Governing Northern Ireland appears to be conducted on the assumption that a sizeable proportion of the Catholic working class is consigned to the role of an effectively excluded under-class.

On the issue of fair employment the British government is at present in danger of creating an explosive mixture of frustrated expectation and fear and resentment. The legislation on fair employment, at present being considered by Parliament, is supposed to strengthen the institutional mechanisms and legal powers dealing with discriminatory employment practices. The proposals have produced predictable responses from the unionist parties while being criticized by the SDLP and Sinn Féin for not going far enough (Jay 1989). The issue is obviously a complex and highly charged one. Yet, as we argued in 1985, it must be at the centre of any reformist agenda for Northern Ireland. It inevitably produces some degree of political polarization. Yet the extent of this will be influenced by the political and economic context in which anti-discrimination measures are introduced. It certainly does not help the process of reform in Northern Ireland if they can be represented as part of some hidden agenda of creeping unification. If at the same time they are to be introduced in the absence of any prospect of substantial new employment opportunities a 'zero-sum' mentality and communal polarization are real dangers.

The Agreement is a reality, or as one local commentator put it,

The task for the next 20 years . . . must not be to continue arguing over whether the Anglo-Irish Agreement can be made to work if it doesn't, or suspended so that something can take its place. Under Thatcherism and Haugheyism at least, it won't and it won't be. (*Fortnight* editorial, January 1989)

The Agreement has ushered in a period of more unstable direct rule—direct rule with a 'green tinge'. It has encouraged a form of managing the Northern Ireland conflict which takes as its prime concern the manipulation of communal identifications. But there is a real limit to the degree to which Catholics can be satisfied by the humiliations and discomfitures of Protestants. Arguably that limit has been reached. If we can, as we must, envisage British and Irish politics after Thatcherism, then there is no reason to assign the same role to the institutions created at Hillsborough. They have not ushered in a 'new dawn' in Northern Ireland. If they continue to be used by constitutional nationalists as a platform from which to attempt to launch even more ambitious 'all-Ireland' constitutional agendas, then the prospects of any progress are slim. At the centre of the tasks of any post-Thatcher government which wants to move out of the present impasse, and we admit that there is a major question mark over any future government's capacity to look critically at the legacy of Hillsborough, must be an attempt to deal with the necessary reformist agenda in a way that clearly separates it from conflicting aspirations on the constitutional future of Northern Ireland. A set of Anglo-Irish institutions within which the British government made clear its commitment to achieving real moves to substantive equality between Protestants and Catholics economically and before the law would entail a break with the present combination of free-market principles and authoritarian statism. While leaving 'ultimate' constitutional aspirations untouched, it would provide for a more expansive and positive form of citizenship within Northern Ireland, whether or not it entailed a substantial increase in public investment for job creation as the essential basis for a serious assault on structural inequality, and legal reforms to improve citizens' rights in relation to the state, including a genuinely independent system for investigating complaints against the police and a Bill of Rights.

In this essay we have deliberately aimed for a certain degree of fluidity and flexibility in our presentation. There is a danger on all sides of the adoption of self-righteous and rigid postures. In our discussion we have mostly confined ourselves to an assessment of what is actually happening—as opposed to those progressive and benign developments that we would like to see happening. We have outlined certain possible paths of development. In our view *any* path of development which might hold out the hope for a modest reduction in sectarian division in Northern Irish society ought to be seriously considered.

Notes

1. Editors' note: The authors' argument only holds true for the short period before and after the Anglo-Irish Agreement. As demonstrated in Appendix 3 violence in the early years of direct rule was far higher than in the years before and after the signing of the Hillsborough agreement.

2. The reference here is to the Campaign for Equal Citizenship (CEC)—an articulate pressure group still led by the high-profile QC Robert McCartney. This group has undoubtedly raised a new issue—the denial of the right of British citizens resident in Northern Ireland to join Tory or Labour Parties if they so wish. The group has, however, also been affected by internal disputes and a certain utopianism, which may reduce its longterm impact. So far its main success has been with the 'quality' British Press—at different times, the *Guardian*, *The Times*, the *Daily Telegraph* and the *Independent* have all carried leaders in support of the CEC's main plank. In the European election of May 1989 the two candidates endorsed by the CEC, L. Kennedy (Conservative) and M. Langhammer (Labour), managed just to exceed the total of the leader of the well-established Alliance Party, John Alderdice. This was a considerable achievement but hardly a dramatic breakthrough. It means that Alliance and the 'equal citizenship' lobby (predominantly Tory) share about a 10% 'middle ground' of the province-wide vote. Neither of these forces has real support west of the Bann, but in the Greater Belfast area it constitutes a considerable slice of non-nationalist opinion. The possibility exists that this constituency will wilt if the Conservatives do not receive the national backing from the Conservative Central Office they are seeking later this year. This would probably be mainly to the advantage of the OUP.
   Editors' note: See ch. 4 for details of the CEC's case.

3. Editors' note: See App. 4 for a discussion of support for political parties in Northern Ireland.

4. For the best review so far, see Bradley (1988).

5. Bew (1980: 127–31) gives the background to this speech.

9

Joint Authority

Anthony Kenny

IF the problems of Northern Ireland are to be solved by constitutional means, there are only four main possibilities of solution.
Northern Ireland may be governed—as it is now—by Britain; or it
may be governed—as it would if Irish nationalists had their wish—
by Ireland. Or it might be governed by neither, and become an
independent state. Or, conceivably, it might be governed by both,
under some system of joint sovereignty or joint authority.

Solutions of the fourth kind have been explored from time to time.
In 1972 the Social Democratic and Labour Party in Northern Ireland,
the constitutional, non-violent, nationalist party, produced a document called *Towards a New Ireland*. This explored the concept of joint
sovereignty, not as a permanent or long-term prospect for Northern
Ireland, but as an interim regime before the advent of the united
Ireland to which nationalists aspired. This document was not much
studied outside the confines of the party which produced it. But
matters changed when, in 1983, the nationalist parties of Ireland,
North and South, gathered together in Dublin to meet in the New
Ireland Forum to spell out the ways in which they hoped to achieve
the unity of Ireland by consent rather than by force. In the context of
the Forum, for the first time, joint authority was considered as a
durable constitution for Northern Ireland.

In November 1983 a submission on the topic of joint sovereignty
was made to the New Ireland Forum by two university teachers of
philosophy, Dr Bernard Cullen from Queen's University Belfast, and
Dr Richard Kearney from University College, Dublin.[1] Cullen, an
executive member of the Belfast Trades Council, had started from a
Unionist background, Kearney, editor of *The Crane Bag Journal of Irish
Studies*, had originally been a believer in a United Ireland. Both had
come to believe that joint sovereignty in Northern Ireland would

provide a framework 'within which the distinctive cultural–historical identity of both major traditions in Northern Ireland may be fully
preserved and advanced'.

The problems of Northern Ireland, they submitted, arose from the
cohabitation of two groups of people with conflicting senses of their
own national and cultural identity. Each community had a set of
traditional ideals, with an ultimate aspiration. The majority of the
Catholics were Irish nationalists, with an ultimate aspiration for a
united Ireland, separate from Britain; but within the Catholic community there were different degrees of commitment to this ideal,
from a vague sentimental wish to a willingness to suffer and kill for
it. On the other hand the majority of the inhabitants see themselves
as Protestants and unionists, and have as their ultimate aspiration
complete constitutional separation from the Republic, as something
alien and threatening, and dependence on Great Britain as the
guarantor of that separation. Any stable governmental institutions
for Northern Ireland must give meaningful expression to both
identities: Irish Catholic and British Protestant.

Kearney and Cullen urged the Forum to realize that the unionists
of Northern Ireland can neither be coerced nor cajoled into a united
Ireland: nor chased out of Ireland. Their British identity must be
accommodated in any new constitutional arrangement. On the other
hand, they said

The long and powerful historical memories of the nationalist community—
closely bound up with the persecution of Catholics in Ireland, and present
even in those who would vehemently deny that they were 'anti-British'—
make any arrangement which excludes the Republic from a say in the affairs
of Northern Ireland ultimately unworkable.

The conclusion was that each community must make concessions,
and renounce the aim of hegemony over the other.

Both communities must renounce the absolute separatism of what we have
called their ultimate aspirations (namely, separatism from Ireland and
Britain, respectively). They can do this, however, without sacrificing the
national identity which they see as guaranteeing their cultural security. In
each case the kernel of their legitimate aspiration is retained, but in a
modified form. The unionists demand British sovereignty over Northern
Ireland. The nationalists demand Irish sovereignty over Northern Ireland. It
is in the light of the foregoing arguments that we are proposing joint British
and Irish sovereignty over Northern Ireland.

Joint governance would involve an equal degree of generosity and an equal degree of concession on both sides: neither side must be seen to 'win'. There followed a sketch of what this would mean in practice: either a British or Irish passport could be carried; there would be two national anthems and two national flags, both equally prominent; the Irish language would be encouraged but not imposed; religious views peculiar to one denomination would not be enshrined in law, whether they concerned sexual ethics or sabbath observance. But once the principle of joint sovereignty was accepted, political, legal, and economic institutions would have to be worked out in negotiations between the two sovereign governments and the two communities in the province. The institutions would have to include a devolved parliament and government, subject to an intergovernmental commission; and the citizens of Northern Ireland would send elected representatives both to Westminster and to Dublin.

What would happen about topics, such as foreign affairs and defence policy, where the two sovereign governments held conflicting views? There are historical precedents for allowing Northern Ireland simply to opt out of such divisive issues (it had, for example, been exempted from conscription and national service in the UK). It would be reasonable to insist that the Republic's neutrality remain intact: perhaps Northern Ireland could be formally declared a demilitarized zone?

For joint sovereignty to be acceptable certain conditions were necessary. First, it must be seen as a durable, not a transitional, solution, not as a stepping-stone to a united Ireland. Secondly, it must not be imposed: once agreed upon by the two sovereign governments, it must be presented to the people of Northern Ireland in a manner likely to secure significant support in both communities. The members of the New Ireland Forum seem to have felt that this might be an impossible task; at all events, the Forum Report does not mention joint sovereignty as one of its proposals for a New Ireland. Apart from practical considerations, there may have been a number of reasons of principle for this.

To many people sovereignty means, in Blackstone's words, 'a supreme, irresistible, absolute, uncontrolled authority'. If understood in this sense, sovereignty must be indivisible; it would be impossible for any region to recognize more than one sovereign. International lawyers often write as if any cession, or sharing, by a

state of supreme jurisdictional competence would be a diminution of
its statehood and a betrayal of its national heritage.

Historically, however, matters have not been so neatly cut and
dried, as has been shown in an instructive, though unfortunately
unpublished, paper by Lord Justice Bingham.[2] Liechtenstein,
Monaco, and San Marino are generally recognized as sovereign
states, though in each case a number of the functions of sovereignty
are exercised by the more powerful adjacent states of Switzerland,
France, and Italy respectively. Bhutan, though not internationally
recognized as a sovereign state, has been treated as such in agreements with the British government between 1910 and 1949 and the
Indian government since 1949, though in each case the external
relations of the state have been subject to control by the treaty
partner.

It is not only states on the margin of international existence, Lord
Justice Bingham continues, which endure what may appear significant derogations from full sovereignty.

By the State Treaty of 1955 Austria was declared to be neutral in the divide
between East and West. Any political or economic union with Germany is
forbidden, the character of her army is defined, and the possession of atomic
weapons or the manufacture of aircraft to German or Japanese design is
prohibited. Whether association with the European Economic Community
would be a breach of Austrian neutrality is a delicate question on which the
Soviet Union has expressed a clear (and adverse) view.

Sovereign states have retained their sovereignty despite the
presence of foreign bases, invitations to foreign states to restore
order, protectorates exercised by imperial powers. Sovereignty can
even survive leases of territory such as the original Panama Canal
Zone treaty in which within the canal corridor Panama ceded all the
rights, power, and authority of 'which the U.S. would possess the
exercise as if it were the sovereign of the territory . . . to the entire
exclusion of the exercise by the Republic of Panama of any such
sovereign rights, power, or authority'.

One of the most striking instances of shared sovereignty occurred
in Egypt between 1882 and 1922, where the Khedive remained ruler
under Turkish suzerainty while the United Kingdom assumed
certain functions. This condominium is described by Lord Justice
Bingham as 'one of the most striking constitutional arrangements of
modern times':

The administration of justice has always been regarded, at least by lawyers, as a function close to the core of sovereign competence, not something a sovereign would lightly delegate to aliens. This is what, in large measure, Egypt did. There were strong historical reasons for doing so, and the change was undoubtedly for the better. Despite that the story is of interest. The Mixed Courts were founded in 1875. The Court of Appeal in Alexandria originally sat with 11 judges, four Egyptian and seven non-Egyptian . . . The judges [of the various courts] were distributed among the 14 capitulatory powers, but were chosen and appointed by the Egyptian government, were irremovable from office and were (like the judges of the European Court of Justice or the International Court of Justice) independent of the countries from which they came. No attempt was made to relate the nationality of the litigant to the nationality of the judge. The Mixed Courts did not (as I understand) assume jurisdiction where the *lis* was between solely Egyptian partners, and their criminal jurisdiction was until near the end very limited. But the Courts lasted, administering the Mixed Codes and earning a high reputation, until 1949—one of the most successful examples of international cooperation in modern times.

In more recent times, the accession of sovereign nations to the European Community has led to concessions of power, and admissions of transnational jurisdiction, which bid fair to exceed any of the instances cited by Lord Justice Bingham. At the time of the New Ireland Forum this might have been expected to be the most relevant example of the divisibility of sovereignty, since Ireland and Britain had just completed a decade of joint membership of the EEC.

None the less, the members of the Forum decided to avoid the prickly question of the nature of sovereignty. Instead they set up a subcommittee to consider the topic of 'joint authority': its eight members included Senator Jim Dooge and Maurice Manning TD of Fine Gael, and Senator Mary Robinson of the Labour Party, then sharing in coalition government with Fine Gael; the Fianna Fáil opposition was represented by Gerry Collins TD and John Wilson TD, and there were two members of the SDLP.

The subcommittee met five times in January and February 1984 and reported on February 7.[3] According to the first paragraph of the report:

Joint authority is the equal sharing of responsibility and authority for all aspects of the government of Northern Ireland by the governments of Great Britain and Ireland. Power over all matters relating to Northern Ireland would be vested in and exercised by an Executive Joint Authority of the two governments. This Executive Joint Authority would appoint a Joint Authority Commission to run Northern Ireland. Beneath this there could be whatever levels of local responsibility that the Executive Joint Authority might wish to establish and were agreed to by local representatives. A binding agreement or treaty between the two governments would establish the Executive Joint Authority.

The subcommittee gave as its reason for choosing to consider joint authority rather than joint sovereignty that a joint authority approach

would avoid the conflict between the provisions of Arts. 2 and 3 of the Irish Constitution [which set out the Irish claim to the entire island] and Section 1 of the Northern Ireland Constitution Act 1973 [which declares Northern Ireland part of Her Majesty's dominions and of the United Kingdom] while preserving the essential element of joint sovereignty—viz: responsibility for all aspects of government and international relations.

Even while distinguishing between joint sovereignty and joint authority, the subcommittee thought that in order to prevent any conflict with the existing Irish Constitution it might be necessary to add an amendment to the following effect:

No provision of this Constitution invalidates laws enacted, acts done or measures adopted by the State necessitated by the Agreement/Treaty on Joint Authority in regard to Northern Ireland entered into by the Irish Government.

Parallel to the establishment of joint authority a comprehensive and enforceable Bill of Rights would be promulgated ensuring the protection not only of individual but also of communal rights. A constitutional court would need to be set up to interpret and enforce the treaty, and carry out the function of judicial review.

The report proposed for consideration two different models of joint authority. One was a system of 'shared direct rule' in which the Joint Authority Commission exercised all executive powers; the other was a system in which certain powers were reserved to the Commission while the main executive authority was exercised by a local executive supported by a locally elected Assembly.

Under the first model the British and Irish governments would appoint two Commissioners with equal responsibility for all matters dealing with Northern Ireland; these, and two Deputy Commissioners, could be drawn from the Irish or British Parliaments or from locally elected representatives. The two Prime Ministers would meet regularly to review the operation of the Executive Joint Authority, but the Commissioners would be responsible for the day-to-day running of the province; legislation would be enacted, at their initiative, by Orders in Council in Westminster and equivalent ministerial orders in the Irish Parliament.

Under the second model the Assembly would have devolved control over housing, physical infrastructure, agriculture, education, commerce, minor taxation, health, and social services. However, either of the two Commissioners appointed by the sovereign governments would have a veto on legislation or action by the Assembly, and they would retain control over international relations, defence and security, police, the franchise, taxation, the overall level of public expenditure, the courts and law officers, and public service appointments and procedures.

The Assembly might be locally elected in the normal way, or might be based on an Anglo-Irish interparliamentary body. An Executive would be formed from the Assembly: the report left open the question whether it should be chosen by majority vote (weighted or unweighted), or along the lines of power-sharing or rolling devolution. If the Executive became deadlocked or collapsed, devolved powers would return to the Joint Authority Commission.

The subcommittee recommended that joint responsibility for internal security and for a criminal justice regime should be a central component of joint authority. A new police force should be established based on secondment from existing police forces in Great Britain and Ireland with a new command structure.

The establishment of a new enlarged police service representative of the whole community of sufficient size and with a high level of training and equipment should remove the present necessity for the permanent presence of a military back-up. In the event of such a back-up being required at any time its constitution would be for determination by the two sovereign governments.

The Treaty was to provide for full recognition and symbolic expression of British and Irish identities: all citizens would have joint citizenship rights; the flags of both states would have equal status; Northern Ireland citizens could use passports and consuls of either jurisdiction; the diplomatic services of both sovereign states would be briefed by the Joint Authority Executive.

On economic arrangements, the subcommittee proposed that

existing tax levels within Northern Ireland should continue to apply. The overall level of public expenditure would be determined by the Joint Authority Executive, taking into account the availability of external funding and trends in both British and Irish economies. The shortfall between revenue and expenditure, which is now borne by Westminster, would be borne by the two states jointly, in proportions to be agreed (various formulas were suggested in a supporting document).

A secretariat working under the direction of the Joint Authority Commission would replace the Northern Ireland Office. Several models were proposed for the resolution of disagreements which might arise between members of the Joint Authority Commission, including the suggestion that an outside arbitrator might be appointed by the EEC.

The subcommittee's report concluded by summarizing the advantages and disadvantages to be expected from the institution of joint authority.

In favour, first, there would be for the first time an adequate political, symbolic, and administrative expression of the rights of Irish nationalists. Secondly, the arrangement would provide structures with which the nationalists in the North could identify, and which might reverse 'their progressive alienation from existing structures'. Thirdly, the Unionists would have their Britishness, Protestantism, living standards, and security upheld by the continuing involvement of Britain.

If both Governments were fully committed it would not be possible for Unionists or Nationalists to block . . . the basic necessary structures [from operating] . . . There need be no weak link, exposed to pressures (such as the vulnerability of the Faulkner Unionists to the Loyalist strike in 1974). If any subordinate structures collapsed, the joint authorities could simply carry on joint direct rule.

Joint authority could be implemented immediately, and could provide a period during which unionist confidence could mature, given experience of good and equitable government by the British and Irish authorities; it would enhance security by providing a superstructure for security arrangements with which nationalists could identify. The financial support of the North could be maintained without unsustainable burdens being placed on the South.

But the subcommittee concluded by very fairly drawing attention to the disadvantages which might follow. Joint authority would fall short of the full nationalist aspiration; and the continued involvement of Britain might detract from the readiness of nationalists to identify with the new structures. Unionists, who had reacted so strongly against Sunningdale, might be even more alienated by the present proposals.

Unionists are already disenchanted with direct rule by English overlords: they could be even less enthusiastic about a form of double direct rule. An absence of identification with the structures could promote greater instability than already exists.

The most fascinating passage in the subcommittee's report considered what should happen if and when nationalists became a majority in Northern Ireland. Perhaps the British would wish to end their presence then, in accordance with Section 1 of the 1973 Act; and indeed nationalists might hope that joint authority might gradually win Protestant confidence and lessen Protestant repugnance to Irish unity.

On the other hand, the British might wish to remain involved even after that point was reached, or might feel obliged to respond to a Unionist wish that they should. It could be argued that if Joint Authority is justified where there is a Nationalist minority of 35–40% it would be equally justified where there was a substantial Unionist minority in the North.

The subcommittee's proposal, however, did not figure, even as an appendix, in the final published Forum Report. Continued Fianna Fáil participation in the Forum was made conditional on the unitary state—the united Ireland of tradition—being given prominence as the Forum's preferred option. The system of joint authority, along with a sketch of a federal/confederal state, were described simply as proposals received as to how unionist and nationalist identities and interests could be accommodated in different ways and in varying degrees in a new Ireland. Only the broad outlines of the concept were set out in the Report.

The Forum Report was published in May 1984 (New Ireland Forum 1984). In its immediate aftermath neither the Irish nor the British government was anxious to explore publicly the possibilities of joint authority. The Irish Prime Minister preferred to emphasize the open-endedness of the Report, summed up in its statement 'that the parties in the Forum remain open to discuss other views which may contribute to political development'. On the British side, while the Northern Ireland Act of 1973 did not expressly rule out that while continuing to be a part of the United Kingdom Northern Ireland should become also part of the Irish Republic, it was quite clear that joint authority as described in the Forum Report would be a violation of the spirit of the Act if imposed without consent and would be unlikely to be endorsed if submitted to a plebiscite. As the Secretary of State, James Prior, said in the Westminster debate on the Forum Report, the Act was meant to guarantee 'The Unionists right . . . not only to belong to the United Kingdom *but to be apart from the Republic'* (*Parliamentary Debates* (Commons), 2 July 1984, col. 25).

Joint authority, in the months after the Forum, received some eloquent support from the SDLP leader John Hume; but in the United Kingdom in general it found almost no welcome. As described in the subcommittee's report it seemed indistinguishable, except in name, from joint sovereignty. Such a significant alteration in sovereignty could not be made without Northern Ireland consent, and such consent was unlikely to be forthcoming.

Moreover, there was little enthusiasm for examples of joint sovereignty elsewhere in the world. The Anglo-French condominium in the New Hebrides was widely regarded as a fiasco; the quadripartite treaty which set up the Republic of Cyprus, and subjected its Constitution to the oversight of guaranteeing powers, had not achieved its aim of facilitating the peaceful coexistence of antagonistic groups. It was not surprising that the Forum's joint authority proposal should have been, along with a united Ireland and a federal Ireland, firmly rejected by Mrs Thatcher in her famous 'Out, out, out' press conference of November 1984.

Some elements of the joint authority model, however, received a cautious welcome in the Report of the Kilbrandon Committee in 1985. This was an independent inquiry, set up by the constitutional expert Lord Kilbrandon at the request of the British Irish Association, to examine the practicability of the Forum proposals. The Committee was drawn from all parties and included a former Conservative Cabinet Minister, David Howell, and Lord Underhill, the Deputy Leader of the Opposition in the Lords. Like Mrs Thatcher and almost everyone else in Britain the Committee considered impracticable each of the three frameworks for a new Ireland put forward in the Report. But it considered that the Forum's proposals on joint authority contained ideas which provided scope for progress in Northern Ireland (Kilbrandon Committee 1984).·

The majority of the Committee, indeed, put forward as their favoured recipe for progress a model which owed much to the Forum subcommittee's work. The option they proposed, which they named 'co-operative devolution' aimed to combine a degree of involvement of the Republic in the affairs of the province with a substantial return of control to locally elected politicians.

To be effective in Northern Ireland a devolved executive must be representative, it must have an effective decision procedure, and it must be made proof against boycott. The Kilbrandon majority proposed that, under overall British sovereignty, the top tier of government within the province was to be a five-man executive, consisting of the Secretary of State or his deputy, the Minister of Foreign Affairs of the Irish Republic, and three members elected by the voters of Northern Ireland, in such a way that two of them were representative of the majority community, and one of them was representative of the minority. (The three European Members of Parliament from Northern Ireland, Paisley, Taylor, and Hume,[4] might fill this role: they had been democratically elected and already had experience of working together to promote the interests of the province within the EEC.) Such an executive would be fairly representative: the majority would be represented 2 to 1 among the local members, and the minority plus their patron would be two-fifths of the body, which is approximately their proportion among the population.

Within the executive, a simple majority of those present and voting should be decisive. The constitution of the executive would be such that it could not be predicted that there would be a uniform voting pattern. No doubt there would be occasions when the British and unionist vote would unite to outvote the nationalist and Irish vote. But nationalists have consistently preferred rule from Westminster to Stormont majority rule: this implies that there are likely to be matters in which Westminster will favour nationalists against unionists. The Secretary of State, or his representative, would, in effect, be holding the balance between the Orange and Green votes: this would reflect the underlying reality of British sovereignty over a divided province, while allowing the fullest practical sharing of power among local representatives. To cover all eventualities, the UK government would no doubt wish to reserve a power of veto, in certain matters, to its own representative.

Such an executive would be comparatively boycott-proof because if all the local representatives adopted a boycott the default position was in effect joint rule by the Westminster and Dublin members. There would, in fact, be little incentive for a single local faction to boycott, since that would involve forfeiting its own share of power and leaving local power in the hands of its opponents.

Parallel to the five-member political executive, the Kilbrandon majority suggested, there should be a co-operative police authority. The Kilbrandon Committee rejected the Forum's proposals for a joint police force, but it thought that there should be representation of the Irish Republic on the police authority to control the RUC. This authority should consist of the Northern Ireland Office Minister responsible for security, the Minister of Justice or his deputy from the Republic, and three Northern Ireland citizens, two to represent the majority and one the minority communities. In present circumstances these should not be elected, but nominated by the Secretary of State in consultation with the authorities in the Republic.

The extent of the powers to be given to the political executive were not specified in detail by Kilbrandon: it was suggested that they should initially be modest and then be increased in the light of experience. At the full extent of devolution, the executive could decide on the allocation of resources to particular departments, within an overall budget to be determined by the UK government. It should be concerned with the matters administered through the six Northern Ireland departments of Finance and Personnel, Economic Development, Environment, Agriculture, Education, and Health and Social Services. Ministers for these departments should be appointed by the executive.

The relation between the devolved executive and the existing Northern Ireland Assembly was left vague by the Kilbrandon proposals. It was suggested that the Assembly should 'scrutinise' the conduct of the executive and its ministers; but it was not explained how this was to be reconciled with the responsibility of the Secretary of State to the Westminster Parliament, nor that of the Irish Minister of Foreign Affairs to the Dáil.

Like the Forum subcommittee, the Kilbrandon majority believed that if any form of joint authority was to be successful, it must fulfil three conditions. First, it must be accepted as a durable solution and not as a method of coercing unionists into a United Ireland. Secondly, it should be enshrined in a form which was formal, transparent, and definitive: a Treaty between the two governments, deposited with the United Nations. Thirdly, it should have the possibility of continuing even if there were to be a majority in Northern Ireland who would favour union with the Irish Republic.

Unlike the Forum subcommittee the Kilbrandon Committee believed that throughout the duration of the Treaty sovereignty should remain with the United Kingdom. Moreover, should the Treaty be revoked, all powers conferred under it on representatives of the Irish government should revert to the United Kingdom government. If a majority of the population of Northern Ireland came to wish it, sovereignty should be transfered to Ireland and the Treaty terminated; but a new and symmetrical joint authority Treaty should then be made between the two sovereign states.

The Kilbrandon Report was a completely unofficial study of the New Ireland Forum Report. The members of the Committee saw it as their task, by spelling out possible British responses, to help ensure that the Report was taken seriously in official circles in the United Kingdom, as an expression of the willingness of Irish nationalists and in particular of the Irish Government of Dr Fitzgerald, to assist in achieving a peaceful settlement in Northern Ireland. The eventual response of the British Government showed that the Irish initiative had been taken very seriously indeed.

On 15 November 1985 Mrs Thatcher and Dr FitzGerald signed an accord at Hillsborough Castle by which, for the first time, the British Government allowed the Government of the Republic a formal role in the provisions for the administration of Northern Ireland. The second article of the agreement established an Intergovernmental Conference concerned with Northern Ireland and with relations between the two parts of Ireland, to deal on a regular basis with political matters, security and related matters, legal matters, including the administration of justice, and the promotion of cross-border co-operation.

The basis of the Conference was set out thus:

The United Kingdom Government accept that the Irish Government will put forward views and proposals on matters relating to Northern Ireland within the field of activity of the Conference in so far as those matters are not the responsibility of a devolved administration in Northern Ireland. In the interests of promoting peace and stability, determined efforts shall be made through the Conference to resolve any differences. . . . There is no derogation from the sovereignty of either the United Kingdom Government or the Irish Government, and each retains responsibility for the decisions and administration of government within its own jurisdiction.

Both governments declared their support for a policy of devolution: if a devolved administration should be established, the devolved matters would be taken out of the purview of the Conference. In the meantime, the remaining articles of the Agreement spelt out the areas of concern: Article 5 spoke of the rights and identities of the two traditions, and the protection of human rights and the avoidance of discrimination; Article 6 spoke of the role and composition of the bodies existing in Northern Ireland to safeguard rights and eliminate discrimination; Article 7 spoke of security policy within the province, Article 8 of the enforcement of criminal law and the administration of justice, Article 9 of cross-border co-operation in security, Article 10 of co-operation in economic and social development. Article 11 read:

At the end of three years from signature of this agreement, or earlier if requested by either Government, the working of the conference shall be reviewed by the two Governments to see whether any changes in the scope and nature of its activities are desirable.[5]

The role accorded to the Irish Government by the British Government at Hillsborough fell far short of joint sovereignty, or joint authority either on the Forum model or on the Kilbrandon model. At no point was the Irish Government or its representatives to be allowed to take part in executive decisions. The Conference was to be a framework in which the Irish Government could put forward 'views and proposals' on matters 'which remain the responsibility of the Secretary of State for Northern Ireland'.

In the debates in the British and Irish Parliaments after the signing of the agreement there was much discussion as to whether the role allotted to the Irish Government was or was not purely consultative. Dr FitzGerald, in the Dáil, described it as 'going beyond a consultative role but necessarily, because of the sovereignty issue, falling short of an executive role' (*Dail Debates*, 19 November 1985, col. 2562). At Westminster, a unionist M.P. quoted an Irish academic lawyer as saying that Northern Ireland 'has become subject to the legal rights of two sovereign governments to determine how all matters which go to the heart of sovereignty in that area shall in

future be determined' (*Parliamentary Debates* (Commons), 26
November 1985, col. 780). But Mrs Thatcher insisted that the Intergovernmental Conference 'will have no executive authority either
now or in the future' (col. 750).

Though not a form of joint authority, the Hillsborough agreement
could claim to have achieved some of the symbolic advantages
claimed for joint authority by its supporters. The agreement represented an acceptance of the legitimacy of the nationalist tradition
in the North, and a recognition of the Irish government as the
natural guarantor of the rights of that tradition. The setting up of a
Conference Secretariat meant that Irish civil servants took up official
residence in Belfast. Almost the entire corpus of principles which the
Forum had specified as the basis of a new Ireland, Dr FitzGerald
could boast, had been incorporated into the Anglo-Irish Agreement.

On the other hand, the British Government could claim that the
Agreement meant that the Government of Ireland had accepted the
legitimacy of the existing institutions of the province, so that the
Catholic community in the North should no longer refuse to identify
with them. The advantages from the British point of view were spelt
out very eloquently, if not entirely accurately, by Mr Haughey, then
leader of the Opposition in the Dáil.

For the first time, the legitimacy of Partition has been recognised by the
Republic; the British guarantee to the Unionists has been reinforced by the
Irish Government; and the Government are also endorsing the British
military and political presence in Ireland. The Irish Government are saying
to the world that Northern Ireland is legitimately part of the British State,
that Northern Ireland is no longer part of the national territory. . . . The
absolute sovereignty of the British Government in Northern Ireland has now
been conceded. (*Dail Debates,* 11 November 1985, col. 2584)

This was not, of course, how the Anglo-Irish Agreement was seen
by unionists in Northern Ireland. From the moment of its signing it
was greeted with outrage, Dr FitzGerald being denounced as a viper
and Mrs Thatcher as a traitor. Given that the very first article of the
Agreement affirmed that any change in the status of Northern
Ireland would only come about with the consent of a majority of the
people, the unionist reaction seemed to many people in Great Britain
to be mere paranoia.

But the Hillsborough agreement was, in sober truth, a one-sided
affair. This can be seen if the provisions of the Agreement are
compared with the proposals of the Kilbrandon Committee. When

the Kilbrandon Report was discussed in the Northern Ireland Assembly it was described by a leading unionist politician as 'fantasy and green dreams'. Yet, in several ways, it was less green than what was agreed at Hillsborough.

The Kilbrandon Committee thought that any offer of participation to Dublin must be balanced with a real, and concomitant, return of power to elected Northern Ireland politicians. The Kilbrandon equivalent of the Intergovernmental Conference had not two but five members: in addition to the London and Dublin ministers it had three locally elected politicians. Moreover, unlike the Intergovernmental Conference it was to be subject to scrutiny by the Northern Ireland Assembly. True, the five-man body proposed by Kilbrandon was to have explicit executive power, which the Intergovernmental Conference does not have; but it was felt by many in Belfast that the 'more than consultative' role at the highest level of government was no less sinister than any explicit and limited role in decision-making.

It is easy to understand why unionists felt that the Hillsborough agreement offered them nothing. The British and Irish Governments had hoped that their coming closer would bring victory nearer in the war against terrorism, both by co-operation in the field and by removing any vestige of legitimacy from the IRA. But as unionists constantly remind us, the number of deaths due to terrorism, which had been decreasing before 1985, has increased since the signing of the Agreement. The Irish Government hoped that unionists would be gratified by its affirmation that a united Ireland needs consent, plus its recognition that a majority does not consent; but the sincerity of these statements was called in question by the ambiguous language of their phrasing, and by the refusal to remove from the Irish Constitution the articles which lay claim to the territory of the North.

As I write, the Anglo-Irish Agreement has completed its third year. It cannot be said that it has fulfilled the hopes of those who drew it up; nor, on the other hand, has it justified the fears of those who opposed it.

Though seen as a great symbolic victory for Catholic nationalism, the Agreement has brought very little improvement in the condition of Catholics in Northern Ireland. The grievances which were placed by the Agreement on the agenda for the Intergovernmental Conference—the Diplock Courts, the continuing discrimination in

employment—remain as grievances as yet unresolved to the satisfaction of the complainants.

The goals of both governments were peace, stability, and reconciliation in the province. In the years since the Agreement the
number of violent deaths has increased rather than diminished;[6]
antagonism between the communities has been tense; no real
progress has yet been made towards the establishment of a stable
internal government for the province. Relations between the governments themselves, after an initial honeymoon period, have been
strained in the Agreement's third year. Those who regarded the
Agreement as a wholly inappropriate method of pursuing its goals
have no difficulty in finding evidence to confirm their initial view.

On the other hand, the worst of the fears expressed, on both sides,
at the signing of the Agreement have not been realized. The
unionists did not take up arms in a civil war, and the Irish Secretariat
remains unharmed in Maryfield. The Agreement has not proved a
means of trundling unionists against their will into a united Ireland.
The Northern Ireland judiciary and the Royal Ulster Constabulary
have shown an admirable impartiality, combined with considerable
courage, in enforcing the law under a superstructure which many of
them must have found deeply distasteful.

The Agreement has survived elections in both nations. Mrs
Thatcher's return to power in Britain quashed the hopes of some
unionists that in a hung parliament they might use their bargaining
power to secure the Agreement's abolition. Mr Haughey, having
come to power, has shown a remarkable willingness to operate an
Agreement which in opposition his party denounced as copper-
fastening partition and violating the Republic's Constitution. It has
been left to maverick unionists to challenge the constitutionality of
the Agreement in the Republic's courts.[7]

The Agreement, as has been said, does not involve joint sovereignty or joint authority. Three years into it, how do matters stand
with regard to these more substantial forms of Irish involvement in
the government of the province? Are arguments in favour of joint
authority stronger or weaker than they were when Cullen and
Kearney gave evidence to the New Ireland Forum in 1983?

At first glance, it must seem that the prospects for successful joint
authority have much worsened. If even the modest degree of Irish
involvement conceded at Hillsborough has proved difficult to

implement, how much more difficult would it be to move towards giving the Irish Republic a share in executive authority! If the unionists have proved so intransigent about allowing even a consultative role to the Republic, would they not rise up, goaded at last beyond endurance, if decision-sharing power were to be vested in an Irish minister sitting on a Belfast executive council?

Moreover, the effect of the history of the Agreement on mainland British opinion may well be thought to be adverse to any prospect of joint authority. Joint authority in the forms considered earlier in this paper involves continued long-term involvement by Britain in the affairs of Northern Ireland, prolonged perhaps even after a referendum had transferred sovereignty from Westminster to Dublin. For many years opinion polls have suggested that a large number, sometimes a majority, of British voters would prefer a British withdrawal in the comparatively near future, with an end to the toll of British lives and the drain on the British exchequer. The conduct of the unionists since the agreement has not served to reinforce the links that bind the province to the United Kingdom. Rather, it has alienated the average British voter from his fellow citizens across the Irish Sea, whatever their religious affiliation.

However, supporters of joint authority can make a strong case in the opposite direction. At the time when joint authority was first proposed in the New Ireland Forum, many of its opponents argued that *any* involvement of the Irish government in the affairs of Northern Ireland would lead to unionist insurrection. Events have shown that this is not so. Since Hillsborough the frightful symbolic barrier has been crossed, and it might be thought that the difference between Irish involvement in an Intergovernmental Conference and Irish involvement in a devolved executive is a matter of degree rather than principle.

What is particularly galling to Unionists about the situation since Hillsborough is the feeling that the province is being governed by the British and Irish Governments in collusion behind their backs. If the province was governed by an executive in which elected unionist politicians sat side by side with representatives of the two governments, that feeling, at least, would be diminished.

Moreover, the principal argument of unionists in the past against sharing power with nationalists has been that they will not share power in a Cabinet with a political party whose fundamental and overriding ambition is to abolish the state of which they are a part, that is the state of Northern Ireland. (This was a point emphasized by Dr Cullen in his evidence to the Forum in 1983.) If joint authority is accepted as a durable solution by Irish nationalists North and South then this basic—and reasonable—argument is undermined.

The fundamental weakness of Hillsborough was indeed that it did not combine the two elements of Irish involvement on the one hand, and return of power on the other, to local, including unionist, politicians. Any form of joint authority after Hillsborough would have to be of the second of the two forms suggested by the Forum sub-committee, with a devolved government rather than shared direct rule.

From the Irish side, the fundamental objection to joint authority at the time of the New Ireland Forum was that it was seen at least by Fianna Fáil as involving a renunciation of the nationalist aspiration to a United Ireland. In their oral examination by the Forum (New Ireland Forum 1983–4, No. 10: 36) Drs Cullen and Kearney argued that what must be given up was not the aspiration to a united Ireland, but to the 'absolute separatism' of that aspiration—the aspiration to a united Ireland in which Britain had no part. By 1988 all the nationalist parties in Ireland have now shown that they are willing to accept, at least in the medium term, co-operation with Britain in the government of the province as an alternative to the wholly separate unitary state.

It is not necessary to accept the argument that if it has proved so difficult for the two governments to make harmonious progress under the auspices of the Intergovernmental Conference, it would be much more difficult for them to co-operate in joint-executive decisions. The reverse may well be the case: joint responsibility might force consensus and decision in areas where the present arrangements allow procrastination to breed suspicion.

Full joint sovereignty seems to me now, as it did when I was Vice-Chairman of the Kilbrandon Committee, to be an impractical proposal. The precedents for condominia are of doubtful relevance. Pocket states such as Andorra, Monaco, and Vatican City serve to illustrate the flexibility of the concept of sovereignty rather than to provide models for the political arrangements of a province with the size and history of Northern Ireland. The most successful instances of joint sovereignty have occurred in colonial, or immediate post-colonial, contexts which would be quite inappropriate in the context of present-day Ireland.

One of the major weaknesses of the joint-sovereignty option for Northern Ireland is that it does not provide a secure default position. This was emphasized by Seamus Mallon, Deputy Leader of the SDLP, during the oral examination of Cullen and Kearney by the New Ireland Forum. He asked the proponents:

The commission which in effect would be the governing commission of the joint sovereignty in Northern Ireland—what role would it play and how would it play it? If the Government that you envisage for Northern Ireland broke down—which is not unknown to happen; and given the pressures that exist it might well happen in this scenario—what would the role of the commission be, and how, in effect, would it play if you did not have joint control of security? (New Ireland Forum 1983–4, No. 10: 27)

This question, or rather pair of questions, was not answered by the proponents. After a paragraph or two of sparring, Dr Cullen answered

We have no easy answer to that. What you are asking us is: 'Tell us what you would do if your proposals fell through'. We could then conceivably revert to the *status quo*. (New Ireland Forum 1983–4, No. 10)

The question which Mallon was asking was one which anyone who seriously puts forward a proposal for the future of Northern Ireland must be prepared to answer. And Dr Cullen's answer is not adequate. The status quo at present is British sovereignty. If this had once been handed over to a joint-authority commission, it is by no means clear that it would be the default position if the joint authority broke down, or that this would be accepted as the default position either by the Irish government or by the two communities in Northern Ireland itself.

For this reason, apart from many others which might be put forward, it seems clear that joint authority could only work, from the present position which must be the starting-point, if it were clearly offered under the overarching structure of British sovereignty, and if it were understood from the outset that if the joint-authority institutions failed it was to the United Kingdom that sovereignty reverted.

But under the aegis of British sovereignty many different models of joint authority are, in theory, conceivable and some may, with goodwill on both sides, be workable in practice. A joint security force is probably a chimerical ideal: but there is no reason why a homogeneous security force, such as the Royal Ulster Constabulary, should not be responsible to a police authority which contains elements from both the United Kingdom and the Irish Republic, as proposed by the Kilbrandon Report.

The Hillsborough agreement, in its eighth article, dealt with co-operation in the enforcement of law through the courts. It read as follows:

The Conference shall deal with issues of concern to both countries relating to the enforcement of criminal law. In particular it shall consider whether there are areas of criminal law applying in the North and in the South respectively which might with benefit be harmonised. The two Governments agree on the importance of public confidence in the administration of justice. The Conference shall seek, with the help of advice from experts as appropriate, measures which would give substantial expression to this aim, considering *inter alia* the possibility of mixed courts in both jurisdictions for the trial of certain offences. The Conference shall also be concerned with policy aspects of extradition and extraterritorial jurisdiction as between North and South.

It is the interpretation of this article which has provided the most fertile field of contention between Britain and Ireland since the signing of the Agreement. Had the proposal for mixed courts been implemented, the Agreement would have led to a genuine measure of joint authority, in the judiciary rather than the executive. But nearly three years later the British single-judge Diplock Courts remain; we are as far as ever not only from mixed courts (with judges from both jurisdictions) but even from three-judge British courts or a return to trial by jury. This fact has led to allegations of bad faith by senior Irish participants in the discussions which led to Hillsborough, and is responsible, as much as anything else, for the feeling among nationalists that the promise of the Anglo-Irish Agreement has not been fulfilled.

Experience in 1988 has shown also that if the nationalist community is to have full confidence in the administration of justice in Northern Ireland, it is necessary for there to be Irish participation not only in the judiciary, but also in the prosecuting authority. Few events in the recent history of the province have led to such discontent among Catholics North and South than the decision of the Northern Ireland Director of Public Prosecutions, on the advice of the United Kingdom Attorney-General, not to prosecute members of the police force whose obstruction of the course of justice had been revealed by the Stalker inquiry. Any worthwhile system of joint authority, henceforth, must include an Irish input to the office of the Director of Public Prosecutions.

No doubt such participation by the Republic would be opposed in Northern Ireland, and in certain quarters in the United Kingdom, on the grounds that it might imperil the confidentiality necessary to the maintenance of security. To this objection the reply must be that there are other political considerations to be taken into account and balanced against claims of security. More importantly, short-term concentration on the maximization of security may imperil the long-term maintenance of security if the measures taken place in jeopardy the confidence of the community in the security forces.

All in all, the arguments for and against joint authority have not changed greatly between 1983 and 1989. Dr Cullen summarized the argument in its favour in his oral evidence to the New Ireland Forum.

On one level our proposal is complicated. On another level it is sublimely simple. If you have something and you want to hold on to it and I also want it, if one or other of us is going to have it to the exclusion of the other, that would involve victory and in the Northern Ireland context, unfortunately it would involve people taking up arms to resist you. The sensible thing to me—in fact the only alternative left if we are to strive for peace and long-term stability—is to share the thing. That is what we are proposing. (New Ireland Forum 1983–4, No. 10: 34)

Given the long memories of Irish people, North and South, no proposal for the future can have any hope of success unless it can strike a chord in the reverberations of the past. In the House of Commons debate on the New Ireland Forum and its proposal of joint authority, John Hume endeavoured to strike the appropriate note. He described a dispute which occurred in the days of St Columba, the founder of the city now named Derry. There was a difference of opinion between the Dalriada, a clan living in the area now represented in Westminster by Mr Paisley, and the clans living in the area now covered by Mr Hume's own constituency of Foyle.

The problem was to whom should the Dalriada pay tribute—the Irish high king or the king of Argyll. The solution was simple. Columba said 'Let them pay tribute to both'. In that way he solved the complex identity problem and preserved the unity of the Irish clans. Since then, he has been known in Irish history as a dove of peace. (*Parliamentary Debates* (Commons), 2 July 1984, col. 58)

Notes

1. The text of the submission has not been published in full; it is here quoted from the typescript. A slightly edited version appeared in *Fortnight*, Feb. 1984, pp. 13–14.
2. The paper was delivered to a conference of the British Irish Association at Balliol College in Sept. 1985. I quote, with permission, from the typescript distributed on that occasion.
3. Its report was not published by the Forum, but it was eventually leaked to the *Irish Times* and published there on the 9 May 1984; it is from this version that I quote.
4. Editors' note: Since June 1989 Northern Ireland's three Members of the European Parliament are John Hume, Ian Paisley, and Jim Nicholson.
5. Editors' note: The Review of the Agreement, carried out under Article 11, is published in App. 2.
6. Editors' note: See App. 3.
7. Editors' note: The constitutionality of the AIA is being challenged by the McGimpsey brothers—Northern Irish unionists availing of their rights as Irish citizens.

10

The Case for Negotiated Independence

Margaret Moore and James Crimmins*

NEGOTIATED independence is not the preferred option of either section of the Northern Irish community and is not currently favoured by the British or Irish Governments. However, it has been suggested as a solution to the province's problems by several distinct groups and individuals, representing a wide range of political opinion.[1] Among unionists, it has been advocated primarily by paramilitary groups, such as the Ulster Loyalist Central Co-ordinating Committee in 1976 and the New Ulster Political Research Group, a think-tank attached to the Ulster Defence Association, in 1979 (NUPRG 1979; Ulster Loyalist Central Co-ordinating Committee 1976). In 1987, a task force of the two main unionist parties argued that the concept of negotiated independence was becoming increasingly attractive among Protestants (Joint Unionist Task Force 1987: 5). Among nationalists within Northern Ireland, an influential section of the SDLP, the largest Catholic party, supported independence in the mid-1970s. They succeeded in having a motion passed at the party's 1976 conference instructing the party's executive to undertake an immediate study of the option (Arthur 1982: 125). In Britain, James Callaghan, the former British Prime Minister and person responsible for introducing British troops into Northern Ireland in 1969, publicly declared his support for independence in 1981 (*The Times*, 3 July 1981) a position subsequently supported in a *Sunday Times* editorial (16 August 1981). Finally, the concept has also attracted support from a number of politicians in the Republic of Ireland.[2]

* The authors would like to acknowledge the generous assistance of John McGarry in the preparation and writing of the chapter.

Despite the diverse nature of this support, the case for independence has not been presented in detail in the academic literature on Northern Ireland. This chapter seeks to fill this gap. More than this, however, it is our concern to set the parameters within which an independent northern state is a viable and sustainable option. Taking into account the political and economic risks associated with the creation and maintenance of an independent Northern Ireland, it is argued that the dangers can be sufficiently minimized and the foundations laid for a peaceful resolution *only* if the British and Irish governments are determined in their commitment to support this particular settlement. Ultimately, everything depends on the willingness of these governments to act in concert toward this end.

1. ALLEGIANCES, ATTITUDES, AND STRATEGIES

Negotiated independence is an intrinsically just solution in so far as it involves the requirement that the most favoured political arrangement of both nationalists and unionists must be withdrawn from consideration, because neither is acceptable to both communities.[3] It requires each side to abandon that which the other objects to—the political link with Britain on the one hand, the so-called 'Irish dimension' on the other. It requires that both groups set aside their differences and forge a new identity for the new state of Northern Ireland on the basis of their common or shared interests. It rules out the unrealistic notion of a political victory for either side and involves concessions from both sides.

As an option for Northern Ireland, independence is usually dismissed without much consideration as unrealistic. This is partly due to a prevailing and often unquestioned orthodoxy that the basis for a common allegiance to a state of Northern Ireland does not exist among the province's warring factions. According to the orthodox view, Northern Ireland's Catholics identify with their co-religionists in the Republic of Ireland and seek unification with them; Northern Ireland's Protestants identify with their co-religionists in the United Kingdom and wish to remain united with them; and the two groups are intensely divided from each other and have little in common. While there is clearly some truth in this, it is exaggerated, and in a way that undermines the case for independence.

Northern Ireland's Protestants do not in fact strongly identify with the people on the British mainland, at least not with the English.

Their loyalty to Westminster has always been conditional in nature—useful in so far as it poses an obstacle to a united Ireland but to be jettisoned if it no longer fulfils that purpose (Miller 1978). Even those Protestants who want to be 'integrated' with Britain do so because they regard that arrangement as the most effective way of preventing rule from Dublin, not because they have any positive desire to be governed from London. Since the abolition of their Parliament by Westminster in 1972, many Protestants have objected to the colonial nature of their subordination to London. They resent being governed by English proconsuls with different accents and values, some of whom have made it clear that they regard their stay in the province as a penance rather than an honour or even a duty. They were distressed when Harold Wilson mocked their self-reliance and ignored their sacrifice in two world wars by dismissing them as 'spongers' during the 1974 workers' strike. They suspect that the 'mainland' British regard the level of political violence as 'acceptable' as long as it is contained in one part of the kingdom, i.e. Northern Ireland.[4] But, most of all, they are profoundly afflicted by the fear of an imminent 'sell-out' by Westminster, an anxiety greatly increased by the signing of the Anglo-Irish Agreement in November 1985. Since that time, Protestant politicians routinely talk of Protestant 'alienation' from the British, a term that hitherto was only used to describe the plight of Catholics.[5]

While the IRA's skilful propaganda has tended to obscure the fact, the aspiration of Northern Ireland's Catholics for the reunification of Ireland is much weaker than is commonly thought outside the province. When offered a choice of options in a poll in January 1986, only 26 per cent of Catholics chose a united Ireland, unitary or federal in structure (*Belfast Telegraph*, 15 January 1986). A large minority of Catholics, possibly as many as 25 per cent, voted against a united Ireland in the 1973 Border Poll, despite being told by their leaders to boycott the poll (Compton 1981: 91). While it is true, of course, that the overwhelming majority of Catholics vote for nationalist parties, this does not mean that they agree with all the policies presented by these parties, or even with those policies deemed central to their respective platforms. Some Catholics vote for nationalist parties because those parties are at least partly concerned with improving the position of Catholics within Northern Ireland, and because they have no desire to vote for unionist parties.

A large proportion of Catholics fear a decline in their living standards in a united Ireland and they are unwilling to be caught in the middle of the civil war that would accompany any attempt to force Protestants into such a settlement.

Nor is it correct to claim that Northern Ireland's Catholics and Protestants have nothing in common. Simply by living together and encountering similar experiences, including the 'troubles', both groups have come to share identities which are exclusive to the province and which distinguish them from people in the Republic and Great Britain. A 1968 survey of community identification in Northern Ireland revealed that 67 per cent of Protestants thought Ulstermen of the opposite religion were about the 'same as themselves', while only 29 per cent thought the same about Englishmen. Similarly, 81 per cent of Catholics regarded Ulster Protestants as about the 'same as themselves' but only 44 per cent thought this about southern Catholics (Rose 1971: 214). In an important study of a rural community in Northern Ireland Rosemary Harris, an anthropologist, found that, despite the social segregation, there was a 'considerable area within which Catholics and Protestants shared a common culture' (Harris 1972: 131; see also Murphy 1979). While Northern Ireland clearly has profound divisions, so have other societies, such as Malaysia, Singapore, India, and Tanzania, which have managed to maintain independence and stability.

The most desirable way to proceed towards an independent Northern Ireland would be for the communal leaders in the province to take the first step. They could hold negotiations to establish if a consensus existed. If such a consensus emerged and looked stable, there would be tremendous pressure on the London and Dublin governments to welcome and assist the establishment of an independent state.

It must be conceded, however, that under the present circumstances there is no realistic possibility of such a spontaneous agreement emerging. Politicians in the province show no sign of being willing voluntarily to abandon their preferred alternatives. Even if they did, there are no guarantees that they would attract enough popular support. Independence as an option enjoys only a low level of support in the province, ranging from 3 per cent in October 1979 to 8 per cent in May 1987. This is partly because the idea has not been seriously discussed and also because the risks and dangers attached to it are more immediately obvious than the benefits and advantages. If independence was widely debated and analysed as a genuine option by political leaders, lawyers, economists, the media, and the general public, many more would certainly favour it, though maybe not a majority of today's electorate. Lack of majority consent in Northern Ireland seems so formidable an objection that it is often used to foreclose any further discussion of a range of options including independence.

If independence is to be realized, therefore, the first steps would have to be taken by the London and Dublin governments. They could justifiably decide, without risk of international opprobrium, that because the Anglo-Irish Agreement had not produced stability and showed no sign of doing so, the time had now come for the people of Northern Ireland to solve their own problems.

The outcome of this decision would depend on the way it was carried out. In the present atmosphere of fear and distrust in the province, the immediate and complete abandonment of Northern Ireland to its own devices would carry with it a serious risk of civil war, the 'malign scenario' regularly predicted by Dr Conor Cruise O'Brien (O'Brien 1974). If the London and Dublin governments are to produce by their actions a stable and reasonably prosperous Northern Ireland, they would have to proceed in the following way. First, the British government would have to agree to withdraw from Northern Ireland at a fixed date in the future, allowing a sufficient transition period for it to develop support for the concept in Northern Ireland. During this transition period, Britain would invite all the important political organizations in the province to attend a conference to devise a constitution for the new state. The British government would have to inform the conference that it would withdraw at the end of the transitional period, whether or not an agreement was reached, leaving the northern Irish to fend for themselves. Secondly, the British government would have to proclaim its willingness to continue its present policy of subsidizing the economy of Northern Ireland for a period of fifteen to twenty years. Without this subvention—£1.7 billion annually at the current rate—the present living standards in Northern Ireland could not be maintained; it would be more difficult to rebuild the economy; and the ensuing competition for scarce resources would put an intolerable strain on intercommunal relations. Thirdly, the Republic of Ireland would have to withdraw its constitutional claim to Northern Ireland

and agree to sponsor, or at least refrain from vetoing, the new state's application for membership of the European Community (EC). If the Republic continued to exercise irredentist claims over Northern Ireland, it would severely damage the prospects for internal accommodation. Northern nationalists would be encouraged to continue working towards, and fighting for, a united Ireland, while northern unionists would continue to regard them as fifth-columnists of a foreign power and oppose their involvement in government. Without access to the EC trading bloc the Northern Ireland economy would be in severe difficulties even if the British subvention continued. Finally, the two governments would have to facilitate internal accommodation by making their sponsorship of the new state conditional upon the Protestant majority agreeing to the establishment of a constitution acceptable to the Catholic minority. Apart from the Republic of Ireland and Great Britain, the other members of the Community, any of whom could veto Northern Ireland's application for membership, would probably also insist that the constitution be acceptable to both Catholics and Protestants.[6]

Until now, both groups in Northern Ireland have enjoyed the advantages of Community membership and the large subvention from Britain, regardless of whether or not they were prepared to accommodate each other. For the first time, both benefits, without which Northern Ireland could hardly survive, would be used in a constructive fashion, to provide powerful, perhaps irresistible, incentives to compromise. If the two governments could agree to proceed in this way, it is likely that both sides in Northern Ireland would be able to achieve a settlement of their differences such as cannot be achieved otherwise.

For the first time, both communities would be faced with the prospect of sole responsibility for the future of the territory they share. Looking at them as they are now, frozen in attitudes which make it impossible for them to contribute rationally to political progress, it may seem that independence would lead to disaster. But until now, neither community has had to face this responsibility. Both sides have been able to avoid compromise knowing that the British government would ensure that the violence would be contained within certain levels, and the economy would be subsidized indefinitely no matter what damage the political impasse did to it. It was the probable therapeutic effects of this scenario that led

James Callaghan to declare his support for independence in 1981 (*Parliamentary Debates* (Commons), 2 July 1981, vol. 7, no. 133, cols. 1046–53). Such a strategy undoubtedly involves some risks but, as will be shown, these risks are not as great as the critics of independence allege.

There are several reasons why Protestant leaders faced with resolute action of this sort by the two governments would want to draw up a constitution acceptable to the Catholic minority. They would be aware that an independent Northern Ireland, denied both the British subvention and access to the EC trading bloc, would be in an unenviable situation. The already stagnant economy, which is heavily dependent on trade, would be put in extremely serious difficulties. Living standards would decline drastically overnight. There would probably be a massive outpouring of the most mobile and well-qualified sections of the population, causing further decline. A constitutional settlement that was unacceptable to the large Catholic minority would help the cause of the IRA and seriously jeopardize the stability of the new regime, posing another tremendous obstacle to any hope of economic recovery. Faced with an economic catastrophe of such magnitude, it is inconceivable that the Protestant leadership in Northern Ireland would resist an internal accommodation with Catholics. This is why they have consistently refused to consider a unilateral declaration of independence, for such an action would produce these same unwelcome consequences.[7] Even if Britain was not prepared to isolate an intransigent Protestant government completely because of the suffering that this would cause, more limited sanctions, perhaps selectively aimed at sectors of the economy in which Protestants dominate, would probably be enough to induce a more conciliatory spirit among their leaders.[8]

In addition, Protestant leaders would be aware, or could be made aware, that the government of the Irish Republic, with its larger population and well-equipped armed forces would 'not stand idly by' and permit a repetition of Stormont-type behaviour towards Catholics. The fact that the British sovereign power would have left the province would free a Dublin government to take whatever action it considered appropriate. It should be remembered that the Republic's Government considered intervening in 1969 to prevent Protestant maltreatment of the minority (Kelly 1971).

Apart from these powerful arguments against intransigence, there are at least two positive incentives to compromise that could be employed. First, by offering to recognize the legitimacy of the new state (i.e. withdrawing its constitutional claim in return for an internal settlement in Northern Ireland) Dublin would have gone a considerable way towards reducing the 'siege mentality' among Protestants that has caused them to refuse to compromise in the past. This siege mentality helps to explain why Protestants excluded Catholics from government in Belfast between 1921 and 1972, and why they discriminated against them in terms of jobs and houses in the hope that they would be forced to emigrate. Secondly, a constitution acceptable to all sections of the community in an independent Northern Ireland would be needed to provide the unity of purpose essential for the reconstruction of the Northern Ireland economy after independence.

It should not be surprising that those Protestants who have seriously considered the option of an independent Northern Ireland have made it perfectly clear that the success of such a state would depend on majority tolerance towards the minority. For example, the UDA document *Beyond the Religious Divide* (NUPRG 1979), which advocated independence, was described by Bernard Crick as 'a genuine attempt to shift religious antipathy into constitutional argument and inter-community self-government' (quoted in O'Malley 1983: 320).[9] While the UDA plan did not provide for mandatory power-sharing in government, provisions in the constitution it proposed, including one stipulating that the election of the pivotal position of Speaker needed a two-thirds majority in the legislature, ensured that the system could not function without the co-operation of both sections of the community. The proposed constitution also provided for a Bill of Rights which could only be mitigated during a period of 'public emergency', and which would require for validation a two-thirds majority of the legislature (NUPRG 1979).[10]

Clearly, not all Protestant leaders would be willing to accommodate Catholics in an independent state but it is likely that a substantial majority would. On this score a prolonged transition period might help to facilitate the emergence of a new group of Protestant politicians to replace those rendered immobile by their past rhetoric of intransigence.

It should be noted that current demographic changes may soon make power-sharing between Catholics and Protestants necessary even if it is not constitutionally entrenched. The proportion of

Catholics in the population of Northern Ireland has been rising strongly in recent decades. Demographers have argued that it will increase from its present level of between 38 and 42 per cent to somewhere between 44 and 51 per cent before stabilizing in the early decades of the next century (Rowthorn and Wayne 1988, app. 7). If elections in an independent Northern Ireland continue to utilize the present system of proportional representation and if non-sectarian parties continue to achieve around 10 per cent of the poll, both reasonable assumptions, neither of the two main factions will be able to govern by itself. As the two populations come closer in size to each other, a multiple balance of power will be created in the province and coalitions of some sort will become necessary. Political scientists regard the presence of such a balance of power to be a very important factor underlying the existence of power-sharing govern-ments in other divided societies (Lijphart 1977: 55–61). The ability of the Unionist Party to win a majority by itself between 1921 and 1972 goes some way towards explaining why its leaders were not prepared to share power with Catholics during that period.[11]

The emergence of a multiple balance of power in an independent Northern Ireland may well be facilitated by the growth of new, non-sectarian parties. The unionists have been able to maintain their dominant position in elections, as one party before 1969 and as a varying number of closely allied parties since then, because of the threat to the border. Despite their monolithic appearance, they are in fact divided by denomination, class, region, and differences of interest between agriculture and industry. On several occasions between 1921 and 1969, especially when the threat of Irish unity seemed weakest, this natural clash of interests threatened to emerge giving rise to class-based politics and parties that could appeal to both sections of the community. The unionists, and their nationalist counterparts, were always saved by the re-emergence of the border as the dominant issue. In an independent Northern Ireland, with its frontiers guaranteed by both London and Dublin, the basis for sectarian politics would be greatly weakened.

Some nationalists have claimed that even if a constitution for an independent Northern Ireland could be agreed to by both com-munities, such a state would be in constant danger of an undemo-cratic Protestant takeover.[12] These fears, however, are greatly exaggerated. Protestant leaders would be aware that such action would be completely unacceptable to London and Dublin, both of whom would continue to have an obvious interest in the stability of a Northern Ireland state. If, in spite of this, such a coup did take place, the Protestant junta that had taken power could be brought to its knees by either the British or Irish governments. If Britain chose to, it could destroy such a government without military action and at no cost to itself, by simply cutting off financial aid and imposing a trade boycott. This would make the new state completely unviable and would force all but the completely irrational to come to terms. An undemocratic Protestant takeover would also invite intervention from the militarily stronger Republic, especially if the coup resulted in harsh treatment for the minority.

The main danger to political accommodation between Catholics and Protestants in an independent Northern Ireland would be continuing paramilitary violence. If this could not be contained, it would polarize the two communities, strengthen the hands of militants, and undermine the position of moderates. Given the violent traditions of both communities, it would be foolish to ignore this danger but it would also be wrong to overestimate the risks. The claim that independence would be followed by continuing or even increased violence rests on the assumption that present paramilitary attitudes would remain unchanged in an independent Northern Ireland. But there are good reasons why this would not be the case. The removal of the British presence resulting from independence would achieve the Provisional IRA's goal of 'Brits out' and would remove a fundamental part of its *raison d'être*. Irish republican extremists, whose support expanded greatly when British troops arrived in the province in 1969, and who are guaranteed sufficient recruits and a sympathetic population while those troops remain, would find it considerably more difficult to keep fighting if both parts of Ireland became republics, both governed by Irish people. Moreover, those who chose to continue fighting for a united Ireland would have to do so without the legitimacy that Articles 2 and 3 of the Republic's Constitution presently lends to their cause. Their position would also be weakened to the extent that Catholics were treated equally with Protestants in the new state. The British government could further undermine support for the militant nationalist cause by making it perfectly clear that the large British subvention would no longer be forthcoming in a united Ireland. Nationalist intellectuals readily admit that a united Ireland would be unviable without this, but wishfully assume that British subsidies would continue to be made available to them (see, for example, Rowthorn and Wayne 1988, and Chapter 2 above).

As for the loyalist paramilitaries, some of these have been among the chief promoters of an independent Northern Ireland acceptable to both communities. They would not want to jeopardize its prospects for success by attacking the minority population. Many loyalists appreciate that, with Britain gone, their only chance of survival in the whole island of Ireland, where they are outnumbered 4 to 1, would be to act responsibly towards the minority population. In an all-Ireland military confrontation provoked by Protestant violence against Catholics, the Protestants could not win. It is their present insecurity resulting both from their fear of a British 'sell-out' and the Republic's constitutional claim that has provoked Protestant paramilitary violence against Catholics in the past. In an independent Northern Ireland, loyalists would be in control of their own relationship with the Irish Republic and would no longer have to worry about deals conducted over their heads or behind their backs, such as the Anglo-Irish Agreement. This new state of affairs would provide a sounder base for a friendly relationship between North and South than is possible under present circumstances.

It could be argued that a British unilateral severance of the Union would provoke a loyalist armed rebellion, such as occurred in 1912 with the organization of the UVF. But a rebellion against whom or what? Loyalists organized in 1912 because they were faced with the imminent prospect of government from Dublin. In the 1990s, faced with the departure of the British and an end to the Republic's constitutional claim over Northern Ireland, any extreme loyalist group inclined towards armed rebellion would have no one and nothing to rebel against. The British would have gone, leaving the northern Irish in complete control of their own territory.

Those Protestants (or Catholics) who could not, under any circumstances, reconcile themselves to forgoing the Union, could be given financial aid to move to Britain. It would have to be made clear—to give the state a chance to succeed and to prevent a mass exodus of skilled labour to Britain—that these grants would continue to be available for a significant period. All Northern Ireland citizens should, of course, continue to have the full rights of British citizens, as the people in the Republic have currently. As Callaghan pointed out, the British 'guarantee' could be switched from the territory of Northern Ireland to the people themselves (*The Times*, 3 July 1981).

Independence, unlike any other option, would present both sets of paramilitaries with a quid pro quo, with both being able to claim a sort of victory. The IRA could claim that while they had not achieved a united Ireland, they had rid the island of the British. The loyalists could claim that they had effectively prevented a united Ireland. This would provide the essential framework for an accommodation between the two groups that could not possibly occur if one side is clearly seen to be the winner and the other side the loser. Hopefully, the leaders of the paramilitary factions could be persuaded to participate in the negotiations leading up to the establishment of the new state.

The prospect of political negotiation among paramilitaries has been increased by recent political developments in the major paramilitary factions. The leaders of these organizations have made serious efforts to promote reconciliation and to confront the problem of sectarianism in Northern Ireland (Rowthorn and Wayne 1988: app. 5). The UDA's document *Common Sense* (Ulster Political Research Group 1987) is the most enlightened and moderate document to have emerged from the unionist side since the troubles began. On the Republican side too, leaders of Sinn Féin have become increasingly vocal in their condemnation of sectarianism, a development which, while uneven, represents a reassertion of the traditional non-sectarian values of the republican movement dating back to the eighteenth century when it was led by Protestants (Rowthorn and Wayne 1988: 7). Such developments indicate a potential for realism and compromise among the paramilitaries on both sides and casts doubt on the inevitability of a sectarian blood-bath in an independent Northern Ireland. It is probable that some members of the paramilitary factions would continue to fight but it is not clear that they would constitute serious threats to the new state. If violence did continue on a significant scale, it may be necessary to import neutral security forces either from EC countries (excluding Great Britain) or from the United Nations to aid the indigenous security forces.

The risk of continuing or increased violence in an independent Northern Ireland has also to be balanced against the dangers involved in accepting the only other options available. There will almost certainly be a full-scale civil war if any attempt is made to force one million Protestants into a united Ireland. On the other hand, the death-toll will continue to mount if the British remain in Northern Ireland.[13]

2. ECONOMIC VIABILITY

One of the most serious objections that has been made to the concept of an independent Northern Ireland is that it would not be economically viable. While every economist who has dealt with the subject agrees that the province would need continuing external aid, some add that it is highly unlikely that such aid would be forthcoming, at least not for the extensive period that would be required to rebuild the Northern Ireland economy. David Blake, the economics editor of *The Times*, wrote that it would be 'unlikely' that Britain would be willing to go on paying large sums to a country with which it had severed links (*The Times*, 3 July 1981). The *Belfast Telegraph* (4 and 9 September 1986) responded strongly to suggestions by UUP deputy leader Harold McCusker's claim that independence might be a viable option by dismissing as 'mere wishful thinking' any notion that long-term British financial support would follow a grant of independence. In an article on independence published in 1982, Paul Arthur also speculated that such aid would not be forthcoming, noting that Britain had not displayed such generosity towards other dependent territories (Arthur 1982: 131).

If British aid was not forthcoming for a prolonged period, an independent Northern Ireland would face severe difficulties. The British subvention—the gap between government spending in Northern Ireland and the amount raised in the province in taxes and levies—is currently £1.7 billion per annum and is likely to increase. The 1984 New Ireland Forum Report estimated that it represented 29 per cent of the province's GDP, and that if the subvention had not existed in 1982–83 taxes would have had to rise by 69 per cent in order to maintain the level of services and expenditure (*The Times*, 15 November 1985). Such an increase in taxes is out of the question. It would only jeopardize further the province's faltering industrial base and result in a sizeable emigration of the most mobile and wealth-producing sections of the population, the middle class and skilled labour. The decline in the economic stability of the state would put a severe strain on political stability. The ability of the British government to curb extremist tendencies in an independent Northern Ireland would be reduced without the economic clout it would possess if it continued to pay the subsidies.

Because Northern Ireland is a part of the United Kingdom at present, it is automatically entitled to British government support.

Outside the UK, this automatic entitlement would cease and would have to be specifically negotiated (Rowthorn and Wayne 1988: 120). The danger of losing the subvention is often used by academics and politicians to discredit serious discussion of any option that does not include continued membership of the UK. However, we would argue that it is highly unlikely that Britain would grant independence to Northern Ireland without also agreeing to continue the subsidies. An economically unstable Northern Ireland on Britain's western flank would not be in that country's strategic interests. Furthermore, Britain could realistically expect to save money from negotiated independence even while continuing to underwrite the Northern Ireland economy. The repatriation of British troops would immediately cut Britain's costs by around £200 million per annum with virtually no negative effect on the local economy (Rowthorn and Wayne 1988: 157). Other sources, such as the USA and EC, would probably be willing to share the burden of aid as the price of a durable peace in an area of some strategic importance. At the end of the 1970s, funds from the EC provided a net addition of nearly 10 per cent to the Irish Republic's budget resources after allowing for that government's financial contribution to the Community. The EC also provides substantial aid to many countries outside its boundaries. Fine Gael's argument that special Community aid would be made available for a transition to a united Ireland clearly also applies to a negotiated independence:

It can scarcely be doubted that, in the event of a political solution being found to the Northern Ireland problem, which is by far the biggest single source of unrest and violence within the frontiers of the present community, that institution would be willing to contribute financially to the transitional arrangements towards such a settlement. (Fine Gael 1979, para. 105)

In the long term, the savings to Britain would be much greater. If it stays in Northern Ireland, it will have to continue paying the subsidy indefinitely. If it withdraws, it could expect to abandon payment after a certain, albeit fairly prolonged, period.[14] As economist John Simpson has pointed out, given a stable independent state, the hope must be that Northern Ireland's dependence on British subsidies would be gradually reduced in the future (NUPRG 1979: 44).[15]

The new state would derive certain economic benefits from independence. It would no longer be susceptible to the deflationary measures which Westminster takes periodically to reduce consumption in the booming south-east of England. It would also have control over economic levers which it does not have presently and which it could use to its advantage. One of the disadvantages to Northern Ireland of its membership of the UK is that it has not been able to pursue an independent exchange-rate policy of its own. A devaluation of the Northern Ireland currency would make it more competitive within the EC and a more desirable location for investment. The state would have some independent borrowing capacity and, freed from the constraints of Whitehall taxation policy, which at present inhibits it from pursuing economic policies that might reinvigorate its economy, it would be able to provide the same type of tax and investment incentives which have enabled the Republic to build up its manufacturing sector so successfully in recent decades. An independent Northern Ireland would also have greater wage and salary flexibility than it has at present and could, if it so chose, set its wages more in line with what it could afford rather than by reference to Britain, a much wealthier country (Rowthorn and Wayne 1988: 138). This would make Northern Ireland more competitive and cut unemployment, though it would also mean a lower standard of living for some, at least in the short to medium term.

If the new state gains full representation in the institutions of the EC, it would be in a position to protect its interests there in a way it cannot at present. Northern Ireland, like the Republic, has a large agricultural sector but is represented at the highest levels in the Community by British spokesmen whose job it is to defend the interests of a country with an overwhelming majority of food-consumers. France, West Germany, Denmark, Italy, the Republic of Ireland, Italy, Spain, and Portugal all have major farming communities. Northern Ireland as an independent member of the EC would increase their political salience. An independent Northern Ireland within the EC could also expect to take 8 or 9 seats in the European Parliament rather than the 3 it currently has as a part of the UK. It would thus benefit from the convention in the Community (a characteristic of many other international organizations) whereby small countries are given disproportionate influence, a convention which works to its disadvantage while it remains part of a large state.

The argument that Northern Ireland is too small for independence need not be taken seriously. Much smaller countries, like Malta, Iceland, and Luxemburg have prospered. The Republic of Ireland, with a population of only three million, managed to flourish despite being born in less than propitious circumstances (Arthur 1982: 117). And a political unit's size is of much less importance today in a world of large trading blocs than it was in 1921. Northern Ireland's small size would only pose serious problems if it was denied access to the EC.

Since the present violence is the chief cause of the economic malaise in the province (Rowthorn 1987: 132), it follows that a peaceful settlement, brought about by negotiated independence, would help to provide the basis for increased investment and an economic recovery in the province. Between 1966 and 1971, multinationals set up 51 new manufacturing units in the province and created 11,600 new jobs. By contrast, between 1972 and 1976, largely due to the 'troubles', they established a mere 15 units and created only 900 jobs (Rowthorn and Wayne 1988: 84–5). With a stable peace, Northern Ireland would start to draw in a significant amount of investment, which in turn would stimulate home-grown firms by providing a demand for locally produced goods and services. It would also give a major boost to the tourist industry and would encourage many of those creative and skilled people who, under present circumstances, want to leave the province to remain (Rowthorn and Wayne 1988: 12).

A peaceful settlement would also allow Northern Ireland to take advantage of its attractiveness as a location for multinational investment. It possesses an educated professional class, a large supply of skilled workers, relatively low wages, and inexpensive land. It covers a small territory and its communications are good, certainly much better than those in the Republic of Ireland. In addition, the province has good leisure facilities and beautiful scenery, which make it a very congenial place for incoming executives to live, an important factor in multinational decisions on where to locate firms. The province also has a much better record of industrial relations than the British mainland. While Northern Ireland suffers the disadvantage of being located on the fringe of Europe, in this respect it is no different from the Republic, which continues to attract considerable foreign investment (Rowthorn and Wayne 1988: 121).

3. BRITAIN AND THE REPUBLIC OF IRELAND

At the moment neither the British nor Irish Governments seem

inclined to take the resolute steps required to establish a stable
independent Northern Ireland. But such steps are not as inconceivable as the critics of independence suggest, and they may be
discussed more seriously as the futility of the alternatives becomes
increasingly apparent. Moreover, promoting such a solution to the
crisis in Northern Ireland may be in the interests of both London and
Dublin.

For Britain, giving independence to Northern Ireland would be no
more than a logical extension of its present policy of keeping the
province apart from the rest of the United Kingdom. Since 1920 the
British government has striven to maintain clear distinctions
between Northern Ireland and Great Britain. It gave the unionists
their own Parliament against their will and played no role in
Northern Irish politics until forced to do so by the events of the late
1960s. The main British political parties, fearful that the Irish
problem would destabilize mainland politics, have refused to
organize in the province, and show no sign of doing so in the future.
Unionist demands that Northern Ireland be governed by the same
procedures that apply elsewhere in the United Kingdom have been
consistently refused. Northern Ireland is clearly not 'as British as
Finchley', as Prime Minister Thatcher declared during the hunger
strikes in 1981. It is inconceivable that London would allow a foreign
government a direct say in the running of Finchley or any other part
of Britain. Yet Dublin has been given such a role in Northern Ireland
under the Hillsborough agreement. This accord indicates that Britain
no longer even bothers to conceal its lack of enthusiasm for keeping
Northern Ireland in the UK. The continuing Protestant reaction to
the Agreement and the prospect of having to subsidize the province
indefinitely further tempers what enthusiasm remains.

Negotiated independence for Northern Ireland has several attractions for the British. It would extricate them with honour from an
area which has been a drain on their resources and a source of
tremendous embarrassment both domestically and internationally. It
would be more palatable to the Tory elements of the British
establishment than the alternative of coercing the northern Irish
Protestants into an all-Ireland Republic. It would also be very
popular with the British electorate. Opinion polls in England,
Scotland, and Wales have shown consistently that granting independence to Northern Ireland is far more popular than keeping it in the
UK or allowing it to become part of a united Ireland. A *New Society*

poll in 1981 found that 37 per cent of respondents in Great Britain favoured independence for Northern Ireland, compared to 24 per cent who thought the province should remain part of the UK and 21 per cent who favoured a united Ireland (*New Society*, 24 September 1981). In 1986 a Gallup poll indicated similar results, 35 per cent favouring independence, 26 per cent the UK option, and 24 per cent a united Ireland (*Irish Times*, 29 May 1986).[16]

British capital has no interest in Westminster maintaining political control over Northern Ireland (O'Leary 1987*b*: 10–11). If the province were admitted to the EC British companies would still be able to trade, invest, or locate there. Nor need the strategic interests which Britain has in Northern Ireland (and which help to explain why it has stayed in the province) be adversely affected by independence.[17] London could insist that Northern Ireland join NATO as a condition for continuing its economic subsidies to the province.[18] As far as the British are concerned, an independent Northern Ireland in NATO would be preferable to allowing Northern Ireland to be united with an Irish state which has long professed its neutrality.[19] This would go some way towards overcoming the main objections of Enoch Powell and others to an independent Northern Ireland.

The attractiveness of withdrawal to the British is such that the policy seems to have been given serious consideration by some policy-makers in the mid-1970s. First, the White Paper of July 1974 setting out the British government's future course after the collapse of the Sunningdale agreement was the first in a series of such documents which did not reiterate the pledge that Northern Ireland would remain part of the UK as long as a majority there wanted it (*The Northern Ireland Constitution* (1974), Cmnd. 5675 (London)). Second, according to Merlyn Rees, the Northern Ireland Secretary from 1974–6, a Cabinet subcommittee under Prime Minister Wilson considered withdrawal at a series of meetings in the 1974–5 period (Bew and Patterson 1985: 76, 106; Langdon 1983). Third, during 1974 republican and loyalist paramilitaries met at several conferences where they seemed to be moving towards agreement on an independent Northern Ireland. These conferences were funded indirectly, via the Northern Ireland Community Relations Commission, by the British government. Fourth, the Provisional IRA claims it received a promise of British withdrawal at the time of the truce in February 1975. Many of its policy documents of this period declared a British withdrawal to be imminent (Bew and Patterson 1985: 80–1). Fifth, in 1975, Sir Frank Cooper, then Permanent Under-Secretary at the Northern Ireland Office, told a group of local editors that he expected British withdrawal in about five years. Finally, as we have seen, James Callaghan, the second most important person in the Labour Government during this period, later publicly declared his support for independence (Whyte 1981: 430). It is surely conceivable that a future British government, or indeed the present one, led as it is by a Prime Minister who does not fear radical initiatives, could not only consider withdrawal leading to independence, but carry through such a policy.

From the British perspective, the main problem with this course of action is the risk of destabilizing the province, further undermining the already weak economy, and perhaps even precipitating a bloody civil war. The likelihood of that occurring would be greatly reduced if the government of the Republic of Ireland also recognized the independent state of Northern Ireland. Some may claim that there is no possibility that this would ever occur; and they are probably correct that there is little incentive, in present circumstances, for Dublin to embark on such a politically risky course. However, there are situations in which such action by the Republic's government may be forthcoming. It would not be necessary for London and Dublin to arrive at the conclusion that negotiated independence is the best and fairest solution to the crisis in Northern Ireland independently of each other and simultaneously. It may be sufficient for the British government to make explicit their firm commitment to independence for Northern Ireland and their unwillingness to enact measures to force the Protestants into a united Ireland after they withdraw. Advocates of a united Ireland admit that active promotion by the British of a united Ireland—e.g. the continuation of the subvention, the disarming of the UDR, trade embargoes to force recalcitrant Protestants into submission—is necessary to facilitate the emergence of a united Ireland, rather than produce a costly, perhaps prolonged, civil war, with uncertain results (see e.g. Chapter 2 above). If the British were to make it clear that their support for such measures would not be forthcoming, the Republic would be faced with the choice either of (1) using its influence to ensure a stable Northern Ireland; or (2) refusing to give its support to the independent state, thereby taking the risk that Northern Ireland would disintegrate into civil war, and be eventually repartitioned. In these circumstances, it would surely be in their interests to support the independence option and work to ensure that the new state embodies institutions and principles that benefit the Catholic community.

While the recognition and sponsorship of an independent Northern Ireland would pose significant problems for the leaders of the Republic, given the tradition of irredentism which exists there, these could be overcome with political will. In any case, contrary to what Anthony Coughlan would have us believe (Chapter 2), the extent of the devotion to Irish unification in the Republic is exaggerated. The commitment to unification is, in fact, extremely shallow and coexists alongside an unwillingness to make the financial sacrifices or the constitutional changes that would almost certainly be required to make it a serious option.[20] As the southern Irish have become more used to partition and more involved in their own considerable problems, and as travel and the media have brought them closer to the reality of the 'troubles' in Northern Ireland, the aspiration to unity has weakened. A 1983 survey shows that support for reunification tended to decrease in the more 'modernized' parts of southern society. Younger age groups and those living in the growing urban areas of the country, especially Dublin, are less attached than older people and those living outside the urban areas to the notion of one indivisible nation (Cox 1985: 38). As this demographic trend continues, support for unity will be further weakened. In these circumstances (providing there were reasonable expectations that the position of the Catholic minority in Northern Ireland would be safeguarded), a declaration of support for an independent Northern Ireland by the Republic's government would be unlikely to provoke intolerable controversy amongst the southern electorate.

The changing nature of the Republic's political élite also offers grounds for optimism among those who favour independence. The revolutionary leaders of the post-1916 era—those who could never accept partition in principle though they were willing to reinforce it in practice by their everyday actions—have been replaced by a generation with different concerns and priorities. While there are notable exceptions, including the present Taoiseach, Charles Haughey, the Republic's leaders lack the value system of their predecessors and, as Garvin notes, are 'more concerned with parochial bread and butter issues, the product of competitive electoral democracy in a rather parochial society rather than the product of the militant and romantic movements in the revolutionary period' (Garvin 1988: 99). Even Fianna Fáil leaders, with a long tradition of unyielding reunificationist rhetoric, have shown themselves in practice to be more concerned with the internal stability of the Republic than with Northern Ireland. Like their counterparts in other southern parties, they have no desire to threaten the peace and homogeneity of what has hitherto been one of the best-integrated societies in Europe.

While for a long time Conor Cruise O'Brien was the only leader in the Republic who publicly accepted that reunification was not a realistic option, recognition of this fact among the Republic's élite is becoming more frequent (Cox 1985: 41; O'Malley 1983, ch. 2). Indeed, the unionists are quite wrong to interpret the Anglo-Irish Agreement as the first step in the Republic's plan to achieve a united Ireland. On the contrary, it is a treaty which is primarily designed to hasten a settlement *within* Northern Ireland (Garvin 1988: 100). The fact that the Agreement has failed to do this, and has illustrated to the southern élite the extent of Protestant resistance to a united Ireland, may make it more likely that Dublin will consider alternative ways to reach an internal settlement.

An independent Northern Ireland, which has certain attractions for Britain, also has advantages for the Republic. Many nationalists there would rejoice because the British presence on the island had been removed at no cost to them in terms of money, lives, or changes in civil law. While Dublin's express withdrawal of the constitutional claim to Northern Ireland (Articles 2 and 3) might incite considerable opposition in the Republic while the British remain in Northern Ireland, it would provoke much less opposition if seen as part of a quid pro quo for British withdrawal. Article 2, which was partly designed to repudiate Britain's colonial presence in a part of Ireland, would be much more difficult to justify if all of Ireland was governed by the Irish. Article 3, with its unrealistic and provocative claim that the Dublin government is entitled to rule Northern Ireland, would, as Senator Whitaker points out in *Beyond the Religious Divide*, 'be an embarrassing anachronism' which the Republic 'would be in haste to bury and forget' (New Ulster Political Research Group 1979: 48).

It would also be possible for a Dublin government committed to recognizing an independent Northern Ireland to claim that this did not rule out the possibility of a united Ireland at some time in the

future. Dublin's recognition would remove pressure from the unionists and would, in fact, make unity more likely in the long term than
would be the case if the Republic was to continue its present policy.
While constitutional nationalists claim that their policy is based on
'unity by consent', it is in fact based on a degree of coercion. The
consistent nationalist strategy, dating from the 1921 treaty negotiations and seen again at Sunningdale and Hillsborough, has been to
force the British to pressure the unionists to accept closer relations
with the Republic. However, this strategy of appealing over the
heads of the unionist leaders has resulted in a deepening of their
mistrust of nationalists and the stiffening of their resistance to any
form of co-operation with them. As it is unlikely that the British can
be persuaded to take the measures necessary to force the Protestants
into a united Ireland (never mind the type of state this would
produce), the present nationalist strategy can be seen as an obstacle
to unity. By recognizing that unity could only come about through
'freely given consent', nationalists would be going some way
towards dissolving the fear and mistrust among Protestants which
presently reinforces partition.

In this transformed atmosphere, a consensus for unity could
emerge at some later time. Some long-term developments in the
Republic are making it a more attractive partner for Northern Ireland
in the future than it is at present. It is becoming more prosperous
and is closing the gap in living standards which exists between it and
the United Kingdom. It is becoming more secular, albeit at a slow
pace, as it continues to be integrated with the European mainstream.
A number of politicians in the Republic are already aware that the
less said about unity, the greater the prospects for attaining it.[21]

4. CONCLUSION

There are risks involved in giving independence to Northern Ireland.
It is possible that the reaction of the northern Irish to such a settlement might not follow the rational course outlined here. If the two
groups could not live together and independence resulted in a full-
scale civil war, the only option remaining would be to partition the
province, as happened in 1974 in Cyprus. Either Britain or the
Republic, preferably both, would intervene to perform the same role
that the Turkish government executed in that situation.

The risks, however, should not be overrated. If the British and

Irish governments could agree to establish the process outlined above, the dangers traditionally associated with independence would be minimized and the prospects for peace and prosperity would be considerably enhanced. In the circumstances created by this process, it is virtually certain that the Protestant majority would be willing to negotiate and abide by a constitution acceptable to the Catholic minority. Unlike any other constitutional arrangement, including the present one, independence would satisfy crucial goals of both the Protestant and Catholic paramilitary factions and would have a reasonable chance of winning their support or at least their acquiescence. There would be no serious risk to the living standards of the northern Irish. On the contrary, the settlement would help to provide a basis for rebuilding an economy which has been severely weakened by two decades of violence. Given the more certain dangers involved in following the only alternatives, i.e. continuing the British presence in Northern Ireland or creating a united Ireland, negotiated independence deserves serious consideration.

Notes

1. This paper has benefited from utilizing the key arguments presented by those individuals and organizations who have advocated independence for Northern Ireland since 1976. Their publications include Murphy (1984); NUPRG (1979); and O'Connor (1984). Rowthorn and Wayne (1988) has also been very useful. While Rowthorn and Wayne state the case for a united Ireland, they also present arguments which are as suited, or more suited, to the case for an independent Northern Ireland.
2. Those from the Republic of Ireland who have supported the concept of an independent Northern Ireland include Euro MP Neil Blaney, Senator T. K. Whitaker, and Senator Trevor West. Whitaker's advocacy of this option can be found in NUPRG (1979: 45–8). For West's views, see West (1975). In addition to Dervla Murphy (Murphy 1984), the Irish writer Desmond Fennell has also supported an independent Northern Ireland. See Fennell (1975a,b).
3. This is a central justificatory argument for the institutions and principles advocated by the well-known moral philosopher John Rawls. See Rawls (1985).
4. This suspicion is fuelled by the provisions of the Prevention of Terrorism Act, which prevents suspected terrorists from entering the British mainland while allowing them to move about freely in Northern Ireland.

5. It was probably this alienation which accounted for the increased support for negotiated independence among Protestants which was discovered by the unionist task force in early 1987. See Joint Unionist Task Force (1987).

6. As Moxon-Browne has pointed out (Moxon-Browne 1977), it has become a well-established tenet of Community philosophy that potential members should observe standards of democracy far in advance of mere majority rule. The Community has suspended benefits to countries during lapses from these standards, e.g. the Colonels' Greece. In the same vein, the Spanish government was made clearly aware of the democratic reforms that were required before its bid for membership could be considered.

7. For a discussion of the disastrous economic consequences of a unilateral declaration of independence, see Gibson (1986).

8. Rowthorn and Wayne (1988: 138–9) advocate the use of a range of similar measures by the British government to force a Protestant government in Belfast that had unilaterally declared independence into a united Ireland. However, as Protestants are much less opposed to internal accommodation with Catholics in Northern Ireland than they are to a united Ireland, such measures have a much greater chance of promoting the former than the latter.

9. Various other Protestant groups which support independence have also recognized the need for power-sharing with Catholics in an independent Northern Ireland. For example, see statements by the Ulster Independence Movement (Ulster Independence Movement 1976); the Ulster Independence Party in *Fortnight*, 12 May 1978; and the Ulster Loyalist Democratic Party in *Ulster*, Jan. 1984.

10. While the UDA's document *Common Sense* (Ulster Political Research Group 1987)—reviewed in ch. 6—called for Cabinet-level power-sharing and a Bill of Rights to be entrenched in a Northern Ireland constitution within a United Kingdom framework, the organization has since stated that an independent Northern Ireland should have a similar constitution (*Ulster*, Sept. 1988, p. 2).

11. Claire Palley uses demographic changes to support her arguments for a united Ireland (Palley 1986; see also ch. 3 of this volume). Palley claims that Protestants would be acting prudently if they started negotiating for a federal Ireland now as they will be voted into a unitary state as soon as Catholics become a majority. However, this line of reasoning is dubious on three counts. First, while the size of the Catholic population is increasing, it is by no means certain that they will ever become a majority. Second, even if Catholics did gain a majority, it is not clear that they would vote for a united Ireland in sufficient numbers, as many, if not most, of them do not support this option at present. Third, and most importantly, even if a Catholic majority did vote for unification, this

would merely replace a United Kingdom which has a large dissentient Catholic minority with a united Ireland which had a large dissentient Protestant minority. On a related point, Rowthorn and Wayne's view (1988: 212) that Catholics may well become a majority of the population in Northern Ireland casts doubt upon their earlier argument (1988: 138) that Catholics would not voluntarily accept independence because it 'would leave them permanently reliant on the goodwill of the Protestant majority'.

12. See Garret FitzGerald's attack on the concept of an independent Northern Ireland from this perspective (*Belfast Telegraph*, 10 Aug. 1979).

13. By the end of 1988, 2,724 people had died in the 'troubles' (see App. 3). British Army generals acknowledge that the Republican campaign of violence will continue as long as there is a British presence in Ireland (see Brigadier James Glover's comments in O'Malley 1983: 263), and the new Northern Ireland Secretary of State, Peter Brooke, has admitted publicly what British politicians have privately said for a long time: the British security forces cannot defeat the IRA militarily.

14. Rowthorn and Wayne (1988: 157–8) use these arguments to back up their claim that British subventions will be forthcoming to a united Ireland. The arguments, however, are at least as plausible in the context of a negotiated independence for Northern Ireland.

15. In this same document (NUPRG 1979), Senator T.K. Whitaker, former Governor of the Central Bank of Ireland and the person responsible for the Republic's economic planning from 1958, expressed his conviction that the British subvention would be continued to an independent Northern Ireland and that the state would be viable (NUPRG 1979: 48). He regarded the continuation of the subvention as contingent on both sections of the community agreeing to a constitution for the new state.

16. While nationalist propagandists (Rowthorn and Wayne 1988: 191) are correct to point out that a majority of the British electorate want to withdraw from Northern Ireland, this does not translate into majority support in Britain for a united Ireland.

17. Nationalists, of course, often claim that an independent Northern Ireland would be a threat to Britain's security. See e.g. Garret FitzGerald's comments to this effect, *Belfast Telegraph*, 10 Aug. 1979.

18. Rose (1976b: 157) has pointed out that Britain could, if it thought it necessary, sign a military treaty with the new state, giving Britain the right to intervene if unfriendly forces involved themselves in Northern Ireland. However, such a derogation from sovereignty might pose an obstacle to gaining internal support for independence, especially from Catholics.

19. Ireland refused to end its neutrality even when Britain promised significant steps towards a united Ireland in 1940 (Bowman 1982: 229–36; see also ch. 1, sect. 4).

20. In one survey 51% of respondents said they would not be prepared to pay heavier taxes to run a united Ireland (Cox 1985: 35). See also ch. 5, Sect. 1 of this volume. In a 1986 referendum a majority of the Republic's electorate voted to retain a constitutional ban on divorce despite warnings by some politicians that this would weaken the prospects for unity.
21. There are potential benefits which would accrue to nationalists if they refrained from putting pressure on unionists (Whyte 1981: 427–8).

11

Conclusion

Northern Ireland's Options: A Framework and Analysis

John McGarry and Brendan O'Leary

> Free institutions are next to impossible in a country made up of
> different nationalities. Among a people without fellow-feeling
> ... the united public opinion necessary to the working of rep-
> resentative government cannot exist.
>
> (John Stuart Mill, *Considerations on Representative Government*)

NORTHERN IRELAND is a segmented society. Segmented societies
are divided into separate subcultures which possess radically different identities and values. The subcultures frequently have their
own network of separate and exclusive voluntary associations, such
as political parties. They enjoy different leisure activities, read
separate newspapers, attend separate educational institutions, and
live in segregated neighbourhoods. The divisions in these societies
may be racial, ethnic, religious, linguistic, or ideological, or some
permutation thereof. Northern Ireland's segmentation is based on
ethnicity and religion, and has its origins in Britain's imperial and
colonial past. The historical province of Ulster was an ethnic frontier
between Britain and Ireland, where Scots and English planters
settled amidst Irish natives (see *inter alia* Buchanan 1982; Lustick
1985; Robinson 1982; Wright 1987).[1]

Segmented societies lack the internal consensus which underlies
political stability in more homogeneous societies.[2] They are inherently unbalanced and often, as in Northern Ireland, exist in an
unstable state ranging from uneasy peace to outright civil war. There

are, however, several strategies available for stabilizing segmented societies, many of which have been proposed for Northern Ireland in the chapters of this book. These strategies can be divided into five basic types: control, assimilation, partition, externally managed arbitration, and power-sharing.[3] This concluding chapter assesses the value and relevance of each of these strategies as a way forward for Northern Ireland.

1. STRATEGIES FOR STABILIZATION

Control

According to the political scientist who pioneered this concept, control involves 'a relationship in which the superior power of one segment is mobilized to enforce stability by constraining the political actions and opportunities of another segment or segments' (Lustick 1979: 328). Historically it has been the most common mode through which segmented societies have been stabilized. Control is most often overtly undemocratic in form, with imperial or authoritarian regimes controlling multicultural territories through élite co-option and/or coercive domination. However, control can also be 'democratic' if the controlling segment has a majority of the population. The classic example of the 'democratic' version of control is Northern Ireland itself, where the Protestant majority used its monopoly of power under the Westminster system of government to rule Northern Ireland between 1921 and 1972. Many unionists, especially in the Democratic Unionist Party (DUP), still demand a return to control in Northern Ireland through the restoration of a devolved government on a majority-rule basis. They believe that Stormont government worked, in the sense that it maintained order, and that it was democratic, because it was based on majority rule.

There are several fundamental problems attached to this option for Northern Ireland. First, it is undesirable: the quality of majority-control democracy is dubious. Majoritarian democracy only works well when key conditions are present: when the exclusion of the minority is temporary; and when the issues dividing the majority from the minority are not fundamental so that the minority can expect their interests to be reasonably well served by government policies. These conditions do not exist in segmented societies.

In Northern Ireland, between 1921 and 1972, the Ulster Unionist

Party was elected to government at every election. It was a hegemonic party that could not be defeated. Historians, government-appointed commissions, political scientists, and Marxists all agree that the majoritarian government used its power in a discriminatory fashion to benefit its supporters at the expense of the minority (see *inter alia* Buckland 1979; Cameron 1969; Darby 1976; Farrell 1976). Arguments that this treatment would not be repeated can be dismissed. Majoritarian governments in segmented societies, their hold on power dependent on segmental cohesion, have no clear incentive to make concessions to minority groups and every incentive to help their own.

Second, the restoration of control is unworkable: there is very little likelihood that a reversion to majority-control democracy would result in a return to the stability of 1921–69 as supporters of the option claim. The control system broke down between 1969 and 1972 as a result of a minority rebellion which still persists. Minority expectations have increased since that period and any attempt to reimpose majority rule would almost certainly provoke a marked increase in violence. The reimposition of control would require much more radical coercion of the insurgent minority. The costs of this strategy in Northern Ireland do not need elaboration. It would also create obvious costs for the British government: a dramatic deterioration of relations with the Irish Republic and poor human-rights publicity in European and North American capitals. The peculiar conditions which allowed control to be maintained between 1920 and 1969 are not likely to be restored.[4]

It is therefore highly unlikely that Westminster could condone such a strategy, although Humphrey Atkins did flirt with the option while Secretary of State in 1979–80. Article 4 (b) and (c) of the Anglo-Irish Agreement states that the only acceptable form of devolution for Northern Ireland is one which would secure the co-operation of both minority and majority (see Appendix 1),[5] which effectively rules out a return to control while the Agreement lasts.

Partition

Partition is a logical solution for the problems of segmented societies. If it is impossible for rival groups to live together in a heterogeneous state, it makes obvious sense for them to live apart in two or more homogeneous states. Liam Kennedy outlines in Chapter 5 a number of different ways in which Northern Ireland could be partitioned, all of which aim at separating the two antagonistic communities, thereby reducing the interactions which precipitate violence.

The major problem with the option of partition when applied to Northern Ireland is that the population there is so interspersed that any attempt to redraw the border will leave a substantial minority of Catholics in the part remaining with Britain and a substantial minority of Protestants in the section ceded to the Irish Republic. Kennedy's paper presents the most plausible case for partition in Northern Ireland to date. But even his most radical attempt to produce two homogeneous Ulsters, a scenario in which West Belfast is added to the Republic in addition to the present border areas, would leave a British Ulster with a 20 per cent Catholic minority and an Irish Ulster with a 16 per cent Protestant minority. It may be possible, as Kennedy claims, to reduce the size of these minorities further with 'generous resettlement grants' but given the attachment of Catholics and Protestants to their territory, the policy would face severe difficulties in implementation. Forced transfers would solve this problem, albeit at the cost of sacrificing many people's human rights. In any case, as most of the Protestants who would have to move from the western counties are farmers and most of the Catholics who would have to move from the eastern counties are urban, any direct exchange would be impractical.

Given the likely existence of continuing heterogeneity in Kennedy's 'two Ulsters' there would be risks attached to a partition settlement along the lines he proposes, especially during the transition period. Both majorities would have an interest in making 'their' Ulster as homogeneous as possible. If the patterns of intimidation established in 1969–70 were followed, Catholics would be forced out of Protestant areas and Protestants would be ejected from Catholic areas. A similar scenario cost half a million lives during the partition of the Indian subcontinent in 1947 (Khoshla 1950: 229). Violent evictions would produce two embittered sets of refugees, posing problems for international relations and security co-operation between Ireland and Britain.

It is true that the pattern of partition of Ireland between 1920 and 1925 was in many senses the most fundamental historical cause of the current conflict. The creation of the home-rule Parliament in Belfast and the territorial demarcation of the new entity of Northern Ireland as six counties of the historical province of Ulster laid the foundations of the system of Stormont control. In historical Ulster, Protestants precariously outnumbered Catholics (56 per cent to 44 per cent), but without Cavan, Donegal, and Monaghan the religious ratio in the rest of Ulster altered dramatically in favour of Protestants (65 per cent to 35 per cent). In negotiations with British governments the territory of Northern Ireland was self-consciously carved out by unionists with a view to winning the maximum sustainable amount of territory. They wanted 'those districts which they could control' (Miller 1978: 122 ff.).

The territorial definition of Northern Ireland was thus an act of domination; it guaranteed an in-built Protestant majority, providing Catholic population-growth did not dramatically exceed that of Protestants. The partition was—and remains—dramatically imperfect for those who sought to legitimize it on national, ethnic, or religious grounds. As John Hume has put it, 'Without a minority in Northern Ireland the 1920 settlement would have been perfect' (O'Malley 1983: 100). The Catholic, and largely Irish nationalist population, not only composed over a third of the entire population, but were also a local majority in two of the six counties (Fermanagh and Tyrone), the second city of the territory (Derry/Londonderry), and in almost all of the local-government jurisdictions contiguous with the border.

The British negotiators of the Anglo-Irish Treaty of 1921 were aware of the injustice of incorporating Fermanagh and Tyrone into Northern Ireland. However, they reassured the Irish negotiators by the promise of a future Boundary Commission and with the thought that the presence of a large minority within Northern Ireland would make the new entity both unworkable and illegitimate. There is little doubt (1) that the establishment of a Boundary Commission was designed to avoid a break in negotiations over the issue of Ulster because that would have seriously embarrassed the British, (2) that Lloyd George assured Unionists that the Boundary Commission would lead to very minor changes, whereas he assured Sinn Féin that it would lead to very substantial changes, and (3) that the Sinn Féin negotiators paid insufficient attention to the precise wording of the Boundary Commission clauses in the Treaty (Pakenham 1967: 166–82). The Boundary Commission, which met in 1925, failed to produce any radical adjustments of the border for complex reasons which we cannot detail here (see *inter alia* Gallagher 1957: 169–76; Gwynn 1950: 202–36; Laffan 1983: 91–105).

Kennedy's proposals are in effect an attempt to rectify the wrongs of 1920–5. Unlike Irish nationalists he does not see any injustice in partition *per se*, but rather in the specific pattern of partition executed in the 1920s. However, the British record in partitioning former colonies (Palestine, Ireland, and the Indian subcontinent)[6] and the practical difficulties in repartitioning Northern Ireland, which have been spelt out by various demographers, geographers, lawyers, and political scientists (Boal, 1982: 249–80; Boyle and Hadden 1985: 34–7; Compton 1981: 74–92; Rose 1976*b*: 160–3; Walsh 1981: 93–9) help explain why there has been no recent move to explore the merits of this option by bilateral discussions between both governments. However, Mrs Thatcher is said to have commissioned papers on repartition (*Sunday Press* (Dublin), 4 November 1984),[7] and it is an option which may increase in attractiveness for the British government if the Anglo-Irish Agreement does not induce a more desirable settlement. As we shall suggest in our summing up, repartition is the most benign of drastic default options if more desirable strategies should fail.

Assimilation

A third strategy for stabilizing segmented societies is to eliminate or reduce substantially the plural character of the society through assimilation or integration. Political stability is produced as a consequence of the disappearance of primordial subnational attachments and their replacement with national loyalty through processes of acculturation and socialization. Assimilation requires at least one segment to replace its identity (or at least that part of its identity which is the cause of the conflict) with the identity of the dominant group, or it requires the creation of a transcendent identity. Advocates of this strategy believe that it is only when integration takes place that 'normal' political development can take place on a left–right basis.

Assimilation options are attractive, as they aim at replacing sectarianism with the creation of a common social will, at creating homogeneity in place of antagonistic heterogeneity. The success of the strategy, however, is dependent on the segmentation in the society being weak to begin with or being merely the temporary segmentation of immigrants who have assimilation as their goal (as in the United States). There is not a single instance of the strategy being successful in historically, deeply segmented bicommunal societies. In societies such as these, any attempt to eradicate the strongly entrenched subcultures not only is unlikely to succeed, especially in the short run, but may stimulate segmental cohesion and intersegmental violence rather than national conciliation. Attempts to ignore the concerns of strong subcultures will result in remedies being unsuccessful and perhaps even counterproductive.

In this volume Anthony Coughlan claims in Chapter 2 that Northern Ireland Protestants could and should be integrated into a united Ireland. According to his thesis, the creation of a unitary Irish state would result in the backward, church-dominated subcultures in both parts of Ireland being transcended by a new national identity and political divisions based on class. This argument is a classic example of 'republican' Irish nationalism. It has its roots in Tone's famous statement that an independent and united Ireland would 'unite the whole people of Ireland . . . abolish the memory of all past dissensions and . . . substitute the common name of Irishman in place of the denominations of Protestant, Catholic and Dissenter'.

For such a thesis to be considered realistic, it is essential that Coughlan demonstrate the brittle nature of the unionist subculture in Northern Ireland. He and traditional Irish nationalists assume that the Protestants are part of the Irish nation who, while presently alienated from their fellow countrymen, would be able to reach a political accommodation with them in the event of a British withdrawal. The 'scales will fall from their eyes' in the latter event, and Protestants would recognize their 'true' national identity. If the British declared their intention to leave, and took appropriate measures to minimize Protestant resistance, such as providing subsidies to the new Ireland and disarming the Ulster Defence Regiment,[8] Coughlan claims there would be no serious internal obstacle to the realization of a united Ireland. In this respect Coughlan's arguments do not depart from those of traditional republicans, such as those in Sinn Féin and the Irish Republican Army (IRA), and also *some* within the Social Democratic and Labour Party (SDLP) and Fianna Fáil. They routinely put more emphasis on seeking a British withdrawal than in attempting to win over unionists, because the latter objective is seen to be a secondary matter and relatively unproblematic 'in the long run'.

The claim that Protestants will not fight (or at least not fight convincingly) to prevent a united Ireland is hypothetical and rests on a contestable and wishful interpretation of Irish history. In the past,

Protestants have been at their most militant whenever unification under an Irish state was considered a serious possibility: when Gladstone converted to Home Rule in 1886, during the Home Rule crisis of 1912 and the civil wars leading to partition in 1920–2, and again during the years between 1972 and 1976 when Protestants feared a British withdrawal. On each of these occasions, Protestants grouped together in tens of thousands to join paramilitary bodies. These facts conflict with the nationalist argument that the British presence is the main obstacle to a united Ireland. There are already some 20,000 armed Protestants in the RUC, the RUC Reserve, and the UDR, and the majority of legally held guns are in Protestant hands. There seems to be no compelling reason why Protestants would not again resort to their traditional method of resisting a united Ireland if it became a declared policy of the British and Irish governments. Nobody should extrapolate from the relatively mild loyalist backlash to the Anglo-Irish Agreement (see Appendix 3) to the assumption that unionists will go quietly into a united Ireland. Arguments like those advanced by Coughlan seem to us to belong to the Gaelic Romantic rather than the Irish Enlightenment strand of Irish nationalism.[9]

Other nationalist intellectuals and politicians now admit that the Protestants are an autonomous subculture who must be persuaded of the benefits of a united Ireland (see, for example, FitzGerald 1972). This realization was the clear message of the New Ireland Forum Report (even if its recommendation of an Irish unitary state as the best solution did not follow from its own prior analysis).

There are obvious and fundamental difficulties with the traditional republican nationalism of authors like Coughlan. The Republic's desire or ability to coerce a large recalcitrant Protestant majority into a united Ireland must be doubted (Cox 1985). Its citizens' desire for Irish unity is a 'low-intensity aspiration' (O'Brien 1980: 39). While it is plausible to conceive of the British reneging on their guarantee to Protestants and withdrawing from Northern Ireland if the violence continues and/or the costs of the British commitment escalate, it is unreasonable to expect that they will also be willing to coerce Protestants into a united Ireland against their will precisely because the costs of such an operation would be even higher. For all these reasons, the most likely consequence of a unilateral British withdrawal is not a united Ireland but a more intense civil war followed by a partitioning of Northern Ireland.

Many unionists parallel the arguments of nationalists in claiming that the Northern Ireland minority can be integrated into the United Kingdom. Like their nationalist counterparts, unionist 'integrationists' typically seek to demonstrate the weakness of the subculture which is to be assimilated. They draw attention to the significant number of Catholics who are unionists and claim that those who are not (including the IRA) would acquiesce if the British would only make it clear, once and for all, that Northern Ireland was to be governed in exactly the same way as other parts of the United Kingdom (McCartney 1986). Such a step, it is claimed, would remove Catholic fears of a return to Protestant majority control and deprive the IRA of its hope of victory (Oliver 1988). If this policy was followed, they claim, communal attachments would gradually give way to normal politics of left and right, as happened in Glasgow and Liverpool earlier in the century.

Integration of Northern Ireland with Britain is indeed a more feasible goal than integration with the rest of Ireland, given the organizational resources of the British state, and given that the Catholic minority are already in the United Kingdom and that a significant proportion of Catholics do not wish to become a part of the Republic. It might have been possible to implement such a strategy peacefully at certain points in the past such as after the partition of Ireland in 1920 or in the late 1960s. It might be possible to achieve it even at some future stage. If it was tried now, however, it would probably result in an increase in support for the large republican subculture, which has been successfully developed and articulated by Sinn Féin in the 1980s. If integration were to promote peace and stability, steps would need to be taken to crush that subculture, steps which liberal-democratic governments are usually unwilling to take. It would also require the unilateral abandonment of the Anglo-Irish Agreement,[10] lead to a breakdown in Anglo-Irish relations, compel the SDLP to become more nationalist, and produce a negative international reaction, especially in the United States but also among European Community members.

Apart from a brief period in the late 1970s, when the Labour minority government expediently granted five more Westminster seats to Northern Ireland, and the Conservatives under their Northern Ireland spokesman, Airey Neave, supported integration, British policy-makers have been anxious to quarantine Irish affairs from mainstream British politics (see *inter alia* Arthur 1985: 37–50;

Boyce 1988). They have no desire to have Northern Ireland affairs permanently debated at Westminster, risk Northern Ireland MPs holding the balance of power there, or permanently coerce the recalcitrant Irish nationalist minority.

Hugh Roberts's paper (Chapter 4), which calls for the British parties to organize in Northern Ireland, can also be included in the assimilation category. Roberts claims that it is the failure of the British parties to organize in Northern Ireland which has perpetuated the sectarian divisions in the province. For him, the unionist and nationalist subcultures can only be transcended and 'normal' political development begin when the British parties organize in the province. Like the other 'nation-building' proposals, Roberts's case rests on proving the brittle nature of the present subcultures. To this end, he presents polls which show that a significant proportion (53 per cent) of the Northern Ireland electorate want the British parties to contest elections in the province and would be prepared to vote for these parties.[11] These findings lead Roberts to conclude that the orthodox view 'that the people of Northern Ireland are obsessed with their religious differences and their communal politics . . . and cannot be induced to set aside these preoccupations . . . [is] . . . groundless' and a 'demonstrable myth'.

However, the claim that the organization of the British parties in Northern Ireland would lead to a breakdown of sectarian politics is valid only if those prepared to vote for the British parties have non-sectarian motives for doing so. As Labour is officially committed to a united Ireland and as the Conservatives more clearly support the Union between Britain and Northern Ireland, Roberts's claims seem less sensible. The viability of his prescription must depend critically not only upon the presence of significant numbers prepared to support the British parties but also upon the existence of significant numbers of Catholic Conservatives and Protestant supporters of Labour. Otherwise, what may appear to be non-sectarian electoral behaviour and non-sectarian responses to poll questions may in fact be deeply sectarian. The poll that Roberts presents does not provide a breakdown of party preference and religious affiliation but a *Belfast Telegraph* poll of October 1988 which does is very revealing (*Belfast Telegraph*, 6 October 1988). It shows that 21 per cent of Catholics would support Labour but only 6 per cent of Protestants would do so. Moreover, 24 per cent of Protestants would vote Conservative but only 6 per cent of Catholics would do so. This differential in support cannot be explained adequately by class differences between the two communities, although that may account for some of it. The poll also reveals that, in the event of British parties organizing in Northern Ireland, 70 per cent of Catholics would continue to vote for parties advocating a united Ireland (35 per cent SDLP, 14 per cent Sinn Féin, 21 per cent Labour) while 81 per cent of Protestants would continue to vote for parties which broadly support the Union (34 per cent OUP, 18 per cent DUP, 5 per cent Alliance, 24 per cent Conservative). This more nuanced poll evidence does not support Roberts's crucial conclusion that popular support for sectarianism is 'anything but immutable'. In these circumstances, it is wishful thinking to claim that the mere organization of British parties in Northern Ireland would result in the Northern Irish adopting British political culture. While there may be solid democratic arguments for requiring the British parties to seek a mandate in the province, given the existence of direct rule, it is extremely doubtful that this step alone would lead to the disappearance of the province's deeply rooted subcultures. Roberts's paper, whilst insightful and principled, displays the critical weakness in his own position. It is evident that the British do not regard Northern Ireland as an integral part of the UK state, let alone the British nation, and, if his own analysis is correct, nothing is likely to shift the British political class from the 'unsound stupidities' which have left Northern Ireland bereft of British political parties.

There is in any case more 'soundness' than Roberts allows in the stupidity of the British political class. The recent conversion of many unionists to integrationist philosophies (Aughey 1989; Wilson 1989) smacks of an Anglo-Irish Agreement—induced conversion rather than a principled political position—although we would exclude Roberts himself from this hypothesis. The character of recent Protestant support for electoral integration is not only of the 'too little, too late' variety, but it also suggests a widespread desire on the part of Protestant unionists to follow any course which enables them to avoid having to do business with their Catholic nationalist minority. Moreover, the new-found enthusiasts for integration blame Northern Ireland's discriminatory system upon the absence of British political parties, thereby displaying wishful thinking about the past as well as the present and future. Finally, in their assumption that the modern state must be based on adversarial two-party politics on the Westminster model they display a parochial British romanticism which mirrors Gaelic Romantics' enthusiasm for the unitary Irish state.

Externally Managed Arbitration

Arbitration is a fourth strategy for stabilizing segmented societies, where conflict is refereed 'by a supposedly neutral authority above the rival subcultures' (Lehmbruch 1975: 378). The authority's dis-interestedness enhances its capacity to act autonomously, unswayed by the partisan preferences of the rival subcultures. The arbiter thereby dampens the violence which would occur in its absence and permits governmental effectiveness to be maintained. The success of this strategy depends, most crucially, on the extent to which the internal antagonistic segments perceive the arbiter as genuinely impartial.

Arbitration has been the dominant strategy employed in Northern Ireland since the abrogation of the Stormont Parliament in 1972, complicated only by the brief power-sharing experiment in the first five months of 1974, and the modifications resulting from the Anglo-Irish Agreement. The British government has claimed to be neutral arbiters in Northern Ireland from their intervention in 1969 at least until 1985. There were four key elements in their arbitration strategy (O'Leary 1989*a*). First, they encouraged the rival subcultures to work together towards a political accommodation, while retaining the position of 'honest brokers'. Their neutrality rested on their refusal to accept unionist extremism (the restoration of majority control) or nationalist extremism (withdrawing from Northern Ireland). Second, they proclaimed the reform of Northern Ireland. Third, after some initial equivocation, they criminalized political violence. Finally, they pursued a bipartisan consensus, to quarantine the affairs of Northern Ireland from the rest of Britain.

Their arbitration strategy enjoyed some success in the late 1970s, with decreasing levels of violence and polls indicating that both communities were prepared to accept (or tolerate) direct rule as a second-best option (Rose *et al.* 1978). Direct rule also won support from iconoclastic Irish politicians, notably Dr Conor Cruise O'Brien, who regarded it as the least bad option, echoing the apologias of British administrators.

However, the arbitration strategy came unstuck in the early 1980s. This was largely because Catholics increasingly perceived it as an option biased towards unionists, even though that group was not enamoured by direct rule. Direct rule was after all British rule. The longer it persisted, the more the British government became the primary target of minority discontent and was blamed for the many continuing discreditable features of Northern Irish society. The British were perceived to rely upon sectarian instruments of coercion: the Protestant-dominated RUC and UDR, and the 'extraordinary' legal system. Roy Mason's years as Secretary of State (1976–9) were not seen as neutral arbitration by the Catholic working class. 'Ulsterization', 'criminalization', and the minority government's expedient concession of extra Westminster seats to Northern Ireland suggested that the British were on the side of the unionists. Above all, the failure of the British to reform Northern Ireland became increasingly evident in Catholic eyes. Catholic unemployment remained dramatically higher than Protestant unemployment, the male Catholic rate being 2.5 times the male Protestant rate, and Catholics blamed the differential on discrimination.[12] Catholics did not see their relative position improving under direct rule and it was widely recognized that Protestants preferred direct rule to power-sharing. Caesar's question *'Cui bono?'*, if asked of direct rule, had an obvious answer to Northern Ireland Catholics.

The government's security policy, its handling of emergency legislation, interrogation procedures, judicial processes, and prison management built support for the Provisionals. The 1980–1 hunger strikes allowed Sinn Féin to emerge as a serious political force. This development, added to the increasingly adverse international reaction to British management of Northern Ireland, forced the government to explore alternative longer-term strategies with the government of the Republic, resulting in the Anglo-Irish Agreement (O'Leary 1987*b*).

It is Bew and Patterson's contention (Chapter 8) that the failure of arbitration by the British government was not inevitable. They attribute its lack of success to the unwillingness of the British state to embark upon a radical reformist programme in Northern Ireland aimed especially at reducing the socio-economic deprivation of the nationalist minority and their lack of confidence in the administration of justice and the security forces.

In their view, the Anglo-Irish Agreement has produced a more unstable system of direct rule, namely, 'direct rule with a green tinge'. The prospects for stability resulting from radical government intervention, already bleak under Thatcherism, have been further reduced because reforms are now linked in unionist minds to 'creeping unification', a process they believe has unified unionism behind its most reactionary elements. To break this stalemate, they propose a twin-track approach. First, the British state should embark upon a radical initiative to create substantial new employment in Northern Ireland with the aim of reducing Catholic deprivation without damaging Protestants. It should also implement legal and security reforms, including a 'genuinely independent system for investigating complaints against the police and a Bill of Rights'. Such reforms, they concede, are unlikely under Thatcherism. Second, in order to strengthen the position of unionist moderates and thus further enhance the prospects for stability, the government should take measures to separate internal reform from 'creeping unification'. As they believe that removal of the Agreement would strengthen Sinn Féin at the expense of the SDLP, Bew and Patterson suggest other ways in which unionists might be placated. These include the holding of another border poll, improvements in the handling of Northern Ireland business at Westminster (for example, by the establishment of a Northern Ireland Grand Committee), and the organization of the Conservative Party in the province.

Bew and Patterson are surely correct to emphasize that in principle there was much greater scope for extensive reform of Northern Ireland under direct rule. However, the question arises why it did not occur. The possibility that the institutions of direct rule continued to entrench traditional Protestant interests seems to escape their analysis. Perhaps 'direct rule with a green tinge', i.e. the Agreement, was essential to restore momentum to the idea of reforming Northern Ireland. Small-scale but significant steps to protect the minority cultural rights and a major new Fair Employment Act (1989) would suggest as much. However, the more incongruous component in Bew and Patterson's prescriptions is the suggestion that more reformist policies should be followed by the Conservative Government, including organizing the Conservative Party in the province. Precisely how this development would add momentum to the reform of Northern Ireland remains obscure.[13]

Power-Sharing

Power-sharing between leaders of the rival subcultures is the final strategy for stabilizing divided societies. Whereas assimilationists seek to erode one or all of the subcultures in a segmented society, advocates of power-sharing reject this plan as unrealistic, at least in the short term, and accept the segmental characteristics of the society as the stable building blocks for the regime. While proponents of power-sharing concede that their preferred option may strengthen and institutionalize sectarianism, especially in the short-term, they claim that power-sharing can create the conditions for assimilation to proceed peacefully at some later stage by resolving some of the major disagreements among the segments and by creating sufficient trust at both élite and mass levels to render power-sharing itself eventually superfluous.[14] In the case of Northern Ireland, advocates of power-sharing suggest that after a successful and extended period of such government two possibilities might become feasible. First, on the national question, sufficient trust might develop for Catholics to accept assimilation into Britain, or for Protestants to accept assimilation into the Irish Republic, or for both communities to build an independent Northern Ireland. Second, the political culture of the province could change, as the conditions for the preservation of sectarianism are eroded and a 'normal' class politics develops.

Power-sharing, or consociation as it is known in political science, is distinguished by sustained co-operation amongst political élites, and requires four basic institutional developments. First, the government must be a power-sharing coalition of the segmental leaders. Second, proportionality must apply throughout the public sector: that is, there must be proportional representation in the electoral systems, in assembly committees, in the policing and judicial apparatuses, in public employment and in the allocation of public expenditure. Third, mutual veto or concurring majority principles must operate (whether they be *de facto* or *de jure*), allowing each subculture, especially the potential minorities, to prevent domination by others. Finally, segmental autonomy must exist, allowing the cultural segments which divide the society sufficient freedom to enable them to make decisions on matters of profound concern to them. In Northern Ireland a certain degree of segmental autonomy already exists in the field of education. A very much more radical version of consociation would entail a situation in which each community polices and judges itself, that is, a literal fragmentation or cantonization of state powers.

In Northern Ireland, power-sharing is the only constitutional option which consistently draws significant support from both sub-cultures. While their proposals differ in important details, power-sharing is supported by the Alliance Party (APNI) and by the SDLP, and has been put forward by members of the Ulster Unionist Party (UUP) and Ulster Defence Association (UDA) (see Chapter 6). Power-sharing is also the official policy of the governments of the United Kingdom and the Republic of Ireland, as stated in the Anglo-Irish Agreement (Article 4). Few non-partisans doubt that a power-sharing settlement, which necessarily would involve the leaders of the two subcultures in the governing of their own province, would be a desirable way forward for Northern Ireland. The key question is whether power-sharing is feasible in the province.

The experience of Northern Ireland since the abrogation of the Stormont Parliament suggests that a power-sharing settlement is unlikely to be attained. This option can be achieved only when certain conditions are present.[15] Political leaders from the rival segments have to be sufficiently motivated to engage in conflict regulation. They must also simultaneously be capable of retaining the support of their followers. This condition is likely to be present where political élites enjoy predominance over a deferential and organizationally encapsulated following and where the subcultures in the segmented society enjoy internal stability.[16] Finally, the nationalism of the rival subcultures must be more cultural than political, for as long as each nation uncompromisingly seeks the political objective of independence or unification with its 'own' state, a power-sharing settlement is neither viable nor sustainable. The absence of these crucial conditions in Northern Ireland explain the failure of attempts to promote power-sharing.

There are four reasons why political élites might consider consociation. They may desire to fend off a common external threat, maintain the economic welfare of their segment, avoid violence, or obtain office. These motivations have evidently not been present in a 'critical mass' amongst Northern Ireland's politicians. There is no agreed external threat. The radical economic decline of the province has not concentrated enough minds on the merits of accommodation. The desire to avoid war has not been sufficiently intense. Despite the historical experience of segmental antagonisms, the strategies of unionist and nationalist leaders between 1969 and 1972 could not have been better designed to create violence. While important elements within all the major parties have been interested in local office at various times since 1972, their desire has not been strong enough to overcome their unwillingness to accommodate each other.

Even if the leaders of the segments are motivated to compromise with each other or become motivated at some time in the future, they must also be capable of persuading their followers to abide by their decisions. Northern Ireland, however, does not possess an élite-dominated political culture. It is democratically egalitarian in so far as leaders' independence from their followers is strictly limited.[17] The system of values there is certainly different from the acqui-escent or deferential political cultures of other societies where power-sharing has been successful, like Malaysia and the Nether-lands, where leaders are expected to lead and followers to follow. Élite autonomy in these countries has given leaders wide indepen-dent authority to act in a manner which they think best. It facilitates mass compliance even when the latter find their leaders' decisions questionable or distasteful.

The absence of an élite-dominated political culture can be seen in intra-party relations in Northern Ireland. One obstacle to power-sharing there is that the parties are highly democratic, in the sense of being representative of and responsive to their members. Rather than the conventional 'iron law of oligarchy', there exists a high degree of 'democracy from below' in the province's political parties. This facet leaves political leaders unwilling to take risks or adopt new policies for fear of provoking a reaction in their own party or a loss of electoral support to other parties within their segment.

The UUP, the once hegemonic party which governed Northern Ireland without serious challenge for fifty years, has forced out four of its five leaders since 1969 (O'Neill, Chichester-Clark, Faulkner, and West), and its present leader (Molyneaux) cannot be described as authoritative, let alone charismatic. The UUP has endured several breakaway factions (Faulkner's Unionist Party of Northern Ireland and Craig's Vanguard Party in the 1970s, and McCartney's integra-tionists in the wake of the Anglo-Irish Agreement). It seems to be in a permanent leadership crisis. The Vanguard Party, one of the breakaway parties, disintegrated in 1976 when its leader suggested a temporary coalition with nationalists. Even Paisley, leader of the Democratic Unionist Party (DUP) and arguably the most hegemonic of Northern Ireland's political élite, does not have an unassailable position within his party.[18]

The leadership of the SDLP also does not seem to enjoy the

security necessary to negotiate freely on behalf of its members. This is contrary to the view expressed in the first study of the party which gave the impression of a modern party with extensive discretion vested in its leadership (McAllister 1977). When its leader, Gerry Fitt, supported the Atkins initiative in 1979, his party disagreed and he resigned. The party leadership, partly because of its constitution, has not always been able to impose its wishes upon its local branches. One prominent example is the SDLP's decision not to contest the by-election in Fermanagh and South Tyrone which saw Bobby Sands elected to the Westminster Parliament. The tension over the relative importance of power-sharing and the Irish dimension, evident in the SDLP's 1979 leadership turmoil, remains latent. The present leader John Hume's decision to engage in talks with Sinn Féin during 1988 brought this tension into the open.

Sinn Féin leaders are incapable of delivering compromise on power-sharing even if they were somehow to be persuaded of its merits. The party's history, since its inception in 1917, is one of internal dissension and fragmentation. There is truth in Brendan Behan's joke that whenever republicans meet, the first item on the agenda is the split.

Even with the existence of the appropriate motivations and dominant élites, power-sharing would not automatically follow. Political élites must be secure in their segmental bases before hazarding compromise. Northern Ireland's political élites have obviously not felt so secure. The twenty-year crisis and the change in the electoral system have encouraged the fragmentation of the rival segments. When the Protestant/unionist monolith collapsed it broke into five fractions (the UUP, DUP, UPNI, APNI, and Vanguard) and then into three (UUP, DUP, and APNI). Competition for hegemony within this segment has weakened any impetus for power-sharing and accommodation. The DUP (and Vanguard before it) forced the UUP to be as bellicosely anti-consociational and loyalist as themselves. Hume considered the debate among unionists in the early 1980s to be a competition to see who could 'out-Paisley Paisley' (O'Malley 1983: 103). The Catholic/nationalist bloc consolidated behind the SDLP (as the civil rights activists and nationalists made their peace) in the early 1970s but then fragmented under the lack of political progress. Competitive pressure, first from the Irish Independence Party and then Sinn Féin, has left the SDLP continuously guarding its nationalist flank.

The Anglo-Irish Agreement was, in part, a new experiment designed to create the requirements for power-sharing to work. Many, though not all, of its architects, on both the British and Irish sides, saw it as a master-plan to coerce key fractions of the unionist bloc into accepting some version of the Sunningdale 1973–4 settlement, as the lesser of several evils. On the one hand, the Agreement confronted the unionists with an Irish dimension, the Intergovernmental Conference, of far greater political salience than the Council of Ireland of 1973–4. On the other hand, the unionists were offered a mechanism for removing the agenda-setting scope of the Intergovernmental Conference, provided they were prepared to bite the bullet of 'agreed devolution', as specified in Articles 4(b) and (c) of the Agreement. The hope was that the SDLP—having secured an Irish dimension (the Intergovernmental Conference)—would be motivated to reach a consociational accommodation. Strengthened in its segmental rivalry with Sinn Féin, the SDLP would be more able to negotiate. The unpalatable choices which the Agreement put before the unionist bloc, by contrast, were designed to force their leaders to rethink their political attitudes, and to sow divisions amongst them in the hope that a significant group would be willing to grasp the nettle of power-sharing. The Agreement was designed to change the structure of the incentives facing the élites of both blocs and to encourage élite autonomy within Northern Ireland's political parties. It was also hoped that the Agreement would affect intrasegmental relations in a way conducive to power-sharing.

It is now clear, of course, that the Agreement has not sufficiently altered élite motivations, élite autonomy, and segmental stability in ways conducive to power-sharing. The APNI remains the only unionist party willing to accept power-sharing under the terms of the Agreement. Unionists still seem to be willing to stay in their current state of disaffection and general withdrawal of consent against the British government in the hope that the Agreement is repudiated. Rather than proclaiming its willingness to promote power-sharing, the SDLP has emphasized the Irish dimension within the Agreement and seems intent on pushing pan-Irish solutions to the conflict. Rather than conducting serious discussions with unionists, Hume spent most of 1988 meeting with Sinn Féin. Whether he was trying to build a nationalist monolith to help achieve an all-Ireland solution, or simply out-manœuvre Sinn Féin, the talks indicate that an internal settlement is not an urgent priority.

The failure of secret discussions at Duisburg in late 1988 suggests that Hume is not prepared to trade even a temporary suspension of the Conference in return for a power-sharing deal (see *Fortnight*, March 1989, pp. 14–15). Northern Ireland would appear to vindicate John Stuart Mill's pessimism about the prospects for representative government in a country made of different nationalities. It does not seem hospitable territory for consociational solutions.

The notions of federalism or confederalism (hereafter con/federalism) are closely related to consociationalism. Both con/federalists and consociationalists reject the majoritarian principles inherent in Westminster government (Lijphart 1979). The consociational principles of segmental autonomy, power-sharing, proportionality, and the mutual veto are related to the con/federal principles of a constitutionally entrenched central–regional division of powers, equal or disproportionately strong representation of the smaller component units in the federal legislative chamber, and the right of the component units to be involved in the process of amending the con/federal constitution. In segmented societies, a con/federal structure can provide a useful institutional framework for implementing consociational or related principles as long as the territorial boundaries in the con/federation approximate the segmental boundaries. It obviously facilitates segmental autonomy but also allows the implementation of the other consociational principles in various formal and informal ways.[19] If, however, the segmental boundaries in a con/federation do not coincide at least roughly with the territorial boundaries, it will be necessary for anti-majoritarian principles to govern segmental relations within the territorial units as well as relations between the units and the centre.

Whereas supporters of consociationalism in Northern Ireland seek to use its principles to achieve internal consensus, supporters of con/federalism direct their attention primarily to external relations between Northern Ireland and the rest of Britain or Ireland. In calling for a federal United Kingdom, some unionists seek to protect Northern Ireland Protestants from majoritarian decisions at Westminster such as the decision to abolish Stormont or impose the Anglo-Irish Agreement, but seek to combine this with majority rule within Northern Ireland (Smyth 1987). Con/federalism, which would apply anti-majoritarian principles at the UK level, would be used by them as a tool to entrench majority control at the level of the Northern Ireland unit. As the serious conflict is between Northern

Ireland's Protestants and Catholics, and not between Northern Ireland's Protestants and Britain, such a strategy obviously would not contribute to stability in the province but would exacerbate the conflict there.

Supporters of a con/federal Ireland, while they normally envisage a power-sharing settlement within Northern Ireland, see the anti-majoritarian principles inherent in con/federalism as facilitating a consensus between Protestants and Catholics on an all-Ireland basis (Fine Gael 1979). In this respect they are firmly part of the Irish Enlightenment tradition of Irish nationalism (Prager 1986). In this volume, Claire Palley (Chapter 3) claims that a con/federal Ireland is an appropriate solution to the Northern Ireland conflict. She argues that con/federal institutions are emergent in Irish political culture and the framework of the Agreement. Her advice to unionists is to bargain now for a con/federal Ireland from a position of relative strength as demographic trends favouring Catholics will eventually lead to their absorption into an all-Ireland state on less favourable terms.

We are not convinced, however, that an Irish confederation (even in the attenuated form suggested by Palley) is the only or even the most likely long-term constitutional development resulting from the Agreement. Long-term developments, such as economic, demo-graphic, political, or cultural trends, are much more difficult to predict than she suggests. The ideas that Palley puts forward, that the 'logic of history' suggests some form of Irish Union as the 'emergent' solution, have been part of nationalist hopes and unionist fears for the best part of this century. In the present circumstances, it is at least as plausible to suggest that unionist agreement on an internal consociation within the terms of the Agreement could strengthen Northern Ireland's position within the United Kingdom. In addition to winning over significant numbers of Catholics, whose long-term economic interests already dispose them towards sup-porting the Union, such a gesture could win support from crucial elements in the British political élite and could have long-term integrationist consequences. Because agreement on consociation within the terms of the Agreement would result in devolution, it might well contribute towards a 'federalizing' process within the United Kingdom, rather than Ireland.[20] Suggestions that an all-Ireland settlement is inevitable are not helpful. They are more likely to increase Protestants' fears and intransigence than promote conciliatory attitudes.

While it is likely that the political parties and politicians in the Irish Republic would be prepared to accept greater co-operation between their government and a Northern Ireland power-sharing government established within the terms of the Agreement, it is by no means certain that they would be willing to suffer the diminutions of sovereignty necessary to allow a meaningful Irish con/federation to emerge. It may be the proclaimed position of Fine Gael, but it remains untested, and unsupported by the other Irish parties. The Republic's largest party, Fianna Fáil, favours a unitary state in principle, but also presumably because its very unrealizability preserves its predominance in the Irish party system.

Palley's defence of a con/federal Ireland does not seem to us to address satisfactorily the objection made by Vile, although she is evidently aware of its importance. Vile asked 'How far can federalism cope with genuinely deep *communal* divisions within a society?', and argued that it can only cope where there are a large number of units in the federation—preventing domination by one unit and enabling shifting coalitions to take place—and where a party system develops which provides political linkages across territorial boundaries (Vile, 1982). Despite this, Palley envisages a two-unit con/federation in which the southern unit would be twice the size of the northern one. She offers no reasons that would lead us to expect the emergence of brokerage parties of the type considered essential by Vile.

2. WHAT IS TO BE DONE?

None of our contributors give Lenin's answer to his own question. Need we adopt an attitude of philosophical despair and conclude that '*the problem is that there is no solution*—at least no solution recognizable in those more fortunate parts of the Anglo-American world that are governed with consensus' (Rose 1976*b*: 139)? The last five chapters in this collection offer proposals which are aimed at breaking the deadlock. They are all attempts, in their various ways, to create the conditions necessary for power-sharing in Northern

Ireland by providing new incentives for the élites to consider a consociational settlement.

Boyle and Hadden (Chapter 7) argue that the stalemate requires a two-pronged approach by the two governments which, if adopted, would enhance the prospects for internal accommodation. First, if the SDLP are to be motivated to compromise, a number of reforms are required to improve the self-esteem of nationalists within Northern Ireland. Such reforms would include measures to give expression to the nationalist culture within the province, to improve nationalist confidence in the security forces and the administration of justice, and to prevent discrimination in employment.

Second, they argue that if unionists are to be reconciled to the framework established at Hillsborough and to arrive at an internal accommodation with nationalists, a number of important changes to the Agreement are required. The Republic should replace its claim to jurisdiction over Northern Ireland, as expressed in Articles 2 and 3 of its Constitution, with a new clause expressing an aspiration to unity. The present system whereby Northern Ireland legislation is passed by Order in Council, a process that does not allow amendments once draft orders are laid before Parliament, should be changed to allow a select committee to consider and amend legislation before the final parliamentary stage. The requirement that representatives of both communities be guaranteed seats in a Northern Ireland executive should be replaced by a more informal power-sharing arrangement in which matters of special concern to the minority would be protected by weighted-majority requirements or entrenched constitutional rights. Finally, the scope of the Intergovernmental Conference, which is at present almost exclusively concerned with Northern Ireland, should be extended to consider the relationships between the two parts of Ireland and those between Ireland and the United Kingdom as a whole. In this context, the Secretariat, presently located outside Belfast, should perhaps be moved or expanded so that it would have offices in Dublin and London.

These suggestions, though reasonable, are likely to encounter significant obstacles. While a Fianna Fáil government committed to amending Articles 2 and 3 would have little difficulty in winning the support of opposition parties and thus ensuring the success of a referendum on the question, it is unlikely that the present party leadership would take such a step.[21] It is also questionable whether the informal power-sharing arrangements proposed by Boyle and

Hadden would be acceptable to moderate nationalists, as they provide for the possibility of an exclusively unionist executive. The SDLP were given executive seats in 1974. It is doubtful whether they could accept anything less and save face. Their ability to do so in any form, as Boyle and Hadden appreciate, must depend crucially on reforms radically improving the conditions of the minority community. Two decades of British reform programmes which have failed to achieve this end can hardly inspire optimism. However, the Fair Employment Act of 1989 is certainly a step in the right direction.

The UDA proposal for power-sharing (Chapter 6) attempts to alter the nature of the incentives facing the rival élites and to win support from moderate groups within each segment while giving them the necessary leeway to compromise without being outflanked by extremists. The centrepiece of the proposal is a Northern Ireland constitution which contains mandatory provisions for power-sharing and which could be amended only by a two-thirds weighted majority. The virtue of such an amending formula is twofold. As it would effectively prevent a united Ireland unless an overwhelming proportion of Protestants supported it, it would remove their most important objections to power-sharing. As the same clause would guarantee the longevity of a power-sharing settlement and prevent a return to majority rule, it would also be attractive to minority representatives.

So far unionist leaders have been unwilling to embrace the UDA initiative, which was first released in January 1987. Many still seek integration with Britain or majority rule, and at any rate the two unionist parties are unwilling to negotiate on substantive questions unless the activities of the Conference are suspended and the presence of the Anglo-Irish Secretariat scaled down. Even if unionists did put forward the UDA package or something similar, it is unlikely that the SDLP would accept it. Nothing in the SDLP's past behaviour, during, for example, the 1974 Executive, the Convention, the Atkins talks, or Prior's initiative in 'rolling devolution', indicates that it might be willing to abandon a strong Irish dimension for an internal settlement, even a guaranteed one. In the Agreement, constitutional nationalists have been ensured power-sharing and/or a role for Dublin in the Intergovernmental Conference. The treaty, unlike the UDA proposal, requires only simple majority consent for unification to proceed. While these alternatives exist, while Sinn Féin remains a potent electoral threat, and while the Dublin govern-

ment continues to encourage all-Ireland solutions, the possibility of
the SDLP accepting even such a moderate unionist proposal seems
remote.

The final two papers advocate alternative, more decisive, ways to
achieve a power-sharing settlement in Northern Ireland. Anthony
Kenny (Chapter 9) proposes that, while maintaining the framework
of British sovereignty in Northern Ireland, Britain should establish a
five-person executive as the top tier of government within Northern
Ireland. This would consist of the Secretary of State or his or her
deputy, the Minister of Foreign Affairs of the Irish Republic, and
three members elected by the voters of Northern Ireland, in such a
way that two of them are representative of the majority community,
and one of them is representative of the minority. This body would
have a relatively effective decision-making procedure because
neither of the Northern Ireland groups would have veto power.
Finally, according to Kenny, it would be boycott-proof because if
either internal group chose this tactic it would leave its rivals in a
majority. If all the local representatives adopted a boycott, the
default position would be in effect joint direct rule by Westminster
and Dublin.

Kenny's proposal would operate on SDLP motivations and
autonomy. The powerful role for the Republic's government, the
guaranteed role for the SDLP in the coalition, and the provisions
which prevent unionists from exercising a veto make this a desirable
arrangement for the constitutional nationalists and one which they
could enter without fearing a loss of support to Sinn Féin.

Kenny's scheme also provides both positive and negative incentives for unionists. The direct involvement of unionists in such a
government would remove one of their chief fears at present,
namely, that Northern Ireland is being governed behind their backs
between two governments in collusion, possibly acting with a secret
agenda. However, Kenny's proposal also attempts to force unionists
into power-sharing by increasing the pressure already implicit in the
Agreement. Whereas the present unionist refusal to consider power-
sharing merely results in Dublin exercising a role which is 'more
than consultative but less than executive' over those matters suitable
for devolution, a boycott of Kenny's structures would leave Dublin
with a full executive role in the government of Northern Ireland, and
nationalists with a majority in that government. According to
Kenny, unionist acceptance of this package would be facilitated by

the fact that the frightful symbolic barrier of Dublin involvement has already been crossed. The increased role for Dublin, he claims, may not unduly perturb unionists as they already fear that Dublin's power approaches that outlined in his scheme. Kenny's reasoning here is problematic. Unionists' claims that the Agreement was joint authority, or the beginning of joint authority, were rejected by British and Irish government statements, and refuted by the way the Agreement has operated in practice. Kenny's proposal is tantamount to informing unionists that their initial paranoia was lucid sanity. What kind of reasonable response can be expected from unionists in these circumstances?

Kenny recognizes that the prospects for the success of his package would be considerably enhanced if it was accepted as a durable solution by Irish nationalists, North and South. This final factor is equally problematic. Even if some nationalists did accept the arrangements as permanent, there is a serious risk that others would not. Besieged unionists in Northern Ireland tend to view the most extreme representatives of nationalism in Ireland as that community's authentic spokesmen and, therefore, might also see such an arrangement as transitional in nature. As Kenny's structures must involve an explicit upgrading of Dublin's power over Northern Ireland, their implementation might produce destabilization and possibly a very violent reaction.

In these circumstances, more malign than those anticipated by Kenny, his scheme does not seem as boycott-proof as he envisages. If the unionists did refuse to take part, the legitimacy of a governmental arrangement for Northern Ireland that includes Dublin, London, and the minority but not the majority of Northern Ireland's population would be undermined, even if the unionist boycott was self-imposed. Moreover, this outcome, joint direct rule by Britain and Ireland, is not attractive to British and Irish politicians. Britain would share power and responsibility with no reduction in costs, whereas Irish politicians would face increased responsibilities without electoral benefits.

Another variant of coercive power-sharing, imposed independence designed to produce internal accommodation, might also be considered a viable strategy on the grounds that nationalists and unionists would have to agree to accommodate each other without Britain's arbitration. This is the option proposed in Chapter 10. According to the authors, the abandonment of Northern Ireland to its own devices by both Britain and the Irish Republic would provide the necessary motives and autonomy for the élites to compromise. For the first time, peace and prosperity would depend on both élites acting responsibly towards each other.

Like joint authority, however, the success of this proposal is dependent on perceptions of its permanence. It is probable that many nationalists, especially republicans, would regard such a settlement as the first step towards a united Ireland and would still seek to bring about that goal by gun and/or ballot. If they did, Protestant paramilitaries would probably retaliate. Even low levels of violence in an independent Northern Ireland would create distrust between the two communities, presenting serious problems for a power-sharing government, even if one could be formed. Nationalist violence, for example, might produce demands for government retaliation which SDLP members of the executive would find difficult to accept. There would be no agreed default position. For Protestants, the default position would be the imposition of majority control whereas for Catholics it would be an appeal to the Republic to complete the unfinished business of 1916–25. Therefore an independent Northern Ireland could become ungovernable and rapidly descend into civil war, with partition the most likely consequence.

Because of these dangers, neither Britain nor the Irish Republic are likely to approve such an arrangement. Other EC countries, fearful of the consequences for separatist groups within their own borders, would counsel caution. Even moderate members of the Republic's governing élite have asserted that an independent Northern Ireland would be unworkable, and when James Callaghan put forward the option in the British House of Commons in 1981, no one embraced it.[22]

3. SUMMARY

Having invited the contributors to this collection to state their preferred solutions to the conflict in Northern Ireland, and having critically evaluated some of the merits and difficulties with their various ideas, it is only fair that we should explicitly indicate where we stand.

We independently arrived at the same normative and empirical conclusions about the Northern Ireland conflict at the same time (McGarry 1988; O'Leary 1989*a*). Our normative conclusions were as follows. Power-sharing or consociation is the best means of stabilizing the Northern Ireland conflict, on the grounds of equity and of adherence to democratic values. By comparison with some of the other options we evaluated, and have examined here, consociation has the following advantages, which are visibly apparent in the Northern Ireland case. First, consociation is based upon agreement rather than coercion (unlike control, coercive integration or assimilation, or enforced partition). Second, it is based upon conflict regulation by the actors themselves rather than by external powers (unlike external management). Third, consociation is compatible with democratic legitimacy, provided the preconceived Westminster norms of what a democratic system must be like are transcended. Northern Irish Protestants look too much to the Westminster model for their picture of the good polity, whereas we believe they would be better advised to examine the democratic systems of Switzerland, Austria, Belgium, or the Netherlands for models worth emulating. Fourth, consociation has a (partially) successful track record in stabilizing potentially violent societies elsewhere in the world. While it is difficult to realize in certain circumstances, its advocates cannot be accused of the utopian assumptions which unfortunately mar the reasoning of many sincere assimilationists, whether of the British or of the Irish variety. Finally, if consociation succeeds, it becomes dispensable; that is, consociational democracy can facilitate a transition to 'normal' democratic competition, in which sectarian or ethnic divisions are diminished or transcended, as has arguably occurred in the Netherlands. Far from 'institutionalizing sectarianism'—as its critics wrongly suggest—consociation is based upon principles of equality, respect, and mutuality, and facilitates the erosion of sectarianism while permitting cultural differences to survive.

However, as we saw in Section 2 of this chapter, we are persuaded that the essential conditions for consociational democracy are not yet present in Northern Ireland, and that the Agreement has not yet worked in ways conducive to the development of these conditions. Do such conclusions suggest that consociationalists should despair? We think not. We believe (in basic agreement with Boyle and Hadden and in partial agreement with Bew and Patterson) that radical reforms, within the framework of the Agreement, have not been tried consistently or for long enough in ways which might be conducive for a consociational settlement.

A policy aimed at promoting consociationalism implies the restructuring and reform of Northern Ireland to make consociation easier to achieve at some point in the future. On the one hand such a strategy would work by persuading Catholics that Northern Ireland can be reformed through programmes of affirmative action—more far-reaching than those envisaged in the Fair Employment Act of 1989—and justly administered through the restoration of civil liberties, the creation of a Bill of Rights, and the reform of the courts;[23] and by persuading Catholics that sacrificing the immediate pursuit of the objective of Irish unity in return for power-sharing is worth while. On the other hand it would work by forcing (what some regard as) disagreeable change in Northern Ireland, persuading unionists that power-sharing is the best way of protecting their interests and weakening the influence of external powers on public policy in Northern Ireland. This strategy was latent in the terms of the Agreement, and deserves to be tried more earnestly than it has been to date.

Although discrimination and civil rights were centre stage when the conflict in Northern Ireland erupted in 1968 the dominant pre-occupation of commentators since then has been to perceive and analyse the problems of Northern Ireland wholly in terms of political institutions and national identity—as is reflected in the contributions to this volume. While we do not dissent from the primacy of political and constitutional problems and solutions we believe that concentration on these questions should not take place at the expense of public-policy problems surrounding discrimination and civil rights. The evidence of recent research (Smith 1987) also shows that a considerable proportion of the Northern Ireland electorate think the same way.

The aim of the Labour Party's front-bench spokespersons on Northern Ireland is to achieve local consociation through radical, reforming direct rule (McNamara *et al.* 1988). It is the case, of course, that Labour is committed to achieving Irish unity by consent, but it is evident from the statements of Labour's spokespersons that Irish unity is not expected within the life-span of one Labour government. In practice, given that consent will not be attained in the foreseeable future, if at all, the task of a Labour government will be to work the Agreement, reform Northern Ireland, and promote a power-sharing government. Given that, for many reasons, Labour is more likely to be enthusiastic about pursuing such objectives than Conservative governments it is possible that the reforming and consociational dimensions of the Agreement will be given renewed vigour by a future Labour government.

We believe that any such strategy, whether pursued by Labour or the Conservatives, should be accompanied by a systematic change in the electoral system in Northern Ireland. All elections, to the European Parliament, Westminster, a new Northern Ireland assembly, and to local councils, should take place under the same system: a party-list system of proportional representation. This change would have a number of advantages. The first is uniformity. Currently, Westminster elections take place under first-past-the-post whereas other elections take place under the STV system. Second, the change would alter élite motivations amongst the UUP. Competition with the DUP, rather than co-operation, at least during the Westminster elections, would become more likely. Third, the list system has the key advantage over STV of enhancing the authority of party leaders as opposed to the voters (Lijphart 1977: 137), which *might* make compromise easier. Fourth, the list system is genuinely proportional, unlike STV, which is a system which counts preference-rankings and the intensity of preferences. Finally, the list system is used in successful consociational democracies elsewhere.

We also believe that any such strategy should be accompanied by a British commitment to persuading the Irish government to entrench unity by consent in its Constitution, that is, as Boyle and Hadden suggest, by replacing Articles 2 and 3 of the Irish Constitution with a declaration which merely aspires to achieving the unification of the island of Ireland into one state. Suggesting this option is not utterly unrealistic. In December 1967 an all-party committee set up to review the Constitution of 1937 proposed that Article 3 be replaced by a new provision:

1. The Irish nation hereby proclaims its firm will that its territory be reunited in harmony and brotherly (*sic!*) affection between all Irishmen (*sic!*).
2. The laws enacted by the Parliament established by this Constitution shall, until the achievement of the nation's unity shall otherwise require, have the like area and extent of application as the laws of the parliament which existed prior to the adoption of this Constitution. Provision may be made by law to give extra-territorial effect to such laws. (Keogh 1987: 72)

Despite its sexism the enactment of this provision would have effectively constitutionally committed the Irish Republic to seeking 'unity by consent'. The provision failed to be enacted because of opposition within Fianna Fáil, primarily orchestrated by Kevin Boland (Kelly, 1987: 211), but there is no reason to suppose that Fianna Fáil is immutably committed to all of de Valera's legacy. A post-Haughey Fianna Fáil might well be more flexible, especially since the party has been working the Anglo-Irish Agreement since February 1987.

A British government intent on producing a consociational settlement should also take advantage of British and Irish membership of the European Community to promote maximum feasible functional cross-border co-operation (in attracting investment and European Social and Regional Fund support, in agricultural policy, energy production and distribution, and public transport) and maximum feasible legal harmonization (in bills of civil and social rights). The direction of more political attention to Brussels, that is, away from London and Dublin, will be triply beneficial. European arbitrators of interests in Northern Ireland are less likely to be regarded as enemies of either segment; greater European integration will make the differences between membership of the British and Irish states less salient over time; and this type of harmonization will make either con/federal or consociational settlements easier to achieve.

If, as we must candidly admit seems unfortunately all too likely at the time of writing, consociationalism cannot be rapidly engineered (if ever), even by a radical reforming British government actively working the Agreement in conjunction with a similarly motivated Irish government, we must ask what are the most likely ways in which the management of the Northern Ireland conflict will develop?

We believe that there are three feasible political and constitutional strategies available for the consideration of British policy-makers. The first entails a retreat towards the status quo ante, maintaining a modified form of direct rule, slowly downplaying the importance of the Agreement, and reverting to the 'crisis management' much criticized by the Irish government before November 1985. We believe that over the longer run this policy is unsustainable. Policymakers in liberal democracies are under constant pressure to 'do something', and the famous fallacy 'Something must be done; this is something; let's do this' operates regularly in politics. British policy-makers want to end a conflict in which they have no major economic, geopolitical, or political stakes—apart from an annual subsidy running at well over £1 billion.

The second option involves a unilateral abandonment of the Agreement by the British government and integrating Northern Ireland with the rest of the British political system. For reasons we have already referred to, we believe this strategy is unlikely to be embarked upon.

While the final feasible initiative, repartition, is not on the immediate agenda, it is clear that should the Agreement fail in the next decade it will become increasingly attractive to British policy-makers. Repartition is, as Kennedy has ably suggested in this volume, the drastic but logical solution to consociational failures. Moreover, since in our judgement and that of many others the outcome of most solutions which entail a British withdrawal from Northern Ireland is another partition of the island, a simple question must arise at least amongst British policy-makers considering this option. 'If repartition is going to happen if we British decide to leave then why shouldn't we organize it in a more civilized way?' We believe that from the point of view of British governments, especially Conservative ones, repartition is an obvious long-run emergent solution, consonant with their interests and beliefs. It would produce a smaller but loyal British Ulster, and transfer most troublesome Irish Catholics to another jurisdiction. We therefore expect support for this option to grow over time, especially if the Agreement fails to produce a consociational settlement.

What are the feasible political and constitutional strategies facing Irish policy-makers? Their first option is also to revert to the status quo ante. In its most radical form this would entail repudiating the Agreement, retaining the irredentist claim over Northern Ireland, and adopting the policy towards the British which has been nicely satirized by Conor Cruise O'Brien as consisting of the exhortation 'Please go, but for God's sake stay'. This option is unlikely to be followed. Fianna Fáil has now accepted the Agreement, and the Agreement has so far withstood constitutional challenges in the Irish courts.

The second Irish option is to use the framework of the Agreement to promote the position of the minority in Northern Ireland and to advocate a consociational settlement within Northern Ireland as a prelude to the eventual achievement of Irish unity by consent. This option was the one to which the Fine Gael and Labour coalition government committed themselves when they negotiated the Agreement. While the present Fianna Fáil government has come to work much of the coalition's strategy in practice, they have not actively encouraged the formation of a devolved government—not surprisingly, given Haughey's oft-repeated claim that 'Northern Ireland is a failed political entity.'

The final semi-feasible strategic option for Irish policy-makers is to try to negotiate Irish unity, of a unitary or con/federal type, through direct talks with Ulster unionists. This idea, aired regularly by Haughey, seems, at least to us, to be deeply unrealistic. Unionists have no interest in negotiating with Fianna Fáil except if that party offers them what it cannot give them: a repudiation of its republican ideals and aspirations.

What is the conclusion following from this mixture of normative and empirical analysis? The British and Irish governments are locked more deeply into the framework of the Agreement than superficial journalistic commentary on the success of the Hillsborough pact might suggest. Both governments should recognize that only the joint pursuit of consociation within Northern Ireland is likely to pay dividends. Both governments need to be persuaded, as we are, that there are only two long-run stabilizing solutions to the Northern Ireland conflict: consociation or repartition. Of these we believe the former has by far the greater merit, but we realize the strengths of the arguments for another partition—even if it poses drastic dangers. Indeed partition is such a drastic solution that threatening a major repartition of Ulster might actually produce the change in élite motivations, élite autonomy and segmental relations required to generate a consociational settlement.[24] It would concentrate nationalist minds in West Belfast, and unionist minds west of the Bann and south of Armagh. The threat would have to be made credible by the appointment of a boundary commission, by a public declaration on the part of both states to carry out some small adjustments (for example, in Crossmaglen) *pour encourager les autres*. Clarification of the choice between partition and power-sharing, through the threat of partition, just might produce a consociational settlement. Focusing people's attentions on the consequences of the former might persuade them of the merits of the latter.

Notes

1. A summary of the evidence of segmentation in Northern Ireland is provided in Whyte (1986).
2. See Lijphart (1977) for a full explanation of this assertion.
3. Lijphart (1977: 44–45) mentions three strategies: assimilation, partition, and consociation. Lehmbruch (1975: 378) mentions two: arbitration and consociation. Lustick (1979) pioneered the concept of control. There are of course other 'strategies' for 'stabilizing' divided societies—compulsory mass emigration or genocide—but we do not consider these for obvious reasons.
4. For a discussion of the external conditions which permitted unionists to maintain control see Ch. 1.
5. In non-attributable interviews conducted in London and Dublin in 1988–9 B. O'Leary was told that one reason for the wording of Article 4(b) was to encourage unionists to accept devolution because it was *British*. The statement that 'The Irish Government support that policy' was intended to indicate British precedence.
6. For a good discussion of British-managed partitions see Fraser (1984).
7. The accuracy of this Press report was confirmed in an interview with Dr G. FitzGerald conducted by B. O'Leary in Dublin in June 1989.
8. This argument is also made by Rowthorn and Wayne (1988), and, of course, by Sinn Féin and the IRA.
9. The ideal-typical and idealist distinction between the Gaelic Romantic and the Irish Enlightenment strands in Irish nationalism is forcefully presented by Prager (1986) in a book which elaborates an argument first developed by Ronan Fanning.
10. The pursuit of integration would be at odds with the spirit of Article 4 of the Anglo-Irish Agreement, which commits both governments to a power-sharing devolved government (see App. 1), and with the entire temper of the Agreement, which recognizes the legitimacy of two traditions, the nationalist and unionist.
11. Roberts displays no scepticism about the meaning of the poll data. Northern Irish polls are especially unreliable because respondents understate their extremism and over-emphasize their moderation and unreasonableness (which is why the scale of electoral support for the DUP and Sinn Féin causes surprise to those who rely on polls).

In the European Community elections of June 1989 Dr Laurence Kennedy, the 'model Conservative' candidate who stood on a platform advocating Conservative organization in the province, lost his deposit, as did two candidates advocating Labour organization. Between them these candidates polled 5% of the vote in an election tailor-made for a 'protest vote'. This set of results suggests a certain naïvety amongst those who believe that British parties will transform the Northern Ireland electorate. However, since Roberts's paper was written the British Conservatives have announced their commitment to contest four Westminster seats in the next general election to be held in Northern Ireland (*Irish Times*, 10 November 1989).

12. Objective analysis demonstrates that indirect discrimination through informal recruitment remains the major factor in explaining differential unemployment. See SACHR (1987) and Smith (1987).

13. It is one of Northern Ireland's more curious ironies that two of its best-known and respected left-wing analysts should appear to welcome the organization of the Conservative Party in the province.

14. Lijphart (1977: 105) points to the Austrian power-sharing experiment of 1945–66, which paved the way for the resumption of a government-versus-opposition pattern of politics without any danger to the regime's stability, and to The Netherlands, where religious divisions gave way to class politics after a prolonged period of power-sharing.

15. Lijphart identifies a number of background conditions which are conducive or favourable to consociationalism, but none of which are essential. The most important of these are: a multiple balance of power among the segments, so that no segment is dominant; an external threat perceived as a common danger by the different segments; some society-wide loyalties; the absence of extreme socio-economic inequalities among the segments; and the existence of prior historical traditions of political accommodation that predispose the segments to power-sharing. It is clear that most of these favourable conditions have been and are absent in Northern Ireland. See e.g. Lijphart (1975), McGarry (1989), and O'Leary (1989a).

16. This is the central theme of Nordlinger (1972).

17. There may be economic reasons for this. Both subcultures in Northern Ireland lack a strong bourgeois élite, although the absence of this group is especially noticeable in the Catholic segment. Religion may also be a factor. Presbyterians, especially, shun élites. While the Catholic religion is more hierarchical, the old clerical élites are not as dominant in Catholic society as they were before the 1960s.

18. After both Paisley and Molyneaux hinted, following talks with Prime Minister Thatcher in Feb. 1986, that they might be prepared to discontinue their campaign against the Anglo-Irish Agreement, they were both forced to 'recant' immediately after meeting with their party members in Belfast (*Fortnight*, 10 Mar. 1986). In 1971, after causing much consternation among his supporters, Paisley also quickly retracted a statement that an accommodation with the Irish Republic might be possible if the influence of the Catholic Church there was reduced (O'Malley 1983: 192).

19. The Canadian federation provides an example of how federalism can be

used to implement consociational-type principles. Most of the country's francophone minority is concentrated in Quebec, where they constitute 80% of the population. In addition to having segmental autonomy, Quebec's population is formally entitled to a proportionate share of seats in the federal legislature and the federal Supreme Court. Quebec's representatives in the federal legislature informally receive a proportionate share of federal cabinet seats. Proportionality is also observed in the federal civil service. An amendment to give Quebec (and each of the other provinces) a formal veto over all significant constitutional changes has been ratified by the Parliament of Canada and the legislatures of 8 of the 10 provinces. If it is approved by the two remaining provinces before June of 1990, it will become part of the Constitution of Canada.

20. Article 10(c) of the Agreement does assert that a Northern Ireland consociational government 'will need to' establish machinery for cross-border co-operation on economic, social, and cultural matters. However, this does not mean that con/federal institutions will have to be established or that the political links between Northern Ireland and the Republic will become more significant than, or equivalent to, those between Northern Ireland and Britain.

21. Bew and Patterson's suggestion of border polls as an alternative way of reducing unionist fears is more realistic, but it addresses only one unionist fear, that of British withdrawal. A border poll would not address unionists' other fear: that the Irish state is committed to their incorporation without their consent. There is undoubtedly tension between Articles 2 and 3 of the Irish Constitution and Article 1 of the Anglo-Irish Agreement.

22. See Garret FitzGerald's comments, *Belfast Telegraph*, 10 Aug. 1979. For the British political élite's reaction to the independence option, see *The Times*, 3 July 1981. The unwillingness of British and Irish politicians to contemplate the independence option proves nothing about the economic viability of an independent Northern Ireland—much smaller micro-states exist in the world—but it does show that it is an 'unthinkable' option for the political class in Dublin and London.

23. We are not persuaded that democracies necessarily have to abandon civil liberties, due process, and trial by jury in order to deal with terrorist attacks. Indeed the Northern Ireland evidence suggests that abandoning these rights and procedures is actually counter-productive for political stability and the legitimation of the existing legal order.

24. The same line of argument might also be suggested with respect to joint authority, i.e. the threat of the latter might generate consociational motivations.

Appendices

1. Agreement between the Government of the United Kingdom of Great Britain and Northern Ireland and the Government of the Republic of Ireland (The Anglo-Irish Agreement, November 1985)

THE Government of the United Kingdom of Great Britain and Northern Ireland and the Government of the Republic of Ireland;[1]

Wishing further to develop the unique relationship between their peoples and the close co-operation between their countries as friendly neighbours and as partners in the European Community;

Recognising the major interest of both their countries and, above all, of the people of Northern Ireland in diminishing the divisions there and achieving lasting peace and stability;

Recognising the need for continuing efforts to reconcile and to acknowledge the rights of the two major traditions that exist in Ireland, represented on the one hand by those who wish for no change in the present status of Northern Ireland and on the other hand by those who aspire to a sovereign united Ireland achieved by peaceful means and through agreement;

Reaffirming their total rejection of any attempt to promote political objectives by violence or the threat of violence and their determination to work together to ensure that those who adopt or support such methods do not succeed;

Recognising that a condition of genuine reconciliation and dialogue between unionists and nationalists is mutual recognition and acceptance of each other's rights;

Recognising and respecting the identities of the two communities in

Northern Ireland, and the right of each to pursue its aspirations by peaceful and constitutional means;

Reaffirming their commitment to a society in Northern Ireland in which all may live in peace, free from discrimination and intolerance, and with the opportunity for both communities to participate fully in the structures and processes of government;

Have accordingly agreed as follows:

A

STATUS OF NORTHERN IRELAND

ARTICLE 1

The two Governments

(a) affirm that any change in the status of Northern Ireland would only come about with the consent of a majority of the people of Northern Ireland;

(b) recognise that the present wish of a majority of the people of Northern Ireland is for no change in the status of Northern Ireland;

(c) declare that, if in the future a majority of the people of Northern Ireland clearly wish for and formally consent to the establishment of a united Ireland, they will introduce and support in the respective Parliaments legislation to give effect to that wish.

B

THE INTERGOVERNMENTAL CONFERENCE

ARTICLE 2

(a) There is hereby established, within the framework of the Anglo-Irish Intergovernmental Council set up after the meeting between the two heads of Government on 6 November 1981, an Intergovernmental Conference (hereinafter referred to as 'the Conference'), concerned with Northern Ireland and with relations between the two parts of the island of Ireland, to deal, as set out in this Agreement, on a regular basis with:

   (i)   political matters;

   (ii) security and related matters;

   (iii) legal matters, including the administration of justice;

   (iv) the promotion of cross-border co-operation.

(b) The United Kingdom Government accept that the Irish Government will put forward views and proposals on matters relating to Northern Ireland within the field of activity of the Conference in so far as those matters are not the responsibility of a devolved administration in Northern Ireland. In the interest of promoting peace and stability, determined efforts shall be made through the Conference to resolve any differences. The Conference will be mainly concerned with Northern Ireland; but some of the matters under consideration will involve co-operative action in both parts of the island of Ireland, and possibly also in Great Britain. Some of the proposals considered in respect of Northern Ireland may also be found to have application by the Irish Government. There is no derogation from the sovereignty of either the United Kingdom Government or the Irish Government, and each retains responsibility for the decisions and administration of government within its own jurisdiction.

ARTICLE 3

The Conference shall meet at Ministerial or official level, as required. The business of the Conference will thus receive attention at the highest level. Regular and frequent Ministerial meetings shall be held; and in particular special meetings shall be convened at the request of either side. Officials may meet in subordinate groups. Membership of the Conference and of sub groups shall be small and flexible. When the Conference meets at Ministerial level the Secretary of State for Northern Ireland and an Irish Minister designated as the Permanent Irish Ministerial Representative shall be joint Chairmen. Within the framework of the Conference other British and Irish Ministers may hold or attend meetings as appropriate: when legal matters are under consideration the Attorneys General may attend. Ministers may be accompanied by their officials and their professional advisers: for example, when questions of security policy or security co-operation are being discussed, they may be accompanied by the Chief Constable of the Royal Ulster Constabulary and the Commissioner of the Garda Síochána; or when questions of economic or social policy or co-operation are being discussed, they may be accompanied by officials of the relevant Departments. A Secretariat shall be established by the two Governments to service the Conference on a continuing basis in the discharge of its functions as set out in this Agreement.

ARTICLE 4

(a) In relation to matters coming within its field of activity, the Conference shall be a framework within which the United Kingdom Government and the Irish Government work together

(i) for the accommodation of the rights and identities of the two traditions which exist in Northern Ireland; and

(ii) for peace, stability and prosperity throughout the island of Ireland by promoting reconciliation, respect for human rights, co-operation against terrorism and the development of economic, social and cultural co-operation.

(b) It is the declared policy of the United Kingdom Government that responsibility in respect of certain matters within the powers of the Secretary of State for Northern Ireland should be devolved within Northern Ireland on a basis which would secure widespread acceptance throughout the community. The Irish government support that policy.

(c) Both Governments recognise that devolution can be achieved only with the co-operation of constitutional representatives with Northern Ireland of both traditions there. The Conference shall be a framework within which the Irish Government may put forward views and proposals on the modalities of bringing about devolution in Northern Ireland, in so far as they relate to the interests of the minority community.

C

POLITICAL MATTERS

ARTICLE 5

(a) The Conference shall concern itself with measures to recognise and accommodate the rights and identities of the two traditions in Northern Ireland, to protect human rights and to prevent discrimination. Matters to be considered in this area include measures to foster the cultural heritage of both traditions, changes in electoral arrangements, the use of flags and emblems, the avoidance of economic and social discrimination and the advantages and disadvantages of a Bill of Rights in some form in Northern Ireland.

(b) The discussion of these matters shall be mainly concerned with Northern Ireland, but the possible application of any measures pursuant to this Article by the Irish Government in their jurisdiction shall not be excluded.

(c) If it should prove impossible to achieve and sustain devolution on a basis which secures widespread acceptance in Northern Ireland, the Conference shall be a framework within which the Irish Government may, where the interests of the minority community are significantly or especially affected, put forward views on proposals for major legislation and on major policy issues, which are within the purview of the Northern Ireland Departments and which remain the responsibility of the Secretary of State for Northern Ireland.

ARTICLE 6

The Conference shall be a framework within which the Irish Government may put foward views and proposals on the role and composition of bodies appointed by the Secretary of State for Northern Ireland or by departments subject to his direction and control including:

    the Standing Advisory Commission on Human Rights;
    the Fair Employment Agency;
    the Equal Opportunities Commission;
    the Police Authority for Northern Ireland;
    the Police Complaints Board.

D

SECURITY AND RELATED MATTERS

ARTICLE 7

(a) The Conference shall consider:

(i)   security policy;
(ii) relations between the security forces and the community;
(iii) prisons policy.

(b) The Conference shall consider the security situation at its regular meetings and thus provide an opportunity to address policy issues, serious incidents and forthcoming events.

(c) The two Governments agree that there is a need for a programme of special measures in Northern Ireland to improve relations between the security forces and the community, with the object in particular of making the security forces more readily accepted by the nationalist community. Such a programme shall be developed, for the Conference's consideration, and may include the establishment of local consultative machinery, training in community relations, crime prevention schemes involving the community, improvements in arrangements for handling complaints, and action to increase the proportion of members of the minority in the Royal Ulster Constabulary. Elements of the programme may be considered by the Irish Government suitable for application within their jurisdiction.

(d) The Conference may consider policy issues relating to prisons. Individual cases may be raised as appropriate, so that information can be provided or enquiries instituted.

E

LEGAL MATTERS, INCLUDING THE ADMINISTRATION OF JUSTICE
ARTICLE 8

The Conference shall deal with issues of concern to both countries relating to the enforcement of the criminal law. In particular it shall consider whether there are areas of the criminal law applying in the North and South respectively which might with benefit be harmonised. The two Governments agree on the importance of public confidence in the administration of justice. The Conference shall seek, with the help of advice from experts as appropriate, measures which would give substantial expression to this aim, considering *inter alia* the possibility of mixed courts in both jurisdictions for the trial of certain offences. The Conference shall also be concerned with policy aspects of extradition and extra-territorial jurisdiction as between North and South.

F

CROSS-BORDER CO-OPERATION ON SECURITY, ECONOMIC, SOCIAL
AND CULTURAL MATTERS
ARTICLE 9

(a) With a view to enhancing cross-border co-operation on security matters, the Conference shall set in hand a programme of work to be undertaken by the Chief Constable of the Royal Ulster Constabulary and the Commissioner of the Garda Síochána and, where appropriate, groups of officials in such areas as threat assessments, exchange of information, liaison structures, technical co-operation, training of personnel, and operational resources.

(b) The Conference shall have no operational responsibilities, responsibility for police operations shall remain with the heads of the respective police forces, the Chief Constable of the Royal Ulster Constabulary maintaining his links with the Secretary of State for Northern Ireland and the Commissioner of the Garda Síochána his links with the Minister for Justice.

ARTICLE 10
(a) The two Governments shall co-operate to promote the economic and social development of those areas of both parts of Ireland which have suffered most severely from the consequences of the instability of recent years, and shall consider the possibility of securing international support for this work.
(b) If it should prove impossible to achieve and sustain devolution on a basis which secures widespread acceptance in Northern Ireland, the Conference shall be a framework for the promotion of co-operation between the two parts of Ireland concerning cross-border aspects of economic, social and cultural matters in relation to which the Secretary of State for Northern Ireland continues to exercise authority.
(c) If responsibility is devolved in respect of certain matters in the economic, social or cultural areas currently within the responsibility of the Secretary of State for Northern Ireland, machinery will need to be established by the responsible authorities in the North and South for practical co-operation in respect of cross-border aspects of these issues.
G

ARRANGEMENTS FOR REVIEW
ARTICLE 11
At the end of three years from signature of this Agreement, or earlier if requested by either Government, the working of the Conference shall be reviewed by the two Governments to see whether any changes in the scope and nature of its activities are desirable.
H

INTERPARLIAMENTARY RELATIONS
ARTICLE 12
It will be for Parliamentary decision in Westminster and Dublin whether to establish an Anglo Irish Parliamentary body of the kind adumbrated in the Anglo-Irish Studies Report of November 1981. The two Governments agree that they would give support as appropriate to such a body, if it were to be established.
I

FINAL CLAUSES
ARTICLE 13
This Agreement shall enter into force on the date on which the two Governments exchange notifications of their acceptance of this Agreement.

310   *Appendix 1*

Notes

1. Editors' note: This text is the British version (Cmnd. 9690), which differs
   from that of the Irish version (Prl. 3684). The British version refers
   throughout to 'The Government of the United Kingdom of Great Britain
   and Northern Ireland and the Government of the Republic of Ireland',
   whereas the Irish version refers throughout to 'The Government of
   Ireland and the Government of the United Kingdom'.
   Legal interpretations of the Anglo-Irish Agreement can be found in, *inter
   alia*, Hadden and Boyle (1989) and Hadfield (1986), whereas political
   interpretations can be found in, *inter alia*, Coughlan (1986), Cox (1987),
   O'Leary, (1987*b*) and Shannon (1986).

2. Review of the Anglo-Irish Intergovernmental Conference (May 1989)

1. In accordance with Article 11 of the Anglo-Irish Agreement, the two Governments have completed a review of the working of the Intergovernmental Conference and have considered whether any changes in the scope and nature of its activities are desirable. In conducting this review the two sides engaged in an assessment of the work of the conference to date under each of the articles of the agreement and examined the overall achievements of the conference in terms of the stated objectives of the agreement and the relationship between the two countries. Their discussions took account of a range of views put to them by interested groups and individuals and they wish to place on record their appreciation of all submissions made to them on the review. The conclusions which the two Governments have reached are set out below in the order in which the various subjects are covered by the agreements.

2. Having conducted the review, the two Governments reaffirm their full commitment to all of the provisions of the agreement and to the shared understandings and purposes set out both in the preamble and in the agreement itself as well as in the Hillsborough Communiqué of November 15 1985. They reaffirm their belief in the need for political dialogue at all levels as an essential element in achieving progress and an end to violence. They reiterate their unyielding opposition to any attempt to promote political objectives by violence or the threat of violence; and they commit themselves to continuing close co-operation in the security field to ensure that those who resort to such methods do not succeed.

The Conference

3. The Intergovernmental Conference has met on 27 occasions since the signature of the agreement. It has provided a valuable forum to address in a regular and organised way the full range of matters covered in the agreement, mainly affecting Northern Ireland, and to promote co-operative action in both parts of Ireland. Through the conference, the Irish Government have put forward views and proposals on these issues for consideration by the British side. Thus, in the development of measures relating to Northern Ireland the conference has played an important role, and both Governments

look forward to working closely together in this way in the future along the lines laid down in the agreement. They acknowledge the valuable contribution of the secretariat in servicing the conference and in providing a readily available and continuing channel of communication between the two Governments on matters covered by the agreement, a role which they will seek to develop as appropriate.

4. With a view to improving the working of the conference as a means of resolving differences between them, both Governments agree that conference meetings in the future should be organised so far as possible on a regular schedule, following the pattern in 1988 when ten meetings were held. In addition to meeting the needs of the regular work of the conference, this pattern should give both sides an opportunity to consider forthcoming developments on a systematic basis, thereby making it more likely that problems can be anticipated and resolved in the spirit of harmony called for by the agreement and reducing the risk of misunderstanding or confrontation arising from particular events. In the interests of ensuring the fullest possible consideration of longer term issues relevant to the agenda of the conference, it was also agreed that at least once each year there will be an informal ministerial meeting.

5. Consistent with their objective of developing the potential of the conference as envisaged in Article 3 of the agreement, both Governments agree in principle that future conference meetings should provide for widened ministerial participation, at the invitation of the joint chairmen, to encourage more structured discussion of a greater range of issues of common interest to both parts of Ireland.

6. The two Governments note that a number of the submissions which they have received emphasise the importance of fuller information about discussions at conference meetings being made public. Both Governments agree that the public should be made fully aware of the contribution which the work of the conference is making and will seek to respond to this point in future communiqués and press conferences.

Devolution

7. It continues to be the British Government's policy, supported by the Irish Government, to encourage progress towards the devolution of responsibility for certain powers to elected representatives in Northern Ireland as set out in Article 4 of the agreement. Both sides recognise that the achievement of devolution depends on the co-operation of constitutional representatives of both traditions within Northern Ireland.

Accommodation of the Rights and Identities of the Two Traditions

8. The two Governments share a common view of the central importance in the implementation of the agreement of measures to accommodate the

rights and identities of the two traditions in Northern Ireland, to protect human rights and prevent discrimination. The Irish Government welcome a number of positive measures which have been implemented by the British Government in this respect since the signature of the agreement. These include the repeal of the Flags and Emblems Act, the enfranchisement of the 'I voters' and the enactment of the Public Order (NI) Order 1987 enhancing the powers of the police to control potentially provocative marches.

9. The introduction of new legislation on fair employment has been the subject of detailed discussion in the conference in the light of the commitment to eliminate discrimination in the workplace and establish fair employment practices in Northern Ireland. The two Governments agree on the importance of ensuring that such legislation shall be an effective means of meeting that commitment and the conference will closely follow developments in this regard. The Irish Government welcome also the launching by the British Government of a programme of action to address the social and economic problems in the most disadvantaged areas of Belfast and other deprived areas.

10. Both Governments reaffirm the fundamental importance of the proper protection of human rights and will continue to discuss through the mechanism of the conference all legislative and other means by which such rights may be better protected in Northern Ireland.

11. The two Governments attach importance to the continuing work for improved community relations through developing increased cross-community contact and co-operation, and to encouraging greater mutual understanding, including respecting the cultural heritage of both traditions. They recognise the valuable role which the education system can play in promoting mutual esteem and understanding between the two traditions, and the Irish Government support the efforts made to reflect this objective in the new curriculum for Northern Ireland currently under preparation. The two Governments recognise also the importance of the Irish language in this context and undertake to support efforts to enhance awareness and appreciation of this particular strand of the cultural heritage.

Public Bodies

12. The two Governments agree on the importance of the principle that public bodies in Northern Ireland should be so constituted as to enjoy the widest possible respect and acceptance throughout the community. Exchanges will continue on ways in which this objective can be furthered. The Irish Government will continue to put forward views and proposals on the role and composition of such bodies for consideration by the British side, which will be ready to consider what means may be available to remedy imbalances arising from the use by others of their existing nominating powers without due regard to fairness or balance.

Confidence in the Security Forces and the System of Justice

13. The two Governments attach great importance to policies aimed at improving relations between the security forces and the community in Northern Ireland and at enhancing respect for the rule of law. They have considered the record of the working of the conference in relation to fostering confidence in the system of justice in all its aspects and ensuring that the security forces are clearly perceived to discharge their duties even-handedly, acting at all times within the law, with equal respect for the unionist and nationalist traditions and with demonstrable accountability for their actions. Special importance is attached to ensuring that representations by the public about the behaviour of members of the security forces are promptly and fully addressed and, in particular, that any allegations of harassment are quickly investigated and that, if complaints are substantiated, the necessary action is taken without delay.

14. A number of new measures affecting these confidence issues have been introduced, including those on marches and other public events, incitement to hatred, police complaints procedures, police/community liaison committees and the need for the police to respect equally the two traditions in Northern Ireland, which is set out in the Code of Conduct promulgated by the Royal Ulster Constabulary. Further work remains to be done and progress achieved will be reviewed on a regular basis at the conference.

15. Following discussion in the conference, further confidence building measures are envisaged or in hand by the relevant authorities, including the following: systematic monitoring of the nature, pattern and handling of complaints by the public about the behaviour of members of the security forces; further effective developments of the policy of ensuring as rapidly as possible that, save in the most exceptional circumstances, there should be a police presence in all operations which involve direct contact between the armed forces and the community; additional safeguards for members of the public being questioned by the police in connection with non-terrorist offences; and the publication of a guide to the operation of the provision of the Emergency Provisions and Prevention of Terrorism Acts.

16. The Irish Government reaffirm the importance they attach to reform of the system of trial under the Emergency Provisions Act 1978 and in particular the introduction of three-judge courts. The British Government are not at present persuaded of the merits of this proposal. While it is recognised that emergency legislation was a response to the campaign of violence and intimidation, it is agreed that both sides will continue through the conference to consider what changes may be desirable in the emergency provisions, the general criminal law or procedure with the aim of securing maximum public confidence in the system of justice.

17. The conference has considered prisons policy. There have been important developments affecting the Northern Ireland prison system, including the special reviews of the cases of the remaining prisoners in special category and those serving sentences at the Secretary of State's pleasure, as well as life sentence review procedures generally, the opening of the new prison at Maghaberry, and matters affecting the prison regime. The two Governments undertake to maintain exchanges on prison matters, given the importance of careful and considered treatment of this sensitive issue.

18. The two Governments are fully agreed on the need for fair and effective procedures for extradition and for the exercise of extra-territorial jurisdiction to ensure that fugitive offenders are brought to justice. There has been extensive discussion of these matters within the framework of the conference. The two Governments will continue their examination of these matters, through their respective law officers and the mechanism of the conference, with a view to ensuring that appropriate arrangements are in place in relation both to extradition and extra-territorial jurisdiction.

19. The two Governments agree that there should be further study of areas of the criminal law applying in the two jurisdictions which might with benefit be harmonised.

Security Co-operation

20. The two Governments condemn in the strongest terms the actions of those who in seeking to promote political ends by violent means cause the most callous loss of life, human misery and wanton destruction. They reaffirm their determination to counter this evil through continuing close co-operation between the security forces on both sides of the border and pay tribute to the commitment of these forces. Cross-border security co-operation has received regular and intensive consideration at meetings within the framework of the Intergovernmental Conference as well as at frequent meetings between the respective police forces. A programme of work between the Commissioner of the Garda Síochána and the Chief Constable of the Royal Ulster Constabulary as envisaged in Article 9 of the agreement was put in hand and substantial progress has been achieved under all of the headings listed.

21. In the light of their common understanding of the scale of the terrorist threat, the two Governments reaffirm their commitments to further and sustained efforts to combat it effectively. They have endorsed a programme of future work between the two police forces to develop their co-operation and to enhance their capacity to protect human life and property from terrorist outrage. They agree that progress in cross-border security co-operation will be reviewed regularly by the conference, which the two Governments will continue to use as a framework to work together to ensure that those who adopt or support violence do not succeed.

Cross-Border Economic Co-operation

22. The two Governments have taken stock of the pattern of cross-border economic co-operation since the signature of the agreement. Apart from the work of the conference, itself, a number of cross-border ministerial meetings has taken place in the framework of the agreement and a cross-border study of social and economic problems in the North West region has been commissioned with assistance from the European Community. The two Governments affirm their conviction that cross-border economic and social co-operation is of obvious benefit to all.

23. They agree that future conference meetings will include a systematic programme of assessment of all the main sectors to determine where the process of co-operation can most fruitfully be expanded. Where appropriate, the responsible ministers North and South will participate in the work of the conference. In a preliminary survey during the review, both Governments have considered an illustrative list of areas which offer scope for further work, including transport, communications, tourism, industry, agriculture, energy and health.

24. The two Governments have considered also the implications of the completion of the internal market in the European Community in 1992. They recognise that these will be far reaching and will generate common opportunities for both parts of Ireland as well as common difficulties arising from peripheral island status and other factors including the increase of competition. They agree that the conference could provide a valuable forum for both sides to consider and assess the cross-border implications of the Single European Market and, consistent with national policies, to maximise the potential benefits. Various practical ways of advancing work in this area will be considered and the continuation of the dialogue on this issue begun at Louvain in December, 1988 will also be encouraged.

International Fund for Ireland

25. In September, 1986 the two Governments, in accordance with Article 10(a) of the agreement, established the International Fund for Ireland with the financial support of the United States, Canada and New Zealand and, from 1989, the European Community. In the interval since its foundation, the fund has committed over £50m Sterling to projects in Northern Ireland and the border counties in the South and has been instrumental in creating a significant number of new jobs. The two Governments express their appreciation of the generosity of the donors to the Fund and will continue to give every support to the work of the fund and the emphasis it is now placing on improving the position in the most disadvantaged areas.

British–Irish Interparliamentary Body

26. The two Governments welcome the progress which has been made

towards the establishment of a British Irish Interparliamentary body of the kind envisaged in the Anglo-Irish Studies Report of November, 1981, which would provide a valuable independent forum for interparliamentary contacts.

Conclusion

27. The two Governments commit themselves to continue to work together through the institutions and procedures of the agreement for the realisation of the fundamental objectives of promoting peace and stability in Northern Ireland; helping to diminish the divisions between the two major traditions in Ireland; creating a new climate of friendship and co-operation between them and improving co-operation in combating terrorism. Reaffirming the right of each tradition to pursue its aspirations by peaceful and constitutional means, they reiterate the objective of the creation of a society in Northern Ireland in which all may live in peace, free from discrimination and intolerance.

28. They agree that the conference, together with its related mechanisms, has proved its value to both Governments in the three years since the signature of the agreement and that, while requiring no fundamental change at present, its role could nevertheless be developed and enhanced in the ways set out above.

29. If in future it were to appear that the objectives of the agreement could be more effectively served by changes in the scope and nature of the working of the conference, consistent with the basic provisions and spirit of the agreement, the two Governments would be ready in principle to consider such changes.

30. The two Governments stress that the agreement does not represent a threat to either tradition in Northern Ireland. On the contrary, it provides a framework which respects the essential interests of both sides of the community and their right to pursue their aspirations by peaceful means. It facilitates co-operation in the fight against terrorism and sets out to create the conditions in which the whole community can live together in peace.

3. Violence in Northern Ireland, 1969–June 1989

Brendan O'Duffy and Brendan O'Leary

OFFICIAL and independent data collections on violence in Northern Ireland are generally reliable even though different methodologies are employed by the two principal monitors: the Northern Ireland police force, the Royal Ulster Constabulary, and the private organization, the Irish Information Partnership. All the data analysis and graphics in this appendix are based on these two data bases. The RUC and IIP data differ very marginally in their aggregate figures on deaths. In their annual death-tolls the difference is generally less than 1 per cent (McKeown 1985: 4). The main difference between the two data-sets is that the IIP is much more exhaustive and illuminating in categorizing the status of victims and in the categorization of agents responsible for violent acts. The RUC data by contrast is less helpful, and in some cases less credible.

1. LONG-RUN TRENDS AND AGGREGATES, 1969–1989

Deaths

The annual death-toll between 1969 and 1988 according to the RUC is presented in Table A3.1 (second column) and in Figure A3.1. As can be seen clearly in Table A3.1, in Figure A3.1, and in Figure A3.2, which presents the cumulative annual death total, over a quarter of all deaths occurred in the first four years of the current wave of troubles, and nearly 61 per cent of all deaths over the two decades occurred in the five years 1971–6. Since 1977 the annual average rate of death due to political violence has been 85 persons per annum, and the numbers killed in the last five years (1984–8) have been 13.5 per cent of the total killed since 1969. This picture suggests a dramatic fall-off in deaths since the early 1970s.

The death-toll after the Anglo-Irish Agreement (AIA) was signed (November 1985) confirms the overall downward trend since the early and mid-1970s *if* one takes a long-term view. An average of 82 deaths in the years 1986–8 compares with an average of 85 deaths per annum since 1977. However, there is a perceptible upward trend in the death-toll after the AIA *if* one takes a short-term view and compares the death-toll in the three years 1986–8 (61, 93, 93) with the toll in 1983–5 (77, 64, 54)—although we shall

TABLE A3.1. *Deaths in Northern Ireland, 1969–1988*

Year	Annual deaths		Cumulative deaths		Five-yearly total	% of total every five years
	No.	% of total	No.	% of total		
1969	13	0.48				
1970	25	0.92	38	1.5		
1971	174	6.40	212	7.9		
1972	467	17.22	679	25.12		
1973	250	9.22	929	34.34	929	34.34
1974	216	7.97	1,145	42.21		
1975	247	9.11	1,392	51.32		
1976	297	10.96	1,689	62.28		
1977	112	4.13	1,801	66.41		
1978	81	2.99	1,882	69.40	1,882	35.15
1979	113	4.17	1,995	73.57		
1980	76	2.80	2,071	76.37		
1981	101	3.73	2,172	80.10		
1982	97	3.58	2,269	83.68		
1983	77	2.84	2,346	86.42	2,346	17.12
1984	64	2.36	2,410	88.78		
1985	54	1.99	2,464	90.77		
1986	61	2.43	2,525	93.20		
1987	93	3.43	2,618	96.63		
1988	93	3.43	2,711	100.06*	2,711	13.47
TOTAL	2,711	100.06*				100.08*

* Figures do not add to 100 because of rounding.
Source: RUC official data.

discuss below whether this upward trend was caused by the AIA. One way to put the apparent impact of the AIA in long-term perspective is by inspecting Figure A3.2, the cumulative annual death-toll. The post-AIA death-toll seems to have restored the post-1976 trend after the brief fall in the years 1983–5.

There are three basic explanations for the fall-off in deaths since the early and mid-1970s. First, loyalist paramilitaries have ceased to engage in sectarian killings of Catholics on the same scale as they did in the years 1971–6. Many of them have been arrested and jailed, and their organizations have become more factionalized, corrupt, and directionless. Second, nationalist paramilitaries have also changed their strategies and organizations in ways which have reduced the annual death-toll. Many of them have also been arrested and jailed; and their organizations have become smaller and structured in cells or 'active service units' (Bishop and Mallie 1987). The 'cell structure' was partly adopted in response to declining popularity in nationalist areas but also for strategic reasons—to avoid penetration by the security forces. The Provisional IRA have aimed primarily

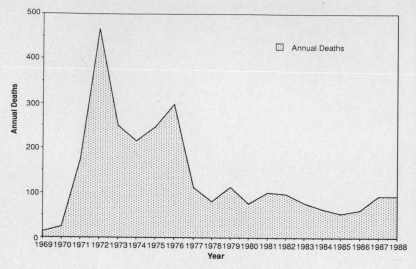

FIG. A3.1. Annual deaths, 1969–1988
Source: drawn from RUC data

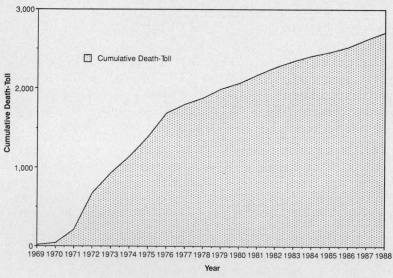

FIG. A3.2. Cumulative death total, 1969–1988
Source: drawn from Table A3.1

to attack 'military targets' (i.e. members of the security forces) since the mid-1970s, and have consequently reduced their use of bombs in urban areas—a tactic which killed many civilians, both Catholic and Protestant, in the early 1970s. Finally, more effective surveillance and knowledge on the part of the security forces may have dampened the potential levels of violence. However, this final explanation has to be qualified in the light of firm evidence that the actions of the security forces have frequently, if sometimes unintentionally, raised the levels of violence.

Time-series trends in deaths are available in a crude form from RUC data. Figure A3.3 confirms the downward trend in civilian deaths since the 1971–6 period—although RUC data do not enable us to follow victims by religious category over time. It also shows a dramatic falling off in the number of deaths sustained by the British Army (excluding the Ulster Defence Regiment). Finally, since the early 1980s the local security forces (the RUC/RUC Reserve and the UDR) have suffered an increasing proportion of the deaths sustained by the security forces. In part this trend reflects 'Ulsterization'—the Northern Ireland Office's policy preference for local as opposed to British forces—but it also suggests a switch in the targets chosen by nationalist paramilitaries. 'Ulsterization' and the rising death-toll of local security forces are naturally and predictably related.

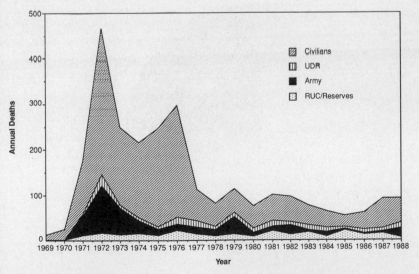

Fig. A3.3. Time-series death data, 1969–1988

Source: RUC

Status of Victims and Responsibility for Deaths

The IIP provide a detailed breakdown of the status of victims, as well as categorizing the agents responsible for deaths (see Table A3.2), whereas the RUC merely record whether or not victims were members of the security forces. We can only speculate as to the reasons the RUC fail to provide similarly detailed information. For the present the IIP data base is of much greater use in clarifying the distribution of victims and of responsibility for their deaths.

Inspection of Figures A3.4–12, all of which are based on the IIP data base (i.e. Table A3.2, which runs from 1969 to June 1989), illustrates the story. Figure A3.4 presents a pie-chart showing the status of victims over the two decades. Surprisingly, in view of British public perceptions, the largest single category of victims has been Catholic civilians (32.5 per cent), who just shade members of the security forces (31.2 per cent). Given that Protestant civilians outnumber Catholic civilians in the Northern Ireland population by approximately 3 to 2, it is evident that Catholic civilians (896 deaths) have suffered both *absolutely* and *relatively* more than Protestant civilians (575 deaths). Catholic deaths have been 59.3 per cent of all civilian deaths whereas Protestant deaths represent 38.1 per cent of all civilian deaths. There are four simple explanations for this variance. First, Catholic

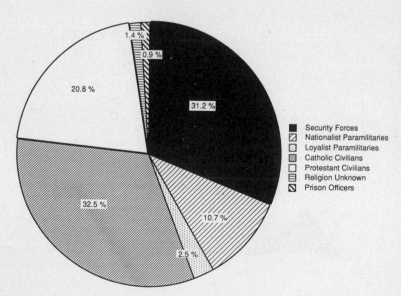

Fig. A3.4. Status of victims, 1969–June 1989
Source: drawn from IIP, *Agenda Database*

TABLE A3.2. *Deaths in Northern Ireland: responsible agent and category of victim, 1969–June 1989*

Category of victim	Agency responsible				Total	As % of total
	Security forces	Nationalist paramilitaries	Loyalist paramilitaries	Others/ unidentified		
Security forces	14	834	10	4	862	31.2
Nationalist paramilitaries	123	146	18	8	295	10.7
Loyalist paramilitaries	12	18	36	3	69	2.5
Civilians						
Catholic	148	173	502	73	896	32.5
Protestant	25	377	100	63	575	20.8
Religion unknown	5	22	11	1	39	1.4
Total	178	572	623	137	1,510	54.7
TOTAL	327	1,593	689	152	2,761	100.0
As % of all deaths	11.8	57.7	25.0	5.5	100.0	
As % of civilian deaths	11.6	38.8	40.7	8.9	100.0	
Civilian deaths as % of all deaths	54.4	37.4	90.7	90.1	55.6	

Source: IIP, *Agenda Database.*

civilians are the primary targets of loyalist paramilitaries (502), whereas the security forces—including the British Army—are the primary targets of nationalist paramilitaries. Second, the local security forces (the RUC, the RUC Reserves, and the UDR) are recruited primarily from Protestant civilians, and thus the simple comparison of Catholic and Protestant civilian death-rates obscures the number of victims suffered by the Protestant community as a whole. Third, a rather high number of Catholic civilians (173) have been killed by nationalist paramilitaries, whether mistakenly, as 'collateral by-products' of other actions, or deliberately in the 'disciplining' of their own community. However, loyalists have also killed a rather high number of Protestant civilians (110). Finally, Catholic civilians are far more likely to be killed, mistakenly or otherwise, by members of the security forces (148) or by nationalist paramilitaries (173), because armed combat between the latter two groupings is more likely to take place in predominantly Catholic areas.

What is also clear from Figure A3.4 is that nationalist paramilitary violence is primarily strategic rather than simply sectarian—especially after 1972–3. More members of the security forces (862) are killed than Protestant civilians (575), and since the former are overwhelmingly killed by nationalist paramilitaries (834, and see Figure A3.8 below), it follows that nationalist paramilitaries partially fulfil their objective of fighting 'a war of national liberation', as opposed to a mere sectarian war. However, Protestants understandably *interpret* killings of Protestant members of the local security forces as sectarian, and, as we shall see nationalist paramilitaries have also killed a very considerable number of Protestant civilians (377, and see Figure A3.12 below).

Figure A3.4 also shows that nationalist (10.7 per cent) and loyalist paramilitaries (2.5 per cent) combined (13.2 per cent) have suffered fewer deaths than either religious category of civilian. They have also sustained fewer deaths than the security forces. The paramilitaries' low share of the overall death-toll presumably explains why their activities are relatively easily sustained—although it is also clear that nationalist paramilitaries have died more than four times as frequently as loyalist paramilitaries.

The pie-chart in Figure A3.5 breaks down the agents responsible for all deaths on the basis of IIP data. It shows, contrary to what Irish-American nationalist propagandists imply, that the security forces have been responsible for only 327 deaths or 11.8 per cent of the overall death-toll. Even if they were to be (wrongly) held responsible for all the deaths by other agencies and by unidentified agents, their overall level of responsibility for deaths would still be considerably less than either of the two categories of paramilitaries. What Figure A3.5 shows is that the security forces kill less than half as many people as loyalist paramilitaries and that loyalist paramilitaries kill less than half as many people as nationalist paramilitaries. It confirms that nationalist paramilitaries are responsible for more than half of

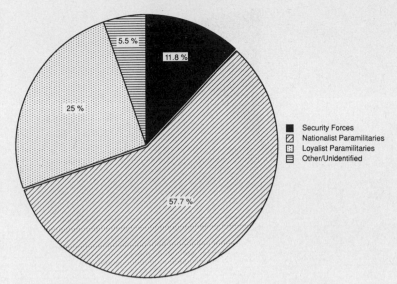

FIG. A3.5. Agents responsible for all deaths, 1969–June 1989
Source: drawn from IIP, *Agenda Database*

all deaths (1,593 deaths in total), partially confirming the British perception that they are the primary antagonists in the conflict.

However, a slightly different picture emerges if we remove deaths suffered by the security forces in order to examine the agents responsible for civilian deaths. The pie-chart shown in Figure A3.6 reveals that loyalist paramilitaries have killed slightly more civilians than nationalist para-militaries (623 compared to 572), and that both sets of paramilitaries have been responsible for nearly 80 per cent of all civilian deaths. Moreover, a very large share of the deaths due to other or unidentified agents (8.9 per cent) can reasonably be attributed to loyalist and nationalist paramilitaries.

Figure A3.7 shows 'Civilian Deaths as a Proportion of Deaths by Agency'. It is perhaps the most revealing bar-chart. It shows that the security forces kill a civilian 1 time in 2, i.e. they are 'efficient and effective'—if not always law-abiding—only 1 time in 2. This demonstrable evidence of incompetence, error, or malevolence (depending upon one's point of view) is made some-what more palatable by the low overall share of the death-toll attributable to the security forces. However, the low ratio of 'appropriate' to 'wrongful' killings—especially the disproportionate wrongful killings of Catholics—helps explain why the security forces are poorly regarded by Northern Ireland Catholics.

Nationalist paramilitaries (the IRAs (both Official and Provisional), INLA, and IPLO), as Figure A3.7 also shows, by far exceed all other agents in

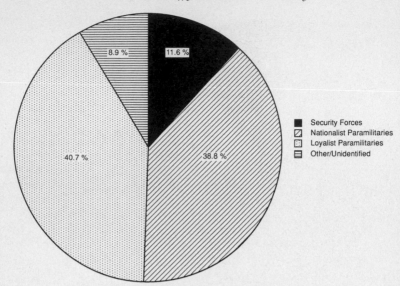

Fɪɢ. A3.6. Agents responsible for civilian deaths, 1969–June 1989
Source: drawn from IIP, *Agenda Database*

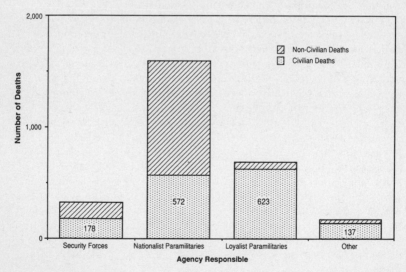

Fɪɢ. A3.7. Civilian deaths as a proportion of deaths by agency, 1969–June 1989
Source: drawn from IIP, *Agenda Database*

responsibility for killings. Moreover, they kill non-civilians just over 3 times in 5, a 'kill ratio' which also indicates a high degree of incompetence, error, or malevolence with respect to civilians. Although they are more likely to kill their declared targets than the security forces it is also true that the absolute level of civilian deaths which they have caused (572) is very close to the number of civilians killed by loyalist paramilitaries (623). Although nationalist paramilitary killings are primarily 'non-sectarian' it is obvious that they also kill a very high number of Protestant civilians. Time-series data (in the IIP database) do show, however, that nationalists have killed proportionately higher numbers of non-civilians in the last decade.

The final striking feature of Figure A3.7 is that loyalist paramilitaries kill civilians almost exclusively. This feature of their activities has been consistent since their first eruption (Boulton 1973; Dillon and Lehane 1973). It is also easy to explain. Catholic civilians are easier to identify than nationalist paramilitaries. They are also softer targets. They are therefore killed in acts of 'representative violence' (Wright 1987) which are meant to deter Catholics from supporting the IRA or other nationalist organizations. Thus although loyalist killing appears more random and less instrumental than nationalist killing it too is generally 'rational', i.e. goal-governed behaviour based upon attention to the consequences of action. This point is reinforced by considerable event-data evidence which shows that loyalists have engaged in systematically 'retributive' rather than purely random killing. However, there have also been a high number of psychopathic killings by supposedly politically motivated loyalists. (The same psychopathic propensity is also true—although to a lesser extent—of nationalist paramilitants.) The most barbaric of these activities were carried out by the 'Shankill butchers' (Dillon 1989).

The next set of Figures (A3.8–12) displays the agents responsible for the deaths of the five main groupings to have sustained high death-tolls (nationalist paramilitaries, members of the security forces, Catholic civilians, Protestant civilians, and loyalist paramilitaries). Figure A3.8 demonstrates a very striking feature of the deaths of nationalist paramilitaries. Nationalist paramilitaries themselves kill almost as many nationalist paramilitaries (146) as all other agencies combined (149). There are three explanations for this surprising fact. First, nationalist paramilitary organizations, like all guerrilla and terrorist organizations, engage in a high degree of 'internal disciplinary' killing, i.e. the execution of (often merely alleged) informants and wayward (or unreliable) members. Second, there has been a high degree of faction-fighting within nationalist organizations. The Provisional IRA and the Official IRA fought one another in the early 1970s. The Official IRA and the breakaway Irish National Liberation Army killed each other's members in 1975, and more recently in the spring of 1987 INLA imploded in an internal feud which accompanied the formation of IPLO. Third, in the racist language of the British security forces, many of the deaths of nationalist

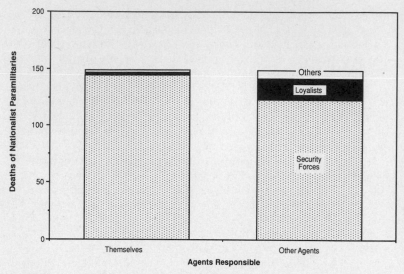

FIG. A3.8. Agents responsible for deaths of nationalist paramilitaries, 1969–June 1989
Source: drawn from IIP, *Agenda Database*

paramilitaries have been due to 'Paddy factors', i.e. bungled actions, such as blowing themselves up by mistake. Such actions were especially common in the Provisional IRA's early days. Since the completion of their organizational 'learning curve' such deaths are now less common, especially given that explosives like Semtex are apparently easier to handle. However, raw and inexperienced IRA recruits are still vulnerable to 'own goals'.

Figure A3.9, which identifies the killers of the security forces, shows that responsibility rests overwhelmingly (97 per cent) with nationalist paramilitaries. The 'Brit factor' ('own goals' or soldiers running amok in barracks) is apparently very low. By contrast Catholic civilians, as shown in Figure A3.10, are killed by a diverse group of agents. Loyalist paramilitaries have killed over half of them. However, nationalist paramilitaries have killed almost 1 in 5 Catholic civilians *and* have killed more of them than members of the security forces. Figure A3.11 shows that nationalist paramilitaries have killed two-thirds of the Protestant civilians who have died in the 'troubles'. However, loyalist paramilitaries have also been responsible for 1 in 5 of the civilian deaths within their own community. This figure includes those killed in error or as part of 'internal disciplining' of their community. Finally, Figure A3.12 demonstrates the remarkable fact that *over half* of all deaths (36 out of 69) suffered by loyalist paramilitaries have been caused by other loyalist paramilitaries.

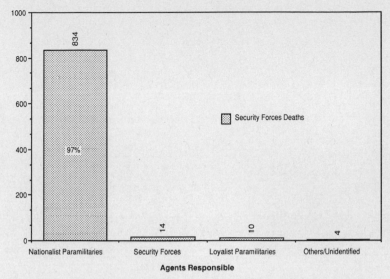

FIG. A3.9. Agents responsible for security forces deaths, 1969–June 1989
Source: drawn from IIP, *Agenda Database*

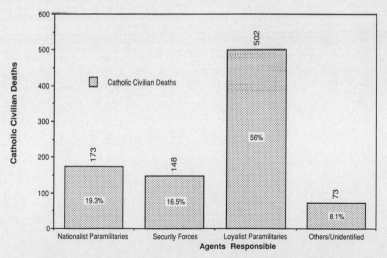

FIG. A3.10. Agents responsible for deaths of Catholic civilians, 1969–June 1989
Source: drawn from IIP, *Agenda Database*

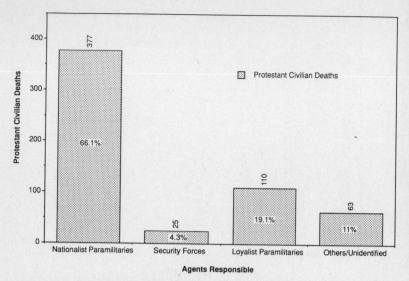

FIG. A3.11. Agents responsible for deaths of Protestant civilians, 1969–June 1989
Source: drawn from IIP, *Agenda Database*

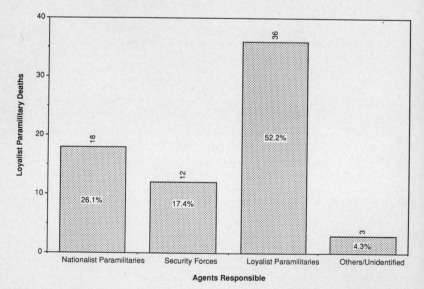

FIG. A3.12. Agents responsible for deaths of loyalist paramilitaries, 1969–June 1989
Source: drawn from IIP, *Agenda Database*

Other Long-Run Indices of Violence

Political violence in Northern Ireland has extended far beyond killings or executions. Data are also available from the RUC on injuries sustained due to the 'troubles', as well as the annual number of explosions, the number of bombs neutralized, the scale of findings of explosives, the number of shooting incidents, the number of firearms finds, the number of armed robberies, and the money taken in armed robberies. The graphics in Figures A3.13–19 illustrate these indicators in turn.

They all show the same pattern as the death-toll data. Very high indicators of violent activity are evident in the years 1971–6 with 'normaliz-ation' thereafter. The years 1976–7 were turning-points in the scale of all violence—not simply deaths—for three main reasons. First, the security forces' improved knowledge and capabilities enabled them to dampen down the levels of violence. In particular the ending of internment without trial appears to have helped reduce nationalist militancy after 1976. Second, loyalist paramilitaries dramatically lowered their assassinations and attacks on Catholic civilians. They did so because they believed that the unionist community had beaten back the threat to the integrity of Northern Ireland posed by the civil rights demonstrations, the abolition of Stormont, and the Sunningdale agreement. The opportunities for easy killings had also been reduced by the very extensive resettlement and segregation of Catholics and Protestants after the early years of the 'troubles'— in fact the largest forced population movements in Western Europe since the aftermath of World War II. Finally, nationalist paramilitaries, especially the IRA, reorganized in 1976–7 and changed their strategy. The new cell structure reduced the scale of IRA activities. Combined with their shift from bombing civilian, shopping, and urban centres to attacking military targets the scale of the violence fell in consequence. The propensity of this 'military' violence to cause deaths or injuries to civilians was much lower than the previous combination of 'economic' and 'military' violence.

Over 20,000 people have suffered serious injuries since 1969. In a small population of one-and-a-half million people the social impact of such violence is easily imagined. The trends in injuries (Figure A3.13) apparently show that civilians have borne the brunt of the conflict over time. However, the RUC data are unhelpful here because they classify both sets of para-militaries as civilians. Moreover, in the first three years (1968–70) the RUC data-set implies that no civilians were injured at all (i.e. no data was collected on the question). The data-set is also unhelpful because the RUC do not declare how they tabulate their figures. Originally they referred to injuries caused by terrorism, whereas they now refer to injuries due to the 'security situation' (*sic!*). In other words it is unclear whether injuries caused by the security forces are included in the figures. It appears that they are,

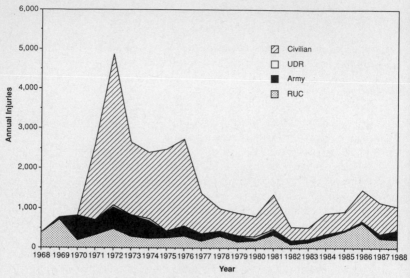

FIG. A3.13. Injuries due to political violence in Northern Ireland, 1968–1988
Source: drawn from RUC data

although this would seem to imply that the RUC used to classify injuries caused by the security forces as due to terrorism!

Figure A3.14, which shows numbers of explosions and bombs neutralized over time, reveals a similar pattern to all other indicators—i.e. peaks between 1971 and 1976 followed by secular declines thereafter. However, there is no evidence from this figure that 'bomb neutralization' has improved. This fact suggests that there was reason in Peter Brooke's controversial declaration in 1989 that the IRA could not be *militarily* defeated. Indeed the data on bomb neutralization appear to suggest a deterioration in the capacities of the security forces after 1986. We are unable to confirm whether this trend may be due to increased supplies of Semtex explosives (which are more difficult to detect), reduced use of warnings by nationalist paramilitaries, or even changes in data collection. The figures on weights of explosives found (Figure A3.15) are of questionable significance because technological changes have made the relationships between bomb weight and potency of bomb somewhat indeterminate.[1] However, explosives finds by the security forces do appear to mirror the general level of violence.

The evidence on 'shooting incidents' and 'shots heard' (apparently a recent distinction in RUC data collection) is presented in Figure A3.16. While showing a similar trend to other patterns of violence such data by its very nature is much less credible than other indicators of violence. The firearms

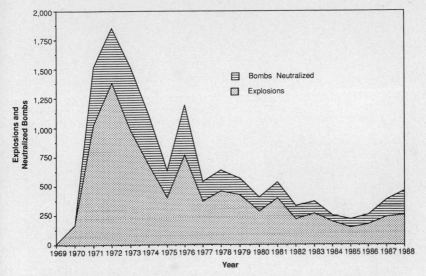

FIG. A3.14. Annual number of explosions and neutralized bombs, 1969–1988
Source: drawn from RUC data

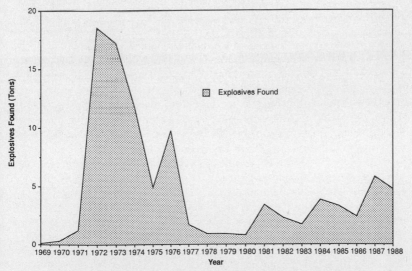

FIG. A3.15. Finds of explosives in Northern Ireland, 1969–1988
Source: drawn from RUC data

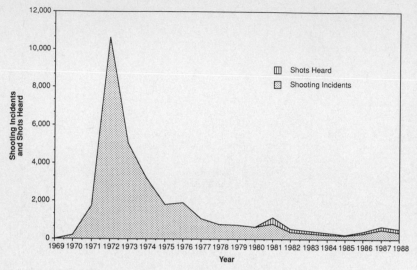

FIG. A3.16. Shooting incidents and shots heard in Northern Ireland, 1969–1988
Source: drawn from RUC data

finds data shown in Figure A3.17 are much more credible and show much the same trend as other indicators of violence, i.e. high figures in the early 1970s followed by decline thereafter. However, whether or not this trend suggests improved control by the security forces or, conversely, greater ability to hide arms on the part of paramilitaries remains a moot point.

The final RUC data on long-run trends in political violence tabulate armed robberies (Figure A3.18). Since Northern Ireland had extraordinarily low rates of 'ordinary, decent' crime before the late 1960s almost all of the rise in armed robberies is attributable to the political climate of the 'troubles'. Armed robberies are one important source of finance for paramilitary organizations. Other sources include genuine voluntary donations, protection rackets, 'legitimate' front enterprises, and, in the case of the IRA, funds from Irish-American organizations (Holland 1987). Unfortunately the RUC data—unsurprisingly—does not break down the agents responsible for armed robberies so we have no way of knowing the relative proportion of nationalist to loyalist armed robberies. However, what is evident is that the trend in armed robberies displays a similar pattern to the other indicators of violence. There also appears to have been a sharp increase in 1986, the year after the Anglo-Irish Agreement—much sharper than the increase in the death-rate. Having adjusted the RUC data we can also see in Figure A3.19 the annual real value of these armed robberies—after adjusting the nominal values into 1985 prices.

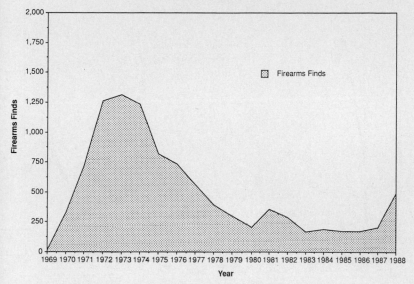

FIG. A3.17. Arms finds in Northern Ireland, 1969–1988
Source: drawn from RUC data

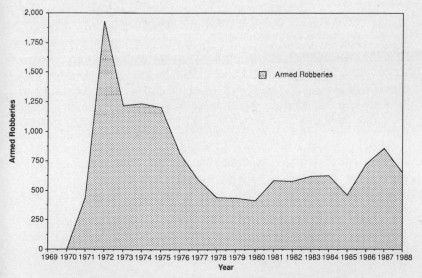

FIG. A3.18. Armed robberies in Northern Ireland, 1969–1988
Source: drawn from RUC data

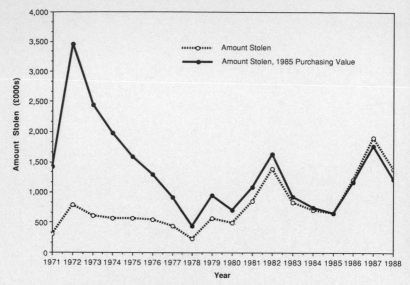

FIG. A3.19. Money taken in armed robberies in Northern Ireland, 1971–1988

Sources: calculated from RUC data and Department of Trade and Industry data (Central Statistical Office)

2. SHORT TERM TRENDS: BEFORE AND AFTER THE AIA, 1983-88

Ultra-nationalists and unionists are both hostile to the Anglo-Irish Agreement. They also share a common interest, albeit for different reasons, in demonstrating that the Anglo-Irish Agreement has not worked in one central respect: the promotion of peace, security, and stability. Consequently these critics of the AIA argue that since November 1985 violence, insecurity, and instability have actually increased. They have some evidence to support their case. Table A3.3 shows that deaths, injuries, shooting incidents, explosions and armed robberies have all gone up significantly in the three years after the AIA by comparison with the three years in the run-up to the Hillsborough accord. Injuries and shooting incidents have gone up by over 50 per cent, armed robberies by 30 per cent and deaths by just over 25 per cent.

There can be no doubt that some of the increased violence is attributable to political reactions to the Agreement. There can also be no doubt that in part the rise in violence is explicable by self-fulfilling prophecy. The paramilitaries hostile to the AIA have been doing their best to undermine it. Moreover, unionist demonstrations against the Agreement restored some of the 'street politics' of the early 1970s, and led to increased injuries. Loyalist

TABLE A3.3. *Indicators of violence before and after the Anglo-Irish Agreement*

Year	Deaths	Injuries	Shooting incidents	Explosions	Armed robberies
1983	77	528	290	266	622
1984	64	875	230	193	627
1985	54	939	196	148	459
Total	195	2,342	716	607	1,708
1986	61	1,462	285	172	724
1987	93	1,146	489	236	858
1988	247	3,661	1,132	661	2,253
Rise	52	1,319	416	54	527
%	26.6	56.3	58.1	8.9	30.85

Source: calculated from RUC data.

paramilitaries also increased their assassinations of Catholic civilians after having been dormant for a long time. They also engaged in large-scale intimidation of Catholic civilians and, in the spring of 1986, of RUC officers.

However, it would be a mistake to attribute all the rise in violence in the three years after 1985 to the Agreement itself, just as it would be a mistake to assume that the decline in indicators of violence before November 1985 would have continued indefinitely had there been no change in the constitutional status quo. The monthly death data in the years preceding and succeeding the AIA are shown in Table A3.4 (second column). They are also represented in the histogram Figure A3.20. Inspecting the data in its raw monthly form makes the upward trend after the Agreement much less evident than in the annual data. Moreover, as inspection of the months for 1987 reveals, it is evident that the monthly death-toll was raised considerably in several cases by episodes which are not directly linked to the Agreement: the INLA feud in the spring, the deaths of an IRA unit in a stake-out at Loughall in early summer, and the (allegedly mistaken) IRA killing of Protestant civilians at Enniskillen in November of the same year.

When the monthly death data are smoothed, using the standard technique in exploratory data analysis of running medians and hanning (Hartwig and Dearing 1979: 36–9), a pre-Agreement downward trend and a post-Agreement upward trend in deaths are much more apparent (see Figure A3.21). However, the rise is not especially dramatic. Indeed much of the deterioration in the smoothed monthly figures comes after the spring of 1986—after the IRA received extensive reinforcements of *matériel* from Libya. Finally, one might even argue that the impact of the AIA has been relatively low-key given the ferocity of unionist opposition to it. The predictions of a loyalist backlash on the scale of the early 1970s have so far not been fulfilled—even though loyalist paramilitary killings have increased since November 1985.

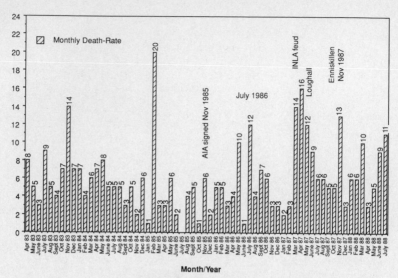

FIG. A3.20. Actual monthly death-rate, April 1983–July 1988

Source: IIP, *Agenda Database*

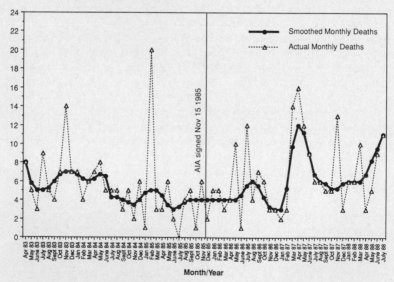

FIG. A3.21. Smoothed monthly death data before and after the AIA, April 1983–July 1988

Source: calculated from IIP, *Agenda Database*

TABLE A3.4. *Smoothing the monthly death-toll, April 1983–July 1988*

Month/year	No. dead	5	3	3R′	(H)	53R′(H)
1983						
April	8	8	8	8		8.00
					6.5	
May	5	5	5	5		5.75
					5.0	
June	3	5	5	5		5.00
					5.0	
July	9	5	5	5		5.00
					5.0	
August	5	5	5	5		5.25
					5.5	
September	4	7	6	6		6.00
					6.5	
October	7	6	7	7		6.75
					7.0	
November	14	7	7	7		7.00
					7.0	
December	7	7	7	7		7.00
					7.0	
1984						
January	7	7	7	7		6.75
					6.5	
February	4	6	6	6		6.25
					6.0	
March	6	5	6	6		6.00
					6.0	
April	7	6	6	6		6.25
					6.5	
May	8	7	7	7		6.75
					7.0	
June	5	7	7	7		6.50
					6.0	
July	5	5	5	5		4.25
					4.5	
August	5	4	4	4		4.25
					4.0	
September	3	3	4	4		4.00
					4.0	
October	5	4	3	5		3.75
					3.5	
November	2	3	4	3		3.50
					3.5	
December	6	5	3	4		4.00
					4.5	
1985						
January	1	3	5	5		4.75
					5.0	
February	20	5	5	5		5.00
					5.0	
March	3	5	5	5		5.00
					5.0	
April	3	5	5	5		4.50
					4.0	
May	6	3	3	3		3.50
					3.0	
June	2	3	3	3		3.00
					3.0	
July	0	4	3	3		3.25
					3.5	
August	4	2	4	4		3.75
					4.0	
September	5	4	4	4		4.00
					4.0	
October	1	4	4	4		4.00
					4.0	
November	6	4	4	4		4.00
					4.0	
December	2	4	4	4		4.00
					4.0	

TABLE A3.4. (*Cont.*)

Month/year	No. dead	5	3	3R'	(H)	53R'(H)
1986						
January	5	4	4	4	4.0	4.00
February	5	4	4	4	4.0	4.00
March	3	5	4	4	4.0	4.00
April	4	4	4	4	4.0	4.00
May	10	4	4	4	4.0	4.00
June	1	4	4	4	5.0	4.50
July	12	7	6	6	6.0	5.50
August	4	6	6	6	6.0	6.00
September	7	6	6	6	5.0	5.50
October	6	4	4	4	3.5	4.25
November	3	3	3	3	3.0	3.25
December	3	3	3	3	3.0	3.00
1987						
January	2	3	3	3	3.0	3.00
February	3	3	3	3	7.5	5.25
March	14	12	12	12	12.0	9.75
April	16	12	12	12	12.0	12.00
May	12	12	12	12	10.5	11.25
June	9	9	9	9	7.5	9.00
July	6	6	6	6	6.0	6.75
August	6	6	6	6	6.0	6.00
September	5	6	6	6	5.5	5.75
October	5	5	5	5	5.0	5.25
November	13	5	5	5	5.5	5.25
December	3	6	6	6	6.0	5.75
1988						
January	6	6	6	6	6.0	6.00
February	6	6	6	6	6.0	6.00
March	10	6	6	6	6.0	6.00
April	3	6	6	6	7.5	6.75
May	5	9	9	9	9.0	8.25
June	9	9	9	9	10.0	9.50
July	11	11	11	11		11.00

Source: (2nd col.) IIP, *Agenda Database.*

Calculated as in Hartwig and Dearing (1979: 36–9).

Judging by the preliminary and unconfirmed figures for 1989, the death-toll in Northern Ireland will fall by comparison with the previous two years—although the IRA have caused many deaths outside Northern Ireland, in places as diverse as England, The Netherlands, and West Germany. Indeed the Provisional IRA may well have decided that campaigning outside Northern Ireland against 'soft' British military targets is a more effective way of destabilizing the AIA. However, within Northern Ireland, policy-makers in the 1990s, benefiting from the improved security co-operation between the British and Irish states, have good reasons to believe that the scale of the conflict can be reduced to its pre-Hillsborough levels—although they have no reason for being too sanguine.

Notes

1. It is wholly unclear from the RUC data whether or not the weight of explosives finds are expressed in TNT impact-weight or simple weight in pounds.

4. Party Support in Northern Ireland, 1969–1989

Brendan O'Leary

THE support for political parties, expressed as a percentage of the total vote (or as a percentage of the total first-preference vote) in the eighteen province-wide elections held between 1969 and 1989, is shown in Table A4.1. It excludes the January 1986 by-elections caused by the resignations of fifteen unionist MPs in protest at the Anglo-Irish Agreement because they did not produce a province-wide election. Table A4.1 breaks down parties and their support into four categories, the unionist bloc, the nationalist bloc, the non-confessional bloc, and a residual 'Other' classification.

The unionist bloc is characterized by an overriding commitment to the Union of Great Britain and Northern Ireland and by its essentially Protestant appeal. Since 1969—and before—its support has been drawn almost exclusively from the Protestant population. However, divisions within the Ulster Unionist Party, which had won all the elections held in the province since the 1920s, were exacerbated by the introduction of the single transferable vote (STV) in 1973, for local-government and Assembly elections, and subsequently in 1979 for European elections. The unionist bloc fragmented into multiple parties during the collapse of the Stormont regime, but eventually realigned into two principal organizations, the UUP (the Official Unionists) and the DUP (the Democratic Unionists).[1] Other unionist organizations which emerged but faded without enduring impact include the Vanguard Unionist Party of Bill Craig (which was militantly loyalist), the Unionist Party of Northern Ireland (which was in favour of power-sharing) and the Ulster Loyalist Democratic Party (which acts as a front for the UDA). The UUP and the DUP differ between themselves, and internally, over the merits of integration, devolution, and power-sharing. However, they are both vehemently opposed to the institutionalization of an 'Irish dimension' in Northern Ireland, and, of course, to the Anglo-Irish Agreement. From its inception the trend in DUP growth at the expense of the UUP was fairly consistent until 1981. Moreover, its leader, Ian Paisley, has enjoyed a huge first-preference vote in every European election since 1979. However, the UUP made a come-back in the early 1980s, and, as we shall see, in the wake of the failure of DUP militancy to break the Anglo-Irish Agreement (see below, and Table A4.4).

TABLE A4.1. *Party support in elections in Northern Ireland, 1969–1989 (percentage of vote).*

Election	Unionist bloc			Nationalist bloc			Non-confessional bloc			Other
	UUP	DUP	Other	SDLP	Sinn Féin	Other	NILP	APNI	WP	
1969 S	61.1	—	6.3	—	—	18.8	8.1	0.0	—	5.7
1970 W	54.3	—	4.5	—	—	23.3	12.6	0.0	—	5.1
1973 LG	41.4	4.3	10.9	13.4	—	5.8	2.5	13.7	—	8.0
1973 A	29.3	10.8	21.8	22.1	—	2.0	2.6	9.2	—	1.0
1974 W	32.3	8.2	23.7	22.4	—	4.5	2.4	3.2	—	3.3
1974 W	36.5	8.5	17.1	22.0	—	7.8	1.6	6.3	—	0.2
1975 C	25.8	14.8	21.9	23.7	—	2.2	1.4	9.8	—	0.4
1977 LG	29.6	12.7	8.5	20.6	—	4.1	0.8	14.4	—	8.3
1979 W	36.6	10.2	12.2	19.9	—	8.2	—	11.8	—	2.1
1979 E	21.9	29.8	7.3	24.6	—	6.7	—	6.8	—	2.9
1981 LG	26.5	26.6	4.2	17.5	—	5.3	—	8.9	1.8	8.2
1982 A	29.7	23.0	6.7	18.8	10.1	—	—	9.3	2.7	0.7
1983 W	34.0	20.0	3.0	17.9	13.4	—	—	8.0	1.9	1.6
1984 E	21.5	33.6	2.9	22.1	13.3	—	—	5.0	1.3	0.3
1985 LG	29.5	24.3	3.1	17.8	11.8	2.4	—	7.1	1.6	1.8
1987 W	37.8	11.7	5.4	21.1	11.4	—	—	10.0	2.6	0.0
1989 LG	31.4	17.8	—	21.2	11.3	—	—	6.8	2.1	9.4
1989 E	21.5	29.9	—	25.5	9.2	—	—	5.2	1.1	5.7

Notes: S = Stormont; W = Westminster; LG = local government; A = Assembly; C = Constitutional Convention; E = European Parliament.

— indicates the party did not exist or did not contest the election.

'Other nationalist' includes the Republican Clubs until 1979.

'Non-confessional bloc' consists of parties who endorse the Union (NILP and APNI), or who accept it for the medium-long term (WP). The APNI, though it endorses the Union, and is therefore 'unionist', is not classified as part of the unionist bloc because its support is bi-confessional. The Workers' Party is separately classified from 1981 in the 'non-confessional bloc'.

Sources: calculated from Flackes and Elliott (1989) and the *Irish Times* (May and June 1989).

The nationalist bloc is characterized by commitment, of some sort, to the political unification of the island of Ireland and by its essentially Catholic appeal. Its internal differences are over how to achieve Irish territorial unification and the nature of post-unification Ireland. The largest party in the nationalist bloc, the SDLP, is constitutionally nationalist and committed to seeking the unification of Ireland by consent. It is a member of the democratic Socialist International. Its support is primarily drawn from the Catholic population, and amongst the Catholic electorate its constituents are disproportionately concentrated amongst the better-off, those who live west of the Bann, and the over-30s. It rapidly consolidated its position as the principal nationalist party after contesting its first province-wide elections in 1973. Its fortunes declined slightly in the early 1980s but it has re-established its position since the Anglo-Irish Agreement (see below). Sinn Féin, the second largest party in the nationalist bloc, supports the insurrectionary activities of the IRA. It has been contesting province-wide elections since 1982. Its rapid growth after 1982 appears to have been halted by the Anglo-Irish Agreement (see below). Other nationalist party organizations to have emerged but which have faded without decisive impact in the last two decades include the Republican Clubs—which is counted as part of the nationalist bloc until 1979 in our classification—and the Irish Independence Party.

The non-confessional bloc is characterized by the (nominally) non-ethnic and non-religious appeal of its parties. The Northern Ireland Labour Party (NILP) and the Alliance Party of Northern Ireland (APNI) sought biconfessional support, and the Workers' Party (WP), since its emergence from the Republican Clubs in the early 1980s, has explicitly sought support as a non-sectarian socialist party. These parties are all tacitly unionist, but not Unionist. Although there are arguments for including these parties in the unionist bloc because they accept the Union, their political appeal, rationale, and biconfessional support count against such a classification. They make no apologies for and do not wish to return to anything like the Stormont regime. In particular both the APNI and the WP recognize, albeit tacitly, the importance of an 'Irish dimension'. The APNI accepts the Anglo-Irish Agreement, and the Workers' Party is organized as an all-Ireland party, with units in both the Republic of Ireland and Northern Ireland.

The simple residual category 'Other', by contrast, includes Independents, Ecologists, and others not easily classifiable into the other three blocs. In recent times it includes the representatives of groups seeking to organize British (i.e. Labour and Conservative) political parties in Northern Ireland.

1. LONG-TERM TRENDS IN PARTY SUPPORT

There are three clear long-term trends in this data-set of province-wide elections since 1969: first, the sustained growth in support for the nationalist bloc; secondly, the intense and volatile competition between the UUP and the DUP for hegemony within the declining Unionist bloc; and finally, the recomposition and fragmentation of the non-confessional bloc, which has waxed but mostly waned.

Nationalist Bloc

The most obvious long-term trend in party support is the growth in size of the nationalist bloc (see Table A4.1 and Table A4.2). In Table A4.2, support for the nationalist bloc is gradually smoothed, using the simple techniques of modern exploratory data analysis, running medians and hanning (Hartwig and Dearing 1979: 36–9). Figure A4.1(*a*) compares the actual nationalist vote (Table A4.2, second column) with the smoothed vote (Table A4.2, last column). The smoothed interpolation indicates a clear and continuous upward trend in the nationalist vote.[2]

TABLE A4.2. *Smoothing the nationalist-bloc vote in province-wide elections, 1969–1989*

Year	%	5	3	3R'	(H)	53R'(H)
1969 S	18.8	(18.8)	(18.8)	(18.8)		18.80
					19.00	
1970 W	23.3	(19.2)	19.2	19.2		20.13
					21.25	
1973 LG	19.2	23.3	23.3	23.3		22.48
					23.70	
1973 A	24.1	24.1	24.1	24.1		24.35
					25.00	
1974 W	26.9	25.9	25.9	25.9		25.45
					25.90	
1974 W	29.8	25.9	25.9	25.9		26.15
					26.40	
1975 C	25.9	26.9	26.9	26.9		26.65
					27.50	
1977 LG	24.7	28.1	26.9	26.9		27.20
					27.50	
1979 W	28.1	25.9	28.1	28.1		27.80
					28.10	
1979 E	31.3	28.1	28.1	28.1		28.35
					28.50	
1981 LG	22.8	28.9	28.9	28.9		29.30
					30.10	
1982 A	28.9	31.3	31.3	31.3		30.50
					31.30	
1983 W	31.3	31.3	31.3	31.3		31.48
					31.65	
1984 E	35.4	32.0	32.0	32.0		32.20
					32.75	
1985 LG	32.0	33.5	33.5	33.5		33.13
					33.50	
1987 W	33.5	33.5	33.5	33.5		33.50
					33.50	
1989 LG	33.5	(33.5)	33.5	33.5		33.65
					33.80	
1989 E	34.7	(34.7)	(34.7)	(34.7)		34.70

Notes: S = Stormont; W = Westminster; LG = local government; A = Assembly; C = Constitutional Convention; E = European Parliament.

Source: Calculated as in Hartwig and Dearing (1979: 36–9) from Table A4.1.

346 Brendan O'Leary

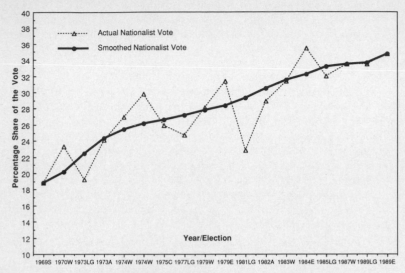

FIG. A4.1(*a*). Actual and smoothed share of the nationalist bloc, 1969–1989

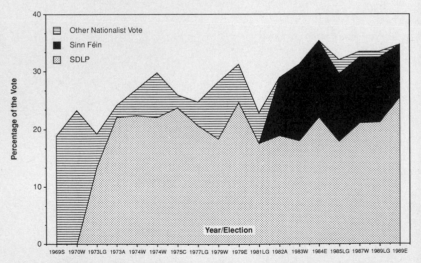

FIG. A4.1(*b*). The distribution of the nationalist vote, 1969–1989

Key: S = Stormont; W = Westminster; LG = local government; A = Assembly; C = Constitutional Convention; E = European Parliament

Source: calculated from Table A4.2.

Performances above trend in the nationalist bloc occurred in the 1974 Westminster elections, the 1979 and 1984 European elections, but only one of these, the 1979 European election, is a standard deviation away from the smoothed data-curve. The deviance of the two European results is explicable through the high personal vote for John Hume, including votes from Catholics who might otherwise have voted for the APNI. However, the nationalist vote in the 1989 European elections seems part of the trend rather than a deviant vote due to Hume's huge personal appeal—although this result may be an artefact of its being the last point in the data-set. The most notable performance below trend in the nationalist bloc vote occurred in the 1981 local-government district elections, which might be symptomatic of a high degree of Catholic electoral alienation at that time—it was the period of the Maze hunger strikes.

Why, as revealed in Figure A4.1(*a*), has the nationalist vote risen consistently? Space precludes a detailed analysis, but there are four distinct yet potentially compatible explanations. First, demographic explanations suggest that because the Catholic population has been growing the nationalist vote has risen in tandem. However, the nationalist vote has risen from just below a fifth to just over a third of the electorate in twenty years, whereas (at most) the Catholic population (as opposed to the electorate) has risen from just over a third to two-fifths of the total population. Therefore, even if a demographic surge has boosted nationalist voting, it is still true that nationalist voting has increased within the Catholic electorate.

Second, psephological explanations suggest that the change in the voting system to STV has increased Catholic voting-participation. However, the nationalist vote has also increased in Westminster elections—where the STV system is not in operation—and it is not very persuasive to suggest that increased nationalist voting in Westminster elections is a by-product of STV-induced higher participation in assembly and local-government elections.

Third, institutional explanations point to the legalization of Sinn Féin, increases in the number of Westminster seats after 1979, and recent reforms giving Irish citizens the right to vote in Northern Ireland in the same way as British citizens as all being of some consequence in increasing the available nationalist electorate. The first institutional change is clearly most important: if Sinn Féin were illegal—as it used to be—nationalist abstentions would be higher. The second fact clearly helps explain the rise in nationalist voting at Westminster elections since 1979—the greater the number of seats the greater probability that one's vote will make a difference—but it can only have been a minor factor. Moreover, the recent change in the status of 'I' voters only applies to local-government elections and cannot be responsible for long-run trends.

Finally, political explanations point to increased nationalist voting as symptomatic of the polarization of Northern Ireland society, under the impact of the Provisionals' paramilitary campaign, assassinations by loyalist paramilitaries, counter-insurgency operations by the security forces, and the failure of British reform programmes. Political explanations suggest that increased nationalist voting in the 1980s is the joint product of two key developments: Sinn Féin's mobilization of previously abstentionist voters, and the failure of British reforms to win the 'hearts and minds' of the Catholic population. Figure A4.1(*b*), which shows the distribution of the nationalist vote over time, shows how Sinn Féin's decision to participate in Northern Ireland elections boosted the total nationalist vote. Those, like the present author, who would place most stress on political explanations also point to the collapse of the NILP, the fall-off in support for the APNI, and the failure of the WP as examples of the same phenomenon: the failure of biconfessional reforming parties to entrench themselves in the Catholic population in a polarized milieu in which such parties appear as at best irrelevant.

Whatever the explanations, however, nationalist voting, *ceteris paribus*, seems destined to continue to rise, especially if current demographic trends continue. Although it is important to recognize that not everybody who votes nationalist (for the SDLP or indeed Sinn Féin) is uncompromisingly committed to a pan-Irish solution to the Northern Ireland conflict, it remains the case that the Catholic population has become both *absolutely* and *relatively* more nationalist in its voting behaviour since 1969.

Unionist Bloc

The percentage share of the Unionist bloc, by contrast, has declined over time (Table A4.1 and Figure A4.2(*a*)), albeit marginally. In the elections held between 1969 and 1979 its mean vote was 59.81 per cent, and its median vote 60.5 per cent, whereas in the elections held between 1981 and 1989 its mean vote was 55.6 per cent, and its median vote 56.95 per cent. However, the end-points of the data-set in Table A4.1 (67.4 per cent in 1969 compared to 51.4 per cent in the European elections, see also Figure A4.2(*a*)) illustrate the decline more starkly—if somewhat misleadingly. It was the departure of Protestant (and Catholic) unionists to vote for the pro-power-sharing APNI which permanently reduced the size of the unionist bloc from the mid-1970s, and even if the APNI has done less well in the polarized voting conditions of the 1980s the unionist bloc is now hovering at just over half of the voting electorate. The other main factor reducing the share of the unionist bloc has of course been the increased nationalist share of the vote (see above). Looking to the future it is also obvious that if the very recently successful (1989) efforts to organize the Conservatives in some Northern Ireland constituencies produce any significant electoral impact then the unionist bloc's support will fall below the 50 per cent level in the early 1990s. In other words the impact of their intervention might well be to give more Westminster seats to the SDLP.

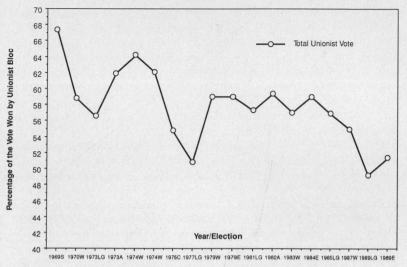

F IG. A4.2(*a*). Voting for the unionist bloc, 1969–1989

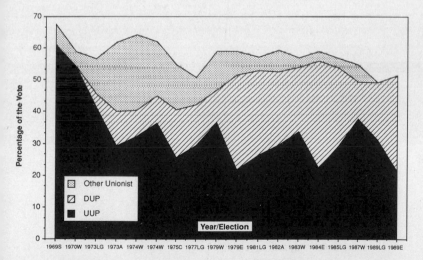

F IG. A4.2(*b*). The distribution of the unionist vote, 1969–1989

Key: S = Stormont; W = Westminster; LG = local government; A = Assembly; C = Constitutional Convention; E = European Parliament

Source: calculated from Table A4.1.

The volatile distribution of the vote in the unionist bloc has been more marked than the gradual decline of the share of the entire bloc. Figure A4.2(*b*) shows the percentage of the vote obtained by the UUP, the DUP, and other unionists between 1969 and 1989. As the graph illustrates, the fragmentation between 1970 and 1975 rapidly gave way to two-party competition within the unionist bloc between the UUP and the DUP. Over time these two parties have absorbed the entire bloc's vote. The competition between the DUP and the UUP for the unionist vote is shown in Table A4.3, and illustrated in Figure 3 which shows the DUP's percentage share of the combined UUP and DUP vote.

Five features of UUP/DUP competition are apparent from Figures A4.2(*b*) and A4.3. First, in the European elections Paisley's performance far exceeds the trend in support for his party. Second, in Westminster elections the UUP outpolls the DUP consistently. They do so for obvious reasons. These elections are held under the plurality-rule system, and therefore the incumbent UUP MPs have benefited from the fear that a vote for the DUP candidate will let in a nationalist-bloc challenger. The logic of plurality rule in Westminster elections has also obliged Paisley, often against the wishes of his party colleagues, to leave the UUP a clear field in certain constituencies. Third, the competition between the UUP and the DUP is fiercest in local-government district and Assembly elections where STV permits freer

TABLE A4.3. *Democratic Unionist Party share as a percentage of DUP + Ulster Unionist Party vote, 1973– 1989*

Year	Body	DUP share as % of DUP + UUP
1973	Local government	9.4
1973	Assembly	26.9
1974	Westminster	20.2
1974	Westminster	18.9
1975	Convention	36.5
1977	Local government	30.0
1979	Westminster	21.8
1979	European	57.6
1981	Local government	50.0
1982	Assembly	43.6
1983	Westminster	37.0
1984	European	59.9
1985	Local government	45.2
1987	Westminster	23.6
1989	Local government	36.2
1989	European	58.2

Source: calculated from Table A4.1.

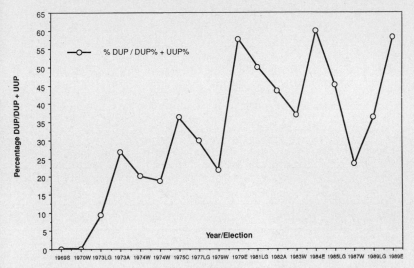

F IG. A4.3. Democratic Unionist Party as a percentage of DUP + Ulster Unionist Party vote, 1973–1989

Key: S = Stormont; W = Westminster; LG = local government; A = Assembly; C = Constitutional Convention; E = European Parliament

Source: calculated from Table A4.3.

competition, and the relevance of Paisley's charisma is less salient. Fourth, the combination of the second and third features mentioned above help explain why the DUP leadership is consistently more enthusiastic about devolution (if not power-sharing) than the UUP, and why the UUP, over-represented at Westminster, is more consistently in favour of integration.[3] Finally, as Figure A4.3 suggests, all the elections held after the Anglo-Irish Agreement (i.e. the 1987 Westminster, the 1989 local-government, and the 1989 European elections) suggest a decline in support for the DUP as compared with the previous directly comparable election. What is suggested in Figure A4.3 is confirmed in Table A4.4. However, it should be noted that in 1983 there was competition between the UUP and the DUP for West-minster seats whereas in 1987 Paisley made an electoral pact with the UUP at the expense of his own party. It is unlikely to be repeated.

The long-term trend in the unionist bloc is very slowly downwards, but it will be the next century before this trend could produce a nationalist-bloc majority. However, the unionist bloc will almost certainly lack a simple majority of votes (more then 50 per cent) in the 1990s—especially if the Conservative Party organizes throughout the province—which may marginally enhance the prospects for consociational coalitions. However,

TABLE A4.4. *Democratic Unionist Party electoral performances before and after the Anglo-Irish Agreement (%)*

Body	Before AIA	After AIA	Net loss
Westminster	1983: 20.0	1987: 11.7	8.3
Local government	1985: 24.3	1989: 17.8	6.5
European Parliament	1984: 33.6	1989: 29.9	3.7

Source: calculated from Table A4.1.

support for the Conservatives amongst Protestants may also have the opposite effect: competition between the UUP and the Conservatives may lead both groups in Northern Ireland to reject 'devolution' and 'power-sharing' with equal vehemence as 'foreign' and 'non-British' ideas.

Non-confessional Bloc

The parties which have not been organized explicitly on the national question and which have sought bi- or non-confessional support, have been squeezed over time since 1969, even though the APNI did experience a surge of support in the mid- and late 1970s. Figure A4.4 illustrates the fortunes of the NILP, the APNI, the WP, and the residual 'Other' category. It demonstrates that peaks of support for this bloc have declined over time, suggesting a steady decline. The NILP, the biggest single party opposing the UUP in the Stormont elections of 1969, was squeezed rapidly in the polarization that accompanied the development of the 'troubles'. It is also evident that the APNI's initial growth has not been sustained, and that the WP have failed to make any serious inroads into the working-class electorate.[4]

Figure A4.4 also shows that four troughs of support have occurred for the non-confessional bloc as a whole. The first was in the deeply polarized conditions of the February 1974 Westminster election, when many APNI voters backed Brian Faulkner's pro-Sunningdale Unionists to keep alive the prospects of power-sharing. The other troughs have occurred in European elections. There are two plausible explanations for this apparently anomalous result. First, the European contests polarize the electorate, *whatever the prevailing political background,* because there are only three seats at stake, and two candidates are likely to achieve a quota on the first count. Therefore, a vote for any candidate from the non-confessional bloc is a wasted vote. Second, one can surmise that some 'natural' APNI voters probably desert their party in European elections, to vote for John Hume of the SDLP (if they are Catholic) or the UUP candidate (if they are Protestant). They desert to strengthen the moderate against the extremist (the SDLP against Sinn Féin, or the UUP against the DUP), but also in Hume's case because he campaigns on a genuinely European manifesto. In other words

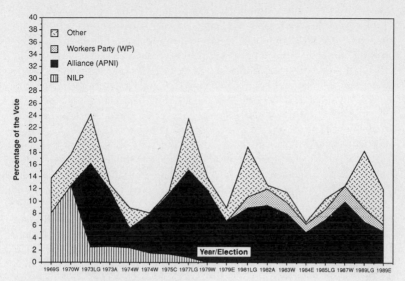

FIG. A4.4. The electoral performance of the non-confessional bloc and others, 1969–1989

Key: S = Stormont; W = Westminster; LG = local government; A = Assembly; C = Constitutional Convention; E = European Parliament

Source: calculated from Table A4.1.

voting behaviour in Northern Ireland is rationally affected by both the voting system and the organization of constituency boundaries. It is not some Pavlovian reflection of the balance of sectarian forces.

2. SHORT-TERM TRENDS: BEFORE AND AFTER THE ANGLO-IRISH AGREEMENT

What has been the impact, if any, of the Anglo-Irish Agreement on party support? This question is of critical importance because the Agreement was intended to shake up trends in party support.[5] The framers of the AIA hoped that its impact on the nationalist bloc would be to stem and to reverse the growth of Sinn Féin, and to stabilize support for the moderate constitutional nationalists within the SDLP. They also hoped that the unpalatable choices which the AIA presented the unionist bloc would encourage divisions which would be productive for power-sharing. The hope was that the AIA would eventually strengthen power-sharing devolutionists within the UUP, at the expense of extremists within the DUP and integrationists within the UUP.

How have actual developments in party support matched the aspirations of the framers of the AIA? Within the unionist bloc, as we have suggested above, the DUP has certainly lost ground since the Hillsborough accord. Tables A4.1 and A4.3, as well as Figure A4.3, show that the DUP's share of the combined DUP and UUP vote fell in the Westminster elections of 1987 and the local government elections of 1989. Table A4.4 demonstrates that in all three elections held after the signing of the Agreement, including the European election of 1989, Paisley's party failed to match the share of the vote it obtained in the corresponding elections held before the Agreement. The overall showing of the unionist bloc in the three elections after the Agreement is also significant. Its share of the vote (at 54.9 per cent in the Westminster election of June 1987, 49.2 per cent in the local-government district elections of May 1989, and 51.4 per cent in the European elections of June 1989) fell from its level in each of the last comparable elections. Indeed the 1989 elections produced the lowest and second-lowest shares for the unionist bloc since the current conflict began (see Figure A4.2(*a*)). Some unionists undoubtedly abstained, some disillusioned with constitutional politics no doubt, but others disillusioned with their natural party's campaign against the AIA.[6] The architects of the AIA could reasonably believe in 1989 that the fluidity it had caused had produced some movement in the direction of squeezing loyalist extremists, but without, as yet, bringing forth a decisive accommodating response on the question of power-sharing from within the UUP. Indeed, it might be argued that the greater degree of support for the UUP since Hillsborough has marked a retreat for the prospects of a power-sharing devolutionary settlement precisely because the UUP are the more integrationist of the two parties. However, on the other hand, optimists observe that the DUP, partly because of the reverses it has sustained after the AIA, and partly under the prompting of Peter Robinson, has shifted away from simple majority-rule devolutionism, and is seeking a devolved government which the minority can accept.

Within the nationalist bloc the AIA has more clearly achieved the objectives of those who brought it into being. First, it has halted the growth of the Sinn Féin vote, and shows some signs of reversing it. Table A4.5 shows that Sinn Féin's vote fell in each of the elections, Westminster, local-government district, and European, held after Hillsborough, by comparison

TABLE A4.5. *Sinn Féin electoral performances before and after the Anglo-Irish Agreement (%)*

Body	Before	After	Net loss
Westminster	1983: 13.4	1987: 11.4	2.0
Local government	1985: 11.8	1989: 11.3	0.5
European Parliament	1984: 13.3	1989: 9.2	4.1

Source: calculated from Table A4.1.

with the corresponding three elections before the accord was signed. Second, the SDLP's position within the nationalist bloc, while not hegemonic, has been decisively restored. Figure A4.5, based on Table A4.6, which interpolates Sinn Féin's share of the combined Sinn Féin and SDLP vote between 1982 and 1989, shows that the SDLP has stemmed and reversed the Sinn Féin tide—albeit within a growing nationalist bloc (see Figure A4.1(*b*)). Within the nationalist bloc the framers of the AIA have some cause for satisfaction. Extremist nationalism has been squeezed, although considerable reform of Northern Ireland will be required to reduce it further.

In conclusion this brief portrait of party support suggests that the prospects for a consociational settlement in the 1990s are limited, but should not be ruled out entirely. The growth of the nationalist bloc and the decline of the unionist bloc is both an opportunity for reaching accommodation as well as a threat that divisions will become even more deeply entrenched. If policy-makers in the next decade can work on the incentives facing devolutionists within the UUP, the DUP, and the SDLP, Northern Ireland's party-political future *might* be less negative and polarized.

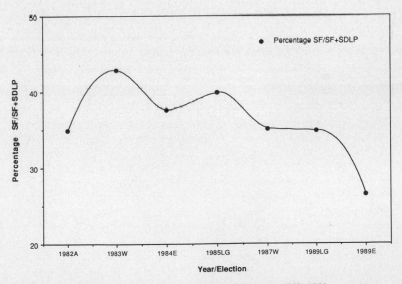

FIG. A4.5. Sinn Féin's share of the SDLP + Sinn Féin vote, 1982–1989

Key: S = Stormont; W = Westminster; E = European Parliament; LG = local government

Source: calculated from Table A4.6.

356 *Brendan O'Leary*

TABLE A4.6. *SDLP and Sinn Féin competition before and after the Anglo-Irish Agreement*

Election	SDLP	Sinn Féin	Combined SDLP+SF	SF/SDLP+SF	Percentage
1982 A	18.8	10.1	28.9	0.3494	34.9
1983 W	17.9	13.4	31.3	0.4281	42.8
1984 E	22.1	13.3	35.4	0.3757	37.6
1985 LG	17.8	11.8	29.6	0.3986	39.9
Agreement 15 November 1985					
1987 W	21.1	11.4	32.5	0.3507	35.1
1989 LG	21.2	11.3	32.5	0.3476	34.8
1989 E	25.5	9.2	34.7	0.2651	26.5

Notes: S = Stormont; W = Westminster; E = European Parliament; LG = local government.

Source: calculated from Table A4.1.

Notes

1. The Alliance Party of Northern Ireland (APNI), founded by former members of the UUP, became a biconfessional party, drawing Catholic as well as Protestant support, and therefore is not classified as part of the unionist bloc.
2. The markedness of the upward trend would be even higher but for the fact that I have removed the Workers' Party from the nationalist bloc after 1981, even though its predecessor (the Republican Clubs) is counted as a constituent component of the nationalist bloc as late as 1979. The Republican Clubs were the political wing of the Official IRA, from whom the Provisional IRA split in 1969. The Republican Clubs, and Official Sinn Féin, have gradually transformed themselves into a Marxist (rather than nationalist) political organization, the Workers' Party, who regard the 'national question' as a distraction from more salient 'class issues'—which is why I have removed them from the nationalist bloc.
3. These tendencies explain why the Editors recommend a change to a PR voting method in Westminster elections (Chapter 11, Section 3). This change would increase DUP/UUP competition, weaken the integrationists in the UUP in favour of the consociationalists, and produce a much more proportional nationalist representation at Westminster.
4. If support grows for Conservative Party organization amongst Protestants it will be a moot point as to whether this development should be

classified as growth of the non-confessional bloc or change within the Unionist bloc.

5. For a more detailed analysis see O'Leary (1987*b*).
6. Aughey (1989: 171–3) also suggests that the low turn-out for unionist MPs was caused by 'free-riding' voters who did not bother to participate in the 1987 election because of the existence of a pact between the DUP and UUP. However, this suggestion overlooks other more plausible explanations and the long-run decline in support for the unionist bloc. It used to command nearly 70% of the electorate under one party—when rational free-riding by Protestant unionists should have been at its highest.

Bibliography

ADAMS, G. (1988), *Signposts to Independence and Socialism* (n.p.).

ARTHUR, P. (1974), *The People's Democracy* (Belfast).

—— (1980), *The Government and Politics of Northern Ireland* (London).

—— (1982), 'Independence', in Rea (1982).

—— (1985), 'Anglo Irish Relations and the Northern Ireland Problem', *Irish Studies in International Affairs*, 2(1): 37–50.

—— (1986), 'Labour and Ireland', *Government and Opposition*, 21(3): 372–6.

—— and JEFFREY, K. (1988), *Northern Ireland since 1968* (Oxford).

AUGHEY, A. (1989), *Under Siege: Ulster Unionism and the Anglo-Irish Agreement* (London).

AUNGER, E. (1975), 'Religion and Occupational Class in Northern Ireland', *Economic and Social Review*, 7(1): 1–17.

BARRITT, D. P. and CARTER, C. F. (1972), *The Northern Ireland Problem: A Study in Group Relations*, 2nd edn. (Oxford).

BARTON, B. (1988), *Brookeborough: The Making of a Prime Minister* (Belfast).

BELL, G. (1976), *The Protestants of Ulster* (London).

—— (1982), *Troublesome Business: The Labour Party and the Irish Question* (London).

BELOFF, M., and PEELE, G. (1985), *The Government of the United Kingdom: Political Authority in a Changing Society* (London).

BEN DOR, G. (1979), 'Federalism in the Arab World', in Elazar (1979a).

BENNETT COMMITTEE (1979), *Committee of Inquiry into Police Interrogation Procedures in Northern Ireland*, Cmnd. 7497 (London).

BEW, P. (1978), *Land and The National Question* (Dublin).

—— (1980), *C. S. Parnell* (London).

—— (1987), *Conflict and Conciliation in Ireland* (Oxford).

—— and PATTERSON, H. (1985), *The British State and the Ulster Crisis* (London).

—— —— (1987), 'Unionism and the Anglo Irish Agreement: The New Stalemate', in Teague (1987a).

—— —— (1988), 'Ireland in the 1990s North and South', in R. Kearney (ed.), *Across the Frontiers: Ireland and Europe in the 1990s* (Dublin).

—— GIBBON, P., and PATTERSON, H. (1979), *The State in Northern Ireland, 1921–72: Political Forces and Social Classes* (Manchester).

BISHOP, P., and MALLIE, E. (1987), *The Provisional IRA* (London).

BOAL, F. W. (1982), 'Segregating and Mixing: Space and Residence in Belfast', in Boal and Douglas (1982).

BOAL, F. W. and DOUGLAS, J. N. H. (eds.) (1982), *Integration and Division: Geographical Perspectives on the Northern Ireland Problem* (London).

BOGDANOR, V. (1986), 'Federalism and Devolution: Some Juridicial and Political Problems', in R. Morgan (ed.), *Regionalism in European Politics* (London).

BOULTON, D. (1973), *The UVF 1966–1973: Anatomy of Loyalist Rebellion* (Dublin).

BOWEN, K. (1983), *Protestants in a Catholic State: Ireland's Privileged Minority* (Dublin).

BOWMAN, J. (1982), *De Valera and the Ulster Question 1917–1973* (Oxford).

BOYCE, D. G. (1988), *The Irish Question and British Politics 1868–1986* (London).

BOYLE, K., and HADDEN, T. (1985), *Ireland: A Positive Proposal* (Harmondsworth).

BRADLEY, C. (1988), *Consensus in Contemporary Irish Nationalism: The Sinn Féin/SDLP Talks and Related Issues*, M.S.Sc. thesis, Department of Political Science, Queen's University, Belfast.

BRITISH LABOUR PARTY (1981), *NEC Policy Statement on Northern Ireland* (Brighton).

BROWNLIE, I. (1988), 'The Rights of Peoples in Modern International Law', in J. Crawford (ed.), *The Rights of Peoples* (Oxford).

BRUCE, S. (1986), *God Save Ulster! The Religion and Politics of Paisleyism* (Oxford).

BRYCE, J. (1901), 'The Nature of Sovereignty', in *Studies in History and Jurisprudence*, ii (Oxford).

BUCHANAN, R. H. (1982), 'The Planter and the Gael: Cultural Dimensions of the Northern Ireland Problem', in Boal and Douglas (1982).

BUCKLAND, P. (1973), *Ulster Unionism and the Origins of Northern Ireland 1886–1992* (Dublin).

—— (1979), *The Factory of Grievances: Devolved Government in Northern Ireland* (Dublin).

—— (1981), *A Short History of Northern Ireland* (New York).

BURGESS, M. (1985*a*), 'Empire, Ireland and Europe', in M. Burgess (ed.), *Federalism and Federation in Western Europe* (London).

—— (1985*b*), 'Federalism and Federation in Western Europe', in M. Burgess (ed.), *Federalism and Federation in Western Europe* (London).

CAMERON COMMITTEE (1969), *Disturbances in Northern Ireland*, Cmd. 532 (London).

CLIFFORD, B. (1985), *Parliamentary Sovereignty and Northern Ireland* (Belfast).

—— (1986*a*), *Government without Opposition* (Belfast).

—— (1986*b*), *Parliamentary Despotism: John Hume's Aspiration* (Belfast).

CLR (Campaign for Labour Representation) (1986*a*), *The Labour Party and Northern Ireland: An Official History* (Belfast).

—— (1986*b*), *Stuart Bell's Northern Ireland Policy* (Belfast).

—— (1987), *McNamara's Ban* (Belfast).

COLLINS, N. (1985), 'Federal Ideas in Contemporary Ireland', in M. Burgess (ed.), *Federalism and Federation in Western Europe* (London).

COMPTON, P. (1978), *Northern Ireland: A Census Atlas* (Dublin).

—— (1981), 'The Demographic Background', in Watt (1981).

—— (1982), 'The Demographic Dimension of Integration and Division', in Boal and Douglas (1982).

—— (1985), 'An Evaluation of the Changing Religious Composition of the Population in Northern Ireland', *Economic and Social Review* 16, 201–24.

—— and POWER, J. (1986), 'Estimates of the Religious Composition of Northern Ireland Local Government Districts in 1981 and Change in the Geographical Pattern of Religious Composition between 1971 and 1981', *Economic and Social Review*, pp. 137–46.

—— COWARD, J., and WILSON-DAVIS, K. (1984), 'Family Size and Religious Denomination in Northern Ireland', *Journal of Biosocial Science*, 137–46.

CONNOLLY, J. (1973), *James Connolly: Selected Writings*, ed. P. B. Ellis (London).

CORRIGAN, A. (1969), *Eye-Witness in Northern Ireland* (Dungannon).

COUGHLAN, A. (1986), *Fooled Again? The Anglo-Irish Agreement and After* (Cork).

COX, W. H. (1985), 'Who Wants a United Ireland?', *Government and Opposition*, 20(1): 29–47.

—— (1987), 'The Anglo Irish Agreement', *Parliamentary Affairs*, 40: 1.

CRONIN, S. (1987), *Washington's Irish Policy 1916–1986* (Dublin).

CURTIN, C., KELLY, M., and O'DOWD, L. (eds.) (1984), *Culture and Ideology in Ireland* (Galway).

DARBY, J. (1976), *Conflict in Northern Ireland: The Development of a Polarized Community* (Dublin).

DAVIDSON, J. (1986*a*), *Electoral Integration* (Belfast).

—— (1986*b*), *Integration, a Word without Meaning* (Belfast).

DEARLOVE, J. and SAUNDERS, P. (1984), *Introduction to British Politics* (Cambridge).

DE PAOR, L. (1970), *Divided Ulster* (Harmondsworth).

DICEY, A. V. (1939), *Introduction to the Study of the Law of the Constitution* (London).

DILLON, M. (1989), *The Shankill Butchers* (London).

—— and LEHANE, D. (1973), *Political Murder in Northern Ireland* (Harmondsworth).

DIPLOCK COMMITTEE (1972), *Legal Procedures to Deal with Terrorist Activities in Northern Ireland*, Cmnd. 5185 (London).

DUCHACEK, I. (1970), *Comparative Federalism: The Territorial Dimension of Politics* (New York).

DUCHACEK, I. (1988), 'Dyadic Federations and Confederations', *Publius*, 18(2): 5–32.

DUP (Democratic Unionist Party) (1984), *Ulster: The Future Assured* (Belfast).

DYAS, E. (1988), *Federalism, Northern Ireland and the 1920 Government of Ireland Act* (Belfast).

ELAZAR, D. (ed.) (1979*a*), *Federalism and Political Integration* (Ramat Gan, Israel).

—— (ed.) (1979*b*), *Self-Rule/Shared Rule: Federal Solutions to the Middle East Conflict* (Ramat Gan, Israel).

EVERSLEY, D., and HERR, V. (1985), *The Roman Catholic Population of Northern Ireland in 1981: A Revised Estimate* (Belfast).

FARRELL, M. (1976, 1980), *Northern Ireland: The Orange State* (London).

—— (1983), *Arming the Protestants* (London).

FENNELL, D. (1975*a*), 'The North: Is Independence the Answer?', *Irish Times*, 29 July 1975.

—— (1975*b*), 'Recognising Both Communities in an Independent N.I.', *Irish Times*, 30 July 1975.

—— (1978*a*), 'A Federal Ireland', *The Irish Times*, 23–4 February 1978.

—— (1978*b*), 'What a Federal Ireland Means', *The Sunday Press*, 4 June 1978.

FINE GAEL (1979), *Ireland: Our Future Together* (Dublin).

FINER, S. (1975*a*), *Adversarial Politics and Electoral Reform* (London).

—— (1975*b*), 'State and Nation-Building in Europe: The Role of the Military', in Tilly (1975*a*).

—— (1980), *The Changing Party System: 1945–79* (Washington, DC).

FISK, R. (1983), *In Time of War: Ireland, Ulster and the Price of Neutrality, 1939–45* (London).

FITZGERALD, G. (1972), *Towards a New Ireland* (London).

—— (1982), *Irish Identities* (London).

FLACKES, W. D., and ELLIOTT, S. (1989), *Northern Ireland: A Political Directory* (Belfast).

FORSYTH, M. (1981), *Union of States: The Theory and Practice of Confederation* (Leicester).

FRASER, T. G. (1984), *Partition in Ireland, India and Palestine: Theory and Practice* (London).

FRIEDRICH, C. J. (1968), *Trends of Federalism in Theory and Practice* (London).

GALLAGHER, F. (1957), *The Indivisible Island: The Story of the Partition of Ireland* (London).

GARDINER COMMITTEE (1975), *Measures to Deal with Terrorism in Northern Ireland*, Cmnd. 5847 (London).

GARVIN, T. (1988), 'The North and the Rest', in C. Townshend (ed.), *Consensus in Ireland: Approaches and Recessions* (Oxford).

GELLNER, E. (1983), *Nations and Nationalism* (Oxford).

GIBSON, N. (1986), 'UDI: A Grim Scenario', *Fortnight*, 27 January, 9 February 1986.

—— and MCALEESE, D. (1984), *New Ireland Forum: The Macroeconomic Consequences of Integrated Economic Policy, Planning and Co-ordination of Ireland* (Dublin).

GOMEZ-IBANEZ, J. D. (1975), *The Western Pyrenees* (Oxford).

GWYNN, D. (1950), *The History of Partition 1912–1925* (Dublin).

HADDEN, T., and BOYLE, K. (1989), *The Anglo-Irish Agreement: Commentary, Text and Official Review* (Dublin).

HADFIELD, B. (1986), 'The Anglo Irish Agreement 1985: Blue Print or Green Print?', *Northern Ireland Legal Quarterly*, 37(1): 1–28.

HARBINSON, J. F. (1973), *The Ulster Unionist Party 1882–1973* (Belfast).

HARRIS, R. (1972), *Prejudice and Tolerance in Ulster* (Manchester).

HARTWIG, F., and DEARING, B. F. (1979), *Exploratory Data Analysis* (Beverly Hills, Calif.).

HEWITT, C. (1981), 'Catholic Grievances, Catholic Nationalism and Violence in Northern Ireland during the Civil Rights Period: A Reconsideration', *British Journal of Sociology*, 32(2): 362–80.

—— (1987), 'Explaining Violence in Northern Ireland', *British Journal of Sociology*, 38(1): 88–93.

HINTZE, O. (1975), *The Historical Essays of Otto Hintze*, ed. F. Gilbert (New York).

HOLLAND, J. (1987), *The American Connection* (Swords, Co. Dublin).

HOPKINSON, M. (1988), *Green against Green: The Irish Civil War* (Dublin).

HUTCHINSON, J. (1987), *The Dynamics of Cultural Nationalism: The Gaelic Revival and the Creation of the Irish Nation State* (London).

HUNT COMMITTEE (1969), *Advisory Committee on Police in Northern Ireland*, Cmd. 535 (London).

IRISH BOUNDARY COMMISSION (1969), *Report*, with an introduction by G. J. Hand (Shannon).

ISLES R. S., and CUTHBERT, N. (1957), *An Economic Survey of Northern Ireland* (Belfast).

JAY, R. (1989), *The Fair Employment Issue in Northern Ireland*, Paper for ISA/BISA Convention, London 29 March, 2 April 1989.

JOINT UNIONIST TASK FORCE (1987), *An End to Drift* (Belfast).

KEDOURIE, E. (1960), *Nationalism* (London).

KELLY, J. (1971), *Orders for the Captain* (Dublin).

—— (1987), 'The Constitution: Law and Manifesto', in F. Litton (ed.), *The Constitution of Ireland, 1937–87*, Special Issue of *Administration*, 35(4): 208–17.

KELSEN, H. (1945), *General Theory of Law and State* (Cambridge, Mass.).

KENDLE, J. (1968), 'The Round Table Movement and "Home Rule All Round"', *Historical Journal*, 11(2): 332–53.

—— (1971), 'Federalism and the Irish Problem in 1918', *History*, 56: 207–30.

KENNEDY, D. (1988), *The Widening Gulf: Northern Attitudes to the Independent Irish State, 1919–49* (Belfast).

KENNEDY, K. A., GIBLIN, T., and MCHUGH, D. (1988), *The Economic Development of Ireland in the Twentieth Century* (London).

KENNEDY, L. (1986), *Two Ulsters: A Case for Repartition* (Belfast).

KENNY, A. (1986), *The Road to Hillsborough: The Shaping of the Anglo-Irish Agreement* (Oxford).

KEOGH, D. (1987), 'The Constitutional Revolution: An Analysis of the Making of the Constitution', in F. Litton (ed.), *The Constitution of Ireland, 1937–87*, Special Issue of *Administration*, 35(4): 4–85.

KHOSHLA, G. D. (1950), *Stern Reckoning* (New Delhi).

KILBRANDON COMMISSION (1973), *Report of the Royal Commission on the Constitution 1969–1973*, i, Cmd. 5460 (London).

—— COMMITTEE (1984), *Report of an Independent Inquiry 'To Consider the Report of the New Ireland Forum, Examine the Practicality of any Proposals Made in the Report by Any Other Sources, and Make Recommendations'* (London).

KING, P. (1982), *Federalism and Federation* (London).

LAFFAN, M. (1983), *The Partition of Ireland 1911–1925* (Dundalk).

LANGDON, J. (1983), 'Labour Thought of Ulster Pull Out', *Guardian*, 19 July 1933.

LANGHAMMER, M., and YOUNG, D. (1987), 'The UDA Plan: Opening for Dialogue or Sectarian Fix?', *Fortnight*, March 1987.

LAWRENCE, R. (1965), *The Government of Northern Ireland* (Oxford).

LEHMBRUCH, G. (1967), *Proporzdemokratie: Politisches System und Politische Kultur in der Schweiz und in Österreich* (Tübingen).

—— (1975), 'Consociational Democracy in the International System', *European Journal of Political Research*, 3(4): 377–91.

LEWIS, W. A. (1965), *Politics in West Africa* (London).

LIJPHART, A. (1975), Review Article: The Northern Ireland Problem; Cases, Theories and Solutions', *British Journal of Political Science*, 5, 83–106.

—— (1977), *Democracy in Plural Societies* (New Haven, Conn.).

—— (1979), 'Consociation and Federation: Conceptual and Empirical Links', *Canadian Journal of Political Science* 12(3): 499–515.

—— (1982), 'Consociation: The Model and its Application to Divided Societies', in Rea (1982).

—— (1985), *Power-Sharing in South Africa* (Berkeley, Calif.).

LUSTICK, I. (1979), 'Stability in Deeply Divided Societies: Consociationalism versus Control', *World Politics*, 31: 325–44.

—— (1985), *State-Building Failure in British Ireland and French Algeria* (Berkeley, Calif.).

—— (1987), 'Israeli State-Building in the West Bank and the Gaza Strip: Theory and Practice', *International Organization*, 41(1): 151–71.

LYNCH, J. (1972), 'The Anglo Irish Problem', *Foreign Affairs*, 50(4): 601–17.

LYONS, F. S. L. (1973), *Ireland since the Famine* (London).

MCALLISTER, I. (1977), *The Social Democratic and Labour Party of Northern Ireland* (London).

MCCARTNEY, R. (1986), *The Case for Integration* (Belfast).

MCCLOSKEY, C. (1989), *Up off their Knees: A Commentary on the Civil Rights Movement in Northern Ireland* (Galway).

MCCRUDDEN, C. (1989), 'Northern Ireland and the British Constitution', in J. Jowell and D. Oliver (eds.), *The Changing Constitution*, 2nd edn. (Oxford).

MACDONALD, M. (1986), *Children of Wrath: Political Violence in Northern Ireland* (Cambridge).

MCGARRY, J. (1988), 'The Anglo Irish Agreement and the Prospects of Power Sharing in Northern Ireland', *Political Quarterly*, 59(2): 236–50.

—— (1989), 'Northern Ireland and the Option of Consociationalism' (mimeo).

MCKEOWN, M. (1984), 'Repartition: The Veto to End All Vetoes', *Fortnight*, January 1984.

—— (1985), *De Mortuis* (Gondregnies, Belgium).

—— (1986), *The Greening of a Nationalist* (Lucan, Co. Dublin).

MCMICHAEL, J. (1987), 'Common Sense Realities', *Fortnight*, April 1987.

MCNAMARA, K., MARSHALL, J., and MOWLAM, M. (1988), 'Towards a United Ireland: Reform and Harmonization, a Dual Strategy for Unification', Front Bench Statement of the British Labour Party (House of Commons, Westminster).

MADDOX, W. P. (1941), 'The Political Basis of Federalism', *American Political Science Review*, 35.

MANN, M. (1986), *The Sources of Social Power* (Cambridge).

MANSERGH, N. (1965), *The Irish Question 1840–1921* (London).

—— (1978), *The Prelude to Partition: Concepts and Aims in Ireland and in India* (Cambridge).

MILLER, D. W. (1973), *Church, State and Nation in Ireland, 1898–1921* (Dublin).

—— (1978), *Queen's Rebels: Ulster Loyalism in Historical Perspective* (Dublin).

MORGAN, M., and TAYLOR, R. (1988), 'Forget the Myths: Here's the Real Story', *Fortnight*, November, pp. 6–7.

MOXON-BROWNE, E. (1977), 'Independent Ulster and the E.E.C.', *Fortnight*, 1 April 1977.

—— (1978), 'Northern Ireland', in M. Kolinsky (ed.), *Divided Loyalties* (Manchester).

MURPHY, D. (1979), *A Place Apart* (Harmondsworth).

—— (1984), *Changing the Problem: Post Forum Reflections* (Mullingar).

MURPHY, J. A. (1975), *Ireland and the Twentieth Century* (Dublin).

MURPHY, R. (1986), 'Walter Long and the Making of the Government of Ireland Act, 1919–1920', *Irish Historical Studies*, 25(97) (May), 82–96.

NELSON, S. (1984), *Ulster's Uncertain Defenders* (Belfast).

NEUBERGER, B. (1979), 'Federalism and Political Integration in Africa', in Elazar (1979*a*).

NEW IRELAND FORUM (1983*a*), *A Comparative Description of the Economic Structure and Situation, North and South (Dublin)*.

—— (1983*b*), *The Economic Consequences of the Division of Ireland since 1920* (Dublin).

—— (1983–4), *Reports of Proceedings*, Nos. 1–13 (Dublin).

—— (1984), *Report* (Dublin).

NORDLINGER, E. (1968), 'Political Development: Time Sequences and Rates of Change', *World Politics*, 20(3): 494–520.

—— (1972), *Conflict Regulation in Divided Societies* (Cambridge, Mass.).

NORTHERN IRELAND ECONOMIC COUNCIL (1984), *Economic Strategy: Historical Growth Performance* (Belfast).

NUPRG (New Ulster Political Research Group) (1979), *Beyond the Religious Divide* (Belfast).

O'BRIEN, C. C. (1974), *States of Ireland* (London).

—— (1980), *Neighbours* (London).

O'CLEIREACAIN, S. (1983), 'Northern Ireland and Irish Integration: The Role of the European Communities', *Journal of Common Market Studies*, 22(2): 107–24.

—— (1985), 'Northern Ireland in the European Community', in M. Keating and B. Jones (eds.), *Regions in the European Community* (Oxford).

O'CONNOR, U. (1984), 'Shared Identity Basis for Ulster Republic', *Irish Times*, 18 April 1984.

O'FERRALL, F. (1985), *Catholic Emancipation: Daniel O'Connell and the Birth of Irish Democracy, 1820–30* (Dublin).

O'HALLORAN, C. (1985), *Partition and the Limits of Irish Nationalism* (Dublin).

O'LEARY, B. (1985), 'Explaining Northern Ireland', *Politics*, 5(1): 35–41.

—— (1987*a*), 'The Accord' in Teague (1987*a*).

—— (1987*b*), 'The Anglo Irish Agreement: Statecraft or Folly?', *West European Politics*, 10(1): 5–32.

—— (1987*c*), 'Towards Europeanization and Modernization? The Irish General Election of February 1987', *West European Politics*, 10(3): 455–65.

—— (1989*a*), 'The Limits to Coercive Consociationalism in Northern Ireland', *Political Studies*, 37(4): 562–88.

—— (1989*b*), 'The Limits to Hegemonic Control: The Impact of British and Irish State- and Nation-Building Failures on Northern Ireland 1920–1972', ECPR Conference Paper, Paris, April.

—— and PETERSON, J. (1990), 'Further Europeanization: The Irish General Election of July 1989', *West European Politics*, 13(1): 124–36.

OLIVER, J. (1988), 'Constitutional Uncertainty and the Ulster Tragedy', *Political Quarterly*, 59(4): 427–36.

O'MALLEY, P. (1983), *The Uncivil Wars: Ireland Today* (Belfast).

OPPENHEIMER, F. (1975), *The State*, introduced by C. Hamilton (New York).

OSBORNE, R. D. (1979), 'The Northern Ireland Parliamentary Electoral System: The 1929 Reapportionment', *Irish Geography*, 12: 42–56.

—— (1982), 'Voting Behaviour in Northern Ireland 1921–1977', in Boal and Douglas (1982).

OSTROM, V. (1973), 'Can Federalism Make a Difference?', *Publius*, 3(2): 197–238.

PAKENHAM, F. (1967), *Peace by Ordeal: The Negotiation of the Anglo-Irish Treaty 1921* (London).

PALLEY, C. (1972), 'The Evolution, Disintegration and Possible Reconstruction of the Northern Ireland Constitution', *Anglo-American Law Review*, 1(3): 462–75.

—— (1981), 'Ways Forward: The Constitutional Options', in Watt (1981).

—— (1986), 'When an Iron Hand Beckons a Federal Union', *Guardian*, 20 January 1986.

PATTERSON, H. (1980), *Class Conflict and Sectarianism* (Belfast).

POUND, N. J. G. (1964), *Poland between East and West* (New York).

PRAGER, J. (1986), *Building Democracy in Ireland* (Cambridge).

PRINGLE, D. G. (1980), 'Electoral Systems and Political Manipulation: A Case Study of Northern Ireland in the 1920s', *Economic and Social Review*, 11(3): 187–205.

PURDIE, B. (1988), 'Was the Civil Rights Movement a Republican/Communist Conspiracy?' *Irish Political Studies*, 3: 33–41.

RAWLS, J. (1985), 'Justice as Fairness: Political not Metaphysical', *Philosophy and Public Affairs*, 14(3): 223–51.

REA, D. (ed.) (1982), *Political Co-operation in Divided Societies: A Series of Papers Relevant to the Conflict in Northern Ireland* (Dublin).

REES, M. (1985), *Northern Ireland, a Personal Perspective* (London).

RIKER, W. H. (1964), *Federalism: Origin, Operation, Significance* (Boston).

ROBERTS, H. (1986), *Northern Ireland and the Algerian Analogy: A Suitable Case for Gaullism?* (Belfast).

ROBINSON, P. (1982), 'Plantation and Colonization: The Historical Background', in Boal and Douglas (1982).

ROKKAN, S. (1975), 'Dimensions of State-Formation and Nation-Building: A Possible Paradigm for Research on Variations within Europe', in Tilly (1975a).

ROSE, P. (1982), *Backbencher's Dilemma* (London).

ROSE, R. (1971), *Governing without Consensus* (London).

—— (1976a), 'On the Priorities of Citizenship in the Deep South and Northern Ireland', *Journal of Politics*, 38(2): 247–91.

—— (1976b), *Northern Ireland: A Time of Choice* (London).

—— (1982), 'Is the United Kingdom a State? Northern Ireland as a Test

Case', in P. J. Madgwick and R. Rose (eds.), *The Territorial Dimension in United Kingdom Politics* (London).

ROSE, R., MCALLISTER, I., and MAIR, P. (1978), 'Is there a Concurring Majority about Northern Ireland?', *Strathclyde Studies in Public Policy*, No. 22.

ROWTHORN, B. (1987), 'Northern Ireland: An Economy in Crisis', in Teague (1987a).

—— and WAYNE, N. (1988). *Northern Ireland: The Political Economy of Conflict* (Cambridge).

SACHR (Standing Advisory Commission on Human Rights) (1987), *Religious and Political Discrimination and Equality of Opportunity in Northern Ireland: Report on Fair Employment* (London).

SCARMAN COMMITTEE (1972), *Violence and Civil Disturbances in Northern Ireland in 1969*, Cmd. 566 (London).

SCHMITT, D. E. (1988), 'Bicommunalism in Northern Ireland', *Publius*, 18(2): 33–46.

SDLP (1972), *Towards a New Ireland* (Belfast).

SHANNON, W. V. (1986), 'The Anglo Irish Agreement', *Foreign Affairs*, 64(4): 849–70.

SINN FÉIN (1971), *Eire Nua* (Dublin).

SMITH, A. (1981), *The Ethnic Revival* (Cambridge).

—— (1983), *Theories of Nationalism*, 2nd edn. (London).

—— (1986), *The Ethnic Origins of Nations* (Oxford).

SMITH, D. (1987), *Equality and Inequality in Northern Ireland*, 3 vols. (London).

SMYTH, M. (1987), *A Federated People* (Belfast).

SMOGORZEWSKI, C. (1934), *Poland's Access to the Sea* (London).

STALKER, J. (1988), *Stalker* (London).

STEINER, J. (1971), 'The Principles of Majority and Proportionality', *British Journal of Political Science*, 1(1): 63–70.

STEWART, A. T. Q. (1986), *The Narrow Ground: Aspects of Ulster History* (Belfast).

TEAGUE, P. (ed.) (1987a), *Beyond the Rhetoric: Politics, the Economy and Social Policy in Northern Ireland* (London).

—— (1987b), 'Multinational Companies in the Northern Ireland Economy: An Outmoded Model of Industrial Development?' in Teague (1987a).

TILLY, C. (ed.) (1975a), *The Formation of National States in Western Europe* (Princeton, NJ).

—— (1975b), 'Reflections on the History of European State-Making', in Tilly (1975a).

—— (1975c), 'Western State-Making and Theories of Political Transformation', in Tilly (1975a).

TITLEY, E. B. (1983), *Church, State and the Control of Schooling in Ireland, 1900–1944* (Montreal).

TODD, J. (1987), 'Two Traditions in Unionist Political Culture', *Irish Political Studies*, 2: 1–26.

TONE, T. W. (1910), *Autobiography 1763–1798*, ed. B. O'Brien (Dublin).

TWO TRADITIONS GROUP (1984), *Northern Ireland and the Two Traditions* (Belfast).

ULCC (Ulster Loyalist Central Co-ordinating Committee) (1976), *Your Future? Ulster Can Survive Unfettered* (Belfast).

ULSTER INDEPENDENCE MOVEMENT (1976), *Towards an Independent Ulster* (Belfast).

UNIONIST JOINT WORKING PARTY (1987), *Unionism: A Policy for All the People* (Belfast).

UPRG (Ulster Political Research Group) (1987), *Common Sense* (Belfast).

VILE, M. (1961), *The Structure of American Federalism* (Oxford).

—— (1982), 'Federation and Confederation: The Experience of the United States and British Commonwealth', in Rea (1982).

WALKER, G. (1985), *The Politics of Frustration: Harry Midgley and the Failure of Labour in Northern Ireland* (Manchester).

WALSH, B. (1981), 'Comment', in Watt (1981).

WATT, D. (ed.) (1981), *The Constitution of Northern Ireland: Problems and Prospects* (London).

WEST, T. (1975), 'An Independent North: The Only Possible Way Forward', *Irish Times*, 2 September 1975.

WHYTE, J. (1978), 'Interpretations of the Northern Ireland Problem: An Appraisal', *Economic and Social Review*, 9(4): 257–82.

—— (1981), 'Why Is the Northern Ireland Problem So Intractable?', *Parliamentary Affairs*, 24(4): 422–35.

—— (1983a), 'How Much Discrimination Was there under the Unionist Regime, 1921–68?' in T. Gallagher and J. O'Connell (eds.), *Contemporary Irish Studies* (Manchester).

—— (1983b), 'The Permeability of the United Kingdom Irish Border: A Preliminary Reconnaisance', *Administration*, 31(3): 300–15.

—— (1986), 'How is the Boundary Maintained between the Two Communities in Northern Ireland?', *Ethnic and Racial Studies*, 9(2): 219–34.

—— (1988), 'Interpretations of the Northern Ireland Problem', in C. Townshend (ed.), *Consensus in Ireland: Approaches and Recessions* (Oxford).

—— (1990), *Interpreting Northern Ireland* (Oxford).

WIDGERY COMMITTEE (1972), *Tribunal of Inquiry into Events of Sunday, 30 January 1972*, House of Lords 101/House of Commons 220 (London).

WILSON, T. (1989), *Ulster: Conflict and Consent* (Oxford).

WRIGHT, F. (1987), *Northern Ireland: A Comparative Analysis* (Dublin).

Index